Contract Law in New Zealand

Contract Law in New Zealand

Fifth Edition

Stephen Todd

This book was originally published as a monograph in the International Encyclopaedia of Laws/Contracts.

Founding Editor: Roger Blanpain
General Editor: Frank Hendrickx
Volume Editor: Jacques Herbots

Wolters Kluwer

Published by:
Kluwer Law International B.V.
PO Box 316
2400 AH Alphen aan den Rijn
The Netherlands
E-mail: lrs-sales@wolterskluwer.com
Website: www.wolterskluwer.com/en/solutions/kluwerlawinternational

Sold and distributed by:
Wolters Kluwer Legal & Regulatory U.S.
920 Links Avenue
Landisville, PA 17538
United States of America
E-mail: customer.service@wolterskluwer.com

ISBN 978-94-035-1158-0

e-Book: ISBN 978-94-035-1168-9
web-PDF: ISBN 978-94-035-1178-8

The Author

Stephen Todd, LLM (University of Sheffield, England), LLD (University of Canterbury, New Zealand), FRSNZ, Barrister (Inner Temple), is Professor of Law at the University of Canterbury.

Stephen Todd has published widely in the area of civil liability. In particular, he is the general editor and principal author of *Todd on Torts* (9th edition, 2023) and joint author of *The Law of Contract in New Zealand* (7th edition, 2022). He has also written *Leading Cases in Song* (2013), a light-hearted rewriting of some leading decisions as songs, with music and illustrations. In 2002, he was awarded an LLD by the University of Canterbury in recognition of his work in the field of torts. In 2006, he was awarded the John G. Fleming Memorial Award for Torts Scholarship. In 2022, he was inducted as a Fellow of the Royal Society of New Zealand.

The Author

Table of Contents

The Author 3

List of Abbreviations 19

General Introduction 23

Chapter 1. The General Background of the Country 23

§1. GEOGRAPHY 23

§2. CULTURAL COMPOSITION 23

§3. OUTLINE OF CONSTITUTIONAL AND LEGAL HISTORY OF NEW ZEALAND 23

Chapter 2. Legal Family 26

Chapter 3. Legislative Supremacy 27

Chapter 4. Position of the Judiciary 28

§1. THE JUDICIARY 28

§2. THE MODERN COURT SYSTEM 29
I. The Supreme Court 29
II. The Court of Appeal 29
III. The High Court 29
IV. The District Court 29
V. Disputes Tribunals 30
VI. Other Courts and Tribunals 30

Chapter 5. Public and Private Law 31

Chapter 6. Civil and Commercial Law 32

Introduction to the Law of Contract 33

Chapter 1. Definition of Contract 33

Chapter 2. Historical Development of Contract Law in New Zealand 35

Chapter 3. Classification of Contracts 38

§1. Deeds 38

§2. Simple Contracts 38

§3. A Law of Contract or Contracts? 39

Chapter 4. Contract and Tort 40

Chapter 5. Contract and Restitution 42

Chapter 6. Contract and the Law of Property 43

Chapter 7. Contract and Trust 44

Chapter 8. Good Faith and Fair Dealing 45

Chapter 9. Style of Drafting 47

Chapter 10. Sources of the Law of Contracts 48

Part I. General Principles of the Law of Contract 51

Chapter 1. Formation of Contract 51

§1. Agreement 51
- I. Offer and Acceptance 51
  - A. General 51
    - 1. Bilateral and Unilateral Contracts Contrasted 52
    - 2. Objective Test for Establishing Contractual Intent 52
    - 3. 'Constructed' or Implied Contracts 53
    - 4. Alternative Objective View of Contract Formation 54
  - B. Definition of Offer 54
    - 1. Offers Distinguished from Invitations to Treat 55
    - 2. Examples 55
  - C. Offers Capable of Giving Rise to More Than One Contract 56
    - 1. Process Contracts 56
    - 2. Collateral Contracts 57
    - 3. Auctions 57

4. Options and Rights of Pre-emption 58
D. Special Cases of Offers 59
1. Standing Offers 59
2. Sale of an Interest in Land 60
3. Ticket Cases 60
E. Offers in Unilateral Contracts 61
F. When Offer Is Effective 62
G. Termination of Offer 62
1. Rejection of Offer 62
2. Revocation of Offer of Bilateral Contract 63
3. Revocation of Unilateral Offers 64
4. Termination of Offer by Effluxion of Time, Change of Circumstances, or Failure of a Condition to Which Offer Was Subject 64
5. Effect of Death or Supervening Incapacity of Offeror or Offeree 65
H. Acceptance Generally 66
1. Acceptance in Retrospective Agreements 66
2. Acceptance in Bilateral and Unilateral Contracts Compared 67
3. Acceptance in Unilateral Contracts 67
4. Acceptance in Bilateral Contracts 67
5. Acceptance Where Means of Acceptance Stipulated 68
I. Communication of Acceptance 69
1. General 69
2. Acceptances by Post and the 'Posting Rules' 70
3. Legislative Regime for Electronic Transactions 71
J. Communications Containing or Imposing Fresh Terms or Conditions 72
1. Counter-Offers and 'Battle of the Forms' 72
2. Counter-Offers Generally 73
K. Revocation of Acceptance 73
II. Incomplete, Indefinite and Conditional Agreements 74
A. Uncertainty 74
1. Matters Left for Future Decision 75
2. Future Agreements 75
3. Contractual Machinery and Its Use 76
4. Uncertainty as to Meaning of Terms of Agreement 77
B. Conditional Contracts 77
1. Conditional Contracts Generally 77
2. Conditional or Provisional Agreements 78
3. Waiver of Conditions in Conditional Contracts 79
4. Obligation to Seek Fulfilment of Conditions 80
III. Intention to Create Legal Relations 80
A. General 80
B. Business Transactions 81
1. General 81

2. Letters of Comfort 82
3. Agreements Between Trade Unions and Employers Outside the Industrial Law Regime 82
C. Domestic Agreements 83
D. Agreements Between Private Individuals and the State 83
IV. The Doctrine of Consideration 84
A. Definition 84
1. Introduction 84
2. Executory and Executed Consideration 84
3. Past Consideration Is No Consideration 85
4. Consideration Must Move from the Promisee 85
5. Adequacy of Consideration 86
6. Forbearance and Compromise 86
B. Performance of Existing Duties 87
1. Performance of Existing Duty under the Law 87
2. Performance of an Existing Contract with a Third Person 88
3. Performance of an Existing Contract with the Promisor 88
4. Part Payment of a Debt 91
C. Promissory Estoppel 92
1. Introduction 92
2. The Traditional View: 'A Shield Not a Sword' 92
3. Modern Developments 94

§2. Formal and Evidential Requirements 97
I. General 97
II. Requirements as to Form in Particular Cases 97
III. Property Law Act 2007 99
A. The Requirement of a Written Contract or Written Record of the Terms of the Contract 99
B. The Requirement of a Signature 100
C. Equitable Doctrine of Part Performance 102
D. Contracts of Guarantee 102
IV. Evidential Requirements 103
A. General 103
B. The 'Parol Evidence' Rule 104
C. Notaries Public 104
D. Burden of Proof 104

§3. Liability and Negotiations 104
I. Pre-contractual Liability 104
II. Breakdown of Negotiations 105
III. Misrepresentation 105
A. Contract Legislation 106
1. Definition of Misrepresentation 106
2. Inducement 108
3. Mental Element 110

4. Misrepresentation Made by or on Behalf of Another Party to the Contract 110
5. Liability in Damages 111
6. Cancellation 112
B. The Fair Trading Act 1986 112
1. Introduction 112
2. Features of the Fair Trading Act 113
3. Remedies 114

Chapter 2. Conditions of Substantive Validity 116

§1. Capacity of Parties 116
I. Minors' Contracts 116
A. Minors' Contracts Legislation 116
B. Tortious Liability of Minors 118
II. Trading Corporations 118
III. Mentally Disordered Persons 119
A. Protection of Personal and Property Rights Act 1988 119
B. Common Law and Equity 120
IV. Drunken Persons 121

§2. Defects of Consent 122
I. Mistake 122
A. Scheme of Contractual Mistakes Provisions in the Contract and Commercial Law Act 2017 122
B. Grounds for Relief 123
1. Meaning of 'Mistake' under the Act 124
2. Classes of Mistake Eligible for Relief 125
3. Requirement of Substantial Inequality of Exchange 126
4. Provisions Allocating Risk of Mistake 126
C. Discretion to Grant Relief 127
D. Remedies Preserved by the Contractual Mistakes Legislation 127
1. Rectification 127
2. *Non Est Factum* 129
II. Misrepresentation 130
III. Improper Pressure 130
A. Introduction 130
B. Economic Duress 131
C. Undue Influence 134
1. Introduction 134
2. Classes of Undue Influence 134
3. Manifest Disadvantage 135
4. Royal Bank of Scotland Plc Etridge (No. 2) 135
5. Proof of Undue Influence 136
6. Effect of Undue Influence 138
7. Suretyship Transactions 139
D. Unconscionable Dealings 141

E. Statutory Unconscionable Conduct 144
IV. Illegality 145
A. General 145
B. Definition of an Illegal Contract 146
C. Contracts Which Are Void Rather than Illegal 147
1. Contracts Ousting the Jurisdiction of the Courts 147
2. Contracts Affecting the Freedom or Security of Marriage 147
D. Illegality at Common Law 148
1. Contracts to Commit a Criminal Offence, a Fraud or a Tort 148
2. Contracts Interfering with the Course of Justice 148
3. Contracts to Defraud the Revenue 149
4. Contracts Which Are Prejudicial to Good Government 150
5. Contracts Promoting Sexual Immorality 150
E. Contracts in Breach of a Statute and the Illegality Provisions of the Contract and Commercial Law Act 2017 151
F. Consequences of Illegality of a Contract 152
G. Relief under the Contract and Commercial Law Act 2017 152
1. Power to Grant Relief Where Contract Is Illegal 152
2. Jurisdiction to Grant Discretionary Relief 153
3. Factors Relevant to the Exercise of the Discretion to Grant Relief 153
H. Contracts in Restraint of Trade 155
1. General 155
2. Reasonable Restraints 155
3. Impact of Illegal Contracts Legislation 157

Chapter 3. The Contents of a Contract 159

§1. THE DIFFERENT CLAUSES 159
I. Ascertaining of Express Terms 159
A. The Parol Evidence Rule 159
B. Collateral Contracts 160
C. Representations and Terms 160
II. Implied Terms 161
A. Custom 161
B. Statute 162
C. The Courts 162
1. Implied by Law 162
2. Implied in Fact 163
III. Exclusion Clauses 165
A. Introduction 165
B. Incorporation into the Contract 166
C. Interpretation 168
D. Fundamental Breach of Contract 169
E. Statutory Control 171
1. Disputes Tribunal Act 1988 172

2. Contract and Commercial Law Act 2017, Section 50 172
3. Fair Trading Act 1986 172
4. Unfair Terms in Consumer Contracts 173
5. Consumer Guarantees Act 1993 174
IV. Penalty Clauses 174
V. Arbitration Clauses 178

§2. INTERPRETATION 179
I. The Rules of Interpretation 179
A. Introduction 179
B. The Matrix of Fact 180
C. Pre-contract Negotiations, Subsequent Conduct 181
D. Business Common Sense 182
E. Evidential Issues 182

Chapter 4. Privity of Contract 184

§1. THE DOCTRINE OF PRIVITY OF CONTRACT 184
I. The Imposition of Contractual Liabilities upon Third Parties 184
II. The Acquisition of Contractual Rights by Third Parties 184
A. Introduction 184
B. Remedies of the Promisee 185
C. Trusts of Contractual Rights 186
D. Exclusion Clauses and Third Parties 187
E. Privity Legislation 188
1. Right of Enforcement to Third Parties 188
2. Variation or Discharge of the Contract 190
3. Defences 191

§2. THE TRANSFER OF CONTRACTUAL RIGHTS 191
I. Voluntary Assignment 191
A. Introduction 191
B. Assignment under the Property Law Act 1952 192
C. Assignment in Equity 193
D. Consideration 193
E. Notice 194
F. Assignment Subject to Equities 194
G. Assignment under the Property Law Act 2007 195
H. Limits on Assignability 197
1. Bare Right to Litigate 197
2. Contracts Involving Personal Skill or Confidence 198
3. Prohibitions on Assignment 198
I. The Transfer of Contractual Liabilities 199
II. Assignment by Operation of Law 201

Chapter 5. The Termination of the Contract 202

§1. Performance and Breach 202
I. Cancellation for Breach 202
A. The Types of Breach 202
1. Repudiation 202
2. Breach of Term 203
B. The Substantiality of Breach 204
1. Essential Term 204
2. Substantial Breach 205
C. Election 206
D. Affirmation 207
E. Cancellation 208
F. The Effect of Cancellation 209
G. Relief under Section 43 211
H. Cancellation for a Bad Reason When a Good Reason Also Exists 212
II. Contracting Out of the Contract and Commercial Law Act 2017 212
III. Savings 213
A. Sale of Goods Act Provisions of the Contract and Commercial Law Act 2017 213
B. Consumer Guarantees Act 1993 214
C. Fair Trading Act 1986 215

§2. Impossibility, Frustration, and Hardship: The Unforeseen 215
I. Definition 215
II. The Threshold 216
III. Express Provision 217
IV. Foreseeability 217
V. Self-Induced Frustration 218
VI. The Effect of Frustration and the Contract and Commercial Law Act 2017 218
VII. Exclusions from the Frustrated Contracts Provisions of the Contract and Commercial Law Act 2017 219

§3. Discharge by Agreement 220
I. Termination by Virtue of Term in Contract 220
II. Bilateral Discharge by Agreement 220
III. Waiver 221
IV. Accord and Satisfaction 222

Chapter 6. Remedies 224

§1. Damages 224
I. Measure of Damages 224
A. Expectation Loss 224
B. Reliance Loss 226

C. Restoration of Benefits 226
D. Consequential Loss 227
E. Relationship Between Different Heads of Loss 228
F. Date of Quantification 228
G. Exemplary Damages 229
II. Remoteness of Damage 230
A. The Rule in Hadley v. Baxendale 230
B. The Scope of the Defendant's Duty 232
C. Upset and Distress 235
D. Failure to Pay Money 236
III. Mitigation of Damage 237
IV. Contributory Negligence 239
V. Damages Fixed by the Contract 240

§2. Cancellation of Contract 240

§3. Specific Performance and Injunction 241

§4. Damages in Substitution for Specific Performance or Injunction 242

§5. Account of Profits 243

§6. Limitation of Actions 243
I. Introduction 243
II. Actions Subject to the Limitation Act 1950 244
III. Actions Subject to the Limitation Act 2010 245
IV. Equitable Relief 247

Part II. Specific Contracts 249

Chapter 1. Agency 249

§1. Introduction 249

§2. Types of Agents 249
I. Mercantile Agents 250
II. Brokers 250
III. *Del Credere* Agents 250
IV. Auctioneers 250
V. Estate Agents 251

§3. Formation of Agency 251
I. Express or Implied Appointment 251
II. Ratification 252
III. Agency of Necessity 253

§4. Authority of Agents 254
I. Express or Implied Actual Authority 254
II. Apparent Authority 254

§5. Duties of the Parties to the Agency Relationship 256
I. Duties of the Agent 256
II. Duties of the Principal 258

§6. Contracts by Agents 259
I. Disclosed Principal 259
II. Undisclosed Principal 260
III. Payment to the Agent 260

§7. Dispositions of Property by Agents 261

§8. Rights of Third Party Against Principal 262
I. Right to Enforce the Contract 262
II. Right to Treat Agent's Knowledge as That of Principal 262

§9. Rights of Third Party Against Agent 263
I. Agent's Liability on the Contract 263
II. Breach of Warranty of Authority 263

§10. Termination of Agency 264

Chapter 2. Bailment 266

§1. Introduction 266
I. Nature of Bailment 266
II. Transfer of Possession 266

§2. Rights and Duties of a Bailee 267
I. Rights of a Bailee 267
II. Duties of a Bailee 268

§3. Rights and Duties of a Bailor 269
I. Rights of a Bailor 269
II. Duties of a Bailor 269

Chapter 3. Gaming and Wagering Contracts 271

§1. Wagering Contracts 271
I. Definition 271
II. Status 271
III. Contracts Collateral to Wagering Contracts 271

Chapter 4. Sale of Goods 273

§1. INTRODUCTION 273

§2. SALE OF GOODS LEGISLATION 274
I. Definition of a Contract for the Sale of Goods 274
II. Formation of the Contract 275
III. Passing of Property in Goods and Risk 275
A. Specific Goods 276
B. Unascertained Goods 276
C. Sale or Return Contracts 277
D. Reservation of Property 277
E. Risk 278
F. Perishing of Goods 279
IV. Sales Without Title 279
A. Nemo Dat Quod Non Habet 279
B. Personal Property Securities 281
V. Terms of the Contract 281
A. Conditions, Warranties and Innominate Terms 281
B. Implied Terms 282
VI. Performance of the Contract 284
A. Seller's Duty to Deliver 284
B. Buyer's Duty to Pay 285
C. Acceptance 285
VII. Remedies 286
A. Seller's Remedies 286
B. Buyer's Remedies 287
VIII. Contracting Out 287

Chapter 5. Consumer Contracts 288

§1. INTRODUCTION 288

§2. THE CONSUMER GUARANTEES ACT 1993 288
I. Application of the Act 288
II. Guarantees in Respect of the Supply of Goods 290
III. Guarantees in Respect of the Supply of Services 291
IV. Rights of Redress Against Suppliers of Goods 292
V. Rights of Redress Against Suppliers of Services 293
VI. Rights of Redress Against Manufacturers 294
VII. Assessment of Damages 295
VIII. Contracting Out 296

Chapter 6. Building Contracts 297

Chapter 7. Leases 299

§1. Definition 299

§2. Term of Lease 299

§3. Creation of Leases 299

§4. Commercial Leases 300
I. Landlord's Obligations and Powers 300
II. Tenant's Obligations 301

§5. Domestic Leases 301
I. Introduction 301
II. Landlord's Obligations and Powers 301
III. Tenant's Obligations 302

§6. Agricultural Leases 303

Chapter 8. Contracts of Suretyship 304

§1. Contracts of Guarantee and Contracts of Indemnity 304
I. Definition 304
II. Formal Requirements 304
A. Requirement of Writing 304
B. Cases Where Oral Guarantee May Still Be Enforceable 305
III. Cases Where Creditor's Conduct May Render Guarantee Unenforceable 306
IV. 'Guarantees' in Consumer Transactions 306

Chapter 9. Contracts of Pledge 307

§1. Contracts of Pledge 307
I. General 307
II. Contracts of Pledge or Pawn 307
A. Things Capable of Being Pawned 307
B. Rights of Parties to Contract of Pawn 308

Chapter 10. Contracts of Loan 309

Chapter 11. Contracts with the Government and Other Public Administrations 310

Chapter 12. Partnerships 312

Chapter 13. Restitution 313

§1. The Traditional Law 313
I. Money Paid by the Plaintiff to the Defendant's Use 313
II. Money Paid under a Mistake 313
III. Total Failure of Consideration 315
IV. Money Paid in Pursuance of a Void Contract 316
V. Money Paid in Pursuance of an Illegal Contract 317
VI. Claims Against Wrongdoers 317
VII. Claims on a Quantum Meruit 317

§2. Restitution Today 318

Selected Bibliography 321

Index 325

Table of Contents

List of Abbreviations

Ad & El	Adolphus & Ellis
All ER	All England Law Reports
Amb	Ambler
B & Ad	Barnewall & Adolphus
B & Ald	Barnewall & Alderson
B & S	Best & Smith
Beav	Beavan
Bing	Bingham
BPR	Butterworths Property Reports
Burr	Burrow
Camp	Campbell
CB	Common Bench
CBNS	Common Bench New Series
Ch	Chancery
Ch App	Chancery Appeals
Ch D	Chancery Division
CJ	Chief Justice
Cl & Fin	Clark & Finnelly
CLR	Commonwealth Law Reports
Cmnd	Command Paper
Co Rep	Company Reporter
CP	Common Pleas
CPD	Common Pleas Division
CRNZ	Criminal Reports of New Zealand
DCR	District Court Reports
De G & J	De Gex & Jones
De G F & J	De Gex, Fisher & Jones
De G M & G	De Gex, MacNaughten and Gordon
DLR	Dominion Law Reports
E & B	Ellis & Blackburn

List of Abbreviations

E & E	Ellis & Ellis
EG	Estates Gazette
Eq	Equity
ER	English Reports
ERNZ	Employment Reports of New Zealand
Exch	Exchequer
Ex D	Exchequer Division
FCR	Federal Court Reports
FLR	Federal Law Reports
H & C	Hurlstone & Coltman
H & N	Hurlstone & Norman
HC	High Court
HCA	High Court of Australia
HL	House of Lords
HL Cas	House of Lords Cases
ILT	Irish Law Times
J	Justice
KB	Kings Bench
Ld Raym	Lord Raymond Law Reports
LJ Ch	Law Journal Chancery
Ll Rep	Lloyds Reports
LR	Law Reports First Series
LT	Law Times Reports
M & S	Maude & Selwyn
M & W	Meeson and Welsby
MR	Master of the Rolls
NE	North Eastern Reports
NZAR	New Zealand Arbitration Reports
NZBLC	New Zealand Business Law Cases
NZCLC	New Zealand Company Law Cases
NZCPR	New Zealand Conveyancing and Property Reports
NZ ConvC	New Zealand Conveyancing Cases
NZELC	New Zealand Employment Law Cases
NZ Jur	New Zealand Jurist Reports
NZLC	New Zealand Law Commission
NZLR	New Zealand Law Reports
NZ Rec Law (NS)	New Zealand Recent Law (New Series)
NZTC	New Zealand Tax Cases
NZULR	New Zealand Universities Law Review

P	President
P	Probate, Divorce and Admiralty Division
PD	Probate, Divorce and Admiralty Division
Ph	Phillips
PRNZ	Procedure Reports of New Zealand
QB	Queen's Bench
QBD	Queen's Bench Division
Qd R	Queensland Reports
Russ	Russell
SA	South African Reports
SC	Session Cases
SCC	Supreme Court of Canada
Sh	Shaw
Sim	Simons
SR (NSW)	State Reports (New South Wales)
TCLR	Trade and Competition Law Reports
TLR	Times Law Reports
Trad LR	Trading Law Reports
TRNZ	Tax Reports of New Zealand
UKPC	United Kingdom Privy Council
UNCITRAL	United Nations Convention on International Contract Sales
Unrep	Unreported
Ves	Vesey
VR	Victorian Reports
WLR	Weekly Law Reports
WTLR	Wills & Trusts Law Reports

List of Abbreviations

General Introduction

Chapter 1. The General Background of the Country

§1. Geography

1. New Zealand lies between the Tasman Sea and the South Pacific Ocean, about 1,600 km south-east of Australia. There are two principal islands (North Island and South Island) and a very large number of smaller islands. The total land area is approximately 267,000 sq. km.

The population of New Zealand in December 2020 was 5.228 million, of whom approximately 15% were of Maori descent.[1]

§2. Cultural Composition

2. New Zealand has three official languages: English, Maori, and New Zealand Sign Language.[2] English is overwhelmingly the language used, and only a small proportion of the Maori population speaks Maori fluently and as a preferred language. However, Maori culture is an important element of New Zealand's overall culture, and various governments have taken a wide range of initiatives for the promotion of Maori language and culture.

There are a significant number of immigrants of various backgrounds – principally Asian, Pacific Island, and European – and these have also been incorporated to a greater or lesser extent in New Zealand culture. These immigrant communities also use various other languages, particularly Chinese and various Pacific Island languages.

§3. Outline of Constitutional and Legal History of New Zealand

3. New Zealand became a colony of Great Britain in 1840, after the signing of the Treaty of Waitangi which was intended, at least by the Maori signatories, to ensure the retention of Maori lands and rights. The Maori populations fell severely

1. https://www.macrotrends.net/countries/NZL/new-zealand/population'>New Zealand Population 1950-2023. www.macrotrends.net. Retrieved 21 Aug. 2023.
2. Maori Language Act 1987; New Zealand Sign Language Act 2006.

during the nineteenth century, largely as a result of epidemics of disease. Large-scale migration, principally from Britain, brought the settler population to over half a million by 1900. In the twentieth century, population growth has been very substantial, and with further large-scale immigration, the overall population is now over 5 million. Early economic and population growth was fuelled by booms in wool, gold and the export of frozen meat and dairy produce. While primary industries of this kind remain very important, forestry products, manufacturing and tourism now create a more balanced economy.

From 1840 to 1852, New Zealand was ruled by a Governor and an appointed Council which exercised both executive and legislative functions. In 1852, a bicameral local parliament was created by a British statute, and internal self-government followed in 1854. Although there was a brief attempt at combining this central legislature with provincial governments, the provincial governments were abolished in 1876, and New Zealand has remained with a single legislature and a National government. In 1947, Britain lost its last remaining powers to legislate for this country.

New Zealand acquired a well-deserved reputation in the period 1890–1940 for innovative and sometimes radical social and political innovations. Examples are the early enfranchisement of women (1893); a state-sponsored structure for conciliation and arbitration in labour disputes (1894); and the creation in the 1930s of a 'welfare state'.

New Zealand has no formal written constitution. Although legislation does provide for many of the critical matters, such as the existence of and elections for a unicameral parliament (the House of Representatives),[3] there is still considerable reliance on constitutional convention. There are few, if any, restrictions on the power of the government of the day, provided it can muster a majority in the House of Representatives.[4]

New Zealand currently has a mixed-member-proportional electoral system, whereby parties receive, more or less, the same proportion of the 120 seats in the House of Representatives as their proportion of the party votes cast by electors. Since the introduction of this system in 1996, New Zealand has been ruled by coalitions of varying political hues. There are seven seats in the House of Representatives elected on a solely Maori roll, but many other Maori are elected through the general system.

Special mention must be made of the position of Maori law and Maori interests. Although the Treaty of Waitangi, signed in 1840 between Maori and representatives of the British Crown, has no formal constitutional or legal status, it has enormous political and cultural significance. It is common for governmental policies to be expressed in terms of a 'Treaty partnership', which at the least involves consultation with Maori interests before major initiatives are taken. Maori law is formally recognized in certain limited fields, such as the determination of ownership of land still held through Maori customary title and the rights of children adopted under Maori custom. However, a factor which is increasingly coming to be recognized as capable of affecting or modifying the existing principles of the common law is

3. *See*, for example, Constitution Act 1986; Electoral Act 1993.
4. For a detailed account, *see* Joseph, *Constitutional and Administrative Law in New Zealand* (5th ed., Thomson Reuters NZ Ltd, 2021).

tikanga Māori. The nature of tikanga and its potential significance in influencing the development of the common law of contract will be explained when considering the sources of the law of contract in New Zealand.[5]

5. *See* para. 27.

Chapter 2. Legal Family

4. Despite some recent innovations, the New Zealand legal system still reflects its English heritage and common law base. While much of the law is statutory, the courts continue to draw heavily on case law precedents from England and other common law systems. The English influence has been very great, and indeed, in the period 1920–1970, it was common to see New Zealand courts depart from earlier decisions of their own in favour of following a more recent English decision. Since then, there has been a significant change in this regard, with the courts being much more ready to prefer local authority to conflicting English case law. There has also been a significantly greater consideration of judicial decisions from Australia and Canada. However, the English inheritance still remains a key conceptual and practical influence on the New Zealand legal system.

Chapter 3. Legislative Supremacy

5. Parliamentary enactments are the highest form of law. Thus, an Act of Parliament can override any rule of the common law or any decision of the courts as to that case law. However, it is clear that any statute which seeks to abrogate significant rights or privileges conferred by the common law will have to be expressed in very clear language.[6]

As New Zealand does not have a written constitution, the judges have no power to strike down parliamentary legislation as inconsistent with the national constitution. The courts are required, where possible, to interpret statutes consistently with the New Zealand Bill of Rights Act 1990, but that act does not have overriding force. In consequence, a statute which clearly is contrary to the NZ Bill of Rights Act will nevertheless be valid. The courts can, and on occasion do, strike down delegated legislation (statutory regulations, bylaws and the like) where these are not in accord with the empowering legislation.[7]

As New Zealand has a unicameral parliament, the only significant limitations on the power of the Government to legislate as it chooses are the need to ensure majority support for legislation and perceptions of political disadvantage. There is a theoretical check-in that legislation must receive the Royal Assent (in practice, given by the Queen's representative, the Governor-General), but this assent has never been withheld in modern times.

---

6. *R v. Pora* [2001] 2 NZLR 37.
7. Joseph, *Constitutional and Administrative Law in New Zealand* Ch. 26 (5th ed., Thomson Reuters NZ Ltd, 2021).

Chapter 4. Position of the Judiciary

§1. The Judiciary

6. As with all common law legal systems, the members of the judiciary are the supreme figures in the court system. They determine cases involving both statute law and common law. As New Zealand has no written constitution, the judges do not have the power to strike down statutes passed by parliament, but the High Court judges can and do determine the validity of subordinate legislation and have also a wide power to review decisions of administrative tribunals and, in some cases, of governmental agencies.

Judges are normally appointed either to the High Court or to the District Court, but there have been a few instances of District Court Judges being raised to the High Court bench. Judges of the Court of Appeal are usually appointed from the ranks of High Court judges, but there have been occasions of direct appointment from the ranks of the legal profession. High Court and District Court Judges must normally have held a New Zealand practising certificate as a barrister and solicitor for at least seven years before being eligible for appointment.[8]

High Court judges may be removed from office only by the Governor-General in response to a motion passed by the House of Representatives alleging misbehaviour or incompetence on the part of the judge.[9] There is no instance of this power being used. District Court judges may be removed by the Governor-General for misbehaviour or incompetence without the intervention of parliament.[10] There have been no recent instances of this power being used. Both High Court and District Court judges are required to retire at the age of 70.[11]

There are also a small number of specialist courts, particularly the Maori Land Court and Maori Appellate Court.[12]

One other tribunal deserves special mention. This is the Disputes Tribunal which can deal with certain civil matters, including contracts, with claims limited to a maximum of NZD 30,000.[13] The referees who sit in the Disputes Tribunal do not have to be legally qualified (although many are) and are appointed for a limited term with a possibility of reappointment. Unlike the judges, therefore, they have no real security of tenure.[14]

---

8. Senior Courts Act 2016, s. 94(1); District Court Act 2016, s. 15(1). A practising certificate in other jurisdictions may qualify in certain circumstances: s. 94(2) and s. 15(2), respectively. In New Zealand, the legal profession is 'fused', in that practitioners may practise as both barristers and solicitors. Most lawyers do practise in both capacities, although a number of lawyers become specialist barristers and this group furnishes many of the judges.
9. Constitution Act 1986, s. 23; Senior Courts Act 2016, s. 134.
10. District Court Act 2016, s. 29.
11. Senior Courts Act 2016, s. 133; District Court Act 2016, s. 28.
12. Te Ture Whenua Maori Act 1993.
13. Disputes Tribunal Act 1988, s. 10(1A)(b).
14. *Ibid.*, ss 10, 13.

§2. The Modern Court System

I. The Supreme Court

7. At the apex of the New Zealand court system is the Supreme Court created in 2003. The Supreme Court consists of the Chief Justice and no fewer than four or more than five permanent judges.[15] The Court may hear appeals from the Court of Appeal or, in exceptional cases, directly from the High Court. Appellants in all cases require the leave of the Supreme Court itself, which will not be given unless the matter is of general public importance, or of general commercial significance, or there is a risk of a serious miscarriage of justice.[16]

II. The Court of Appeal

8. For most practical purposes, the dominant court is the Court of Appeal. It consists of the President of the Court of Appeal and no fewer than five or more than nine other judges.[17] High Court judges may also be called upon to sit where necessary. The Court of Appeal will normally sit in a number of benches of three, although a full court of five may sometimes be assembled.[18] The Court of Appeal has a very wide jurisdiction, as appeal lies to it as of right from all civil and most criminal decisions of the High Court, as well as from some criminal matters tried in the District Court.

III. The High Court

9. The High Court consists of the Chief Justice and up to fifty-five other judges.[19] The High Court is a superior court of record, and as such can hear appeals from the District Court. It has original jurisdiction in a range of civil matters, most materially those where a sum of more than NZD 350,000 is in dispute. Juries are only used in criminal cases and in defamation, false imprisonment and malicious prosecution cases, so that in civil matters such as contract, the judge will decide all matters of both fact and law.

IV. The District Court

10. The District Court is the principal workhorse of the New Zealand court system. It deals with an enormous volume of criminal and family litigation, as well

15. Senior Courts Act 2016, s. 66(2).
16. *Ibid.*, ss 73, 74.
17. *Ibid.*, s. 45.
18. *Ibid.*, ss 50, 51.
19. *Ibid.*, ss 6, 7.

as with civil cases where amounts up to NZD 350,000 are in dispute.[20] There are up to 182 District Court judges.[21]

V. Disputes Tribunals

11. The Disputes Tribunal, which has the power to hear and determine small disputes,[22] is not a court as such. The referees need not be legally qualified, and the procedure of the Tribunal is deliberately informal. Most significantly, a Disputes Tribunal Referee is required to have regard to the law but is not obliged to apply it strictly.[23] An appeal lies to the District Court, but only on the grounds of procedural fairness and not as to the substance of any decision.

VI. Other Courts and Tribunals

12. There are a number of other specialist courts which have jurisdiction in special circumstances. One of the most important is the Employment Court, set up under the Employment Relations Act 2000, which has a specialized jurisdiction over industrial law issues and disputes arising from contracts of employment. There is also a Maori Land Court to deal with issues as to ownership of land held under Maori customary law.[24]

There are a number of specialized tribunals set up under statute with limited jurisdiction over matters arising from certain trades or professions, although the fact that these tribunals exist does not deprive the ordinary courts of jurisdiction. Thus, the Motor Vehicle Disputes Tribunal may entertain cases concerning aspects of sales of vehicles by licensed motor vehicle dealers, but a disgruntled purchaser might equally well bring a case in the District Court or the Disputes Tribunal, as appropriate.

20. District Court Act 2016, s. 74(1).
21. *Ibid.*, s. 12.
22. *See* para. 6.
23. Disputes Tribunal Act 1988, s. 18(6).
24. Te Ture Whenua Maori Act 1993, s. 6.

Chapter 5. Public and Private Law

13. New Zealand law does not make a distinction between 'public' and 'private' law in a way that is found in some European countries. All tribunals (save those with a specialized jurisdiction drawing on Maori law) apply the same corpus of law. It is, however, common in New Zealand legal parlance to make a distinction between 'public' or 'public and administrative' law on the one hand and 'private' law on the other. Public or public and administrative law deals with the relations of the individual and the state, and therefore includes the substantial body of statute and case law which governs proceedings before administrative tribunals and the procedures by which the courts may review such proceedings. Private law, however, is primarily concerned with the relationships of private individuals, and thus takes in the law of contract, torts, trusts, company law, and indeed family law. As New Zealand is a small state in which the Government plays a major economic role, there will be many instances where 'private' law issues actually arise between the Government and the individual. The position as to contracts between individuals and the state is discussed in more detail elsewhere.[25] Where the Government is acting in this quasi-private character, there is no significant difference in the form of the proceedings or the manner in which cases are dealt with by the courts from that which prevails in cases between private litigants.

25. *See* paras 76, 342.

Chapter 6. Civil and Commercial Law

14. New Zealand has no special commercial courts or codes of commercial law. The same general law is applied in all the courts of general jurisdiction. It is commonplace to use 'commercial law' as a convenient term of reference to denote areas of the general law such as that governing the sale of goods, contracts of insurance, banking, agency and the like. These areas of law have largely developed from the general law of contract over the last century or so. In many cases, the development has been reflected in the passage of statutes embodying the principles developed by the courts.[26]

26. *See*, for example, the former Sale of Goods Act 1908 (now Part 3 of the Contract and Commercial Law Act 2017), discussed in Part II, Specific Contracts, Ch. 4.

Introduction to the Law of Contract

Chapter 1. Definition of Contract

15. A contract is an agreement between two or more parties which is intended to create rights and obligations enforceable at law. From this perhaps a deceptively simple definition may be drawn a number of the separate threads which together make up the basic principles of the law of contract. First, there must be something which the law regards as a sufficient agreement. This is usually to be determined by looking for a point at which it can be said that, viewed objectively, there has been an offer in sufficiently definite terms by one party which has been unconditionally accepted by the party to whom it was made. This in turn entails the courts determining whether particular communications do or do not amount to offers or to acceptances.

However, an agreement alone will not be sufficient to constitute a contract. There must also be an intention that the transaction has legal effect – what is usually referred to as 'an intention to create legal relations'. Lastly, it must be shown that there is an element of exchange or mutuality in the transaction so that each party is furnishing consideration for the other's promises or acts.

The courts may also be called on to determine the precise scope of the contract and whether particular written or oral communications are or are not terms of the agreement. This may involve both interpretation of the parties' actual statements and consideration of any further provisions which the courts may imply in the agreement. Again, the courts may need to determine precisely the parties who are, or are not, intended to receive enforceable rights under the agreement. The resolution of any questions which arise as to any one or more of these issues will be necessary before the court can be satisfied there is an agreement which is clearly capable of enforcement and was intended to be enforced.

It is common for one or more parties to the transaction to allege that the law should not give effect to the apparent contract. In most cases, this will be because it is alleged that the relevant party (or parties) should not be held to the transaction because the surface appearance of consent did not represent the reality. The relevant party may claim a lack of capacity to consent, or that he or she was pressured or improperly influenced to enter the agreement, or that an apparent consent was the result of a mistake or of misrepresentation by another party. It may also be alleged that an agreement to which the parties had given actual and unimpeachable consent should not be enforced because it is contrary to law.

Lastly, the courts must consider whether a contract has been properly performed and/or properly terminated, as both a failure to perform contractual obligations and an attempt improperly to bring them prematurely to an end may involve a breach of the rights of the other party. Should the court find there have been some such breach of one party's rights, it must consider what remedy that party may receive under the terms of the contract and/or under the general law.

Chapter 2. Historical Development of Contract Law in New Zealand

16. At the time of its founding as a new colony, New Zealand inherited the laws of England so far as they were applicable to the circumstances of the colony. As a part of this inheritance came the common law of contract as it had developed to 1840.[27] The law of contract was at this time almost entirely a creation of the common law, of centuries of judicial decisions which had gradually developed and refined key principles. As that history is traversed in the volume on England, only a very brief account is given here.

Certain key features of the development of contract deserve attention. The common law of contract as it evolved into the nineteenth century took the shape it did in large part as a result of developments which were perceived by litigants to produce a more efficient and effective body of rules by which their disputes might be resolved. Expediency and pragmatism were far more important than principle or theory. For example, the medieval actions for debt or covenant, both of which required certain matters to be proved by writing, were largely replaced by the general law of contract under which oral agreements could be enforced. Again, in the place of pre-stated penalties in written bonds came general contractual rules allowing, eventually, recovery of damages for both obligations incorrectly performed and obligations not performed at all.

By the nineteenth century, the courts had largely ceased to compete with each other for the business of litigants, and national trade had meant the clear primacy of the common law over remnants of local custom. A rather more coherent, if not entirely consistent, body of principles relating to the enforcement of contract then came to develop. For the most part, the judges of the era started from the premise that society was best served where the law enforced agreements freely entered into by competent persons – a theory sometimes called the doctrine of freedom of contract.[28] The emphasis on enforcement of contracts properly entered into focused attention on factors which could allow the challenge to the reality of consent or the competence of the parties. The modern law of misrepresentation, fraud, undue influence, and contractual capacity all owe much to the judges of the nineteenth century. While much of that development occurred after 1840 when Britain acquired sovereignty over New Zealand, the settler courts largely adopted English developments without question.

Contract law in New Zealand has been resolutely monocultural: there has been no attempt in practice or in theory to draw on Maori custom or law. The settlers from 1840 brought with them and applied such parts of the law of England as could apply to the colony, which in the case of the law of contract appears to have been

27. English Laws Act 1858. For the current position as to inherited British law, *see* Imperial Laws Application Act 1988.
28. For a fascinating study, *see* Atiyah, *The Rise and Fall of Freedom of Contract* (OUP 1979).

effective transplantation of virtually the entire corpus of the law. The settler Parliament appears to have lacked interest in altering to any great extent the substantive principles, with only an occasional statute replicating contemporary English legislation.[29]

However, in the twentieth century, governments and parliament proved readier to countenance and encourage changes in the law of contract. In particular, where governments sought regulation to minimize economic disruption caused by war or depression, it was common for legislation to have some significant impact on particular kinds of contract. For example, legislation in the 1930s allowed mortgagees to have the terms of their mortgages reviewed and, frequently, revised in the mortgagees' favour.[30]

A different kind of legislative influence was found in the period 1969–1986 when an important series of statutes revised and amended significant parts of the general law of contract. The Minors' Contracts Act 1969 was followed by the much more influential and far-reaching Illegal Contracts Act 1970, and then by the Contractual Mistakes Act 1977, the Contractual Remedies Act 1979 and the Contracts (Privity) Act 1982. In addition, the Fair Trading Act 1986, while primarily a consumer protection measure and thus not specifically aimed at contract law, has had a very significant practical effect on the law of misrepresentation. Several of these statutes gave the courts wide discretionary powers to grant relief to persons who would have been unreasonably disadvantaged by the application of common law rules or principles. As noted below, most of these Acts have been consolidated into a single statute.

Developments at the end of the twentieth century and the beginning of the twenty-first have further watered down the principle of freedom of contract. A number of statutes have imposed mandatory obligations on contracting parties and have prevented them from contracting out of liability. Examples are the Consumer Guarantees Act 1993[31] and the Credit Contracts and Consumer Finance Act 2003, giving a court the power to reopen a credit contract which it finds to be harsh and oppressive. Indeed, by an amendment introduced in 2013, the Fair Trading Act 1986 gives power to the courts to declare a term in a standard form 'consumer' contract to be unfair and unenforceable.[32]

Most recently, various contract statutes, including those mentioned (but not the Fair Trading Act and the Consumer Guarantees Act), have been repealed and re-enacted in one omnibus statute called the Contract and Commercial Law Act 2017. This new Act is a revision Act that is not intended to change the law but to re-enact it in an up-to-date and accessible form.[33]

While there is some evidence that in the nineteenth century, the law as applied by the settler courts was shaped by the special conditions of the colony,[34] it must be said that until the latter part of the twentieth century, the New Zealand judges, and the legal profession generally, generally seemed readier to apply English law than

29. *See*, for example, the Sale of Goods Act 1908 and the Frustrated Contracts Act 1944.
30. Mortgagors Relief Act 1931.
31. *See* Part II: Specific Contracts, Ch. 5.
32. Fair Trading Act 1986, s. 46I; *see* para. 180.
33. Contract and Commercial Law Act 2017, ss 3 and 4.
34. Finn, 'Early Contract Law in Canterbury' [2002] NZLJ 229.

to develop a body of law with a distinctly New Zealand character. In recent decades, a more independent perspective has prevailed, and some quite distinctive bodies of principle have been developed. Examples are the law relating to uncertainty and conditional contracts for the sale of land. Nevertheless, it is fair to sum up the history of New Zealand contract law as being one of the adoptions of English case law, but increasingly mitigated or overtaken by local statutory reforms. It is the latter which have created the most distinctive aspects of New Zealand's contract law.

Chapter 3. Classification of Contracts

17. There is a distinction between a simple contract and a contract by deed. The most important difference is that a simple contract requires consideration to render it binding, whereas a deed does not.

§1. Deeds

18. A seal is not necessary to constitute a deed except where the party to be bound is a corporation. By section 9 of the Property Law Act 2007, all that is necessary is that the deed should be signed by the party to be bound and attested by one witness who adds his address and calling. In addition, the parties must *intend* the document to operate as a deed.[35] Usually, that intention is evinced by the use of the descriptor 'deed' in the document itself. Otherwise, it must be derived by a process of construction in which extrinsic evidence may play a part.[36] The ancient requirement that a deed must be 'delivered' now only means that the document be handed over to the other party with the intention that it becomes binding immediately or, if the obligation is conditional on the occurrence of some event, when that event occurs.[37]

The absence of the requirement of consideration in a deed means that a gratuitous promise by deed is binding. There is also authority that since a deed does not require the element of bargain, one party could in theory be bound immediately to sign it even though the other party has not yet signed.[38]

§2. Simple Contracts

19. Simple contracts can be in writing or by word of mouth.[39] They require consideration to render them binding. Simple contracts are, therefore, bargains whereby each party gains, and each party receives, something. Simple contracts can be unilateral and bilateral. A unilateral contract is a promise in return for an act, and a bilateral contract is a promise in return for a promise. The rules for unilateral and bilateral contracts are the same, but the practical application of those rules can differ.

---

35. *Domb v. Owler* [1924] NZLR 524; *Hawken v. Inland Revenue Commissioner* [1960] NZLR 865; *Morley v. Spencer* [1994] 1 NZLR 27. Note that an agreement not validly executed as a deed may sometimes be enforceable as a contract, *see*, for example, *ANZ Bank New Zealand Ltd v. Calvert* [2013] NZHC 3169, at [25].
36. *Morley v. Spencer* [1994] 1 NZLR 27.
37. Property Law Act 2007, ss 9 and 10.
38. *Naas v. Westminster Bank* [1940] AC 366.
39. For instances where writing is required, *see* paras 90–93.

§3. A Law of Contract or Contracts?

20. In New Zealand law, one starts from the position that in principle the law of contract is the same for all contracts. Nevertheless, contracts are of such different types, and cover such a variety of subject matter, that the statement that the same general law governs all of them, while essentially true, needs some qualification.

The distinction between commercial contracts involving large business corporations and consumer contracts involving individual citizens has had some impact. While, certainly, most of the general principles of the law of contract do apply to both, judges and Parliament have both been astute to see that the differences in bargaining power are appropriately recognized. Thus, the judges sometimes adopt an approach more protective of the consumer when they are construing written consumer contracts, particularly those involving harsh or oppressive terms.[40] Parliament, as noted elsewhere,[41] has also intervened to offer a measure of consumer protection, both generally, as in the Consumer Guarantees Act 1993, and specifically in relation to particular types of contracts. 'Freedom of contract' is thus a less meaningful aphorism in relation to many consumer contracts than it is to commercial contracts.

Further, certain types of contracts have over a long period built up their own specific rules. Some of these clusters of rules are very detailed. While most of them are consistent with, and merely *supplement* the general law and define its application to the specialist subject matter, a few of them vary it in matters of detail. In the case of shipping contracts, for example, centuries of mercantile practice and litigation have shaped a very specialist body of law. Contracts of insurance are another example. The statute has actually codified rules for some of these specialist contracts: the Sale of Goods Act 1908 (now Part 3 of the Contract and Commercial Law Act 2017) and the Marine Insurance Act 1908 are examples.

In other types of contracts, detailed standard-form written contracts are in common use. In some cases, these standard forms not only add considerable detail to the general principles but also actually vary them. The standard form conveyancing and construction contracts are examples. This merely illustrates one of the law of contract's most fundamental general principles, namely that parties are free to contract as they wish.

---

40. *See* para. 174.
41. *See* paras 16, 27.

Chapter 4. Contract and Tort

21. A tort is a civil wrong. It is the breach of a non-contractual obligation which one citizen owes to another. Examples of torts are negligence, nuisance, battery, false imprisonment, defamation. The expanding ambit of the tort of negligence in particular means that the boundary between contract and tort is less clearly defined than was once the case.

First, there are cases where, even though the plaintiff and defendant are not in a contractual relationship, the law of tort imposes a liability not dissimilar to liability for breach of contract. Thus, in *Meates v. Attorney-General,*[42] it was held that even though the parties had no concluded contract, the defendant could be liable to the plaintiff in respect of a negligently made statement of intent on which the plaintiff had relied to his detriment. This is equivalent to allowing an action in respect of a non-contractual promise, provided that promise was carelessly made. Indeed, the Privy Council later said that it did not find it 'altogether easy to follow the reasoning' in the case.[43]

Second, the law of negligence may confer on parties to a contract rights and duties vis-à-vis third persons who are not parties to the contract. Thus, a solicitor who fails to carry out his or her client's instructions to draft a will may be liable in tort to the intended beneficiaries,[44] and a negligent builder can be liable to a subsequent purchaser of a defective house[45] or defective commercial building.[46] Indeed, the manufacturer of defective components used in constructing buildings arguably may be liable as well.[47]

Third, there are situations where the defendant's negligent act is also a breach of a term, express or implied, in the contract. If, for example, a solicitor negligently performs work for a client and as a result causes the client loss, the solicitor is in breach of his or her contractual duty to the client to act with proper care and skill, but the solicitor's conduct also constitutes the tort of negligence. There is no reason in principle why the plaintiff should not have alternative causes of action in both contract and tort. However, in both the United Kingdom[48] and New Zealand,[49] the rule formerly was that the contractual relationship was exclusive, and the client had no alternative action in tort. But in a decisive case in 1995,[50] the House of Lords held that there may be concurrent duties in contract and tort and that the plaintiff may choose to sue in either. However, if the contract is inconsistent with the alleged

42. [1983] NZLR 305. *See also Shing v. Ashcroft* [1987] 2 NZLR 154 at 158.
43. *Meates v. Westpac Banking Corporation* [1991] 3 NZLR 385 at 402.
44. *Gartside v. Sheffield Young and Ellis* [1983] NZLR 37. *See Todd on Torts* (9th ed., Thomson Reuters, Wellington, 2023) at [4.9.4(2)].
45. *Invercargill CC v. Hamlin* [1996] 1 NZLR 513; *North Shore City Council v. Body Corporate 188529 (Sunset Terraces)* [2011] 2 NZLR 289.
46. *North Shore CC v. Body Corporate 207624 (Spencer on Byron)* [2013] 2 NZLR 297.
47. *Carter Holt Harvey Ltd v. Minister of Education* [2017] 1 NZLR 78. *See Todd on Torts* (9th ed., Thomson Reuters, Wellington, 2023) at [5.4.3], [5.4.4], [5.5.3].
48. *Bagot v. Stevens Scanlon & Co* [1966] 1 QB 197.
49. *McLaren Maycroft & Co v. Fletcher Development Co Ltd* [1973] 2 NZLR 100.
50. *Henderson v. Merrett Syndicates Ltd* [1995] 2 AC 145.

tortious duty, the contract must prevail. In such a case, 'the parties must be taken to have agreed that the tortious remedy is to be limited or excluded'.[51]

After a number of indications that the old rule was ripe for consideration, the New Zealand Court of Appeal aligned itself with the House of Lords.[52] Thus, concurrent liability in contract and tort is accepted as a matter of principle,[53] but not where it would permit a plaintiff to circumvent or escape a contractual exclusion or limitation of liability.[54]

51. *Ibid.*, at 194 per Lord Goff.
52. *Riddell v. Porteous* [1999] 1 NZLR 1 at 9; *Allison v. KPMG Peat Marwick* [2000] 1 NZLR 560 at 582; *Price Waterhouse v. Kwan* [2000] 3 NZLR 39 at 44.
53. *See generally* Taylor, 'Concurrent Duties' (2019) 82 MLR 17.
54. *Rolls Royce New Zealand Ltd v. Carter Hold Harvey Ltd* [2005] 1 NZLR 324; cf. *RM Turton & Co Ltd v. Kerslake & Partners* [2000] 3 NZLR 406, where it was held that imposing a tortious duty vis-à-vis a building contract would be to cut across the overall contractual structure. Where concurrent duties in tort and contract are owed, it will be most unusual for there to be any difference in the standard of care required: *Frost & Sutcliffe v. Tuiara* [2004] 1 NZLR 782.

Chapter 5. Contract and Restitution

22. Sometimes, the law comes to the aid of a person who has been unjustly deprived of property. The expression 'quasi-contract' formerly was used to describe the basis of the plaintiff's action, but the term was a bare fiction, for such claims are not based on agreement. The expression 'quasi-contract' has thus gone out of favour, and modern works use 'restitution' or 'unjust enrichment' instead. The topic is covered briefly in the final chapter of this book.[55]

55. *See* Part II, Specific Contracts, Ch. 13.

Chapter 6. Contract and the Law of Property

23. A contract must be distinguished from a conveyance of property which passes title to the purchaser. Usually, a contract precedes the conveyance, but not always: a conveyance can be by way of gift.

Sometimes, a contract can have a similar effect to a conveyance. For example, a contract to sell real estate which is specifically enforceable creates an equitable interest in the purchaser,[56] and an agreement to lease which is specifically enforceable likewise gives the lessee an equitable interest, thus leading to the aphorism that 'an agreement to lease is as good as a lease'.[57] A contract for the sale of specific goods passes the property in the goods to the buyer,[58] so it is effectively the same as a sale.

In leases, there has always been a distinction between 'privity of contract' and 'privity of estate'. The original landlord and tenant have contractual rights inter se, but assignees of both are bound by covenants relating to the land because of the respective estates they hold rather than by virtue of being parties to a contract. The same is now also true of covenants relating to land in other contexts. A covenant relating to land of the covenantor and intended to benefit the owner for the time being of other land runs with the covenantor's land and is binding in equity on purchasers of that land.[59]

Some rights created by a contract – for example, debts – can be transferred from one person to another. They are regarded as a type of property and are known as *things in action* or *choses in action.* The rules about assignment of things in action are complex; they are dealt with briefly below and in books on personal property and contract law.[60]

---

56. *See*, for example, *Bevin v. Smith* [1994] 3 NZLR 648.
57. *Walsh v. Lonsdale* (1882) 21 Ch D 9; *Rewiri v. Eivers* [1917] NZLR 479; *De Luxe Confectionery Ltd v. Waddington* [1958] NZLR 272; *Inglis v. Clarence Holdings Ltd* [1977] 1 NZLR 268 at 272.
58. Contract and Commercial Law Act 2017, s. 146, rule 1.
59. Property Law Act 2007, ss 301–307.
60. Property Law Act 1952, s. 130 and Property Law Act 2007, ss 50, 51; and *see* paras 199, 203, and Todd and Barber, *Law of Contract in New Zealand* Ch. 17 (7th ed., 2022).

Chapter 7. Contract and Trust

24. A contract must also be distinguished from a trust. In a trust, one person (the trustee) holds property on behalf of another (the beneficiary) and is bound to deal with it for the benefit of that other. While the trustee is the legal owner of the property, the beneficiary is said to have beneficial, or equitable, ownership of it.

A contract creates rights in personam; a trust creates equitable rights which can be equivalent to rights in rem. If A and B enter a contract whereby money is to be paid to C, C at common law had no right of action to enforce the promise, and even now can only do so if the criteria stipulated in the privity provisions in the Contract and Commercial Law Act 2017 are met. But if it can be shown that A and B have created a trust for C, C can, and always has been able to, enforce it personally.[61] The courts are, however, not willing to find the existence of such a trust.[62]

Unlike a contract, a trust does not depend on agreement and requires no consideration to establish it. A declaration by one person, the seller, that he or she holds property in trust is sufficient.[63] The parties to a contract can cancel it by agreement, but a settlor cannot revoke a completely constituted trust unless the trust document reserves a power of revocation.[64]

61. For example, *Tomlinson v. Gill* (1750) Amb 330.
62. For example, *Swain v. Law Society* [1983] 1 AC 598.
63. *Milroy v. Lord* (1862) 4 De G F & J 264 at 274. To be effective, a declaration of a trust of land must be evidenced in writing: Property Law Act 2007, s. 25(2).
64. *Henry v. Armstrong* (1881) 18 Ch D 668.

Chapter 8. Good Faith and Fair Dealing

25. The United Kingdom Supreme Court has affirmed that there is no general principle of good faith in contracting in English law.[65] There is no well-developed doctrine of good faith in New Zealand law either. It has been held that even an express agreement to *negotiate* in good faith is unenforceable. The Court of Appeal has said:[66]

> Good faith in this context is essentially a subjective concept, as the House of Lords pointed out in *Walford*. There is thus no sufficiently certain objective criterion by means of which the Court can decide whether either party is in breach of the good faith obligation. The Court is unable in such cases to resolve the question whether a particular negotiating stance was adopted in good faith. The law regards the task of reconciling self-interest with the subjective connotation of having to act in good faith as an exercise of such inherent difficulty and uncertainty as not to be justiciable. The ostensible consensus is therefore illusory.[67]

Different considerations apply to good faith in the *performance* of a contract. Sometimes parties expressly contract that they will act in good faith forwards each other in performing their contract, or in performing certain obligations under it. The Courts in New Zealand have as yet had few opportunities to define good faith in this context, but have indicated it can only be given a meaning in the context of the contract in which it appears. Older cases have seen ‘good faith’ as excluding a wide range of types of bad faith, such as endeavouring to frustrate the joint venture by trying to terminate it in a manner inconsistent with the terms of the agreement, or by failing to make any attempt to ensure the happening of an event in which future performance depends.[68] A more recent decision[69] has adopted the view of the Canadian Supreme Court[70] that a duty of good faith requires the parties to perform their contractual duties honestly and reasonably, not capriciously or arbitrarily, and also requires each party to have regard to the legitimate contractual interests of the other party and not to dishonestly undermine them.

Sometimes, a court will imply an obligation of good faith in a contract, using the standard tests for implying terms in contracts. The Court of Appeal has implied an undertaking into a joint venture contract,[71] and Elias J has said it can be implied in

---

65. *Times Travel (UK) Ltd v. Pakistan International Airlines Corp* [2021] UKSC 40, [2021] 3 WLR 727 at [27], [95].
66. *Wellington City Council v. Body Corporate 51702* [2002] 3 NZLR 486 at 495–496.
67. It has been held that when parties are negotiating for a contract, any attempt to use the tort of negligence to make up for the lack of a process contract should be rebuffed: *Prime Commercial Ltd v. Wool Board Disestablishment Co Ltd* (2006) 7 NZCPR 697.
68. *Symphony Group Ltd v. Pacific Heritage (Auckland) Developments Ltd* HC Auckland CP 362/98, 17 Aug. 1998; *NZ Licensed Rest Homes Associated Ltd v. Midland Regional Health Authority* HC Hamilton CP 34/97, 15 Jun. 1999; affd CA 170/99, CA 268/99, 17 Jul. 2000.
69. *Heli Holdings Ltd v. The Helicopter Line Ltd* [2016] NZHC 976.
70. *Bhasin v. Hrynew* (2014) 379 DLR(4th) 385; 2014 SCC 71.
71. *Kiwi Gold NL v. Prophecy Mining NL* CA 30/91, 18 Jul. 1991.

a contract to sell on commission, and other contracts which are 'predicated on mutual confidence'.[72] The Privy Council, on appeal from New Zealand, had said it is not prepared to rule out the existence of an implied term of good faith in a franchise contract.[73] A requirement of good faith is statutorily imposed in employment contracts.[74]

One New Zealand judge, Thomas J, would have gone further and supported a general doctrine of good faith in contract law.[75] He noted that a number of doctrines of our contract law are based on a latent premise not unlike good faith, for example, the rule invalidating penalties, the law providing for relief against forfeiture, and rules of construction like the *contra proferentem* rule. So far, Thomas J has had little support for such a general rule.

It should be noted that the Fair Trading Act 1986 section 9 prohibits conduct in trade which is misleading or deceptive or likely to mislead or deceive. This has overtones of good faith.

72. *J L Stanley Ltd v. Fuji Xerox Ltd* HC Auckland CP 479/96, 5 Nov. 1997.
73. *Dymocks Franchise Systems (NSW) Pty Ltd v. Todd* (2002) 10 TCLR 527 at 548.
74. Employment Relations Act 2000, s. 4.
75. *Livingstone v. Roskilly* [1992] 3 NZLR 230 at 238; *Bobux Marketing Ltd v. Raynor Marketing Ltd* [2002] 1 NZLR 506 at 513–517.

Chapter 9. Style of Drafting

26. Many contracts, in particular long-standing standard forms of contract, are drafted in a very wordy and detailed way. That is so of some insurance contracts, mortgages, and construction contracts. This style is largely the result of a number of influences: the at times overly literal approach to interpretation adopted by the courts in times past; the disinclination of the courts to imply terms in contracts; the need to amend the document when decisions of the courts have revealed gaps in the current version; and the fear (usually exaggerated) that simplification of established wording will unsettle the meaning and thus create uncertainty.

Thus, some forms of contract have become, over the years, inelegant and unwieldy. Sentences can be very long – sometimes several hundred words.

As against that, contracts drafted by business people who are not lawyers can be remarkably brief. Some 'heads of agreement' are only a page long. Today, the courts are showing more inclination to uphold even bare and open-ended contracts, provided the intention to contract is clear. To some extent, they always have: they have not wished 'to incur the reproach of being a destroyer of bargains'.[76]

Today, there is a strong movement towards 'plain English' drafting. Parliamentary counsel has led the way, and modern New Zealand statutes are much more clearly, coherently, and (often) briefly drafted than their predecessors. Some modern contracts have followed this lead. For example, the newest version of one of the standard construction contracts is in much plainer English than were earlier editions.[77] Some insurance companies take pride in marketing their 'plain English' policies. This movement invites a more purposive approach to interpretation by the Courts, and by and large, this is happening.

76. *Hillos & Co Ltd v. Arcos Ltd* (1932) 147 LT 503 at 512 per Lord Tomlin. *Cf. Fletcher Challenge Energy Ltd v. Electricity Corporation of New Zealand* [2002] 2 NZLR 433 and *Tower Insurance v. Nicon Ltd* [2019] NZCA 332.

77. For example, *Conditions of Contract for Building and Civil Engineering Construction* (NZS 3916: 2013).

Chapter 10. Sources of the Law of Contracts

27. The New Zealand law of contract is based on English common law. By the Imperial Laws Application Act 1988, the common law of England (including the rules of equity) continues to be part of the law of New Zealand. Until the second half of the twentieth century, the New Zealand courts followed the precedents of the English courts closely; indeed, they regarded themselves as absolutely bound by the House of Lords and would almost never depart from the English Court of Appeal. There is not the same binding authority these days, but decisions of the English Courts are still treated with great respect, and very recent developments in England (e.g., in the field of consideration and contract interpretation) have been followed here.

In the first half of the twentieth century, the New Zealand legislature enacted a number of statutes relating to the law of contracts which were virtually exact replicas of English legislation, among them the Sale of Goods Act 1908 and the Frustrated Contracts Act 1944. But in more recent times, New Zealand started enacting its own contract legislation which codified and in some cases substantially modified the common law. They included the Minors Contracts Act 1969, the Illegal Contracts Act 1970, the Contractual Mistakes Act 1977, the Contractual Remedies Act 1979, and the Contracts (Privity) Act 1982. As was noted earlier, all of these statutes plus some others have been brought together and re-enacted in the Contract and Commercial Law Act 2017. In the following pages, the background to this new Act in the earlier statutes will be explained where necessary, but references to the present law will be to the provisions of the 2017 Act.

In addition, there are a number of acts of a consumer protection nature which have substantial implications for the law of contract. They include the Credit Contracts and Consumer Finance Act 2003, the provisions in the Fair Trading Act 1986 concerning unconscionable conduct,[78] and most importantly, the Consumer Guarantees Act 1993.[79] Both Acts make significant changes to consumer law in New Zealand.

The New Zealand law of contract is thus a mixture of common law and statute. Occasionally, the relationship between the two, and the extent to which a particular statute has entirely revoked the common law in the area to which it relates, can cause problems.[80]

A further factor which is increasingly coming to be recognized as capable of affecting or modifying the existing principles of the common law, or even as a separate source of law, is tikanga Māori. The significance of tikanga in New Zealand law has been acknowledged by the courts on frequent occasions,[81] and recently, in *Ellis*

78. Fair Trading Act 1986, ss 7 and 8; *see* Ch. 2, §2.III.D.
79. *See* Part II, Specific Contracts, Ch. 5.
80. This happened on a number of occasions in relation to the Contractual Remedies Act 1979 (now replaced by ss 33–59 of the Contract and Commercial Law Act 2017): *see*, for example, *Thompson v. Vincent* [2001] 3 NZLR 355 and *Garrett v. Ikeda* [2002] 1 NZLR 577.
81. *See*, in particular, *Te Weehi v. Regional Fisheries Officer* [1986] 1 NZLR 680 (HC); *Attorney-General v. Ngati Apa* [2003] 3 NZLR 643 (CA); *Takamore v. Clarke* [2012] NZSC 116, [2013] 2 NZLR 733 at [94], [150].

v. R,[82] the Supreme Court examined the question and also, in an appendix to the decision, provided a *Statement* explaining the concepts relevant to the debate.[83]

The *Statement* says that tikanga is the Māori 'common law'.[84] It is a system of law that is used to enhance predictability and to provide templates and frameworks to guide actions and outcomes. Although there is increasing published material on tikanga, it is lived and exists as unwritten conventions. The term 'tika' means 'to be right'. Tikanga Māori therefore means the right Māori way of doing things. It is what Māori consider is just and correct and is comprised of both practice and principle. That is, it includes both the rules (what you should and should not do) and the principles that inform the practical operation and manifestation of the rule. Tikanga includes certain fundamental principles which are identified and explained in the *Statement* and which can be applied in determining disputes.[85] These include 'hara' (the commission of a wrong, the violation of tikanga resulting in an imbalance); 'ea' (the state achieved when balance is restored); 'mana' (concepts of power, presence, authority, prestige, reputation, influence and control); 'whakapapa' (genealogy and kinship relationships); and 'whanaungatanga' (the maintenance of properly tended relationships in a matrix of relationships and collectives).

Ellis did not raise any issue of liability in contract,[86] but all members of the court were agreed that tikanga played an important part in influencing the development of the common law in New Zealand. Taking Winkelmann CJ's judgment, her Honour recognized that the common law was generated by the work of the courts, while tikanga flowed out of the matrix of iwi (tribe), hapū (sub-tribe) and whānau (family) relationships that fundamentally framed the Māori world. But while each system was grounded in its own cultural and constitutional context, there was a growing relationship between them. Tikanga was the first law of New Zealand and was not displaced or extinguished by the arrival of the English common law. Tikanga concepts and values had shaped and contributed to broad social norms and values and had come to regulate the behaviour of non-Māori in many contexts. It was relevant to the development of the common law because the common law had to serve all in society. Looking to tikanga in the development or application of the law was not to break with the continuity of the common law. Indeed, in the instant case, it had provided new concepts that helped shape the principles to be applied. It had also provided a new vocabulary for existing concepts within the common law, and by providing that vocabulary, produced fresh insights.[87]

---

82. *Ellis v. R* [2022] NZSC 114; [2022] 1 NZLR 239.
83. *Statement of Tikanga of Sir Hirini Moko Mead and Professor Pou Temara* SC 49/2019, 31 Jan. 2020, which was prepared following a wānanga (gathering of experts) which had been convened for the purpose of assisting counsel involved in conducting the appeal in that case. It comprises an agreed series of statements which speak to the overall place of tikanga in Aotearoa/New Zealand, the intersection between tikanga and the state legal system, the nature of tikanga (and its associated principles), and the key tikanga principles relevant to the case at hand.
84. *Statement* at [24].
85. *Statement* at [55]–[105]. The *Statement* is clear that it does not purport to provide an exhaustive account of tikanga principles.
86. It was concerned with the question of whether an appeal against a criminal conviction could continue notwithstanding the death of the convicted person. The Supreme Court held that the appeal could continue, and was influenced by tikanga principles in reaching that result.
87. At [168]–[176].

Where a matter has not been determined, or where an existing principle is challenged, the common law often works by drawing upon disparate sources in determining the principles that should apply to the case at hand, and to this extent, the judgments can be recognized as applying established reasoning. As for the relevance of tikanga in this process, and as regards contract law in particular, the approach mapped out in *Ellis* so far has had only minimal application, although it seems likely that this will gradually start to change. Some initial steps perhaps may be taken in relation to the interpretation of contracts, by drawing upon tikanga principles as providing the background or surrounding circumstances in checking whether some modification to the natural and ordinary meaning of the contract was intended.[88] Indeed, by taking incremental steps in recognizing the value of tikanga in influencing the direction of the common law, the courts will promote the inclusive nature of the common law for the benefit of the community as a whole.

---

88. *See* para. 185.

Part I. General Principles of the Law of Contract

Chapter 1. Formation of Contract

§1. Agreement

I. Offer and Acceptance

A. General

28. A legally binding contract requires there to have been an express or implied agreement between two or more parties of competent capacity, an intention to create legal relations and consideration. The requirements of capacity, consideration, and intention to create legal relations are considered elsewhere.[89] The question of contract formation requires discussion of the paradigm case of a bilateral express agreement,[90] and then of certain special cases including agreements made when the parties are at a distance,[91] 'constructed' or implied agreements[92] and cases where the courts use an objective assessment to determine agreement has been achieved.[93]

In most cases, an agreement which may give rise to a contract will have been reached by an exchange of promises by the parties[94] during which one party makes an offer and the other party or parties accept that offer.[95] Where this analysis is applied, the courts will scrutinize the parties' dealings and communications to discover whether one party has made a contractual offer to the other. They have to determine whether there has been at some point an expression of willingness by one party, the offeror, to be contractually bound to the other (the offeree) upon sufficiently definite terms,[96] and an acceptance of that offer by the offeree. If so, an agreement capable of having contractual force comes into existence.

89. *See* paras 118–123 (capacity), 77–89 (consideration), 71–76 (intention to create legal relations).
90. *See* para. 29.
91. *See* paras 57, 58.
92. *See* para. 31.
93. *See* para. 30.
94. *Air New Zealand v. New Zealand Air Line Pilots' Association Inc* [2016] 2 NZLR 829, at [47].
95. *Boulder Consolidated Ltd v. Tangaere* [1980] 1 NZLR 560 at 566–567.
96. As to the requirement of certainty, *see* para. 62.

1. Bilateral and Unilateral Contracts Contrasted

29. New Zealand law recognizes both unilateral and bilateral (or more properly synallagmatic)[97] contracts, although there are differences in the law relating to the two forms. In a unilateral contract, only one party makes a promise – for example, to pay money for the return of lost property – and the contract is formed when the promise is accepted by an act by the other party or parties, in our example, by returning the lost property. By contrast, in a bilateral or synallagmatic contract, there is an agreement which results from an exchange of promises, as in the case of a promise to deliver goods, which is met by a promise to pay money once the goods have been delivered. In a unilateral contract, only one party makes a promise, and the other party both accepts the contract and performs that party's obligations under it by performing the stipulated act. In a bilateral or synallagmatic contract, both sides make promises, and performance of the contractual obligations will inevitably follow behind the formation of the agreement.

2. Objective Test for Establishing Contractual Intent

30. Although New Zealand inherited from England the common law view that contract required a 'consensus ad idem' or meeting of the minds, the law has moved on. While consensus or actual or subjective agreement is an important indicator of contractual agreement, it is no longer essential.[98] What is now required is that there is an *appearance* of agreement. The behaviour of the parties must be such that a reasonable bystander would believe that there has been acceptance by one party of an offer by the other, upon which the courts will treat the parties as having reached actual agreement. Thus, in *Robinson v. Hemachandra Holdings (NZ) Ltd*,[99] it was held that a person signing an agreement for sale and purchase, though placing a future date beside his signature, was contractually bound by the agreement because an objective bystander would have seen the date as entered in error and the signature on the document as indicating an acceptance of the offer it contained. If, however, the conduct of one or both parties indicates a lack of agreement – for example, by indicating a term of the offer is not accepted and a different term is sought – there is no contract, but rather the creation of a counter-offer which might in turn be accepted.[100] Similarly, if one party has indicated that, although the substantive terms

97. This term was preferred by Diplock LJ in *United Dominions Trust (Commercial) Ltd v. Eagle Aircraft Services Ltd* [1968] 1 WLR 74 at 82.
98. *Mechenex Pacific Services Ltd v. TCA Airconditioning (New Zealand) Ltd* [1991] 2 NZLR 393 at 396.
99. (2006) 7 NZCPR 245; compare *Boulder Consolidated Ltd v. Tangaere* [1980] 1 NZLR 560 at 566–567.
100. *See*, for example, *Cross v. Davidson* (1899) 17 NZLR 576; *Reporoa Stores Ltd v. Treloar* [1958] NZLR 177 at 187; *Frampton v. McCully* [1976] 1 NZLR 270; and *see* para. 60.

of the offer are acceptable, they will not consider themselves bound until further steps have been taken by the other party, there is no binding agreement until those steps are taken.[101]

The courts will not allow the objective test to apply so as to impose contractual obligations on an offeree whose conduct may, objectively viewed, have given rise to an appearance of agreement if the offeror has actual knowledge that no acceptance was intended. Thus, in *Airways Corporation of New Zealand Ltd v. Geyserland Airways Ltd,*[102] the respondent airline operators, the offerees, had refused to pay charges demanded by the appellant offeror for the provision of its services, even though the respondents continued to seek and to receive the services in issue. It was held that no contract came into existence, because the offeror had actual notice that the offerees were not minded to accept the offer, even though an objective bystander might have thought that an agreement had been reached.

The objective view of agreement does not always provide a satisfactory analytical framework. It must, for example, be stretched considerably to fit contracts concluded through the post or by other long-distance communications[103] or to deal with 'constructed' or implied contracts[104] or retrospective contracts.[105] There are also some cases where the New Zealand courts have decided a sufficient agreement has been reached, although there is neither discoverable offer nor any acceptance.[106]

3. 'Constructed' or Implied Contracts

31. There have been a number of cases where the courts have found, and given effect to, 'agreements' which appear to represent the wishes of the parties even though it is difficult if not impossible to spell out a clear offer and a clear acceptance. In *NZ Shipping Co Ltd v. A M Satterthwaite and Co Ltd,*[107] the Privy Council, by a majority, held a contract had come into existence between stevedores unloading the cargo of a ship and the shipowner, although no explicit offer had been addressed to the stevedores. It is also hard to fit within the 'offer and acceptance' analysis cases such as *Clarke v. Dunraven,*[108] whereby one entrant in a sporting contest (in that case, a yacht race) was held by the fact of the entry into the contest to be contractually bound to other contestants, despite the fact the contestants had never communicated with each other but only with the organizers. However, as Lord Wilberforce said in *Satterthwaite*:[109]

101. *Wilmott v. Johnson* [2003] 1 NZLR 649; *Kop-Coat NZ Ltd v. Incodo Ltd* [2018] NZCA 430, at [34].
102. [1996] 1 NZLR 116 at 125.
103. *See* paras 57, 58.
104. *See* para. 31.
105. *See* para. 51.
106. *See* para. 32.
107. [1975] AC 154.
108. [1897] AC 59.
109. [1975] AC 154 at 157.

English Law, having committed itself to a rather technical and schematic doctrine, in application takes a practical approach, often at the cost of forcing the facts to fit uneasily into the marked slots of offer, acceptance and consideration.

4. Alternative Objective View of Contract Formation

32. In a number of cases, the New Zealand courts have been prepared to depart from the traditional 'offer and acceptance' analysis and instead to consider the entire transaction between the two parties and to determine whether, viewed objectively and as a whole, a concluded agreement was reached.[110] This alternative approach, which has been discussed more often than actually applied, is perhaps most likely to apply if the parties have negotiated extensively for a period of time, with no apparent expectation that the negotiations will be concluded by a recapitulation of the terms on which the parties are to be bound, nor any marking of agreement by the execution of some particular document.[111] If, however, the parties have intended their negotiations to range over a number of matters but to be concluded by specific agreement on essential matters, there is no contract until that actual agreement is reached.[112]

B. Definition of Offer

33. An offer is an expression, by one person or group of people (the offeror or offerors) or by agents on the offeror's behalf, made to another (the offeree) of the offeror's willingness to be bound to a contract with the offeree on terms either certain or capable of being rendered certain. An offer may be made to an individual or to a group of persons or to the world at large.[113] If an offer is made only to a particular class of persons, it cannot be accepted by persons outside that class.[114]

An offer will normally be made in more or less express words, but this is not legally necessary. An offer may be implied from a combination of express words and conduct, or indeed from conduct alone – as with a would-be purchaser in a self-service store who collects goods and places them on the shop counter or checkout area.[115]

---

110. *Boulder Consolidated Ltd v. Tangaere* [1980] 1 NZLR 560 at 563; *Meates v. Attorney-General* [1983] NZLR 308 at 377; *Powierza v. Daley* [1985] 1 NZLR 558 at 563; *see also Wilmott v. Johnson* [2003] 1 NZLR 649. The result of this process may be the same as would be reached by a conventional offer and acceptance analysis, *see Ngoi v. Wen* [2017] NZCA 519; (2017) 19 NZCPR 1, at [47]-[51].

111. *See*, for example, *Paper Reclaim Ltd v. Aotearoa International Ltd* [2006] 3 NZLR 188 (CA); (2006) 11 TCLR 544; compare *Meates v. Attorney-General* [1983] NZLR 308 at 378.

112. *Electricity Corporation of New Zealand v. Fletcher Challenge Energy Ltd* [2002] 2 NZLR 433.

113. For offers to all the world, *see* para. 43.

114. *McMahon v. Gilberd* [1955] NZLR 1206.

115. *See*, for example, *Rao v. Police* (1988) 3 CRNZ 697 (a criminal case), applying *Pharmaceutical Society of Great Britain v. Boots Cash Chemists (Southern) Ltd* [1953] 1 QB 401.

1. Offers Distinguished from Invitations to Treat

34. An offer capable of giving rise to acceptance to a contract requires both a sufficient indication of the terms the offeror will accept and an indication or apparent indication that the offeror is willing to enter into a legally binding arrangement on those terms. The former without the latter is merely an invitation to treat. It is a statement designed to allow negotiation of the terms of a future agreement, without an indication of willingness at that time to be bound to any specific terms. In a leading New Zealand case, *Boulder Consolidated Ltd v. Tangaere*,[116] the supply by the appellant of a list of sections of land available for purchase, together with their respective prices, was not an offer to sell any one of the sections but merely an invitation to treat for the sale of any particular section the respondent might wish to buy.

The critical question is the intention, or apparent intention, of the person making the statement in question.[117] An undisclosed reservation or intention not to contract will not prevent a communication which, objectively viewed, appears to indicate a contractual intention from having effect as an offer.[118]

2. Examples

35. The courts have provided illustrations of the general principles distinguishing offers from invitations to treat in a number of common situations.

An advertisement or another call for tenders normally signifies only that the advertiser wishes to ascertain whether others might be interested in coming to a suitable agreement; that is, the advertisement or call is only an invitation to treat. Any tenders received are therefore offers, and the person soliciting tenders may accept them or reject them as he or she chooses.[119] Thus, while it is customary in any call for tenders to stipulate that the highest or any tender will not necessarily be accepted, such a statement is not necessary.[120] If, however, the person calling for tenders departs from the normal practice and indicates a definite commitment to accept the lowest tender, or lowest tender conforming with the tender specifications, that call for tenders becomes an offer which is accepted by the appropriate tender.[121] The call for tenders may, however, also have as an offer, made to

116. [1980] 1 NZLR 560.

117. *Ibid.*, at 566–568.

118. *Andrews v. Colonial Mutual Life Assurance Society Ltd* [1982] 2 NZLR 556 at 566.

119. *Gregory v. Rangitikei District Council* [1995] 2 NZLR 208 at 221.

120. *Pratt Contractors Ltd v. Palmerston North CC* [1995] 1 NZLR 469 at 483–484; *Transit New Zealand v. Pratt Contractors Ltd* [2002] 2 NZLR 313 at 329. The point was not in issue on appeal; *see Pratt Contractors Ltd v. Transit New Zealand* [2005] 2 NZLR 433.

121. *Transit New Zealand v. Pratt Contractors Ltd* [2002] 2 NZLR 313 at 332–333. The point was not in issue on appeal; *see Pratt Contractors Ltd v. Transit New Zealand* [2005] 2 NZLR 433. In such cases, the party calling for tenders may be able to cancel the contract if it is discovered that the tender did not conform to the stated conditions: *Rankin Construction Ltd v. Ontario* (2014) 376 DLR (4th) 697; 2014 ONCA 636.

would-be tenderers, of a 'preliminary' or 'process' contract as to the manner by which tenders received will be evaluated.[122]

An advertisement for goods or services will not normally have an effect other than as an invitation to treat. However, the use of sufficiently specific wording, or the nature of the subject matter of the advertisement, may cause the advertisement to be treated as an offer. Thus, an offer of refrigerators for sale will normally be an invitation to treat, while an advertised promise that the first four refrigerators sold will be at half-price might well be considered to have effect as an offer. Similarly, an advertisement offering a reward for the return of a lost item might be considered to be an offer. Certainly, it is more likely that an advertisement which contemplates the formation of a unilateral contract will be considered to have effect as an offer than one contemplating a bilateral contract.

Displays of goods within a shop window[123] or on the shelves of shops[124] will usually amount to no more than invitations to treat. The normal analysis is that the would-be purchaser must approach the shop owner (or that person's employee or agent) and indicate a willingness to purchase the goods in question. The shop owner or employee or agent may then choose whether to accept or reject the customer's offer.

C. Offers Capable of Giving Rise to More Than One Contract

1. Process Contracts

36. The New Zealand courts have on a number of occasions recognized and upheld what are sometimes referred to as 'process' contracts; that is, contractually binding arrangements governing the process by which an individual will determine whether to accept a particular offer, or which of several offers will be accepted. In *Markholm Construction Ltd v. Wellington City Council,*[125] the defendant had advertised specified parcels of land for sale, stipulating that if more than one offer to purchase at the nominated price was received for any section, a ballot would be held to determine the offer to be accepted. It was held that this statement, while not an offer to sell any parcel of land, did give rise to a contractual obligation to hold the ballot when more than one offer was received for each section.

Liability may attach under statute for a failure to adhere to advertised methods for dealing with applications or tenders, even if there is no contractual obligation.[126]

122. *Pratt Contractors Ltd v. Transit New Zealand* [2005] 2 NZLR 433 at 438 (PC). Paragraphs 36 and 38 provide examples of advertisements giving rise to such 'process' contracts governing negotiations for substantive contracts.

123. *Fisher v. Bell* [1961] 1 QB 394.

124. *Pharmaceutical Society of Great Britain v. Boots Cash Chemists (Southern) Ltd* [1953] 1 QB 401.

125. [1985] 2 NZLR 520. Such a 'preliminary' or process contract was held to be normal in cases where tenders were called: *Pratt Contractors Ltd v. Transit New Zealand* [2005] 2 NZLR 433 at 438 (PC).

126. For example, Fair Trading Act 1986, s. 9, discussed in *Gregory v. Rangitikei District Council* [1995] 2 NZLR 208.

2. Collateral Contracts

37. A somewhat similar situation may arise where the parties have conducted themselves so as to have two apparent agreements concerning the same subject matter but on different terms. If the terms of the second transaction cannot stand together with those of the first (i.e., if the express terms of the one contradicts those of the other), the second must be taken to be a variation of the terms of the first.[127]

However, if the terms of the two transactions can stand together and there is a clear intention by the parties to be bound to more than one transaction, there may be two separate contracts. The principal contract contains the primary obligations of the parties, while a second – the 'collateral' contract – provides for one party to undertake further obligations in return for the other party entering the principal contract.[128] A good example is provided by *Industrial Steel & Plant Ltd v. Smith,*[129] where it was held that when a finance company was negotiating with a borrower company to restructure the latter's debts, a promise made by a director of the borrower to guarantee the borrower's debts if the restructuring transaction went ahead created an enforceable collateral contract of guarantee.

Collateral contracts are of particular importance where the principal contract contains terms limiting or excluding legal liability for breach of contract or for negligence. The collateral contract will normally not contain any such terms, and therefore it may be relied on where an action for breach of the principal contract would not provide a remedy.[130] There will also be cases where the collateral contract is relied on because the principal contract cannot be enforced because of a defect of form or illegality.[131]

3. Auctions

38. By statute, a bid made at an auction sale is an offer to purchase the thing for sale; acceptance of any particular bid or offer occurs when the auctioneer, acting on behalf of the vendor, indicates acceptance of the bid.[132] Unless the sale is subject to a reserve price (as discussed below), the normal expectation is that acceptance will be of the highest bid made. These rules are developed from, and consistent with, the rule that an auctioneer's call for bids is merely an invitation to treat. A bid, like any other offer, may be withdrawn before it is accepted.

---

127. *Lysnar v. National Bank of New Zealand Ltd* [1935] NZLR 129.
128. *See generally Mouat v. Betts Motors Ltd* [1959] AC 71; *A M Bisley & Co Ltd v. Thompson* [1982] 2 NZLR 696; *Lysnar v. National Bank of New Zealand Ltd* [1935] NZLR 129; *Industrial Steel & Plant Ltd v. Smith* [1980] 1 NZLR 545; *Crown Melbourne Ltd v. Cosmopolitan Hotel (Vic) Pty Ltd* [2016] HCA 26.
129. [1980] 1 NZLR 545.
130. *A M Bisley & Co Ltd v. Thompson* [1982] 2 NZLR 696.
131. *Industrial Steel & Plant Ltd v. Smith* [1980] 1 NZLR 545; *Mouat v. Betts Motors Ltd* [1959] AC 71.
132. The statutory provisions governing auction sales are the Fair Trading Act 1986, ss 36X–36ZF and the Property Law Act 2007, s. 42.

This conceptually simple legal position becomes much more complex if the sale is subject to a reserve price or if the vendor has reserved the right to bid at the auction. An auctioneer is obliged to inform potential bidders whether or not the sale is without reserve.[133] That notification puts actual or potential bidders on notice that the auctioneer will not necessarily accept the highest bid made.

Difficulties therefore arise if an auctioneer seeks to refuse to accept the highest bid made at an auction which has been advertised as 'without reserve', as a refusal to accept the bid, or a withdrawal of the goods from sale, is inconsistent with the expectation that the highest bid will be accepted. Yet, as the offer to purchase has not been accepted, there is no contract of sale. The courts have found a satisfactory solution by holding that the advertisement of a sale as 'without reserve' constitutes an offer to potential bidders that the highest bid will be accepted; the making of a bid is an acceptance of that offer. If the auctioneer does not sell to the highest bidder, the auctioneer is liable on this secondary contract, and damages (which may be substantial) are recoverable.[134]

4. Options and Rights of Pre-emption

39. An 'option', or more correctly a 'contract of option', is a specialized form of agreement whereby one party (the grantor of the option) sets out a contractual offer containing (in sufficiently definite form) the terms on which the grantor is prepared at some future time to contract with the other party (the option-holder), and further agrees, in contractually binding fashion, to give up the right to withdraw the offer prior to acceptance.[135] As an option is a form of contract, there must be consideration for it. Further, the offer which is being kept open must be in terms which are sufficiently definite to allow the courts to give it contractual effect. In particular, it must not leave any matters to be decided solely by the parties at some later stage.[136]

An option-holder who seeks to exercise the option must comply fully and strictly with its terms and with any conditions for its exercise. In *Gulf Corporation Ltd v. Gulf Harbour Investments Ltd*,[137] it was held an option had not validly been exercised because the letter purporting to exercise it did not precisely correspond with the terms of the option, although the differences were commercially insignificant and in no way altered the substance of the bargain.

---

133. Fair Trading Act 1986, s. 36ZB(2)(b).
134. *See Barry v. Davies* [2000] 1 WLR 1962; compare *Warlow v. Harrison* (1859) 1 E & E 309. There is a direct analogy with the 'process' contracts discussed at para. 36.
135. *Alexander v. Tse* [1988] 1 NZLR 318 at 324–325; *Murray v. Scott* [1976] 1 NZLR 643 at 655–656; *Jane v. Ben Hall Properties Ltd* [1979] 2 NZLR 68 at 73 per McMullin J. In Australia, Gibbs J. in *Laybutt v. Amoco Australia Pty Ltd* (1974) 4 ALR 482 at 494–498 advanced an alternative view that an option is truly a form of conditional contract. No practical difference is likely to result from the adoption of one view rather than the other.
136. *Willetts v. Ryan* [1968] NZLR 863; *Barrett v. IBC International Ltd* [1995] 3 NZLR 170. A provision leaving a matter for future agreement but allowing a machinery provision to operate in default of agreement is not objectionable on this ground (*see* para. 65).
137. [2006] 1 NZLR 21. For a forceful criticism of the decision, *see* McLauchlan, [2005] NZLJ 300.

The grantor is under a contractual obligation, so a revocation of the offer of the major contract during the currency of the option will be a breach of contract for which damages may be awarded, although specific performance is not available.[138] Where the option is for the sale of land, the option-holder acquires a caveatable interest in the subject land.[139]

By contrast, a contractual right of pre-emption is created when one party (the grantor) makes a contractual promise to the holder of the right that if at some future time covered by the contract the grantor should seek to enter into a contract in relation to a specific matter or service, the grantor will make his or her first offer as to that future contract to the holder of the right of pre-emption.[140] It is, therefore, essentially a contractual right of first refusal. Unlike an option, a right of pre-emption gives the holder no right to compel the grantor to enter into the future contract. A further difference is that where an option requires the terms to be certain, a right of pre-emption does not need to do so. Instead, the terms may be left to be determined by the grantor, although if this is done, the terms of the offer must be those which the grantor would offer to any other potential contracting party.[141]

No specific forms of words are required for an option or for a right of pre-emption, and in determining whether one or other has been created, the courts will look to the substance of the contract and not the description given by the parties.[142]

D. Special Cases of Offers

1. Standing Offers

40. While normally an offer will be either accepted or rejected, and its status as an offer thereby terminated, it is possible to have a 'standing offer'. This is an offer which may be accepted more than once, with each acceptance giving rise to a discrete contract. This will occur where the offeror has manifested a continuing willingness to supply on definite terms specified goods or services, in whatever quantity or frequency the offeree may seek from time to time.[143]

---

138. As to remedies for breach of an option contract, *see generally Alexander v. Tse* [1988] 1 NZLR 318.
139. *See* Land Transfer Act 1952, s. 137; *Willetts v. Ryan* [1968] NZLR 863.
140. *See Adaras Developments Ltd v. Marcona Corporation* [1975] 1 NZLR 324. The grantor of a right of first refusal may trigger the right, in the absence of any third party involvement, by making a fair and reasonable offer to the grantee: *see MacMillan v. Covic* [2004] 2 NZLR 106 and *Johnstone v. Macassey* (2004) 6 NZCPR 118. However, the right of pre-emption will not be triggered upon the grant of an option to buy that same property: *McLachlan v. Mercury Geotherm Ltd (in receivership)* [2006] UKPC 27; (2006) 7 NZCPR 135 (PC).
141. *Smith v. Morgan* [1971] 2 All ER 1500.
142. *Kean v. Dunfoy* [1952] NZLR 611; *Adaras Developments Ltd v. Marcona Corporation* [1975] 1 NZLR 324 at 332; compare *Woodroffe v. Box* (1954) 92 CLR 245.
143. *See Gilmour v. McLeod Bros* (1893) 12 NZLR 335 and *Great Northern Rly Co v. Witham* (1873) LR 9 CP 16; compare *Aotearoa International Ltd v. Scancarriers A/S* [1985] 1 NZLR 513. The Court of Appeal has also used the phrase 'standing offer' to describe an offer, such as is made in

2. Sale of an Interest in Land

41. In New Zealand, formal exchanges of contracts are uncommon, it being the usual practice for both buyer and seller to sign a single contract.

In the case of residential properties and even of smaller commercial properties, the contract will normally be created by the parties signing a standard form agreement (perhaps modified by some special provisions). The most common is a form jointly developed and agreed by the Real Estate Institute of New Zealand and the Auckland District Law Society.

Oral agreements for the sale of an interest in land will not be enforceable in the absence of a written memorandum or of part performance.[144] However, where the subject matter of the contract is more substantial – as with a sale of a substantial area of farmland – it is common for the parties to sign a specially prepared contractual document. Because of this practice, the Court of Appeal held in *Carruthers v. Whitaker* that there is a rebuttable presumption that the parties to such substantial or complex transactions do not intend to be bound until the formal document is prepared and signed.[145] The inference may be rebutted on the facts.[146]

3. Ticket Cases

42. It is commonplace for a ticket, or another similar document, to be passed to one of the parties to an alleged contract at or close to the time when it is alleged the contract was concluded, and for it then to be alleged that terms or conditions printed on the ticket are terms or conditions of the contract. Several different possibilities must be considered.

First, there are the simple cases where one party specifically tenders a ticket in circumstances where, objectively viewed, the ticket is to be seen as containing any terms upon which the offeror wishes to insist. The taking of the ticket is then an acceptance of the offer.[147]

Second, there is the position where the contract is concluded by an offer and an acceptance before any reference to a ticket, or any terms on it, takes place. In such cases, the ticket will not be part of the contract and will therefore not bind the party

---

a copyright licensing scheme, which can be accepted by any one or more of the class of persons to whom it is made without further negotiation of the terms, *see Copyright Licensing Ltd v. University of Auckland* [2015] NZCA 123, [56].

144. Property Law Act 2007, s. 24 and *see* discussion at paras 92–94.

145. [1975] 2 NZLR 667; compare *Spengler Management Ltd v. Tan* [1995] 1 NZLR 120; *Verissimo v. Walker* [2006] 1 NZLR 760; and *Smada Group Ltd v. Miro Farms Ltd* [2007] NZCA 568. The same presumption applies to complex commercial contracts: *Holmes v. Australasian Holdings Ltd* [1988] 2 NZLR 303; *Shell Oil Ltd v. Wordcom Investments Ltd* [1992] 1 NZLR 129.

146. *See*, for example, *Newton-King v. Wilkinson* [1976] 2 NZLR 321; *France v. Hight* [1990] 1 NZLR 345; *Cromwell Corporation Ltd v. Sofrana Immobilier (NZ) Ltd* (1992) 6 NZCLC 67,997 at 68,015.

147. *Chapelton v. Barry UDC* [1940] 1 KB 532; compare *Holmes v. Burgess* [1975] 2 NZLR 311.

to whom it was issued.[148] The position will be different if that party had noticed that certain terms would be imposed and had reasonable notice of what those terms were.[149]

Third, account must be taken of the cases where an offer to purchase goods or services is met with the presentation of a ticket or other document which contains terms which represent a significantly different set of obligations from those contained in the offer. In such cases, it would be proper to consider the presentation of the ticket or document as a counter-offer which must in turn be accepted before there is a contract. This will often be most important where the document proffered contains terms limiting or excluding legal liability which the party offering the document would otherwise incur.[150]

There are unresolved questions relating to the use of automatic or programmed machines which dispense tickets as part of the provision of goods or services. One possibility is that the owner of the machine, by providing a facility to acquire the goods or services from the machine, makes an offer which is accepted by the tender of payment in cash or otherwise. If so, the contract is concluded prior to any ticket or other document being produced by the machine, and therefore any limiting terms or conditions not otherwise brought to the offeree's attention are not effective. However, it may be that the tender of cash or other payment is an offer to purchase which is then accepted by the machine. In this case, the issuing of the ticket may itself represent the acceptance.[151] This latter analysis seems more appropriate in cases where the machine is programmed so that it may accept or reject particular forms of payment tendered.

E. Offers in Unilateral Contracts

43. An offer may be made to the world at large.[152] The issue of whether or not a statement amounted to an offer to the world will generally arise in the context of a claim that a unilateral contract came into existence.[153] In particular, the issue is likely to occur in cases where an advertisement indicates that the advertiser will be bound should someone else act in reliance on the advertisement by doing some specified act, for example, by returning lost property or providing information to the police.[154]

---

148. *Holmes v. Burgess* [1975] 2 NZLR 311.
149. *Harvey v. Ascot Dry Cleaning Co Ltd* [1953] NZLR 549 at 552–553.
150. *See*, for example, *Parker v. South Eastern Railway Co* (1877) 2 CPD 416; *Thompson v. London, Midland and Scottish Railway Co* [1930] 1 KB 41. Exclusion and limitation clauses are discussed at paras 172–181.
151. *See* the views of Lord Denning MR in *Thornton v. Shoe Lane Parking Ltd* [1971] 2 QB 163 at 169.
152. *McMahon v. Gilberd & Co Ltd* [1955] NZLR 1206; *Carlill v. Carbolic Smoke Ball Co* [1893] 1 QB 256.
153. For the distinction between unilateral and bilateral contracts, *see generally* para. 29.
154. *R v. Clarke* (1927) 40 CLR 227.

While it is possible to have an 'offer to the world' to enter into a bilateral contract,[155] it is certainly much more likely that an advertisement which requires a reader of the advertisement to negotiate a bilateral agreement with the advertiser will be held only to amount to an invitation to treat, and not an offer.[156]

However, there is a significant class of case where the advertisement may be held to have two functions in law – as an invitation to treat as to the substantive bargain which the parties might reach, but as a contractual offer to all the world as to how any negotiations towards the substantive bargain will be handled. This class of case is often called a 'process' contract. For example, in *Markholm Construction Ltd v. Wellington City Council,*[157] an advertisement which stated that a municipal body would hold a ballot among prospective purchasers of lands to be sold was held to be an 'offer to the world' capable of being accepted and giving rise to a contract.

F. When Offer Is Effective

44. The objective theory of contract formation requires that an offer be communicated, and there be an appearance of acceptance. Until the offer is communicated, there can therefore be no acceptance. However, if the communication of the offer was not authorized, the apparent offer cannot be accepted.[158]

Once the offer has been communicated, it can be accepted at any time until it is brought to an end by rejection, revocation, expiry, or a supervening incapacity of the offeror. These possible forms of termination of the offer are discussed seriatim below.

G. Termination of Offer

1. Rejection of Offer

45. An offer is terminated as soon as the offeree communicates to the offeror the offeree's rejection of the offer.[159] The making of a counter-offer acts as a rejection of the offer, thus also terminating it.[160]

The fact of rejection means there is no longer any offer capable of acceptance. Any purported later acceptance will be ineffective, unless the offer has been

---

155. For example, an offer made under a copyright licensing scheme to grant a contractual licence to any one or more of the class of persons to whom the offer is directed without further negotiation of the terms: *Copyright Licensing Ltd v. University of Auckland* [2015] NZCA 123, [56].
156. As to invitations to treat, *see* paras 34, 35.
157. [1985] 2 NZLR 520; compare *Pratt Contractors Ltd v. Transit New Zealand* [2005] 2 NZLR 433 at 438. For contracts so constituted, *see* para. 36.
158. *Wilson v. Belfast Corporation* (1921) 55 ILT 205.
159. *Powierza v. Daley* [1985] 1 NZLR 558; compare *Shaw v. Jones* [1924] NZLR 1133.
160. *Cross v. Davidson* (1899) 17 NZLR 576; *see also Powierza v. Daley* [1985] 1 NZLR 558; *Pascoe Properties Ltd v. Attorney-General* [2014] NZCA 616.

expressly or impliedly renewed[161] or, most unusually, it contains express words indicating rejection is not to terminate it.

Care must be taken to distinguish between statements by the offeree which indicate that the offeree will not contract on the offeror's terms – thus rejecting the offer – and statements which merely seek to elucidate the terms of the offer or even to discover whether opportunity exists to reach agreement on other possible terms of a contract. If a reasonable bystander would not think the offeree was insisting on new terms but merely exploring possible alternative terms, there is no rejection of the offer.[162] The addition of words which do not affect the terms of the proposed bargain will not be a counter-offer.[163]

2. Revocation of Offer of Bilateral Contract

46. An offeree may revoke an offer, bringing the offer to an end and making a purported later acceptance ineffective.[164] No particular form of words is needed, and revocation may be by implication rather than in explicit terms, provided the fact of revocation is unequivocally conveyed.[165]

The offeror normally has the right to revoke an offer at any time, even if he or she has indicated it is to endure for some longer period. A standing offer may be revoked, provided there is no contract not to revoke it.[166] However, there are two important exceptions to the right to revoke at will. First, as indicated above,[167] where the offeror has granted an option, withdrawal of the offer may prevent the offer from being accepted, but such a revocation will give rise to liability for breach of the option contract.

The second exception arises in relation to offers which could give rise to a contract for the international sale of goods. The Contract and Commercial Law Act 2017[168] adopts the United Nations Convention for the International Sale of Goods, which provides in Article 16(2)(a) that an offer which is indicated to be irrevocable, either by an express statement to that effect or by an indication that the offer is open for a fixed period, cannot be revoked once it has been communicated to the offeree. Nor may any offer in relation to an intended contract for the international sale of goods be revoked if the offeree has reasonably assumed it was irrevocable and has acted in reliance on that belief: Article 16(2)(b). An offer not expressed to be irrevocable, and not conveying that impression, can be revoked by actual notice to the

161. *Shaw v. Jones* [1924] NZLR 1133; compare *Livingstone v. Evans* [1925] 4 DLR 769.
162. *Attorney-General v. Whangarei District Council* (2006) 6 NZCPR 561.
163. *Coughlan v. Cox* [2014] NZCA 617, [56]–[57], where the clarification of the identity of a party to an agreement did not amount to a material alteration and was not a counter-offer.
164. *Routledge v. Grant* (1828) 4 Bing 653; *Wynes v. Lingard* (1909) 29 NZLR 1.
165. *Manchester Diocesan Council for Education v. Commercial and General Investments Ltd* [1969] 3 All ER 1593; *King v. Homer* (1913) 33 NZLR 222.
166. *Cook Islands Shipping Co Ltd v. Colson Builders Ltd* [1975] 1 NZLR 422.
167. *See* para. 39.
168. Section 204. The Contract and Commercial Law Act 2017, ss 202–206 replace the earlier Sale of Goods (International Conventions) Act 1994.

offeree: Article 16(1). In the normal case of an offer of a bilateral contract, revocation of an offer is effective only when the revocation has been communicated to the offeree, either by the offeror personally or by an authorized agent.[169] Thus a communication by post, or other method of communication requiring transmission, will only be effective when the revocation is received.[170]

If an unauthorized third party communicates to the offeree the offeror's revocation, the offer is terminated if the information has an appearance of reliability such that the offeree should be expected to accept its accuracy.[171]

3. Revocation of Unilateral Offers

47. While it is clear that an offer to enter into unilateral contracts can be revoked before the offeree has commenced the required act of acceptance,[172] there is no New Zealand authority which has sought to answer a related question of some theoretical and practical difficulty. Can an offer of a unilateral contract be revoked when the offeror is aware the offeree has commenced performance? Overseas authorities have canvassed a range of possible answers, from permitting revocation at any time prior to completion of the stipulated act to denying that the offer may be revoked once acceptance has started.[173] It seems probable that the better view is that there is no rule one way or the other, and that whether the offer is revocable will depend on the circumstances of the transaction and the intentions of the parties.[174]

An offer to all the world, which must be made by publication of the offer rather than by individual communication, may be revoked by publication of the revocation in a manner equivalent to that by which the offer was made.[175]

4. Termination of Offer by Effluxion of Time, Change of Circumstances, or Failure of a Condition to Which Offer Was Subject

48. If an offer is made in terms which leave it open only for a specific period of time, it will cease to be capable of acceptance once that time limit has been reached.

169. *Somerville v. Rice* (1912) 31 NZLR 370; *cf. Henthorn v. Fraser* [1892] 2 Ch. 27.
170. *Byrne & Co v. Van Tienhoven & Co* (1880) 5 CPD 344. An offeree whose own conduct unreasonably prevents the revocation being communicated may not be able to assert the revocation was ineffective: *see* the discussion in *Tenax Steamship Co Ltd v. Brimnes (owners), The Brimnes* [1975] QB 929.
171. *King v. Homer* (1913) 33 NZLR 222; *Dickinson v. Dodds* (1876) 2 Ch D 463.
172. *Carlill v. Carbolic Smoke Ball Co* [1893] 1 QB 256.
173. Compare *Petterson v. Pattberg* 161 NE 428 (NY CA 1928), with *Daulia Ltd v. Four Millbank Nominees Ltd* [1978] Ch. 231.
174. *See Mobil Oil Australia Ltd v. Lyndel Nominees Pty Ltd* (1998) 153 ALR 198, 223–229.
175. *Shuey v. United States* 92 US 73 (US SC 1875).

If no time limit is specified, the offer will come to an end at the expiry of a reasonable time,[176] this being judged in relation to the nature of the transaction and of the parties.[177]

If an offer would, in the eyes of a reasonable observer, have been intended by the offeror to be subject to the continued existence of certain circumstances, the offer will lapse where those circumstances are fundamentally changed, whether that change involves a single event or by a cumulative process.[178]

If the offer is expressly or impliedly subject to a condition requiring the occurrence or non-occurrence of some event, failure of the condition will mean the offer comes to an end.[179]

5. Effect of Death or Supervening Incapacity of Offeror or Offeree

49. If the offeror dies before a revocable offer is accepted or rejected, it appears that the offer will be terminated if the intended contract was one dependent on the personal efforts or contributions of the offeror.[180] If it was of a nature which did not involve the personal input of the offeror, the result may be different, and the offer may remain open if this was the apparent intent of the offeror.[181]

It would appear that essentially the same principles apply to cases where the offeree dies before the offer is accepted. If the intended contract requires the offeree's personal contribution or the existence of the offeree is essential, the offer cannot be accepted by the offeree's estate.[182] However, there may be cases where the offer is in such terms that it will survive the offeree's death.[183]

If the offeror ceases to have legal capacity to contract, the offer will terminate,[184] and logically, if the offeree loses contractual capacity prior to acceptance, he or she cannot then validly accept the offer. If neither party ever had the requisite legal capacity, it is likely that no binding contract could ever come into existence.[185]

---

176. While the rule result is clear, its theoretical basis is controverted. The offer may be seen as lapsing (*Kean v. Dunfoy* [1952] NZLR 611 at 612, *Dencio v. Zivanovic* (1993) 105 FLR 117), or as being impliedly rejected by the offeree (*Manchester Diocesan Council for Education v. Commercial and General Investments Ltd* [1970] 1 WLR 241 at 247–248), or perhaps as being impliedly revoked by the offeror.
177. *Kean v. Dunfoy* [1952] NZLR 611; *Ramsgate Victoria Hotel Co Ltd v. Montefiore* (1866) LR 1 Exch 109.
178. *Nielsen v. Dysart Timbers Ltd* [2009] 3 NZLR 160; [2009] NZSC 43. As the division of opinion in that case shows, determining whether such a condition is to be implied is not an easy task.
179. *Financings Ltd v. Stimson* [1962] 3 All ER 386.
180. *Bradbury v. Morgan* (1862) 1 H & C 249 at 255.
181. *Coulthart v. Clemenston* (1879) 5 QBD 42 at 46 per Bowen J; and *see Re Silvester, Midland Railway Co v. Silvester* [1895] 1 Ch. 573.
182. *Sommerville v. National Coal Board* 1963 SC 666.
183. Compare *Re Adams and Kensington Vestry* (1884) 27 Ch D 394 and *Re Irvine* [1928] 3 DLR 268.
184. *Official Assignee of Fretwell v. Fretwell* [1927] NZLR 637.
185. For discussion of capacity to contract, *see* paras 119–124.

H. Acceptance Generally

50. On the objective view of contract formation, an acceptance occurs when the offeree manifests, expressly or impliedly, an intention to be bound to the offeror on the terms expressed in the offer.[186] Thus, the contract comes into existence at the time and place that the acceptance has effect.[187] This is a matter of substance, not of language. The use of words of acceptance when in fact no acceptance is manifested does not amount in law to an acceptance.[188] However, an objective appearance of an intention to accept will not have effect as an acceptance if the offeror knows the offeree is not intending to accept the offer.[189]

An offer may only be accepted by the offeree. If the offer was made personally to one person, that person can accept but another cannot.[190] Similarly, if the offer was addressed to a class of persons, only a person within that class can validly accept it.[191]

Although an offer will normally terminate on acceptance, standing offers do endure after acceptance, and as such may be accepted on more than one occasion.[192]

1. Acceptance in Retrospective Agreements

51. While there is no New Zealand authority directly on the point, the overseas authority has held that an agreement may expressly provide that a contract resulting from it will have retrospective effect.[193] Authority is divided over whether such a term could be implied if the contract contains no such express term.[194]

If one or both parties have acted in reliance on the (ultimately unfulfilled) expectation a retrospective contract would be forthcoming and in doing so have conferred a benefit on the other party, but no such contract is concluded, the courts may in appropriate cases give some remedy to the party or parties, by finding a limited contract covering matters where there has been performance[195] or by allowing recovery on a quantum meruit action.[196]

---

186. *Byrne & Co v. Van Tienhoven & Co* (1880) 5 CPD 344; *Manchester Diocesan Council for Education v. Commercial and General Investments Ltd* [1969] 3 All ER 1593.
187. *J A Redpath & Sons Ltd v. Melville Ford & Co Ltd* [1950] NZLR 362.
188. *Broadcasting Corporation of New Zealand v. Daniels* (1988) 2 NZBLC 103, 535 at 103, 541.
189. *Airways Corporation of New Zealand Ltd v. Geyserland Airways Ltd* [1996] 1 NZLR 116.
190. *Lee v. Sayers* (1909) 28 NZLR 804.
191. *McMahon v. Gilberd & Co Ltd* [1955] NZLR 1206.
192. *Cook Islands Shipping Co Ltd v. Colson* [1975] 1 NZLR 422; for offers to all the world *see* para. 43.
193. *Newlands v. Argyll General Insurance Co Ltd* [1959] SR (NSW) 130 (FC).
194. In *Newlands v. Argyll General Insurance Co Ltd, ibid.*, it was held an express term was required, but a term as to retrospectivity was implied in both *Trollope & Colls Ltd v. Atomic Power Constructions Ltd* [1962] 1 WLR 333 at 339 and *City of Box Hill v. E W Tauschke Pty Ltd* [1974] VR 39. As to implied terms *see* paras 167–171.
195. *Mercurius Ventures Ltd v. Waitakere City Council* [1996] 2 NZLR 495, 501; *Turriff Construction Ltd v. Regalia Knitting Mills Ltd* (1971) 222 Estates Gazette 169.
196. *British Steel Corporation v. Cleveland Bridge and Engineering Co Ltd* [1984] 1 All ER 504. As to quantum meruit generally *see* para. 350.

2. Acceptance in Bilateral and Unilateral Contracts Compared

52. In a bilateral contract, the offeror's promise of future performance is accepted by the giving by the offeree of the offeree's own promise of future performance. By contrast, in a unilateral contract, the offeror makes a promise of future performance, but this is accepted by the offeree actually performing in the way required by the offer, not by a promise to do so in the future.

3. Acceptance in Unilateral Contracts

53. An offer of a unilateral contract is accepted by conduct which both performs the acts required by the offer and is done in response to the offer. The doing of the acts alone is not sufficient: there must be an intention on the part of the offeree to bring himself or herself within the terms of the offer. Thus, if the required act is done without the knowledge of the offer,[197] or without an intention to accept it,[198] there is no acceptance and no contract.

The required conduct must be done within the currency of the offer. As we have seen, there is some uncertainty as to the legal position where the offeror seeks to withdraw the offer after the offeree has commenced performance.[199]

4. Acceptance in Bilateral Contracts

54. Acceptance in a bilateral contract occurs when the offeree manifests an intention to accept the offer by making a promise which corresponds to the offer and is in response to it. There must be some words or conduct, usually in the form of notice to the offeror, which manifests to the objective observer the intention to accept the offer. It is not sufficient that the offeree determines to accept the offer but does nothing to show this intention has been formed.[200] This is so even if the offeror has stated that silence will be taken as acceptance, as the law will not permit an offeror to seek to bind the offeree in this manner.[201] It is the manifestation of an

197. *McMahon v. Gilberd & Co Ltd* [1955] NZLR 1206, applying *R v. Clarke* (1926) 40 CLR 227; *see also NZ Shipping Co Ltd v. A M Satterthwaite and Co Ltd* [1975] AC 154.
198. *Airways Corporation of New Zealand Ltd v. Geyserland Airways Ltd* [1996] 1 NZLR 116; compare *Magnum Photo Supplies Ltd v. Viko New Zealand Ltd* [1999] 1 NZLR 395 at 400.
199. *See* para. 47.
200. *Braund v. Mutual Life and Citizens' Assurance Co Ltd* [1926] NZLR 529; *Stevenson Brown Ltd v. Montecillo Trust* [2017] NZCA 57; *Brogden v. Metropolitan Railway Co* (1877) 2 App Cas 666 at 692 per Lord Blackburn.
201. *Felthouse v. Bindley* (1862) 11 CBNS 869; compare *Fairline Shipping Corporation v. Adamson* [1975] QB 180. The United Nations Convention on Contracts for the International Sale of Goods (in force in New Zealand under the Contract and Commercial Law Act 2017, s. 204) specifically provides in Art. 18(1) that in an offer for a contract for the international sale of goods an offer can stipulate that silence amounts to consent. Nevertheless, there may be some exceptional cases (most of those reported deal with offers of insurance cover) where the nature of the transaction and the parties' history of prior dealings will mean that silence by the offeree in the face of the offer is still effective as an acceptance. *See*, for example, *Lundberg v. Royal Exchange Insurance Co* [1933]

intention to accept, rather than the use of any particular method of acceptance or the use of any particular form of words, that is essential.[202] There will also be cases where the offeree's acceptance is inferred from conduct without communication of acceptance.[203] However, there may be cases where the offeror has required specific words to be used, or, more commonly, the use of a specific method of communicating acceptance. Such requirements are discussed separately below.[204]

A corollary of the requirement that the acceptance be in reliance on the offer is that no contract is created by 'cross-offers' – where A makes an offer to B of a contract on terms X, simultaneously B makes an offer to A of a contract on terms X. Neither communication is a response to the other's offer; neither is a valid acceptance, and further effective communications will be needed before a contract can result.[205]

5. Acceptance Where Means of Acceptance Stipulated

55. Difficulties may sometimes arise if an offeror has stipulated a specific procedure for acceptance or a particular method of communicating acceptance.

The first question for the court is whether there was an apparent intention that the offer could only give rise to a contract if the specified procedure or means of communication was followed. As we have seen, the grantor of an option may stipulate the way in which it must be exercised, and the courts will require strict compliance with the terms of the option.[206] However, the principle can apply to contracts of all kinds. An example is *Wilmott v. Johnson*,[207] where the vendors had indicated they would only consider themselves bound when a change to a particular document had been signed and changes initialled by the parties.

These cases must be distinguished from the perhaps more common position where the offeror has stipulated for acceptance to be made in a particular fashion, so that any acceptance will be received more quickly or with greater assurance

---

NZLR at 614–615; *Taylor v. Allon* [1966] 1 QB 304 at 311; but compare *Braund v. Mutual Life and Citizen's Assurance Co Ltd* [1926] NZLR 529. If an offeree has knowingly allowed the offeror to rely on silence as being an acceptance, questions of estoppel may arise: *Spiro v. Lintern* [1973] 1 WLR 1002.

202. *Broadcasting Corporation of New Zealand v. Daniels* (1988) 2 NZBLC 103, 535 at 103, 541; *Manchester Diocesan Council for Education v. Commercial and General Investments Ltd* [1970] 1 WLR 241; compare *Lundberg v. Royal Exchange Insurance Corporation* [1933] NZLR 605.

203. *See* para. 56.

204. *See* para. 55.

205. *Tinn v. Hoffmann & Co* (1873) 29 LT 271; compare *Holwell Securities Ltd v. Hughes* [1974] 1 WLR 155.

206. *Gulf Corporation Ltd v. Gulf Harbour Investments Ltd* [2006] 1 NZLR 21. For options generally *see* para. 39.

207. [2003] 1 NZLR 649. *See also Corrick v. Silich* [2018] NZCA 221; (2018) 24 PRNZ 210, at [42]-[43].

against mishap than might otherwise be the case. If the stipulation is for this purpose, an acceptance by any other method which is at least equally effective and speedy (so it is not less advantageous to the offeror) will be effective.[208]

In accordance with the general principle, a purported acceptance which does not comply with a mandatory procedure for acceptance might itself amount to a counter-offer which could be accepted by the original offeror.[209]

I. Communication of Acceptance

1. General

56. As acceptance requires the offeree to make a promise in return for, and in response to, the offeror's promise, the principle dictates that the offeree's promise should have to reach the offeror (or the offeree's agent)[210] before it can take effect. If the offeree attempts unsuccessfully to communicate the acceptance, there is no contract.[211] This general principle has been applied by the courts,[212] but with some important exceptions, which are discussed below.

There are three main exceptions to the general rule requiring communication of the acceptance of an offer:

(1) The offeror may be held to have waived the requirement, either expressly or impliedly. In such cases, there may be a sufficient manifestation of an intention to accept by doing other acts evincing an intention to contract. Thus, in *Commerce Commission v. Telecom Mobile Ltd,*[213] it was held that the vendor of packaged mobile telephones had impliedly waived any requirement for communication by purchasers of acceptance of the vendor's terms for providing telephone services. Consequently, the breaking of the seal on the packaged telephone amounted to acceptance by the consumer of those terms.
(2) The special rules governing postal communications may apply.[214]
(3) The offeror may be estopped from denying the efficacy of an acceptance which was not communicated to the offeror because of the offeror's own fault or error.[215]

---

208. The relevant principles and authorities are conveniently discussed in *Manchester Diocesan Council for Education v. Commercial & General Investments Ltd* [1970] 1 WLR 242.
209. *Wettern Electricity Ltd v. Welsh Development Agency* [1983] QB 796.
210. *Powierza v. Daley* [1985] 1 NZLR 558; *Ngoi v. Wen* [2017] NZCA 519; (2017) 19 NZCPR 1.
211. *Entores v. Miles Far East Corporation* [1955] 2 QB 327 at 332–333.
212. *Soares v. Simpson* [1931] NZLR 1079; *Kennedy v. Thomassen* [1928] 1 Ch. 426.
213. [2006] 1 NZLR 190; (2005) 2 NZCCLR 486; compare *Thomson v. Burrows* [1916] NZLR 223 (acceptance of an offer to purchase goods by the dispatch of the goods in question without direct communication to the offeror).
214. *See* para. 57.
215. *Entores v. Miles Far East Corporation* [1955] 2 QB 327 at 333; *Holwell Securities Ltd v. Hughes* [1974] 1 WLR 155; *Brinkibon Ltd v. Stahag Stahl und Stahlwaren GmbH* [1983] 2 AC 34.

2. Acceptances by Post and the 'Posting Rules'

57. New Zealand courts have been called on to apply, but have never seriously questioned, the principles applied in English cases concerning the effect of acceptances communicated through the post. The first question for the court is whether the English 'posting rules' apply to the communications in question. This is determined by looking first to see whether the offeror has expressly or impliedly stipulated the rules do not apply,[216] and where this is not determinative, by looking to whether use of the post was reasonable in the circumstances.[217] Where the 'posting rules' do apply, the courts will hold that a letter of acceptance is effective from the time it is placed in the post, not from the time it reaches the offeror or is read by the offeror.[218] The rationale for the rule is pragmatism rather than logic.[219]

Once it is accepted that the acceptance is effective from posting – or at least from posting to the correct address of the addressee and in accordance with the requirements of the Post Office[220] – it follows that the acceptance is effective even though it is lost in transit and never received.[221] Equally, it is effective if it is posted before the offeree learns of a revocation of the offer dispatched before the acceptance was posted.[222]

The posting rules were applied to telegrams,[223] a means of communication now effectively obsolete, but the courts declined to extend them to communications by telephone and telex transmissions.[224] Facsimile transmissions are usually treated as not falling within the posting rules.[225] Communications by electronic mail are governed by a statutory regime.[226]

---

216. A simple form of express stipulation is where the offeror requires acceptance actually be communicated, as with a requirement that any acceptance be 'in writing to the offeror'; compare *Holwell Securities Ltd v. Hughes* [1974] 1 WLR 155. If the offer is made by a much speedier form of communication than the post, there might be an implied stipulation that the acceptance be by an equally speedy method, and therefore the posting rules are not to apply. The relationship of the parties may also be such that neither can be assumed to accept that communications not actually received are effective: *Tallerman & Co Pty Ltd v. Nathan's Merchandise (Victoria) Pty Ltd* (1957) 98 CLR 93.
217. *Henthorn v. Fraser* [1892] 2 Ch. 27; compare *Household Fire and Carriage Accident Insurance Co Ltd v. Grant* (1879) 4 ExD 216.
218. *Adams v. Lindsell* (1818) 1 B & Ald 681; *cf. Henthorn v. Fraser* [1892] 2 Ch. 27.
219. *Brinkibon Ltd v. Stahag Stahl und Stahlwaren GmbH* [1983] 2 AC 34.
220. *Korbetis v. Transgrain Shipping BV* [2005] EWHC 1345 and *Re London & Northern Bank, ex p Jones* [1900] 1 Ch. 220, respectively.
221. *Household Fire and Carriage Accident Insurance Co Ltd v. Grant* (1879) 4 ExD 216 at 221.
222. *Sommerville v. Rice* (1912) 31 NZLR 370; *Byrne & Co v. Van Tienhoven & Co* (1880) 5 CPD 344.
223. *See Stevenson v. McLean* (1880) 5 QBD 346; *Cowan v. O'Connor* (1888) 20 QBD 640; *Henkel v. Pape* (1870) LR 6 Exch 7; *Shortal v. Buchanan* [1920] NZLR 103.
224. *See* respectively *Union Steamship Co v. Ewart* (1894) 13 NZLR 9; *Entores Ltd v. Miles Far East Corporation* [1955] 2 QB 327; *Brinkibon Ltd v. Stahag Stahl und Stahlwaren GmbH* [1983] 2 AC 34.
225. *Designer Salads Ltd v. Foodtown Supermarkets Ltd* (1990) 4 PRNZ 644; compare *Reese Bros Plastics Ltd v. Hamon-Sobelco Australia Pty Ltd* (1988) 5 BPR 11,106.
226. Contract and Commercial Law Act 2017, Part 4, discussed at para. 58.

The posting rules do not apply to contracts for the international sale of goods, where the United Nations Convention on the International Sale of Goods provides its own regime.[227]

3. Legislative Regime for Electronic Transactions

58. The New Zealand courts have only rarely been required to determine the status and effect of electronic communications such as e-mail messages in the formation of contracts. The matter is now determined by statute. Part 4 of the Contract and Commercial Law Act 2017[228] provides a number of 'default rules' that apply to transactions which in whole or in part are created by electronic communications. If the parties so choose, they may create their own regime to determine when and how any electronic message has effect.[229] Where this is not done, the following default rules will apply (unless a specific statute provides otherwise):

(1) An electronic message is dispatched at the time it enters an information system outside the control of the originator.[230] This will usually be the time at which the message is sent from the originator's computer system to an internet service provider. In cases where a party makes use of a network of computers, there may be interesting questions to be resolved as to the point at which the originator no longer has control of the information system.
(2) Where an addressee has designated an information system for the purpose of receiving communications, a message is deemed to be received when it enters the relevant information system. If the addressee has not designated an information system for the purpose of receiving communications, the electronic message is received only when the communication actually comes to the attention of the addressee.[231] Given that the use of an e-mail address will almost certainly amount to the designation of an information system for the purpose of receiving communications, the statute will almost inevitably mean that an e-mail message is taken to be received when it reaches the addressee's internet service provider; the addressee therefore runs the risk of any breakdown in transmission from that point.
(3) An acceptance of an offer via an electronic communication takes effect from the time the communication enters the offeror's information system, unless the parties have agreed otherwise or a statute provides otherwise.[232]

---

227. *See* Arts 18(2), 21 and 24. The Convention is in force in New Zealand by virtue of the Sale of Goods (United Nations Convention) Act 1994.
228. This part replaces the Electronic Transactions Act 2002.
229. Contract and Commercial Law Act 2017, s. 212.
230. Contract and Commercial Law Act 2017, s. 213.
231. Contract and Commercial Law Act 2017, s. 214.
232. Contract and Commercial Law Act 2017, s. 216.

(4) Electronic communications are taken to be dispatched from the originator's place of business and received at the addressee's place of business, respectively. There are further default provisions where this rule would not be effective, so, for instance, where there is more than one place of business, the messages are sent or received at the place of business having the closest relationship with the transaction.[233]

It must be remembered that there will be a significant number of cases where electronic transactions involve a purchaser of goods or services making purchases through a website operated by the vendor. In most if not all such cases, the vendor will have imposed a set of standard terms and conditions to which the purchaser must give, or will be deemed to have given, consent. In such cases, the specific terms and conditions of the vendor will operate, and the provisions of the Contract and Commercial Law Act 2017 will apply only to any matters left unresolved by the vendor.

J. Communications Containing or Imposing Fresh Terms or Conditions

1. Counter-Offers and 'Battle of the Forms'

59. The general rule is that a response to an offer which purports to accept it but introduces a new term or condition into the transaction is not in law a valid acceptance. If the response seeks to require the offeror to commit to different terms from those contained in the offer, the communication is in fact a counter-offer, and brings the offer to an end.[234]

The problem of fresh conditions or terms is particularly likely to arise in cases where there is a so-called battle of the forms – that is, where the parties each desire to contract on their own sets of terms and conditions as contained in standard form contractual documents, and each seeks to have the contract incorporate its standard terms. Questions may arise as to when, if ever, a contract has been concluded, for if both parties insist on their own terms, each is making a counter-offer to the other's proposals.[235] It may, however, be possible to identify some manifestation of acceptance to one such counter-offer; the contract is then concluded on the terms of that counter-offer.[236] The issue has caused difficulty in other jurisdictions, but there is no New Zealand authority in point.

There have been exceptional cases where new terms or conditions stated in the response did not in fact alter the substance of the bargain as stated in the offer. In these cases, the courts have been content to regard the response as a conditional

233. Contract and Commercial Law Act 2017, s. 215.
234. *Reporoa Stores Ltd v. Treloar* [1958] NZLR 177; *Cross v. Davidson* (1898) 17 NZLR 576; *Katz v. Jones* [1967] NZLR 861.
235. *Johnson Matthey Bankers Ltd v. State Trading Corporation of India* [1984] 1 Ll Rep 427.
236. *BRS v. Arthur v. Crutchley Ltd* [1968] 1 All ER 811; *Muirhead v. Industrial Tank Specialties Ltd* [1986] QB 507 at 530; but compare *Butler Machine Tool Co Ltd v. Ex-Cell-O Corporation (England) Ltd* [1979] 1 WLR 401; *Air Studios (Lyndhurst) Ltd v. Lombard North Central Plc* [2012] EWHC 3162.

acceptance which did not have legal effect as an acceptance until the condition was fulfilled, but equally did not amount to a counter-offer.[237]

2. Counter-Offers Generally

60. A statement by the offeree which indicates an unwillingness to be bound by the terms suggested by the offeror but manifests a willingness to be bound by other terms is a counter-offer, and not an acceptance of the offer received.[238] Insistence on even a very minor change to the terms is a counter-offer.[239] A counter-offer can be accepted so as to give rise to a binding contract.

The making of a counter-offer terminates the original offer so that the original offeree cannot seek to return to and accept the original offer if the counter-offer is not accepted.[240] If the original offeree expressly or impliedly renews the original offer, the offeree may then validly accept.[241]

Care must be taken to distinguish between a response to an offer which merely seeks elucidation of the offer or questions whether other terms might be negotiated or adds words which do not affect the material terms of the proposed transaction[242] – which will not be a counter-offer – and an insistence on different terms – which is a counter-offer.[243]

K. Revocation of Acceptance

61. Where acceptance must reach the offeror, a communication which would have effect as an acceptance on receipt by the offeror may be revoked prior to the acceptance being received.[244] The position is much less clear where the acceptance need not reach the offeror to be effective. Can a legally effective acceptance of which the offeror knows nothing be deprived of legal effect by a later, speedier, communication which is received before the acceptance comes to the offeror's knowledge? One old New Zealand case,[245] of less than compelling clarity, would answer the question in the negative; older Scots authority is the other way.[246] If the issue arises for decision, it might be thought the most practical solution would be to allow the first communication received by the offeror to be effective.

237. *Frampton v. McCully* [1976] 1 NZLR 270; compare *Takapuna Borough v. Australian Mutual Provident Society* [1916] NZLR 256. As to counter-offers generally *see* para. 60.
238. *Reporoa Stores Ltd v. Treloar* [1958] NZLR 177; cf. *Powierza v. Daley* [1985] 1 NZLR 558.
239. *Pascoe Properties Ltd v. Attorney-General* [2014] NZCA 616.
240. *Hyde v. Wrench* (1840) 3 Beav 334; *Shaw v. Jones* [1924] NZLR 1133.
241. *Livingstone v. Evans* (1925) 4 DLR 762.
242. *Coughlan v. Cox* [2014] NZCA 617, [56]-[57] (adding names of trustees of a trust which was to be a party to the transaction did not materially affect the terms proposed and was not a counter-offer).
243. *Attorney-General v. Whangarei District Council* (2006) 6 NZCPR 561; *Powierza v. Daley* [1985] 1 NZLR 558.
244. *Re National Savings Bank Association, Hebb's Case* (1867) LR 4 Eq 9; *A to Z Bazaars (Pty) Ltd v. Minister of Agriculture* (1974) 4, SA 392.
245. *Wenckheim v. Arndt* (1873) 1 NZ Jur 73.
246. *Countess of Dunmore v. Alexander* 1830 9 Sh (Ct of Sess) 190.

II. Incomplete, Indefinite and Conditional Agreements

A. *Uncertainty*

62. An agreement can only have contractual force if its terms are sufficiently certain that the court can ascertain with sufficient precision the obligations being undertaken or to be undertaken by the parties. The New Zealand courts have over the recent years developed a distinctive body of case law in this area, which provides flexible but logical principles by which such issues can be approached. The principles were extensively discussed in the leading case of *Electricity Corporation of NZ v. Fletcher Challenge Energy Ltd.*[247] In that case, the parties had negotiated 'Heads of Agreement' for an intended contract for the long-term supply of large quantities of natural gas. The Heads of Agreement drawn up by the parties noted agreement on most matters, but indicated one item was 'to be agreed' and others were marked 'not agreed'. There were mutual promises to negotiate a final contract. When these negotiations (in which matters indicated in the Heads of Agreement as agreed were revisited) failed, the respondents sought to enforce an agreement allegedly constituted by and recorded in the Heads of Agreement. The Court of Appeal held that no binding contract had ever been concluded.

The Court indicated that where issues of uncertainty or finality of an agreement arose, the first question to be determined was whether the parties had intended their transaction to be legally binding at the point it was alleged a contract had arisen. In deciding this, the court may look at the factual matrix in which the agreement was made, including evidence as to any earlier negotiations between the parties, and it might have regard to subsequent conduct. There should be neither a presumption in favour of an intention to create a contract nor a presumption to the reverse effect.

Once the court was satisfied that there was an intention to create a legally binding contract, the issue shifted to whether the parties' dealings had allowed the court to establish with sufficient certainty all matters which were legally essential or were considered by the parties as essential to their agreement. In regard to this question, the courts should not be neutral, but should rather lean towards fulfilling the parties' expectations and should therefore not lightly hold terms were insufficiently certain. No guidance was given as to what matters were 'legally essential', and it seems probable that these may vary between contracts of different natures, but it would seem the expression must encompass the core issues as to the identity of the parties[248] and the subject matter, the consideration to be furnished by the parties and the time for performance of the contractual obligations.[249] The Court in *Electricity Corporation of NZ v. Fletcher Challenge Energy Ltd* was at pains to point out that

247. [2002] 2 NZLR 433. For a similar approach, *see Carlylev. Royal Bank of Scotland plc* [2015] UKSC 13 at [29].

248. Identity may be proved by evidence: *Sunnyvale Property Trust Ltd v. Liu* [2015] NZHC 2804 at [38], applying *The Starsin* [2003] UKHL 12, [2003] 1 Lloyd's Rep 571 at [175].

249. For example, in a contract for the sale of land the essential terms for are 'parties, property and price': *SM &T Homes Ltd v. Nguyen* [2015] NZHC 3228 at fn 5. In a sale of farmland, the date of taking possession or whether a deposit was payable may be seen as essential; *see Fraser v. McHardy* [2018] NZCA 545, at [28]-[29].

these essential matters need not be stated explicitly in any agreement; it was sufficient if there was some machinery[250] or process to which recourse could be had to determine any matters not expressly agreed and stated. Most importantly, the court indicated that leaving a matter for future agreement between the parties did not of itself mean the agreement lacked sufficient certainty.[251]

1. Matters Left for Future Decision

63. Contractual theory requires that the process of offer and acceptance should lead the parties to agreement on every aspect of the intended contract, or at least to a position where there has been agreement on some process or machinery provision[252] which may be used to determine matters not actually agreed by the parties. On that basis, the courts felt compelled to hold no contract had come into existence if some matter had been left for future agreement between the parties.[253] However, the courts have preferred pragmatism to strict adherence to contractual theory. In *Electricity Corporation of NZ v. Fletcher Challenge Energy Ltd,*[254] the Court of Appeal held that the critical question is not the use of words such as 'to be agreed', but whether the parties intended that any matter left for the future be settled solely by the parties themselves, or whether there was a common intention that if no actual agreement was forthcoming, the matter could be resolved by reference to some machinery provision. For example, a term in the agreement that payment be at 'fair market value' was sufficiently certain because, in default of agreement on such value, the court could do so using objective criteria.[255]

If the parties intended that some matter be settled by the parties, and by the parties only, there is no contract until and unless the parties actually reach the requisite agreement. An agreement 'in principle' will normally indicate further matters are to be agreed before a contract is reached.[256] By contrast, if the parties intended that they should seek to reach agreement but that the matter could be settled objectively by a third party or a machinery provision, the use of 'to be agreed' will not be fatal. There is a close parallel here with the approach taken in cases involving inherently defective machinery provisions, although that link was not expressly explored in *Electricity Corporation.*

2. Future Agreements

64. Even though the New Zealand courts have relaxed the strictures of the older case law concerning matters which may be left for future agreement, the

250. *See* para. 65.
251. *See* para. 63.
252. As to which *see* para. 65.
253. *Willetts v. Ryan* [1968] NZLR 863; *Barrett v. IBC International Ltd* [1995] 3 NZLR 170.
254. [2002] 2 NZLR 433. *See also Wellington City Council v. Body Corporate 51702 (Wellington)* [2002] 3 NZLR 486.
255. *Worldwide NZ LLC v. NZ Venue and Event Management Ltd* [2014] NZSC 108.
256. *Plowman v. Franklin District Council* [2010] 1 NZLR 537 (HC).

requirement of agreement on essential matters means the courts will not recognize as valid and effective an agreement requiring the parties to reach a future contractual agreement.[257] It is clear that the parties to such an agreement would each be reserving to themselves the right to determine whether the contemplated future agreement was one to which they were willing to be bound. There is therefore no intention to undertake binding obligations, and as all the obligations of the parties would need to be settled, no common intention to leave unresolved matters to be determined by some express or implied machinery provision.

If the parties wish to secure legally binding commitments as to the future, they must enter into some sufficiently detailed current obligations, for example, by entering into an option contract or a contract giving pre-emptive rights[258] or a conditional contract.[259]

3. Contractual Machinery and Its Use

65. The common law has long recognized that an agreement intended to have contractual force is not rendered invalid or ineffective because a matter has been left to be determined at some future time by a specified process or by the application of a specific formula.[260] A simple example is a contract for the sale of property at a value to be determined by a specific valuer. Contractual provisions which contain the terms for such a process or a formula to be used are frequently referred to as 'machinery' provisions. A very wide range of machinery provisions are to be found in the cases, and there is no basis in principle for restricting the parties' own ingenuity in devising a process which will satisfy their aims. Thus, a matter may be left by the parties to a sufficiently designated third party, such as a solicitor who is to settle the final form of an agreement by using terms common in the area or profession,[261] or there may be a provision for the use of a sufficiently widely drafted arbitration clause.[262]

Difficulties may arise where the machinery which the parties have provided does not operate adequately or is discovered to be inherently unworkable. It is clear that in general the courts may step in after a machinery provision proves defective in operation and impose some alternative method of determining the matter which the machinery provision was to settle[263] – although the courts cannot do so if the use of the stipulated machinery was essential to the parties.[264] The New Zealand courts

257. *Wellington City Council v. Body Corporate 51702 (Wellington)* [2002] 3 NZLR 486 at 495–496; compare *Walford v. Miles* [1992] 2 AC 128.
258. As to which *see* para. 39.
259. *See* para. 68.
260. The common law applied the maxim '*certum est quod certum reddi potest*' (i.e., certain which can be made certain). The leading New Zealand cases are *Attorney-General v. Barker Bros* [1976] 2 NZLR 495 and *Money v. Ven-Lu-Ree Ltd* [1988] 2 NZLR 414; affirmed [1989] 3 NZLR 129 (PC).
261. *Robertson Enterprises Ltd v. Cope* [1989] 3 NZLR 391; *Coachman Properties Ltd v. Panmure Video Club Ltd* [1984] 2 NZLR 200.
262. *Attorney-General v. Barker Bros* [1976] 2 NZLR 495.
263. *Sudbrook Trading Estates Ltd v. Eggleton* [1983] 1 AC 444.
264. *Nelson v. Cooks McWilliams Wines Ltd* [1986] 2 NZLR 215.

have extended this remedial principle to apply to cases where the machinery provision was inherently defective or incomplete, provided there was a clear mutual intention that the matter to be determined by the machinery provision was to be settled on an 'objective' or 'market' basis.[265]

4. Uncertainty as to Meaning of Terms of Agreement

66. An agreement can only be enforced as a contract if its terms are sufficiently clear that the courts can be certain of the scope of the obligations the parties are undertaking.[266] But if the parties had clearly intended their agreement to have contractual force, the courts will try to find sufficient certainty as to its terms so that the contractual intent is not frustrated.[267]

Any ambiguity or uncertainty as to the meaning of a term in a written agreement may be dispelled by the use of the *contra proferentem* rule of interpretation[268] or by the use of parol evidence.[269] In appropriate cases, uncertain express terms may be rendered certain by the implication of terms to arrive at the most reasonable common expectation of the parties in the circumstances of the contract.[270]

In rare cases, a vague and uncertain provision which is of no significance to the substance of the bargain may be excised so as to leave the agreement in sufficiently definite terms to be enforced.[271]

B. Conditional Contracts

1. Conditional Contracts Generally

67. New Zealand has developed, with some significant influence from Australian law, a coherent and practical body of principles which allow parties to enter into binding contracts while making performance of the more onerous aspects of the transaction dependent on the outcome of events which one or both parties see as

---

265. *Money v. Ven-Lu-Ree Ltd* [1988] 2 NZLR 414, affirmed [1989] 3 NZLR 129. *See also Worldwide NZ LLC v. NZ Venue and Event Management Ltd* [2014] NZSC 108.
266. *Attorney-General v. Barker Bros* [1976] 2 NZLR 495 at 498–499. For example, in *Svenson v. Ngakuru* [2008] 2 NZLR 149, an alleged agreement for sale and purchase failed because the area of land to be sold was not adequately identified.
267. *Electricity Corporation of NZ v. Fletcher Challenge Energy Ltd* [2002] 2 NZLR 433; *see also Tower Insurance v. Nicon Ltd* [2019] NZCA 332.
268. *Anderson v. Tuapeka County Council* (1900) 19 NZLR 1. The *contra proferentem* rule whereby words are construed against the interest of the party introducing them to the agreement is considered further at para. 174.
269. *Quainoo v. New Zealand Breweries Ltd* [1991] 1 NZLR 161; compare *Jenkins v. Harbour View Courts Ltd* [1966] NZLR 1.
270. *GTV Holdings Ltd v. Harris* [2018] NZCA 95, at [27]-[29]. For a recent English decision to the same effect, *see Devani v. Wells* [2019] UKSC 4; [2019] 2 WLR 617, at [33].
271. *See Nicolene Ltd v. Simmonds* [1953] 1 QB 543; *Van Der Hulst v. Tainui Corporation* [1998] 2 NZLR 359.

essential.[272] It is clear that in many cases the New Zealand law is very different from the law and practice in other jurisdictions. It is common in New Zealand for agreements for sale and purchase of real estate to be subject to conditions such as the purchase being subject to loan finance being available,[273] or subject to the approval of the solicitor for one or other parties,[274] or subject to the grant of some necessary approval as to land use or development or the like.[275] The presence of such conditions does not prevent the agreement having contractual force – there will, for example, be binding obligations to seek fulfilment of the condition and to act reasonably when considering whether such conditions have been satisfied[276] – but the major elements of performance are suspended until the condition is fulfilled. Should the condition not be fulfilled, the contract will become either void or voidable, depending on what the parties have provided in their agreement.[277] A misrepresentation made by one party or its agents who induce the other party to believe a condition has been met and therefore consequently confirm the contract rather than leaving it to terminate will give rise to an action in misrepresentation.[278]

2. Conditional or Provisional Agreements

68. An agreement in sufficiently detailed terms is nevertheless only enforceable if there is an intention that it be binding.[279] While in the majority of simple contracts there will be no difficulty in ascertaining that contractual intent was present, cases not infrequently arise where the language used by the parties, or the nature of the transaction, means the issue must be explored.

One of the commonest methods by which parties indicate that they are postponing giving any contractual effect to an agreement is by the use of words such as 'subject to contract'. Where a phrase of this kind appears, the courts will presume that the parties did not intend the agreement to have contractual effect until some formal contractual document had been drawn up and signed by the parties; each is therefore free to withdraw from the arrangement until such a document is executed. However, the presumption that legal effect is being postponed is rebuttable, and

272. The leading cases are *Neylon v. Dickens* [1978] 2 NZLR 35; *Provost Developments Ltd v. Collingwood Towers Ltd* [1980] 2 NZLR 205; *Connor v. Pukerau Stores Ltd* [1981] 1 NZLR 384; *Globe Holdings Ltd v. Floratos* [1998] 3 NZLR 331.
273. *Connor v. Pukerau Stores Ltd* [1981] 1 NZLR 384.
274. *Provost Developments Ltd v. Collingwood Towers Ltd* [1980] 2 NZLR 205. Such a term means approval may be withheld on technical legal grounds, but not on the basis of the transaction being a bad bargain. For the application of a similar principle to approval by an expert of other matters, *see Lerner v. Schiehallion Nominees Ltd* [2003] 2 NZLR 671.
275. *Neylon v. Dickens* [1978] 2 NZLR 35; *North Shore Demolition Ltd v. McKay* [1978] 1 NZLR 454.
276. *See* para. 70.
277. *See* in particular *Neylon v. Dickens* [1977] 1 NZLR 595; affirmed [1978] 2 NZLR 35; *Moreton & Craig v. Montrose Ltd (in liquidation)* [1986] 2 NZLR 496.
278. *Vining Realty Ltd v. Moorhouse* [2010] NZCA 104, [43] and [51]. For the law as to misrepresentation generally *see* paras 102–108.
279. *Electricity Corporation of NZ v. Fletcher Challenge Energy Ltd* [2002] 2 NZLR 433; and *see Tower Insurance v. Nicon Ltd* [2019] NZCA 332.

there have been cases where the circumstances have shown that a 'provisional agreement' which is subject to contract was nevertheless intended to have immediate legal effect.[280]

The New Zealand courts have gone further than this, and have created a rule whereby in large-scale transactions concerning land or commercial dealings where the transaction is of a kind normally evidenced in a formal document drawn by lawyers, the courts will apply a presumption against liability being intended prior to the execution of the formal document even where the parties have not used any words such as 'subject to contract'.[281] The presumption is rebuttable.[282]

3. Waiver of Conditions in Conditional Contracts

69. Both parties to the contract may waive a condition to which it is subject by mutual agreement. However, the issue of waiver will more normally arise where one party wishes to waive a condition, but the other party does not agree. A party to a conditional contract may unilaterally waive a condition in the contract where it is solely for the benefit of that party.[283] Whether or not the condition is solely for the benefit of the party seeking to waive it is determined first by any term of the contract as to the status of the condition, or, where there is no contractual statement, by looking at the actual effect of the condition in the factual matrix within which the contract is to operate.[284] Thus, while a condition relating to planning or land use approvals will normally be solely for the benefit of the purchaser (as affecting the value of the bargain to the purchaser), the position is different if the vendor has a continuing interest in the land as mortgagee so that the planning or land use approvals will affect the worth of that security.[285]

Any waiver must be adequately communicated to the other party before the time fixed for the fulfilment of the condition.[286]

---

280. *Reid Motors v. Wood* [1978] 1 NZLR 319; *Walmsley v. Christchurch City Council* [1990] 1 NZLR 199, *cf. Branca v. Cobarro* [1947] KB 854.
281. As to the presumption in contracts for the sale of land *see Carruthers v. Whitaker* [1975] 2 NZLR 667; *Spengler Management Ltd v. Tan* [1995] 1 NZLR 120; *Verissimo v. Walker* [2006] 1 NZLR 760 (CA) and *Smada Group Ltd v. Miro Farms Ltd* [2007] NZCA 568. For its operation in commercial transactions not involving land *see Concorde Enterprises v. Anthony Motors* [1981] 2 NZLR 385, *Holmes v. Australasian Holdings Ltd* [1988] 2 NZLR 303; *Shell Oil Ltd v. Wordcom Investments Ltd* [1992] 1 NZLR 129; *Kop-Cote New Zealand Ltd v. Incodo Ltd* [2018] NZCA 430.
282. *France v. Hight* [1990] 1 NZLR 345; *see also Cromwell Corporation Ltd v. Sofrana Immobilier (NZ) Ltd* (1992) 6 NZCLC 67,997; *Newton-King v. Wilkinson* [1976] 2 NZLR 321.
283. *Connor v. Pukerau Stores Ltd* [1981] 1 NZLR 384.
284. *Globe Holdings Ltd v. Floratos* [1998] 3 NZLR 331.
285. *Moreton & Craig v. Montrose Ltd (in liquidation)* [1986] 2 NZLR 496; *Karangahape Road Village International Ltd v. Holloway* [1989] 1 NZLR 83.
286. *Williams v. Kirk* [1988] 1 NZLR 452; *Valentines Properties Ltd v. Huntco Corporation Ltd* [2001] 3 NZLR 305 at 313. Communication of the waiver to a common agent of both parties suffices: *BS Developments No. 12 Ltd v. PB & SF Properties Ltd* (2005) 6 NZCPR 741; upheld (2006) 7 NZCPR 603.

4. Obligation to Seek Fulfilment of Conditions

70. The contract will usually place on one party or the other the obligation to seek fulfilment of the condition within the period stated within the contract.[287] There may be an express statement of the degree of effort expected of that party to obtain fulfilment of the condition, in which case the contractual standard must be met, even if it becomes very onerous.[288] Where the contract is silent, the court will imply a term requiring reasonable efforts to be made to fulfil the condition.[289]

If the party on whom the obligation is placed does not comply with the contractually required standard of endeavour, the condition will be treated as having been fulfilled.[290]

The New Zealand courts have steadily moved towards imposing an objective standard of reasonableness on parties who have stipulated for conditions to be met to that party's satisfaction, for example, that an engineer's report as to the condition of a dwelling is 'satisfactory to the purchaser'.[291] This is so even if the condition in question is stated to be for the sole benefit of one contracting party.[292] The imposition of the objective standard is intended to ensure that parties are not able to insert provisions requiring some subjective standard of satisfaction and thereby escape contractual liability.[293]

III. Intention to Create Legal Relations

A. General

71. An agreement will not have effect as a contract unless the parties to it have an actual or imputed intention that the agreement gives rise to legally binding obligations.[294] This requirement is usually referred to as an 'intention to create legal relations'.

---

287. If no time limit is stated, the courts will imply a requirement of fulfilment within a reasonable period: *Mt Pleasant Estates Co Ltd v. Withell* [1996] 3 NZLR 324. A party seeking to terminate the contract because the other party, on whom the obligation to fulfil the condition rested, has not fulfilled the condition within a reasonable time must give notice to the other party of a date which the would-be terminating party considers will conclude the period of 'reasonable time' to fulfil the condition: *Steele v. Serepisos* [2007] 1 NZLR 1.

288. *Innes v. Mars* [1982] 2 NZLR 68; *Innes v. Ewing* [1989] 1 NZLR 598.

289. *Connor v. Pukerau Stores Ltd* [1981] 1 NZLR 384; compare *North Shore Demolition Ltd v. McKay* [1978] 1 NZLR 454 and *Mana v. Fleming* (2007) 8 NZCPR 469; [2007] NZCA 324.

290. *Provost Developments v. Collingwood Towers Ltd* [1980] 2 NZLR 205; *Firestone Tire & Rubber Co NZ Ltd v. Harvard Construction Ltd* (1997) 3 NZ ConvC 192,665. The party alleging failure to make sufficient endeavour to fulfil the condition must prove it: *Ansley v. Prospectus Nominees Ltd* [2004] 2 NZLR 590, 602.

291. *Lerner v. Schiehallion Nominees* [2003] 2 NZLR 671 at 678; *Arcadia Homes Ltd (in liquidation) v. More To This Life Ltd* [2013] NZCA 286; [2013] ANZ Conv R 13-020; leave to appeal refused [2013] NZSC 117.

292. *Gilbert v. Manninen* (2009) 10 NZCPR 209 (HC) at [4].

293. *Arcadia Homes Ltd (in liquidation) v. More To This Life Ltd* [2013] NZCA 286; [2013] ANZ Conv R 13-020; leave to appeal refused [2013] NZSC 117.

294. *Fleming v. Beevers* [1994] 1 NZLR 385.

In the majority of cases, the courts are concerned with ascertaining the parties' actual intentions, but it must be remembered that on the normal objective view of contract formation,[295] the parties will be considered to have made an agreement if an objective bystander would so conclude from their communications and conduct. If one party does not actually intend to be contractually bound by an agreement, but his or her conduct would suggest to a bystander that the agreement was intended to have contractual force, the courts will treat it as having been intended to have contractual effect.[296]

The older English cases made a convenient, if imprecise, distinction between 'business' agreements (being those of generally commercial nature) and 'domestic' agreements (those between spouses or other family members or between close friends).[297] While these cases suggest that there is a rebuttable presumption in favour of an intention to create legal relations in business arrangements, and equally a presumption against such an intention in domestic arrangements, the Court of Appeal held in *Fleming v. Beevers*[298] that in domestic arrangement cases, the courts should not have recourse to a presumption, but rather ascertain the apparent intention of the parties from a careful scrutiny of the facts.

B. *Business Transactions*

1. General

72. It is normally reasonable to draw an inference that a business transaction between strangers was intended to have legal effect.[299] It will not necessarily matter that the value of the transaction is not great.[300] However, the parties can by the use of sufficiently specific language demonstrate that the agreement was not intended to be binding.[301] Such a result will be unusual. It is the overall intention of the parties that matter, and the court may disregard words indicating an unwillingness to create a legal obligation if the transaction was nevertheless intended to be contractual in nature.[302]

---

295. *See* para. 30.
296. *Paulger v. Butland Industries Ltd* [1989] 3 NZLR 549.
297. *See Rose and Frank Co v. J R Crompton and Bros Ltd* [1923] 2 KB 261; *Balfour v. Balfour* [1919] 2 KB 571.
298. *Fleming v. Beevers* [1994] 1 NZLR 385 at 389.
299. *Fleming v. Beevers* [1994] 1 NZLR 385 at 389.
300. *Esso Petroleum Ltd v. Customs and Excise Commissioners* [1976] 1 WLR 1.
301. *Rose and Frank Co v. J R Crompton and Bros Ltd* [1923] 2 KB 261. For a recent example *see*: *X v. Mid Sussex Citizens Advice Bureau* [2012] UKSC 59, [2013] 1 All ER 1038, at [2] (document specifically stating no contract of employment existed). A separate agreement that an apparent contract will never be enforced will demonstrate a lack of intention to create legal relations in relation to the apparent contract: *Maan v. Keys* [2017] NZHC 1967.
302. *Edwards v. Skyways Ltd* [1964] 1 WLR 349.

It is also important to note that there will be transactions where the parties to an agreement clearly contemplate that at a future time their agreement will have contractual force, but do not intend that it be currently binding in law. By far, the most common instance of such transactions is the agreements 'subject to contract', which have been discussed earlier.[303]

2. Letters of Comfort

73. A 'letter of comfort' is a document provided to a bank or other financier by a person or company able to control the activities of a company which has sought financial aid, usually by way of a loan, from the bank or financier. It will typically contain some assurance that the writer will seek to have the borrower meet any liabilities to the lender, but the letter will not contain any promises which might amount to a formal guarantee. Attempts to claim that letters of comfort have effect as if they were contractual guarantees have usually failed,[304] and on occasion, this has been said to be because the writer of the letter of comfort has not intended the parties to enter into any legally binding obligations. A better view is that such letters are usually intended to have some legal effect but to confer only very limited legal rights.[305]

3. Agreements Between Trade Unions and Employers Outside the Industrial Law Regime

74. New Zealand has a statutory regime whereby trade unions and employers can agree on terms and conditions for workers in particular industries.[306] These agreements are enforceable through specialized tribunals and courts, and must naturally be considered to have been intended to have legal effect. However, the status of agreements between unions and employers outside this specialized regime is more difficult to establish. It has been held that such agreements will be unenforceable because the parties cannot have intended to create legal relations, but the reasoning in the case is not compelling, and it might be that a different view would now be taken.[307]

---

303. *See* para. 68.
304. Letters of comfort are extensively discussed in *Bank of New Zealand v. Ginivan* [1991] 1 NZLR 178 and *Kleinwort Benson Ltd v. Malaysia Mining Corporation Berhad* [1989] 1 WLR 379. It is noted in *Bank of New Zealand v. Ginivan* at 179 that a letter of comfort need not be shown on the writer's own financial statements, whereas a guarantee must be so shown.
305. Compare *Kleinwort Benson Ltd v. Malaysia Mining Corporation Berhad* [1988] 1 WLR 799 at first instance with the judgment of the Court of Appeal [1989] 1 WLR 379, where some, very limited, effect was given to the letter of comfort.
306. Employment Relations Act 2000.
307. *Re Andrew M Paterson Ltd* [1981] 2 NZLR 289. Compare *Ford Motor Co v. AUEFW* [1969] 2 All ER 481. One reason given in *Re Andrew M Paterson Ltd* drawing the inference that no legal effect was intended was that workers would not be able in law to enforce promises made in agreements between a union and their employer, but that argument is now untenable given ss 10–20 of the Contract and Commercial Law Act 2017. Those provisions are discussed at paras 195–197.

C. Domestic Agreements

75. Whether a 'domestic agreement' between spouses, family members or close friends will be considered to have been intended to give rise to legal consequences must be determined by careful scrutiny of the facts of the particular case.[308] As a general rule, the more substantial or important the subject matter of the agreement, the more likely the courts will give effect to the agreement as a contract. Thus, agreements involving substantial assets such as real property are likely to be treated as having been intended to be legally binding, as are agreements affecting important legal rights or obligations.[309] While older cases placed significant stress on the legal status of married couples, this is no longer the case. It seems likely that the courts have been influenced in this change by a consistent legislative policy over recent decades which has favoured the creation and recognition of agreements regulating property or other rights of married persons or those living in long-term relationships.[310]

Similar principles appear to apply to agreements between friends, although perhaps the threshold at which an intention to create legal relations will be found is lower. For example, agreements to divide winnings in competitions have been held to be intended to be contractual in nature.[311]

D. Agreements Between Private Individuals and the State

76. On rare occasions, the courts may be called upon to decide whether an agreement between an individual and the government was intended to create legal relations. The rarity that such matters arise is not because few such agreements are made but because in the overwhelming majority of cases it is obvious that the parties did intend legal consequences. Thus, agreements which provide for the myriad routine activities of any large organization – for employment, for purchase of equipment or supplies, for the supply of accommodation or specialized services – which would have contractual effect if between private individuals are equally considered to have legal effect if made between an individual and the government.[312] Agreements whereby the state offers an individual a commercial opportunity or privilege in return for payment have also been treated as contractual.[313]

Different considerations apply where the agreement impacts upon matters of governmental policy or ministerial discretion, and here the courts will presume the agreement was not intended to have contractual effect.[314]

308. *Fleming v. Beevers* [1994] 1 NZLR 385 at 389–390.
309. *See* for example *Fleming v. Beevers* [1994] 1 NZLR 385; *Philips v. Philips* [1993] 3 NZLR 159.
310. In particular *see* the Property (Relationships) Act 1976 (passed in 2001 when the earlier legislation was radically altered).
311. *Welch v. Jess* [1976] 2 NZ Rec Law (NS) 185; compare *Simpkins v. Pays* [1955] 1 WLR 975.
312. *Rothmans of Pall Mall (NZ) Ltd v. Attorney-General* [1991] 2 NZLR 323 at 326.
313. *Rod Milner Motors Ltd v. Attorney-General* [1999] 2 NZLR 568.
314. *Meates v. Attorney-General* [1979] 1 NZLR 415.

IV. The Doctrine of Consideration

A. *Definition*

1. Introduction

77. New Zealand law requires consideration for the formation of a simple contract, although not for a deed. Gratuitous promises, other than by deed, are not enforceable. In this New Zealand law follows the common law of England, where consideration was accepted as a necessity from the seventeenth century.

The concept is not susceptible of ready definition. In nineteenth-century England, it tended to be defined in terms of a benefit to the defendant, or detriment to the plaintiff, in return for the defendant's promise. 'Consideration means something which is of value in the eye of the law, moving from the plaintiff: it may be some detriment to the plaintiff or some benefit to the defendant.'[315] However, there has always been artificiality about this analysis, particularly in the case of the bilateral contract, where the consideration for each party's promise is the promise of the other. To say that the 'benefit' and 'detriment' derive from the binding nature of the mutual promises is to assume what one has set out to prove. So a more satisfactory definition would appear to be that formulated by Sir Frederick Pollock and adopted by the House of Lords in 1915:[316] 'An act or forbearance of one party, or the promise thereof, is the price for which the promise of the other is bought, and the promise thus given for value is enforceable.' This 'price of the promise' definition has been preferred in New Zealand.[317] It has the additional advantage that it emphasizes the necessary element of return which binds the consideration and the promise together.

2. Executory and Executed Consideration

78. Consideration is called 'executory' when it consists of a *promise* in return for the other party's promise. It is the type of consideration which exists in a *bilateral* contract. The classic example is the agreement to sell where the property is to be delivered, and the price paid, at a future time. Consideration is *executed* when it consists of the performance of an *act* in return for the other party's promise. It is the type of consideration which exists in a *unilateral* contract. Examples are a promise to pay a reward for the supply of information,[318] and a promise to find a person employment if a period of training is undertaken.[319]

315. *Thomas v. Thomas* (1842) 2 QB 851 per Patteson J.
316. *Dunlop v. Selfridge* [1915] AC 847 at 855.
317. *Attorney-General for England and Wales v. R* [2002] 2 NZLR 91 at 106 per Tipping J (affirmed [2004] 2 NZLR 577 (PC)).
318. For example *R v. Clarke* (1927) 40 CLR 227.
319. *Holloway v. Attorney-General* [1994] 2 ERNZ 528.

3. Past Consideration Is No Consideration

79. Past consideration is no consideration. A promise made to recompense a party for a gratuitous favour done in the past is not enforceable. It is not part of any bargain.[320] However, if the act done in the past was done at the request of the party who later promises to pay, the result may be different, at least if the act is of a kind which is normally paid for. In that case, it may be possible to imply from the request a promise to pay for the service when it is rendered. Sometimes, for example, it may be possible to imply a promise that interest will be paid on a loan.[321]

There are certain statutory exceptions to the rule that past consideration is no consideration. Section 27 of the Bills of Exchange Act 1908 provides that any antecedent debt or liability is sufficient consideration to support a bill of exchange, and under section 3(2)(a) of the Law Reform (Testamentary Promises) Act 1949, a promise to make testamentary provision is binding although the services may have been rendered prior to the making of the promise.

4. Consideration Must Move from the Promisee

80. At common law, a person cannot sue on a promise for which the consideration was supplied by someone other than himself or herself.[322] There has been some debate as to whether this is the same thing as privity of contract, i.e., the rule that only a party to a contract can sue on it. In respect of this latter rule, the position was ameliorated by the Contracts (Privity) Act 1982, the provisions of which are now contained in Part 2, subpart 1 of the Contract and Commercial Law Act 2017. They give rights to third persons to enforce contracts made for their benefit provided certain conditions are fulfilled. The Committee which recommended the 1982 Act clearly believed that it would modify not just privity of contract but also the rule that consideration must move from the promisee.[323]

Sometimes, a person who at first sight appears to be a stranger to the consideration turns out on the proper construction of the contract to be a party to it, to be supplying consideration, and thus to be entitled to enforce it without the assistance of the Contract and Commercial Law Act. One such case is that of joint promisees where a promise is made to two persons jointly, in return for a consideration provided on behalf of both of them.[324] The fact that the consideration is actually provided by only one of the two is then irrelevant.

320. *Tranzequity Holdings Ltd v. Malley* (1990) 5 NZCLC 66343.
321. *Casey v. Commissioner of Inland Revenue* [1959] NZLR 1952. *See also Johnson v. Bucko Enterprises Ltd* [1975] 1 NZLR 311. Cf. *Teo Tipene v. Mere te Puhi* (1904) 23 NZLR 1079.
322. *Tweddle v. Atkinson* (1861) 1 B &S 393.
323. *Privity of Contract, Report of the Contracts and Commercial Law Reform Committee* (1981), Chs 1 and 2.
324. For example *Coulls v. Bagot's Executor and Trustee Co Ltd* [1967] ALR 385.

5. Adequacy of Consideration

81. As a rule, the courts are not concerned to see that the consideration for a party's promise is equal in value to the value of the promise. The parties themselves are the sole judge of value. Thus, a promise to sell property for a nominal price is just as valid and enforceable as one to sell it for a price which represents its true value.[325]

Parties sometimes take advantage of this rule to render binding a promise which would otherwise be gratuitous: for example, an option to purchase land for a consideration of NZD 0.10, and an agreement to lease land for a peppercorn rental. In such a case, the significance of the 'consideration' is little more than to demonstrate the intent of the party that his or her promise is binding.

Adequacy of consideration can, however, be relevant if the question is whether a contract should be set aside as having been procured by unconscionable conduct such as preying on some special weakness (such as senility) of the other party.[326]

6. Forbearance and Compromise

82. Consideration may consist in forbearing, or promising to forbear, from doing something a party was otherwise at liberty to do. Forbearance as consideration is seen most often in the cases on forbearance to sue and compromise of suit. Forbearance to sue arises when A owes B a debt, and, in consideration of B's refraining from suing A for a time, promises to grant B a benefit such as a security over his or her property. The period of forbearance need not be for any particular time, provided there is some degree of forbearance, and there need not be an express promise to forbear provided it can be inferred that the forbearance which in fact results was the direct consequence of an arrangement between the parties.[327] A compromise of suit arises when two parties settle a disputed claim by one against the other for an agreed payment. In this case, the consideration is the abandonment by one party of the right to sue the other on the original claim.

These two categories of case raise the same question, i.e., as to whether consideration is supplied if the original claim was of doubtful validity in law, and might have failed had it been brought to trial. In such a case, it might be argued that the party abandoning the claim, or forbearing to sue on it, is giving up nothing of value. But in New Zealand, the courts have taken the pragmatic view that provided the party honestly believes he or she had a chance of success, the forbearance or compromise is good consideration. The party is giving up what he or she perceived as a chance of success. In *Couch v. Branch Investments Ltd*,[328] Mr and Mrs C promised, in consideration of B Ltd forbearing for one month to take action against them

325. *Re Murphy* [1933] NZLR 583; *Airways Corporation of NZ Ltd v. Geyserland Airways Ltd* [1996] 1 NZLR 116 at 127.
326. *See* paras 137–144.
327. *Paulger v. Butland Industries Ltd* [1989] 3 NZLR 549; *Attorney-General for England and Wales v. R* [2002] 2 NZLR 91 (affirmed [2004] 2 NZLR 577).
328. [1980] 2 NZLR 314.

on a hire-purchase agreement, to give a mortgage over their two houses. This promise was held binding even though the validity of the hire-purchase agreement was suspect. Cooke J has said:[329] 'The Courts are very slow to reject a compromise of a bone fide claim as consideration on the mere ground that on subsequent analysis it may be seen to have had small prospects of success.'

B. Performance of Existing Duties

1. Performance of Existing Duty under the Law

83. If all that the plaintiff has supplied in return for the defendant's promise is doing, or promising to do, an act which the law of the land already required of him or her, the plaintiff has not provided good consideration. He or she is doing no more than he or she was already bound to do. Thus in one case payment to a worker of a sum due under workers' compensation legislation was held to be no consideration for an agreement to discharge the worker's entitlements.[330]

However, if the plaintiff supplies or promises to supply more than the law obliges him or her to do, he or she does supply good consideration. The plaintiff is then doing something he or she need not otherwise have done. The courts appear to be ready to find, on the true construction of the agreement, that the plaintiff is in fact exceeding his or her existing obligations. Thus, in *Glasbrook Bros v. Glamorgan County Council*,[331] a colliery owner wanted a permanent garrison of police stationed on its premises during a strike, but the police superintendent thought a mobile force was enough. He finally acceded to the owner's wishes in return for a promise to pay GBP 2,200. It was held that although the police were bound by law to provide protection, the superintendent had discretion as to the type of protection, and providing more than he deemed necessary constituted good consideration for the promise to pay. In *Black White and Grey Cabs Ltd v. Reid*,[332] the provision by a taxi company to its drivers of a more extensive radio-telephone communication service than the Transport Act required it to provide was held to be good consideration for a return promise by the drivers.

Statements have occasionally been made, for example, by Denning LJ in *Ward v. Byham*,[333] that even if the promisee is doing no more than he or she was obliged to do, he or she ought, at least in some cases, to be deemed to be supplying consideration, simply because the other party is getting what he or she wanted. While this view cannot be said formally to represent the law at the moment, the developments discussed in paragraph 85 below show that it is now not far from the truth of the matter.

---

329. *Moyes & Groves Ltd v. Radiation NZ Ltd* [1982] 1 NZLR 368 at 371.
330. *Hamilton v. Straits Air Freight Express Ltd* [1960] NZLR 1147.
331. [1925] AC 270.
332. [1980] 1 NZLR 40.
333. [1956] 2 All ER 318.

2. Performance of an Existing Contract with a Third Person

84. The next type of case is where the plaintiff performs, or promises to perform, for the defendant an obligation already imposed on him or her by a contract previously made with a third person.

The situation, in other words, is where C promises A some benefit if A performs, or promises to perform, a contract which A has previously made with B. Perhaps paradoxically, the law has always held that in such a case A does provide good consideration. The law goes back to the nineteenth century, in particular, the English cases of *Shadwell v. Shadwell* in 1860,[334] and *Scotson v. Pegg* in 1861.[335] The view of the law taken in those cases was adopted by the Privy Council, on appeal from New Zealand, in *New Zealand Shipping Co v. A M Satterthwaite & Co (The Eurymedon).*[336] The essential facts of that case were that the plaintiff made an offer to the defendant that if the defendant would unload the plaintiff's goods from a ship (which the defendant was already bound to do by a contract with a third party), the plaintiff would treat the defendant as exempt from any liability for damage to the goods. The majority of the Judicial Committee of the Privy Council had no doubt that the defendant's act of unloading the ship was good consideration. They said:

> An agreement to do an act which the promisor is under an existing obligation to a third party to do, may quite well amount to valid consideration … the promisee obtains the benefit of a direct obligation which he can enforce.[337]

In *Pao On v. Lau Yin Long* the Privy Council said:[338] 'Their Lordships do not doubt that a promise to perform, or the performance of, a pre-existing contractual obligation to a third party can be valid consideration.' The matter may thus be regarded as settled. However, in this area of the law, as in others, the exercise of economic duress in procuring the promise will be a ground for setting it aside.[339]

3. Performance of an Existing Contract with the Promisor

85. If B promises A an additional benefit if A performs, or promises to perform, an existing contractual obligation which A owes to B, traditional theory holds that A supplies no consideration for B's new promise. A is doing no more than he or she was already bound to do. A variation of one party's contractual obligation requires a corresponding variation on the other side. In *Stilk v. Myrick,*[340] two seamen deserted during a voyage, and the captain promised the remainder of the crew that if they would perform the extra duties, the wages of the two deserters would be divided amongst them. It was held that the promise was not binding because they

334. (1860) 9 CBNS 159.
335. (1861) 6 H & N 295.
336. [1974] 1 NZLR 505.
337. [1974] 1 NZLR 505 at 511 per Lord Wilberforce.
338. [1980] AC 614 at 634 per Lord Scarman.
339. *See* para. 136.
340. (1809) 2 Camp 317.

had in their original agreement undertaken to do all they could in the emergencies of the voyage. Likewise, in *Cook Islands Shipping Co Ltd v. Colson Builders Ltd,*[341] a shipping company contracted to carry goods at a set freight. On encountering difficulties, it indicated it would only be prepared to proceed if the other party paid an additional sum over and above the freight. The other party agreed. It was held that this promise was not binding because the shipping company was doing no more than it was already obliged to do under the original contract.

However, if in return for B's promise A promises something over and above his or her existing obligation, there is good consideration. In accordance with principle, this extra performance need not be large. In *Moyes and Groves Ltd v. Radiation (NZ) Ltd,*[342] a buyer ordered goods from a seller for the price of NZD 400. The goods had to be imported from India, and contrary to expectations they did not arrive for nearly three years. Not only had the parties actually forgotten about the contract in the interim: the cost of the goods was now NZD 2,700. The buyer eventually agreed to pay NZD 2,700. It was held that this promise to increase the price was enforceable: the seller had an arguable claim that because of the long delay, the original contract had been abandoned, and his giving up this claim was consideration for the buyer's new promise.

More recently, however, there has been a significant shift in this area. Not only do these recent developments lead to decisions more in accordance with commercial reality: they require a more relaxed view of consideration.

The most significant is *Williams v. Roffey Bros & Nicholls (Contractors) Ltd.*[343] A contractor, employed to refurbish a block of flats, subcontracted the carpentry work to the plaintiff at a price of GBP 20,000. When it became clear in the course of doing the work that the plaintiff would not be able to finish at this price, the parties mutually agreed to raise it by another GBP 10,500, payable in instalments on the completion of each flat. It was held by the English Court of Appeal that the new arrangement was enforceable, and that the Judge's finding that there was consideration for raising the price should not be disturbed. The new arrangements benefited both sides. In particular, the head contractor, having ensured that the plaintiff could not complete the subcontract, would avoid having to pay penalties for late completion, and would not have to expend time and trouble searching for a replacement subcontractor. These practical benefits were sufficient to constitute consideration for the rise in payment. As Glidewell LJ put it, the head contractor had obtained, in practice, a benefit, or obviated a 'disbenefit'. It is this emphasis on the practical consequences of the arrangement which is new. Nevertheless, as the Court of Appeal obviously realized, the new approach is susceptible of abuse, and if it can be shown that the plaintiff has extracted the promise of extra payment by duress, the promise will be unenforceable.

The doctrine in *Williams v. Roffey* was followed in New Zealand in the High Court case of *Machirus Properties Ltd v. Power Sports World (1987),*[344] *Ltd*, where

341. [1975] 1 NZLR 422.
342. [1982] 1 NZLR 368.
343. [1991] 1 QB 1.
344. (1999) 4 NZ Conv C 193,066.

a lessor was held bound by an arrangement allowing the lessee certain rent concessions. Thus, as the Court said, 'Machirus would have been faced with an empty shop, a duty to mitigate loss by reletting – at the then market rental – and no prospect at all of Power Sports renewing the lease after October 1994 … .' The doctrine also has received support from the New Zealand Court of Appeal. There was cautious endorsement in *United Food and Chemical Workers Union of NZ v. Talley,*[345] where the Court suggested that the same principle might apply where there was continued performance of an employment contract following a variation such as a voluntary pay increase, or a practical benefit to the employer in the employee's willingness to continue to serve in the light of such as incentive. There was a more unequivocal support in *Attorney-General for England and Wales v. R,*[346] where Tipping J, in a judgment with which Keith and McGrath JJ agreed, said the *Williams v. Roffey* approach paid attention to practical realities rather than legal niceties; 'a practical benefit will qualify as consideration as well as the legal benefit of an enforceable promise'.[347]

It remains to be seen how far the *Williams v. Roffey* doctrine will be taken, and what inroads it will make on the doctrine of consideration in other contexts. It has been held by the Court of Appeal in England that it cannot operate to affect the longstanding rule laid down in *Foakes v. Beer*[348] that part payment of a debt does not extinguish the whole debt,[349] although recently, in *MWB Business Exchange Centres Ltd v. Rock Advertising Ltd,*[350] the UK Supreme Court left the question open. In this case, Rock Advertising made a contract with MWB to occupy premises which contained a 'no oral modification' clause. The parties later made an oral agreement to reschedule licence fee payments for the premises after Rock got into financial difficulty. The agreement provided for Rock initially to pay less than originally agreed but later to pay more, and Rock also paid the first instalment due under the revised agreement. The Supreme Court held that effect should be given to the requirement of writing and that the revised agreement was invalid,[351] making it unnecessary for the court to deal with the consideration issue. The Court of Appeal had held that there was a consideration to support the variation, on account of the practical benefit to MWB from the prompt payment of part of the arrears and the promise of the balance, and from Rock remaining a licensee and continuing to occupy the premises.[352] However, in the Supreme Court, Lord Sumption said only that the issue was a difficult one, the problem being that that benefit was the very thing which the House of Lords held not to be adequate consideration in *Foakes v. Beer.*[353] His Lordship thought that the decision probably was ripe for

345. [1993] 2 ERNZ 360 at 376.
346. [2002] 2 NZLR 91 (affirmed [2004] 2 NZLR 577).
347. *Ibid.*, at 109; and *see also Kain v. Wynn Williams & Co* [2013] 1 NZLR 498, at [65], [66]; leave to appeal to the Supreme Court was refused: *Kain v. Wynn Williams & Co* [2013] NZSC 26.
348. (1884) 9 App Cas 605; *see* para. 86 below.
349. *Re Selectmove Ltd* [1995] 1 WLR 474.
350. [2018] UKSC 24, [2019] AC 119.
351. *See* further para. 164 below.
352. *MWB Business Exchange Centres Ltd v. Rock Advertising Ltd* [2016] EWCA Civ 553, [2017] QB 604.
353. As to which *see* para. 86 below.

re-examination, but this should be before an enlarged panel and in a case where the decision would be more than obiter dictum.

In *Antons Trawling Co Ltd v. Esperance Fishing Co Ltd,*[354] the New Zealand Court of Appeal agreed with the *Williams v. Roffey* approach but wondered whether a better explanation might be simply that a variation of contract does not require consideration at all.[355] Indeed, in *Teat v. Willcocks,*[356] the Court of Appeal was attracted to the alternative view expressed in *Antons*, which reflected the reality of what had happened in the instant case – a variation that had been proposed and willingly accepted. Whether this more radical solution will win acceptance remains to be determined.[357]

4. Part Payment of a Debt

86. A promise by a creditor to accept less than the amount of a debt from a debtor is not binding because it is not supported by consideration. The debtor, who is actually paying less than he or she is obliged to do, supplies no consideration in return for the creditor's promise to relieve him or her from a portion of the debt. This rule, originally laid down in *Pinnel's* case,[358] was affirmed by the House of Lords in *Foakes v. Beer.*[359]

The rule has not been popular, for it extends a principle originally fashioned for formation of contract. A number of exceptions have grown up. The first is peculiar to New Zealand, and is of considerable importance. Section 27A of the Property Law Act 2007 (formerly section 92 of the Judicature Act 1908) provides that an acknowledgement in writing by a creditor, or any person authorized by the creditor, of the receipt of part of the debt in satisfaction of the whole debt operates as a discharge of the whole debt. However, the section only applies where the acknowledgement is in writing, and where part payment has actually been received.[360] It thus does not completely do away with the rule in *Foakes v. Beer.*

Second, the rule in *Foakes v. Beer* only applies to liquidated debts. If the amount of the debt is unliquidated, or in dispute, an acceptance of a payment in full settlement serves as an accord and satisfaction, or compromise, which extinguishes the debt.[361]

354. [2003] 2 NZLR 23.
355. *Ibid.*, at 45–46 per Baragwanath J. In *Ma Hongjin v. SCP Holdings Pte Ltd* [2020] SGCA 106, the Singapore Court of Appeal favoured retaining the doctrine of consideration in the context of contractual variations. By contrast, in *Rosas v. Toca* 2018 BCCA 191 at [176], the British Columbia Court of Appeal held that a lack of consideration would not prevent the enforcement of variations of contract.
356. [2013] NZCA 162 at [54].
357. *See* the discussion in *Gloria Jean's Coffees International Pty Ltd v. Daboko Ltd* [2020] NZHC 29, [2020] 2 NZLR 488 at [19]–[32].
358. (1602) 5 Co Rep 117a.
359. (1884) 9 App Cas 605.
360. *Re Goile* [1963] NZLR 666; *Chambers v. Commissioner of Stamp Duties* [1943] NZLR 504; *Meikle v. Wellington Loan Co Ltd* (1911) 31 NZLR 217.
361. *Homeguard Products (NZ) Ltd v. Kiwi Packaging Ltd* [1981] 2 NZLR 322.

Third, if the debtor pays part of the debt in a different way (e.g., in kind, or at an earlier time, than that at which the debtor was obliged by the contract to pay), he or she will be discharged;[362] the new element amounts to consideration for the discharge. Again, in *MWB*,[363] in the Court of Appeal, Arden LJ said that where a variation agreement was entered into not simply to accommodate the debtor but was accompanied by other benefits – in this case to avoid the property being unoccupied – then the other benefit was good consideration.

Fourth, there are some exceptions which do not sit comfortably in terms of logic, but which have been deemed necessary to prevent fraud on third persons. Thus, if a part payment in full satisfaction is made by a third person rather than the debtor himself or herself, it discharges the debt,[364] as does a compromise with a number of creditors whereby each creditor agrees to accept part of his debt in full satisfaction.[365]

Fifth, in *Collier v. P & MJ Wright (Holdings) Ltd,*[366] Arden LJ in the Court of Appeal in England considered that *Foakes v. Beer* operated subject to the doctrine of promissory estoppel. As will be explained below, if this is right, it will substantially limit the practical application of the *Foakes* rule.

C. Promissory Estoppel

1. Introduction

87. The doctrine of promissory estoppel, as expounded by Denning J in the *High Trees* case,[367] can provide a way of holding a promisor to his or her promises despite the absence of consideration. Initially, the doctrine was limited to a defensive operation by preventing a promisor acting inconsistently with a promise not to enforce his or her strict contractual rights against the other party. However, recent decisions in New Zealand and Australia show that the doctrine is capable of creating a cause of action. The full implications of such a development have yet to be worked through.

2. The Traditional View: 'A Shield Not a Sword'

88. In *Central London Property Trust Ltd v. High Trees House Ltd,*[368] Denning J introduced promissory estoppel to modern law. In that case, the plaintiff had leased to the defendant a block of flats at a rental of GBP 2,500 per annum. When it became difficult for the lessee to let the flats profitably during the war, the lessor

---

362. *Vanbergen v. St Edmunds Properties Ltd* [1933] 2 KB 223.
363. [2016] EWCA Civ 553, [2017] QB 604, at [85]–[86]; above para. 85.
364. *Hirachand Punamchand v. Temple* [1911] 2 KB 330.
365. *Cook v. Lister* (1863) 13 CBNS 542.
366. [2008] 1 WLR 643.
367. *Central London Property Trust Ltd v. High Trees House Ltd* [1947] KB 130.
368. [1947] KB 130.

wrote to the lessee agreeing to accept a reduced rent of GBP 1,250 per annum. The reduced rent was paid, and accepted, until the beginning of 1945, at which time the flats were all let again. An action was brought to recover GBP 625, being the difference between the rental stated in the lease and the reduced rental for the quarters ending in September and December 1945. Denning J held that the full rental was payable for the period covered by the action, but said that despite the lack of consideration for the landlord's concession, the full rental would not have been recoverable during the war when the flats were not full. He expressed the doctrine on which he relied as follows:[369] '... a promise intended to be binding, intended to be acted on and in fact acted on, is binding as far as its terms properly apply'. Denning J derived this principle from earlier cases in equity. Among them was *Hughes v. Metropolitan Railway Co* in which Lord Cairns had said:[370]

> if parties ... enter upon a course of negotiation which has the effect of leading one of the parties to suppose that the strict rights arising under the contract will not be enforced ... the person who otherwise might have enforced those rights will not be allowed to enforce them where it would be inequitable having regard to the dealings which have thus taken place between the parties.

In other words, the *High Trees* doctrine can operate to release a person from performing his or her obligations, even though there is no consideration for that release.

The New Zealand Courts accepted the *High Trees* doctrine but initially were very cautious in doing so. They imposed various limitations:

(1) The doctrine applied only where the parties were in a contractual relationship, and one released the other from part of his or her contractual obligation.[371]
(2) It did not constitute a cause of action in itself: it was 'a shield not a sword'.[372]
(3) It could operate to release a party from an obligation in advance of its falling due, but not to extinguish a debt already accrued due.[373]
(4) The person to whom the promise of release was made must have altered his or her position in reliance on it to his or her detriment. It was held that simply failing to pay money was not a sufficient act in reliance.[374]
(5) The promise to release someone from an obligation could be withdrawn, and the original obligation reinstated, provided that could be done without causing inequity to the promisee. If the obligation could not be reinstated without causing inequity the release was permanent.[375]

369. *Ibid.*, at 136.
370. (1877) 2 App Cas 439 at 448.
371. *McCathie v. McCathie* [1971] NZLR 58.
372. *Combe v. Combe* [1951] 2 KB 215.
373. *Homeguard Products Ltd v. Kiwi Packaging Ltd* [1981] 2 NZLR 322 at 331.
374. *Commissioner of Inland Revenue v. Morris* [1958] NZLR 1126.
375. *Ajayi v. R T Briscoe (Nigeria) Ltd* [1964] 1 WLR 1326.

3. Modern Developments

89. In recent times, there have been strong indications that promissory estoppel is capable of considerable expansion, and the Courts have been prepared to loosen some of the shackles indicated in the previous paragraph. Of considerable influence has been the fact that another manifestation of estoppel – i.e., proprietary estoppel – has long had far greater strength than the courts were initially prepared to accord promissory estoppel. In essence, proprietary estoppel provides that if an owner of land leads another to believe that that other may have an interest in the land, and on the faith of that understanding the other expends money on the land, the owner of the land will be prevented from denying that that interest exists.[376] The law has developed a range of remedies to enforce, or compensate for, the other's disappointed reliance.[377] Proprietary estoppel thus is capable of giving rise to a cause of action. It is immediately apparent that there are close affinities between proprietary and promissory estoppel. Both depend on persons suffering detriment through reliance on another's word. In recent years, the New Zealand Courts have indicated that both are manifestations of a single doctrine based on unconscionability.

In *Gillies v. Keogh*, Cooke P said:[378]

> The tide is setting or has set, I think, against the view … that proprietary estoppel and promissory estoppel are entirely separate and take their origins from different sources.
>
> [A broader approach] identifies a general principle asserting the unfairness or injustice of resiling from underlying assumptions that have been acted upon.

In *National Westminster Finance NZ Ltd v. National Bank of NZ Ltd,*[379] the Court of Appeal acknowledged 'a single doctrine of estoppel with a variety of manifestations'.

It is apparent from this eclectic view of estoppel that key limitations on the scope of promissory estoppel have disappeared. In particular, the courts have abandoned the limitation that promissory estoppel only applies when there is a pre-existing contractual relationship. In *Harris v. Harris,*[380] for instance, the plaintiff was held to an understanding communicated before a contract was entered into that an obligation to pay money under it would not be enforced. Again, in *Krukziener v. Hanover Finance Ltd,*[381] the Court of Appeal stated that promissory estoppel is no longer confined to promises affecting pre-existing rights.

376. *See Thomas v. Thomas* [1956] NZLR 785; *Thorner v. Major* [2009] 1 WLR 776.
377. *See Guest v. Guest* [2022] UKSC 27, [2022] 3 WLR 911 for discussion of the proper approach to the remedy to be awarded.
378. [1989] 2 NZLR 327 at 331.
379. [1996] 1 NZLR 548 at 549 per Tipping J.
380. (1989) 1 NZ ConvC 190,406.
381. [2010] NZAR 307 at [38].

Even more significantly, it has been said by the Court of Appeal that 'any suggestion that estoppel is available only as a shield has disappeared'.[382] And in Australia, the High Court has gone a considerable distance and has awarded monetary compensation to the plaintiff, using estoppel as a cause of action in this regard.[383]

Recent decisions identify four elements for promissory estoppel to apply.[384] They are as follows:

(a) The party against whom the estoppel is alleged has acted in a clear and unequivocal manner that has caused the claimant to have a certain belief or expectation.
(b) The claimant has reasonably relied upon that belief or expectation.
(c) The claimant has suffered detriment by relying on the belief or expectation.
(d) It would be unconscionable for the party against whom the estoppel is alleged to depart from the belief or expectation.

How these factors apply to the facts of a particular case will determine the effect of the estoppel and the remedy which ought to be awarded. In *Wilson Parking New Zealand Ltd v. Fanshawe 136 Ltd*,[385] the Court of Appeal concluded that the modern focus was on what was necessary for all the circumstances to satisfy the equity arising from a departure from the expectation engendered by the relevant assurance, promise or conduct on the part of the defendant. The clearer and more explicit the assurance was, the more likely it was that a court would be willing to grant expectation-based relief. Similarly, the greater the degree and consequences of detrimental reliance by the claimant, the more likely it was that the court would be prepared to hold the defendant to the promise rather than make an award (generally of a more limited nature) designed to compensate for reliance-based losses. An assessment of the nature and extent of the element of unconscionability formed part of the analysis. The cases showed a wide variation of approach, and a definitive or exhaustive statement of the principles was likely to be elusive given the fact-dependent nature of the cases. The emphasis was on a broad consideration of the relief necessary to achieve a just and proportionate outcome.

Promissory estoppel may even be available to reduce a debt which has fallen due for repayment, at least in the opinion of Arden LJ in *Collier v. P & J Wright (Holdings) Ltd*.[386] Collier together with two partners consented to an order in the County Court that they jointly pay debts owed to Wrights in monthly instalments. C paid

382. *Gold Star Insurance Co Ltd v. Gaunt* (1991) [1998] 3 NZLR 80 at 86.
383. *Waltons Stores (Interstate) Ltd v. Maher* (1988) 76 ALR 513.
384. See *Wilson Parking New Zealand Ltd v. Fanshawe 136 Ltd* [2014] NZCA 407, [2014] 3 NZLR 567 at [44]; *Hansard v. Hansard* [2014] NZCA 562, [2015] 2 NZLR 158 at [5]; *Infinity Enterprises NZ Ltd v. Kinara Trustee Ltd* [2020] NZCA 309, [2020] 3 NZLR 626 at [98]–[104]; *Doig v. Tower Insurance Ltd* [2019] NZCA 107, [2021] 2 NZLR 127 at [22] and [32]; *Creative Development Solutions Ltd v. Chorus New Zealand Ltd* [2021] NZCA 178 at [41].
385. *Ibid.*
386. [2008] 1 WLR 643; but *see MWB Business Exchange Centres Ltd v. Rock Advertising Ltd* [2018] UKSC 24, [2019] AC 119; above para. 85.

off one-third of the debt, but his partners became bankrupt. W served a statutory demand on C to recover the balance, but C argued that W had promised to treat him as a several debtor and that his obligation had been met on paying his one-third. The court held that the agreement alleged by C was merely an agreement to accept payment from a joint debtor of his proportionate share and, applying *Foakes v. Beer*, this was not binding since there was no consideration to support it. However, Arden LJ accepted that where a creditor voluntarily accepted a debtor's offer to pay part only of the amount owed, and, relying on the creditor's acceptance, the debtor paid that part of the amount in full, the creditor would be estopped from claiming the whole debt, since for the creditor to resile from his promise would be inequitable. Longmore LJ agreed that the case was arguable, but found the promissory estoppel point 'more difficult'. But the Court held that C had raised a triable issue, and the statutory demand was therefore set aside.

Clearly, the doctrine of estoppel has much potential, as well demonstrated by *Collier*. If Arden LJ's wide view is followed in New Zealand, then the impact of *Foakes* will be limited to cases where estoppel cannot operate.

We should note finally that to the extent that the requirement for consideration is relaxed, as in *Williams v. Roffey*, there is a lesser need for a separate doctrine of estoppel. Seemingly, the *High Trees* decision itself could now be argued as a case where consideration was provided: the lessor obtained a 'practical benefit' from reducing the rent, as he did not need to go to the trouble and expense of finding another tenant. However, if there was no consideration in *MWB Business Exchange Centres Ltd v. Rock Advertising Ltd*,[387] the Court of Appeal considered that the promise could not be upheld by estoppel, for it was not inequitable to go back on the promise. On the facts, there was no agreement to forgo any part of the licence fees but only to give time to pay in accordance with the agreed payment schedule; the licensee immediately made a payment under the schedule but incurred no detriment because it was part of the existing arrears; two days later the licensor sought to re-impose its original legal rights and gave reasonable notice to this effect; and the licensee could not say that it had suffered any prejudice by relying on the further agreement.[388] In the Supreme Court, Lord Sumption similarly affirmed that the minimal steps taken by Rock Advertising were not enough to support any estoppel defences. His Lordship added that the scope of estoppel could not be so broad as to destroy the whole advantage of certainty for which the parties stipulated when they agreed upon terms including the No Oral Modification clause. At the very least: (i) there would have to be some words or conduct unequivocally representing that the variation was valid notwithstanding its informality; and (ii) something more would be required for this purpose than the informal promise itself.[389]

387. Above para. 85.
388. [2016] EWCA Civ 553, [2017] QB 604, at [63].
389. [2018] UKSC 24, [2019] AC 119, at [16].

§2. Formal and Evidential Requirements

I. General

90. New Zealand law generally recognizes as valid contractual agreements which have usually been called simple contracts – that is, agreements made either by word of mouth or in writing, but without any specific formalities or in a particular form. It is the element of exchange or bargain which provides the rationale for the courts to enforce the contract. However, there are some types of contracts which must be made in writing or evidenced in writing to be effective, in particular, contracts affecting interests in land. There are also specific rules requiring contracts by certain persons to be made in writing.[390]

Much less commonly, there are a small number of transactions which are required to be made by deed. If the transaction is contractual in nature, the contract will have to be made in a form which has effect as a deed.[391] The formality of a deed is required for the disclaimer of rights to land, for the disclaimer of certain rights of inheritance or succession, and for an approved compromise with creditors by a bankrupt.[392]

If a natural person would be required to make a particular contract in the form of a deed, a company will be required to formalize the contract by making it as a contract under seal.[393] The concept of a 'contract under seal' has otherwise largely lost any practical relevance. A statutory entity will, however, be able to make such a contract in writing without the formality of a deed.[394]

The use of a deed will also allow a person to make legally binding a non-contractual promise emanating from the maker of the deed, but such cases fall outside the purview of the law of contract.

II. Requirements as to Form in Particular Cases

91. New Zealand law does not normally require a contract to be made in any particular form nor for any particular formalities to be observed in its making. Thus, for the most part, the parties may choose to make a contract orally, or in writing, or partly in writing and partly orally. However, there are a number of important exceptions to this general principle.

First, as we have seen, where the agreement is concerned with substantial areas of land or large-scale commercial dealings, there is a rebuttable presumption that the agreement is 'subject to contract' and therefore that the creation of contractual obligations is to be postponed until a formal document is executed.[395]

390. *See* paras 91–93.
391. The required formalities are set out in the Property Law Act 2007, s. 9.
392. *See* Property Law Act 2007, s. 17; Administration Act 1969, s. 81; Insolvency Act 2006, s. 317.
393. Companies Act 1993, s. 180; Charitable Trusts Act 1957, s. 19; Public Bodies Contracts Act 1959, s. 3.
394. Crown Entities Act 2004, s. 127.
395. *See* para. 68.

Second, there are a small number of transactions, which may or may not be contractual in nature, which are required by statute to be performed by the execution of a deed.[396]

Third, there is a very much larger and heterogeneous class of contracts which legislation requires be made in writing if they are to be valid. In some cases, such as contracts for direct, uninvited sales, the requirement of writing is clearly intended to complement the consumer protection aspects of relevant legislation.[397] In other cases, the requirement for the contract to be in writing is directed to the need for clear evidence of the rights and obligations created by the agreement, as with agreements as to the division of matrimonial or relationship property, or bills of exchange and promissory notes.[398] If a principal contract is required to be in writing, the requirement will not extend to any agreement collateral to the principal contract.[399]

Fourth, there are a significant number of cases where a requirement for the contract to be in writing arises because of the status of one of the contracting parties. A very large number of organizations created by statute are required by their founding enactment to make contracts for more than a stipulated sum in writing if the contract is to be effective.[400] Other entities, such as local bodies and limited liability companies, are also subject to statutory regimes as to the making of certain contracts.[401]

Lastly, there are those cases covered by the Property Law Act 2007, sections 24–27 (the current New Zealand successor to the English Statute of Frauds 1677), which requires that contracts for the sale or other disposition of interests in land be in writing or that there be a written record of the terms of the contract which has been signed the party against whom the contract is to be enforced, and that contracts of guarantee be in writing and signed by the guarantor.[402] In some cases, the person seeking to enforce the contract can gain assistance from the equitable doctrine of part performance.[403] A defendant must specifically plead any claim that a contract is unenforceable under the Property Law Act.[404]

---

396. *See* para. 90.
397. Fair Trading Act 1986, s. 36L(1). Consumer protection is also the basis for the requirement under the Credit Contracts and Consumer Finance Act 2003, s. 32, that disclosure of certain matters relating to the contract must be in writing. Similarly, writing is required under the Building Act 2004, s. 362F for residential building contracts for work over a prescribed monetary limit.
398. Property (Relationships) Act 1976, s. 21; Bills of Exchange Act 1908, ss 3 and 84.
399. *Industrial Steel and Plant Ltd v. Smith* [1980] 1 NZLR 545. As to collateral contracts generally *see* para. 37.
400. By way of example, *see* Historic Places Act 1993, s. 59; Royal New Zealand Foundation for the Blind Act 1963, s. 18.
401. Public Bodies Contracts Act 1959, s. 3; Companies Act 1993, s. 180.
402. Property Law Act 2007, ss 24 and 27.
403. *See* para. 94.
404. High Court Rules 2008, Rule 5.19; *Boviard v. Brown* [1975] 2 NZLR 694; *cf. Whiting v. Diver Plumbing and Heating Ltd* [1992] 1 NZLR 560.

III. Property Law Act 2007

A. *The Requirement of a Written Contract or Written Record of the Terms of the Contract*

92. The Property Law Act 2007, sections 24–27 largely repeat the basic principles of the predecessor statute, the Contracts Enforcement Act 1956, but with some changes which may mean the law has been amended. But clearly no radical reform was intended. The starting point is that a contract for the sale or other disposition of an interest in land will only be enforceable against a party to the contract where the whole contract is in writing, or where there is a document signed by that party containing the terms of the contract.[405] A contract of guarantee is only enforceable where the actual contract has been signed by the guarantor.[406] It should be noted that where an unsigned agreement which contains a term requiring a party to enter into a contract of guarantee is enforced by way of an order for specific performance, the party against whom the order is made is compelled to enter into the contract of guarantee, including signing in compliance with the statute.[407] The rule is easily applied where there is a document prepared and executed as a contract – which is, of course, the normal position in New Zealand practice. Under the Contract and Commercial Law Act 2017, an electronic record of the transaction will fulfil the requirements of the Property Law Act for a document in writing, and an electronic signature can meet the requirement for a document to be signed.[408]

Where there is a contractual document, it must be complete in the sense that it does not leave any matter to be decided in the future by the parties themselves, although it has been held that it is not fatal that a commencement date had not been inserted where there was an existing common intention as to that date.[409]

In the case of contracts for the sale of land where there is no written and signed contract, the party seeking to enforce the contract may rely on a document which records the terms of the contract and which is signed by the party against whom the contract is to be enforced. The document must have been made after the alleged contract was concluded, unless it is a written offer which was allegedly accepted orally.[410] Whatever the nature of the document, it must contain terms identifying

---

405. This is so whether the party relying on the agreement is seeking to enforce it or is raising it by way of defence or counterclaim: *Country Club Apartments Ltd v. MFT Properties Ltd* [2011] NZCA 560, [44]–[45].

406. Property Law Act 2007, s. 24 and s. 27 respectively.

407. *Chambers v. Chatfield* [2016] NZHC 1871 (2016) 10 NZBLC 99-723. For specific performance *see* para. 252.

408. As to electronic documents as 'writing', *see* Contract and Commercial Law Act 2017, ss 221 and 222; as to electronic signatures *see* Contract and Commercial Law Act 2017, s. 225, *Welch v. Gatchell* (2007) 5 Conv C 194,549, para. [61]; *Wilfred v. Lexington Legal Ltd* [2016] NZHC 1469 (in which a distinction was drawn between an automatically generated name or message in an e-mail and one specifically entered by the sender to indicate confirmation of the text of the message); *Banbrook v. Tan Che Hoe & Sons (Pte) Ltd* [2019] NZHC 1415.

409. *See Barrett v. IBC International Ltd* [1995] 3 NZLR 170; *Madden v. UDC Finance Ltd* [1996] 1 NZLR 542 at 546.

410. *Boote v. R T Shiels & Co Ltd* [1978] 1 NZLR 445, 451; *Geneva Healthcare Ltd v. Essential Assets Ltd* [2014] NZHC 3236.

both the parties, by name or in some other appropriate manner,[411] and the subject matter of the contract. In contracts for the sale of land, the consideration for the contract must be set out, but in the case of contracts of guarantee, this is not necessary.[412] Under the previous law, a very wide range of documents have been accepted, from letters to pleadings in a legal action, and there seems no reason to believe the law has changed here, except that the documents relied on must have been signed.

Under the previous statute, the courts would accept two or more linked documents which collectively satisfied the requirements of the statute, as in *Saunderson v. Purchase*,[413] where a written offer which lacked certain details was coupled with a written receipt for moneys paid which recorded the other necessary details. It would appear that under the Property Law Act 2007, a court could accept two or more linked documents, but each would have to have been signed by the party against whom the contract is sought to be enforced.

A document which incorrectly records the actual agreement, or omits terms which were in fact agreed, may be rectified by the court and then enforced.[414]

B. The Requirement of a Signature

93. The Property Law Act requires that the contract, or the written record of its terms, be signed by the party against whom the contract is sought to be enforced.[415] The meaning of a 'signature' in this context was helpfully discussed in *Welch v. Gatchell*:[416]

> A signature is a distinct and personal act that identifies the party to be charged and evidences his or her intention to be bound by the contents of the document. For that reason, a name need not be interpreted as a signature where it serves some other purpose, as in the case where it appears as part of the substantive content. A signature may appear in any position, but it must govern the whole. A name, initials, or other mark that identifies the party to be charged may suffice as a signature. It need not be hand-written; in particular, it may be stamped or typed.

The common law had developed a number of rules which allowed enforcement of contracts where there was no signature in the normal meaning of the word. It is

---

411. *Rossiter v. Miller* (1878) 3 App Cas 1124. Misdescription of the parties need not be fatal if they can still be identified: *Cooke v. Duntroon Station Holdings Ltd* (1985) 2 NZCPR 264, affirmed NZCA 58/85, 5 Jun. 1987.
412. Property Law Act 2007, s. 27(3).
413. [1958] NZLR 588. *See also Timmins v. Moreland Street Property Ltd* [1958] Ch. 110; *Elias v. George Sahely & Co (Barbados) Ltd* [1983] 1 AC 646.
414. *Whiting v. Diver Plumbing and Heating Ltd* [1992] 1 NZLR 560; *Samson v. Butt* [1927] NZLR 119. As to rectification generally, *see* para. 132.
415. Property Law Act 2007, s. 24 and s. 27.
416. [2009] 1 NZLR 241, at para. [51]. *See also Doughty-Pratt Group Ltd v. Perry Castle* [1995] 2 NZLR 398 at 403.

not entirely clear that all of these rules will continue to apply to the rather different wording of the Property Law Act provisions.

The first issue is whether a document is to be taken as 'signed' by the party to the contract if the signature is in fact that of an authorized agent. It would certainly be most inconvenient were such signatures not effective. Most cases involving agents have turned on whether it has been shown that the agent is properly authorized to sign the document in question,[417] but other issues have arisen. It has, for example, been held that the agent whose signature is relied on must have been acting solely for the party who is allegedly bound by the signature; the signature of a person acting as agent for both parties is not sufficient.[418] The most substantial discussion of the actual requirement of signature by an agent came in *Parkin v. Williams*,[419] where the Court of Appeal held that it was not necessary that the agent should have personally signed the relevant documents; it sufficed that the actual signing had been sub-delegated to another person who was performing a purely ministerial act and had no discretion as to the content of the documents. This decision may need to be revisited in the light of the changed statutory wording.

The change in statutory wording will also call into question the validity of a device developed at common law, the so-called fiction of the authenticated signature which had on occasion been recognized and applied by New Zealand courts as a way of satisfying the statutory requirement for a signature. The device permitted the court to treat a printed or written statement of the party's name in the contractual document as being equivalent to the party's own signature. It required that there be a document on which there is printed or written the name of the party who is to be 'charged' or sued on the contract, and that the document had been prepared by that party or his or her agent and sent to the other party to the contract with an intention apparent from the document or the circumstances that the sending of the document was done with the intention that there would be a complete and binding contract when signed by the party to whom it was sent. Documents prepared for other purposes did not suffice.[420]

If the authenticated signature fiction has survived the changes to the statute, it is clear that the scope of its application is limited. It will not apply, for instance, to the automatic inclusion of the sender's name or e-mail address in an e-mail,[421] nor to the automatic inclusion of the sender's details in the heading of a fax message.

417. *See New Lynn Borough v. Auckland Bus Co* [1965] NZLR 542; *Savill v. Chase Holdings (Wellington) Ltd* [1989] 1 NZLR 257.
418. *Bank of New Zealand Ltd v. Mulholland* (1991) 3 NZBLC 101,970; affirmed (1991) 3 NZBLC 102,251 (CA).
419. [1986] 1 NZLR 294.
420. As to the authenticated signature fiction generally *see T A Dellaca Ltd v. PDL Industries Ltd* [1992] 3 NZLR 88; *Sturt v. McInnes* [1974] 1 NZLR 729; *Van der Veeken v. Watsons Farm (Pukepoto) Ltd* [1974] 2 NZLR 146.
421. *J Pereira Fernandes SA v. Mehta* [2006] 2 All ER 891 at 899; *Welch v. Gatchell* [2009] 1 NZLR 241, para. [76].

C. *Equitable Doctrine of Part Performance*

94. Experience in England showed that on occasion the requirement of the Statute of Frauds 1677 that certain contracts be evidenced in writing could lead to injustice or be used to assist fraudsters. Equity developed in response to the doctrine of part performance whereby it would in some circumstances enforce oral agreements relating to land which had been partly performed by the party seeking to enforce the agreement. The Property Law Act 2007 does not affect the law relating to part performance, so in appropriate circumstances, the doctrine can be used to enforce oral agreements which do not comply with the Act.[422] As part performance is an equitable doctrine, it must be shown that the circumstances call for the intervention of equity, which will require it to be shown that in the circumstances it is inequitable or unconscionable for the defendant to rely on the statutory rule in the Property Law Act.[423]

The doctrine first requires proof of an oral agreement meeting all the requirements of a contract. There must then be proof that the party seeking to enforce the oral contract has done one or more acts which can be accepted as having been done in part performance of the contract. It is at this point that the law becomes less than completely clear. The doctrine requires conduct which is both an element of performance of a contractual obligation or done in the exercise of a contractual right[424] and also appears, when viewed objectively, to be something which was on the balance of probabilities done on the basis that there was an oral contract in the terms alleged. What can amount to part performance must then depend on the nature of the alleged contract and its terms. The courts have accepted a very wide range of acts as meeting the first limb of the test, but it is usually much more difficult to show that the conduct in question meets the second limb.[425]

D. *Contracts of Guarantee*

95. A contract of guarantee is one in which A (the guarantor) agrees to accept a liability to B (the other contracting party) as to a debt, default or liability owed by C (a third party) to B. The Property Law Act 2007 provides that contracts of guarantee are only enforceable where the contract itself is in writing and that contract

---

422. Property Law Act 2007, s. 26. Where a partly performed oral contract has later been varied orally, part performance of the varied agreement will have to be shown: *Street v. Fountaine* [2018] NZCA 55; (2018) 19 NZCPR 236, at [131].

423. *Fleming v. Beevers* [1994] 1 NZLR 385; *Mahoe Buildings Ltd v. Fair Investments Ltd* [1994] 1 NZLR 281.

424. The relevant conduct need not be to the detriment of the party so acting: *Country Club Apartments Ltd v. MFT Properties Ltd* [2011] NZCA 560, [56]; leave to appeal refused [2012] NZSC 9.

425. For the operation of the doctrine generally *see Fleming v. Beevers* [1994] 1 NZLR 385; *Mahoe Buildings Ltd v. Fair Investments Ltd* [1994] 1 NZLR 281; *T A Dellaca Ltd v. PDL Industries Ltd* [1992] 3 NZLR 88. Payment of money is particularly likely to give rise to problems under the second limb; *see Anae v. Lambert* (1985) 2 NZCPR 315; *Steadman v. Steadman* [1976] AC 536 but payment of a deposit may suffice: *Nguyen v. SM & T Homes Limited* [2016] NZCA 58.

has been signed by the guarantor. However, there is no need for the consideration for the guarantee to be stated in the document.[426]

Whether a contract is a contract of guarantee is a matter of substance, not of form.[427] The essence of the guarantee is that the guarantor is promising to discharge the debt or liability of the third party. If there never was a third party to the transaction, or if the transaction involved the discharge of any third party's liability entirely, it is not a guarantee and the Property Law Act requirements need not be met. However, where a contract contains both a guarantee and the giving of some other security for a debt, the requirement as to writing applies.[428] Disputes may sometimes occur as to whether a person who has signed a written guarantee was signing it as guarantor or in some other capacity. In particular, difficulties may arise where a company shareholder or director signs a guarantee of the company's indebtedness, as it is possible for a single signature by such an individual to amount to both a witnessing of the document and a signature undertaking the onerous role of guarantor.[429] It is not clear whether a shareholder or director who mistakenly believes that a signature will have effect only as an attestation and that he or she will not thereby incur personal liability as a guarantor will be able to seek relief under the law relating to mistake.[430]

IV. Evidential Requirements

A. *General*

96. In general, a contract may be made orally or in writing or by a mixture of oral and written terms. There are a significant number of contracts which must be made in writing, or where enforceability requires a written record of the terms of the contract.[431] However, where there is no legal requirement that the contract be in writing, proof of the oral terms of the agreement will suffice. Proof of the existence of a contract and of its terms in such cases is therefore a matter of proof of the necessary facts by the party alleging the contract existed. Such facts will need to be proved on the balance of probabilities, that being the standard required in civil proceedings in New Zealand.

---

426. Property Law Act 2007, s. 27. The writing must contain the essentials of the obligation undertaken by the guarantor: *Brougham v. Regan* [2020] NZSC 118, [2020] 1 NZLR 315 (B signed a loan agreement as the guarantor, but the agreement did not itself set out any provisions under which he would be liable as guarantor). The section does not save a purported contract which is invalid for other reasons: *Radius Residential Care Ltd v. Krishna* [2013] NZHC 2886, [17].
427. *Jenkins v. NZI Finance Ltd* (1991) 3 NZBLC 102,199.
428. *Scott v. Broadlands Finance Ltd* [1972] NZLR 268.
429. *Doughty-Pratt Group Ltd v. Perry Castle* [1995] 2 NZLR 398; *Vuletic v. Contributory Mortgage Nominees Ltd* (2006) 7 NZCPR 552.
430. Contrast *Chiswick Investments Ltd v. Pevats* [1990] 1 NZLR 169 with *Trotter v. Avonmore Holdings Ltd* (2005) 8 NZBLC 101,646, [32]–[33], and *see also* [118].
431. *See* paras 91–93.

B. The 'Parol Evidence' Rule

97. There is a rule of the common law called the parol evidence rule, which is to the effect that where a contract is completely recorded in writing, oral evidence is not admissible to add to, vary or contradict the written terms. That rule is in force in New Zealand, but the rule has been significantly limited by judicial decisions. The rule and its limitations are discussed in detail elsewhere.[432]

C. Notaries Public

98. New Zealand law does not require the involvement of persons of official standing as a condition of contractual validity. There is therefore no necessity for a contract to be witnessed or attested by a solicitor or other professional, although it is common for such a practice to be followed as a method of providing a greater degree of evidential certainty as to the transaction. In Europe, it is normal for the notary to have an obligation to ensure the parties appreciate the effect of the transaction into which they are entering. There is no such obligation on a New Zealand solicitor witnessing a document signed by a person who is not a client of that solicitor.

Although there are a number of persons in practice in New Zealand who are qualified as notaries public, the qualification must be obtained from an authority outside New Zealand, and the principal function of such notaries public is in connection with documents intended to have legal effect in other jurisdictions. There is nothing in New Zealand law which requires their involvement.

D. Burden of Proof

99. Proof of the existence of a contract and of its terms in such cases is therefore a matter of proof of the necessary facts by the party alleging the contract existed. Such facts will need to be proved on the balance of probabilities. No distinction is made in this regard between different kinds of obligation contained within the contract.

§3. Liability and Negotiations

I. Pre-contractual Liability

100. There can be liability for misrepresentations which induce a party to enter a contract. However, liability for misrepresentation is dependent on the existence of a subsequent contract. There is a range of remedies available to a party who has suffered loss in the course of dealings which have not resulted in a completed contract.

---

432. *See* para. 164.

Restitution may be available if money has been paid in anticipation of a contract which does not materialize, and an action for quantum meruit allows reasonable remuneration for work done in such circumstances.[433] The doctrine of promissory estoppel may allow relief to a party who has been misled to his or her detriment by assurances given by the other: cases in both Australia and New Zealand have allowed monetary compensation in such a case.[434] The Fair Trading Act 1986 empowers a court to grant relief to a party against another who has engaged in conduct which is misleading or deceptive or likely to mislead or deceive. This might entitle a party to monetary or other relief in respect of misleading advertising or misleading conduct in the course of abortive negotiations.[435] There is also the possibility of a tortious action in negligence if carelessly misleading statements, or even promises, are made by one party to the other.[436] Finally, the courts also may be prepared to find and enforce 'process' contracts which prescribe the process to be followed by the parties before entering into a substantive contract. Contracts prescribing the process by which tenders are to be submitted and assessed are the best-known example of such process contracts: if the person calling for tenders does not follow the advertised procedure, a tenderer who fails to secure the substantive contract may have a remedy for loss of a chance.[437]

II. Breakdown of Negotiations

101. In general, no liability attaches for the breakdown of negotiations prior to the formation of a legally enforceable contract. New Zealand law does not yet recognize a general doctrine of good faith, and a party can withdraw from negotiations for any reason. Even if the parties have expressly undertaken to negotiate in good faith, such an undertaking will be found too vague to enforce unless the parties have themselves defined what they mean by it, and the steps they must respectively take.[438] However, as pointed out above, liability may sometimes attach for misleading statements made in the course of negotiations by virtue of estoppel, negligence, or the Fair Trading Act.

III. Misrepresentation

102. A misrepresentation is a false statement of present or past fact which induces a party to enter into a contract. In New Zealand, the law on liability for misrepresentation has been greatly simplified by two statutes, the Contractual

433. *Dickson Elliott Lonergan Ltd v. Plumbing World Ltd* [1988] 2 NZLR 608.
434. *Waltons Stores (Interstate) Ltd v. Maher* (1988) 76 ALR 513; *Dowell v. Tower Corporation* [1991] ANZ Conv R 177.
435. Section 9. *See* for example *Gregory v. Rangitikei District Council* [1995] 2 NZLR 208.
436. *Hedley Byrne & Co Ltd v. Heller & Partners Ltd* [1964] AC 465; *Boyd Knight v. Purdue* [1999] 2 NZLR 278; *NRAM Ltd v. Steel* [2018] UKSC 13, [2018] 1 WLR 1190; *see Tort Law in New Zealand* Kluwer, 4th ed., 2022), paras 90–99.
437. *Pratt Contractors Ltd v. Palmerston North City Council* [1995] 1 NZLR 469. In *Prime Commercial Ltd v. Wool Board Disestablishment Co Ltd* (2006) 7 NZCPR 697 the Court of Appeal declined to use the tort of negligence to make up for the lack of a process contract.
438. *See* para. 25.

Remedies Act 1979, recently re-enacted in Part 2, subpart 3 of the Contract and Commercial Law Act 2017, and the Fair Trading Act 1986. In essence, a misrepresentation is redressable by damages and, in serious cases, by cancellation of the contract.

A. *Contract Legislation*

1. Definition of Misrepresentation

103. Section 35 of the Contract and Commercial Law Act 2017, formerly section 6 of the Contractual Remedies Act 1979, gives a remedy in damages for misrepresentation. The section applies to all contracts, including contracts for the sale of goods and contracts of insurance.[439] However, it does not define what a misrepresentation is. The long-standing judicial definitions thus apply.

First, a representation usually will involve an explicit statement, whether written or oral. However, as will be seen, a representation sometimes can be implied from the words used by one of the parties, and, similarly, can be inferred from a party's conduct.[440]

Second, misrepresentation is a statement of past or present fact. That statement needs to be qualified somewhat as a court may see a statement as to the legal position as being one of fact or mixed fact or law, and thus actionable as a misrepresentation if it is inaccurate.[441] It may be of a continuing nature.[442] A statement of future intent does not qualify, and will be actionable, if at all, only if it is a promise which forms part of a contract. However, there are two exceptions to this basic proposition. The first is that if a party does not have the intention which he or she has proclaimed, that amounts to a misrepresentation of that intention: '[t]he state of a man's mind is as much a fact as the state of his digestion'.[443] The second is that a statement which is ostensibly about the future can sometimes imply a statement about the present.[444] Thus, a statement by the vendor of a kiwi fruit orchard that the orchard would be producing by 1982 was held to imply a statement that the vines were presently of such quality that they were capable of producing by the time stated.[445] And a 'budget forecast' for a company was held to imply that the present state of the company was such as to justify the forecast.[446]

Third, a statement of opinion which turns out to be erroneous is not actionable as a misrepresentation. Thus, a vendor's estimate of the sheep-carrying capacity of a farm, the purchaser knowing the vendor had not farmed sheep, was held to be a

439. As to the latter, *see Taylor v. Asteron Life Ltd* [2019] NZHC 978 at [69].
440. *McAlister v. Lai* [2018] NZCA 141 (2018) 14 TCLR 765 at [44].
441. *Fonterra Co-operative Group Ltd v. McIntyre and Williamson Partnership* [2016] NZCA 538.
442. *Cramaso LLP v. Ogilvie-Grant* [2014] UKSC 9, [2014] AC 1093.
443. *Edgington v. Fitzmaurice* (1885) 29 Ch D 459.
444. *Do Yay Ltd v. Wei* [2020] NZHC 759 at [33].
445. *Ware v. Johnson* [1984] 2 NZLR 518.
446. *New Zealand Motor Bodies Ltd v. Emslie* [1985] 2 NZLR 569.

statement of opinion only and not to be actionable.[447] However, as with the last criterion, a statement of opinion may sometimes imply a statement of fact. That is particularly so where the maker of the statement has greater knowledge or expertise than the recipient so that the latter is relying on the former. In such a case, the courts are ready to imply an assurance that the holder of the opinion has taken proper care, and is in possession of facts which justify the opinion.[448]

Fourth, 'mere puff', or exaggerated sales talk, is not treated by the law as misrepresentation; to hold that it was would put a stop to age-old advertising practice. But where the assertion goes beyond generalities and refers to verifiable particulars, it may become a representation.[449]

Finally, generally speaking, silence is not a misrepresentation. A seller who stands by, saying nothing, and allows a purchaser to deceive himself or herself about the qualities of what is for sale does not commit an actionable misrepresentation.[450] However, in certain circumstances, silence may be actionable.[451] First, silence may distort a positive representation: to tell only half the story, and leave out material qualifications, may result in a representation which is not really the truth. Thus, a statement that the nearest competition to a food bar was one mile away was held to be a misrepresentation because it omitted to state that a licence had just been granted for one to open around the corner.[452] Again, an insurance company was found to have misrepresented the amount that could be claimed by a policyholder by deliberately failing to disclose matters which might have shown a larger sum was due.[453] Second, a statement which is true when it is made becomes a misrepresentation if the facts later change in a material way before the contract is finally made; in such a case, the maker of the statement is under an obligation to inform the other party of the change.[454] Third, there may be cases, although they will be rare, where a vendor's silence will be taken to affirm a misapprehension induced in a buyer by the appearance of the property. Thus, in one case, the positioning of a fence, driveway and garden led the purchaser to assume the fence was on the boundary of the property; in fact it was not. It was held that this misleading appearance, coupled with the vendor's silence, was a misrepresentation.[455]

447. *Bisset v. Wilkinson* [1927] AC 177; and *see* for example *Shen v. Ossyanin* [2019] NZHC 135 (statement that a house was not prone to leaking was an honestly and reasonably held statement of opinion and not an innocent misrepresentation of fact); compare *Ridgway Empire Ltd v. Grant* [2019] NZCA 134, para. 104 below.
448. *New Zealand Motor Bodies Ltd v. Emslie* [1985] 2 NZLR 569; *Premium Real Estate Ltd v. Stevens* [2009] 1 NZLR 48.
449. *See* for example *Closurepac NZ Ltd v. WS 2014 Ltd* [2015] NZHC 1587 at [93]-[104] (discussion whether 'excellent' was puffery or misrepresentation); *Gillette v. Green* [2019] NZHC 946 (no misrepresentation where figures could be confusing and misunderstood, and plaintiff had failed to seek clear information).
450. *Deverick v. Hedley* (2000) 9 TCLR 326.
451. *See generally Amaltal Corp Ltd v. Maruha Corp* [2007] 1 NZLR 608, at [47] (on appeal [2007] 3 NZLR 192 (SC)).
452. *Wakelin v. Jackson* (1984) 2 NZCPR 195; *see also Thompson v. Vincent* [2001] 3 NZLR 355.
453. *Dodds v. Southern Response Earthquake Services Ltd* [2019] NZHC 2016, [2019] 3 NZLR 826.
454. *With v. O'Flanagan* [1936] Ch. 575; and *see Cramaso LLP v. Ogilvie-Grant* [2014] UKSC 9.
455. *King v. Wilkinson* (1994) 2 NZ Conv C 191828; *see also Adele Holdings Ltd v. Westpac Finance Ltd* (1988) ANZ Conv R 20.

Where silence contributes to a misleading impression, there may be a question as to whether it is a misrepresentation if the speaker was unaware of the facts he or she did not disclose. On one view, there must be deliberate non-disclosure before there can be liability, on the basis that it would not serve the policy of the Act, or satisfy the requirement of inducement, if the non-disclosure of facts unknown to the representor could constitute a misrepresentation.[456] However, it has been said that half-truth cases involve both silence and positive representation. Innocent half-truths were not simply representations by silence, and the need for deliberate non-disclosure might not be applicable in this case.[457]

At common law, there are a few types of contracts, known as contracts *uberrimae fides*, where one party is obliged to disclose facts to the other; the best known of such type of contract is the contract of insurance. However, the remedy for non-disclosure in such cases has always been rescission only, and it is doubtful whether such non-disclosure is a 'misrepresentation' for the purposes of the Contractual Remedies Act or the Contract and Commercial Law Act. However, the New Zealand Court of Appeal has regarded this as an open question.[458]

2. Inducement

104. For a misrepresentation to be actionable under section 35 of the 2017 Act, it must have induced the representee to enter the contract. There is no requirement that the misrepresentation be the sole inducement – it is enough if it is one of several inducements. Thus, in a case where a 'rosy' budget forecast induced the buyer to purchase a business, it did not matter that the buyer had other motives as well, for example, a desire to rationalize the industry.[459] While the onus is on the plaintiff to show that the misrepresentation induced entry into the contract, that onus is not difficult to satisfy. However, the plaintiff will fail if he or she was unaware of the existence of the misrepresentation or if he or she knew it was false;[460] or if he or she did not allow it to affect his or her judgment. In relation to the last of these situations, the plaintiff will be disentitled to relief if he or she did not rely on the defendant's statement, but independently checked the information and pronounced himself or herself satisfied with his or her own enquiries.[461]

At common law, it was a requirement that the representation must be *material*.[462] Section 35 contains no express requirement of materiality, but no doubt a plaintiff will have difficulty proving inducement if the representation made to him or her was

456. *Ladstone Holdings Ltd v. Leonora Holdings Ltd* [2006] 1 NZLR 211.

457. *Clarkson v. Whangamata Metal Supplies Ltd* HC, Auckland, CIV 2003-404-6869, 8 Jun. 2006 (on appeal [2008] 3 NZLR 31 (CA)).

458. *Scales Trading Ltd v. Far Eastern Shipping Co Public Ltd* [1999] 3 NZLR 26. The matter was left open by the Privy Council ([2001] 1 NZLR 513).

459. *New Zealand Motor Bodies Ltd v. Emslie* [1985] 2 NZLR 569.

460. But *see Zurich Insurance Co plc v. Hayward* [2016] 3 WLR 637.

461. *Attwood v. Small* (1838) 6 Cl & Fin 232.

462. *See BV Nederlandse Industrie v. Rembrandt Enterrpises Inc* [2019] EWCA Civ 596, [2020] QB 551 (representee required to prove that the misrepresentation had materially influenced his decision to make the contract, in the sense that it had been actively present to his mind, but did not have to show that he would not otherwise have entered the contract).

trivial and apparently irrelevant. In one case, a claim of misrepresentation based on certain relevant projections failed because the judge found that no sensible person in the plaintiff's position would have regarded the document as comprehensive or exact: it contained obvious approximations and omissions.[463]

Inducement and reasonable reliance were both in issue in *Vining Realty Group Ltd v. Moorhouse*.[464] Purchasers of a farm were misled about the farm's water permits by the vendors' real estate agents referring to permits that were no longer current and the vendors' solicitors in approving the agreement, and by the local council in its provision of wrong information about the permits in the Land Information Memorandum (LIM). The agents and the solicitors argued, *inter alia*, that the purchasers had instructed their own expert to advise on the suitability of the land, that the agreement was subject to solicitors' approval and to the purchasers' due diligence in satisfying themselves as to the relevant rights, that it was obvious that the agents were not the official source of the information but were passing it on second hand, and that the LIM superseded the agents' earlier statements. However, the Court of Appeal held that the purchasers were relevantly induced by the misrepresentations to enter the contract and that their reliance was reasonable. The court pointed out that where a clear and unequivocal representation was made, the representee should normally be able to take it at face value. Furthermore, it did not normally sit well in the mouth of someone who had been guilty of misrepresentation to blame the other person for believing the misrepresentation. Here, the purchasers could reasonably rely on the agents' representations, on the basis that the agents were part of the process from beginning to end and that their 'significant and explicit' statements would not have been made without checking with the vendors.[465]

Several recent decisions have concerned leaky buildings. In *Magee v. Mason*,[466] the vendor of a house stated in answer to a question of whether the property was a leaky home, 'absolutely not, we have never had any issues with the property'. The purchaser drew the inference that the house was not prone to leak, but the court held that this resulted from an assumption, for which the vendor was not responsible, that the vendor would otherwise have experienced weather-tightness problems. By contrast, in *Ridgway Empire Ltd v. Grant*,[467] the claimant purchaser was held to be entitled to rely on a clear and unqualified assertion by the vendor that the property did not leak.

Knowledge of the untruth of a representation normally is a bar to relief since, in most cases, the plaintiff cannot assert that he or she has been induced to act by the statement, even if made fraudulently. Exceptionally, however, a plaintiff who knows that a representation is false or who does not believe that it is true can still complain

463. *Harrison v. Amcor Trading (NZ) Ltd* HC Auckland, HC 167/97, 13 May 1999.
464. [2010] NZCA 104.
465. An appeal in this case was allowed on a different issue: *see Marlborough District Council v. Altimarloch Joint Venture Ltd* [2012] 2 NZLR 726, where the Supreme Court held that in the circumstances the vendors could not claim a contribution from the council. For discussion of this aspect of the case, *see International Encyclopaedia of Laws: Tort Law in New Zealand* Part VI, Ch. 4, §3 (2017).
466. [2017] NZCA 502; and *see Shen v. Ossyanin* [2019] NZHC 135.
467. [2019] NZCA 134.

about it, for it is not necessary as a matter of law for the plaintiff to believe that a representation was true. So an insurance company was induced to settle a claim notwithstanding that it did not believe the claimant's account, for there was a risk that the claimant might be believed by the judge on the matter going to trial.[468]

3. Mental Element

105. Section 35 of the 2017 Act expressly provides that a remedy lies for misrepresentation, whether that misrepresentation was innocent or fraudulent. What matters is the effect of the statement on the recipient, not the state of mind of the person who made it. However, there has been some discussion of whether, to be actionable, a misrepresentation has to be made with the *intention* of inducing the recipient to enter the contract. The Court of Appeal has held that *either* the person making the representation must have intended to induce the contract *or* the representation must have been such as would induce a normal person to contract.[469] As was said in *Bonz Group Pty Ltd v. Cooke*,[470] what is required is an element of actual or constructive intention as to result.

4. Misrepresentation Made by or on Behalf of Another Party to the Contract

106. The plaintiff will only have a remedy under section 35 if the misrepresentation was made by or on behalf of another party to the contract. A party is liable for a misrepresentation made by his or her agents. In a number of cases, a vendor has been held responsible for misrepresentations made by the land agent employed to sell the property.[471]

However, the party's liability is confined to statements made within the real or apparent authority of his agent. If an agent made a statement which is beyond the authority of such an agent, the party will not have it attributed to him or her. It can be a matter of difficulty to decide the ambit of an agent's authority for this purpose.

A land agent's position has been described in the following way by Bacon V-C:[472]

> A man employs an agent to let a house for him: that authority, in my opinion, contains also an authority to describe the property truly, to represent its actual

468. *Zurich Insurance Co plc v. Hayward* [2016] UKSC 48, [2017] AC 142.

469. *Savill v. NZI Finance Ltd* [1990] 3 NZLR 135 at 145 per Hardie Boys J; *Magee v. Mason* [2017] NZCA 502 at [42]. And *see BV Nederlandse Industrie v. Rembrandt Enterrpises Inc* [2019] EWCA Civ 596, [2020] QB 551, recognizing that at common law there was an evidential presumption of fact, very difficult to rebut, that the representee would have been induced by a fraudulent misrepresentation that was intended to cause him to enter the contract.

470. (1996) 5 NZBLC 104 188 at 104, 192 per Gault J.

471. For example *Wakelin v. Jackson* (1984) 2 NZCPR 195; *Sheppard-Johnson v. Lucy* (1990) 1 NZ ConvC 190, 741.

472. *Mullens v. Miller* (1882) 22 CLD 194 at 199.

> situation, and, if he thinks fit, to represent its value ... I think the principal ... authorizes the agent to state any fact or circumstance which may relate to the value of the property.

Bacon V-C said that the same principle applied where the agent was employed to sell rather than let. In *McAlpine Snowline Ltd v. Wethey,*[473] Henry J held, applying this principle, that an agent was not acting within the scope of his authority when he told a prospective buyer that finance should be available and that the buyer should have no difficulty obtaining suitable tenants. Neither of these statements really related to the property in the sense referred to by Bacon V-C.

Merely passing on a statement made by someone else – acting as a 'conduit' it has been said – will not amount to a misrepresentation. The defendant must adopt the statement as his or her own.[474]

5. Liability in Damages

107. Section 35 provides that a party to a contract (A) who has been induced to enter it by a misrepresentation made to him by or on behalf of another party to that contract (B) is entitled to damages from B in the same manner and to the same extent as if the representation were a term of the contract that has been breached. The damages are available as of right. The party is not entitled to damages from the other party for deceit or negligence.[475] However, the prohibition on suing in tort is confined to actions against the other party or parties to the contract. If the misrepresentation was made by an agent who is not himself or herself a party, a tort action will probably lie against that agent.[476]

Section 35 does not equate a misrepresentation to a contractual term for all purposes: for example, an exclusion clause excluding liability for misrepresentation might well be construed as not applying to contractual terms. But for the purposes of liability in damages, the two are equated. Thus, in a claim for damages for misrepresentation, the damages awarded will be the contract measure. Normally, that will be the sum required to put the plaintiff in the position he or she would have been in had the representation been true. Thus, damages will normally be the difference between the value of the subject matter had the representation been true, and its value as in fact it is.[477] Consequential losses may also be recoverable, provided they satisfy the standard tests of remoteness and causation.[478] Damages for stress

473. (1986) 2 NZCPR 388. *See also Power v. Atkins* [1921] NZLR 763 at 764.
474. *See* for example *Provincial Finance Ltd v. Trowbridge* (2002) 10 TCLR 405; and *see Body Corporate 202254 v. Taylor* [2009] 2 NZLR 17; *Red Eagle Corporation Ltd v. Ellis* [2010] 2 NZLR 492, at [38]; *McAlister v. Lai* [2018] NZCA 141 at [29].
475. Section 35(1)(b). For possible difficulty flowing from the non-availability of the tort action, *see Cygnet Farms Ltd v. ANZ Bank New Zealand Ltd* [2017] 2 NZLR 538.
476. *Wakelin v. Jackson* (1984) 2 NZCPR 195; *Shing v. Ashcroft* [1987] 2 NZLR 154 at 158; *Zhang v. Yu* [2018] NZHC 2215 at [48].
477. *Walsh v. Kerr* [1989] 1 NZLR 490.
478. *Crump v. Wala* [1994] 2 NZLR 332 at 340; *A v. Attorney-General* [2018] NZHC 986, [2018] 3 NZLR 439.

have occasionally been awarded,[479] but they are 'not easily recoverable'.[480] Damages are a flexible remedy, and sometimes instead of the 'difference in value' measure, the court may decide to award a measure based on the amount needed to enable the plaintiff to have the contract performed.[481]

6. Cancellation

108. If a party has been induced to enter a contract by a misrepresentation, he or she may cancel the contract if:[482]

(1) the parties have expressly or impliedly agreed that the truth of the representation is essential to the cancelling party; or
(2) the effect of the misrepresentation is:
   (a) substantially to reduce the benefit of the contract to the cancelling party; or
   (b) substantially to increase the burden of the cancelling party under the contract; or
   (c) in relation to the cancelling party, to make the benefit or burden of the contract substantially different from that represented or contracted for.

The provision applies the same tests of cancellation to misrepresentation as to breach of contract, and the consequences of cancellation are the same in both cases. This is significant, for it means that in New Zealand, cancellation for misrepresentation is not rescission *ab initio* as it was in equity, but cancellation *de futuro*. A full discussion of cancellation will be reserved for the section on breach of contract.[483]

B. *The Fair Trading Act 1986*

1. Introduction

109. Section 9 of the Fair Trading Act 1986 provides: 'No person shall, in trade, engage in conduct that is misleading or deceptive or likely to mislead or deceive.' This provision obviously has a very wide reach. Indeed it extends beyond the boundaries of contract altogether. But it is obviously apt to cover misrepresentation by a person in trade which induces another to contract. In such a case, section 43 of the Act confers on the court power to award a range of remedies. They include power to order the person who engaged in the conduct to pay the amount of the loss

479. *Snodgrass v. Hammington* (1994) ANZ Conv R 159.
480. *Crump v. Wala* [1994] 2 NZLR 332 at 340 per Hammond J.
481. *Marlborough District Council v. Altimarloch Joint Venture Ltd* [2012] 2 NZLR 726.
482. Contract and Commercial Law Act 2017, s. 37(2).
483. *See* paras 210–220.

or damage to the other; to declare a contract to be void (including a power to retrospectively declare it to have been void *ab initio*); to vary a contract; and to order the refund of money paid and the return of property transferred.

There is clearly an overlap between the Fair Trading Act and section 35 of the Contract and Commercial Law Act, although there are significant differences between them.

2. Features of the Fair Trading Act

a. In Trade

110. Unlike section 35, the Fair Trading Act only applies where the conduct is 'in trade', that is to say, in the course of 'any trade, business, industry, profession, occupation, activity of commerce, or undertaking relating to the supply or acquisition of goods or services, or to the disposition or acquisition of any interest in land'.[484] It thus does not apply to private sales or other transactions where the party engaging in misleading conduct is not doing so in the course of a business. And the courts have taken a broad approach to the definition of 'in trade'.[485] For example, conduct in trade may include one-off sales of a business asset.[486] Further, the person making the misleading statements need not be in trade *on his or her* own account. The 'in trade' requirement can be met even though he or she is an agent and director of a company.[487]

b. Misleading or Deceptive or Likely to Mislead or Deceive

111. In *Red Eagle Corporation Ltd v. Ellis,*[488] Blanchard J in the Supreme Court said that section 9 is directed to promoting fair trade by proscribing conduct which, objectively, is deceptive or misleading in particular circumstances. That will depend on the context, including the characteristics of the person or persons said to be affected. Conduct towards a sophisticated businessman may, for instance, be less likely to be objectively regarded as capable of misleading or deceiving such a person than similar conduct directed towards a consumer or, in an extreme case, an individual known to have intellectual difficulties.

Any misrepresentation is, by very definition, misleading. But one question is whether the expression used in the Fair Trading Act can go wider and cover, for example, statements of future intent or instances of silence or inaction which would

---

484. Fair Trading Act 1986, s. 2.

485. *Body Corporate 202254 v. Taylor* [2008] NZCA 317, [2009] 2 NZLR 17 at [78]; *Adventurer Hobson Ltd v. Cockery* [2020] NZHC 675, [2020] 2 NZLR 554 at [46]–[56].

486. *Artifakts Design Group Ltd v. NP Rigg Ltd* [1993] 1 NZLR 196; *Gloken Holdings Ltd v. The CDE Co Ltd* (1997) 6 NZBLC 102,272.

487. *Body Corporate 202254 v. Taylor* [2008] NZCA 317, [2009] 2 NZLR 17.

488. [2010] 2 NZLR 492.

not come within the concept of misrepresentation under the Contract and Commercial Law Act. While there are judicial statements which seek to equate the two concepts,[489] there is another view which holds that one should interpret the Fair Trading Act without reference to other concepts, and should simply apply its words in their natural and ordinary meaning. In so doing, it may be that some instances of silence,[490] and some statements of intent, can in all the circumstances of the case be regarded as misleading. However, in almost all the reported cases, the same result would have been achieved whichever of the two approaches was adopted. Thus, in *Smythe v. Bayleys Real Estate Ltd,*[491] a property for sale was described as a 'quality investment'. It was said that the tenant was in nationwide business and that the rent was NZD 80,000. In fact, the tenant was insolvent, and had requested a reduction in the rent. The failure to disclose this information was held to render the description misleading. In *Hieber v. Barfoot & Thompson Ltd,*[492] the plaintiff bought a waterfront property described as having 'magnificent sea views'. The agent failed to tell the plaintiff that a yacht club was going to move its clubhouse to a position which would obstruct the view. Again, it was held that the agent's conduct was misleading. In *Commerce Commission v. Telecom Mobile Ltd,*[493] the telephone company was held to have been in breach of the Fair Trading Act when it failed to tell consumers that the agreement to sell a mobile phone was subject to the Door to Door Sales Act 1967; it had led them to believe that once they opened the package containing the phone, they could no longer return it.

c. Mental Element

112. Intention to mislead is not relevant for the purposes of the Fair Trading Act. What matters is the impact on the misled party and whether it was reasonable for that person to be misled.[494] However, there are some cases where a court may be reluctant to impose liability for silence if the party concerned was unaware of the facts he or she failed to disclose. Elias J has said that 'no policy of the Act is served by imposing liability for an omission which is wholly unconscious'.[495] However, everything depends on the circumstances of the particular case, and on whether those circumstances, and the conduct of the defendant, create a misleading impression.

3. Remedies

113. The remedies available under the Fair Trading Act (FTA) differ from those under the Contract and Commercial Law Act (CCLA).

---

489. For example *Unilever NZ Ltd v. Cerebos Greggs Ltd* (1994) 6 TCLR 187 at 192 per Gault J: *Taco Co of Australia v. Taco Bell Pty Ltd* (1982) 4 ATPR 40-303.
490. *McAlister v. Lai* [2018] NZCA 141 at [27].
491. (1993) 5 TCLR 454.
492. (1996) 5 NZBLC 104,179.
493. [2006] 1 NZLR 290.
494. *AMP Finance NZ Ltd v. Heaven* (1998) 8 TCLR 144 at 152; *Lane Group v. DI & L Paterson Ltd* [2000] 1 NZLR 129 at 148.
495. *Des Forges v. Wright* [1996] 2 NZLR 758 at 765–766.

a. Damages

114. Whereas under section 35 of the 2017 Act, the plaintiff is entitled to damages as of right, under the Fair Trading Act, they are one of a range of remedies which the court *may* award.[496] Moreover whereas under the CCLA damages are available only against the other party to the contract, under the FTA they lie against the party who engaged in the misleading conduct.[497] Thus whereas an agent cannot be sued personally under the CCLA, he or she can be under the FTA. Moreover, the measure of damages differs. Under the FTA, damages are not based on the contractual measure. The Act gives a remedy for loss resulting from the misrepresentation, not the remedy based on what the position would have been had the misrepresentation been true.[498] In other words, the wrong consists in engaging in misleading conduct; there is no duty to make the misrepresentation good. Thus, in *Cox & Coxon Ltd v. Leipst,* the plaintiff was unable to recover a projected loss of profit under the FTA.[499] However, in one respect, the court has more flexibility under the FTA: it can reduce damages if the plaintiff's own conduct or the conduct of other persons contributed to the loss.[500]

b. Avoidance and Variation

115. The court has power under the FTA to declare a contract void, or to vary it, because there has been misleading conduct.[501] The powers have been little used.[502] The power to void the contract and transfer money and property can give a result not unlike cancellation, although it is less attractive in that it requires a court order; cancellation under the CCLA is achieved by an act of the party himself or herself.

c. Contracting Out

116. There is only a limited ability to contract out of liability for misrepresentation under the CCLA.[503] Again, it is not generally possible to contract out of the operation of the Fair Trading Act 1986, but this is subject to an exception where both parties are in trade.[504]

---

496. Fair Trading Act 1986, s. 43. In *Red Eagle Corporation Ltd v. Ellis* [2010] 2 NZLR 492, at [29], Blanchard J said that the court must first ask itself whether the particular claimant was actually misled or deceived by the defendant's conduct, and if satisfied on this point it must then ask whether the conduct was an operating or effective cause of the claimant's loss or damage.
497. *Ibid.*
498. *Gavigan v. Eichelbaum* [2017] NZCA 212, [2018] 2 NZLR 530.
499. [1999] 2 NZLR 15. Followed in *Harvey Corporation Ltd v. Baker* [2002] 2 NZLR 213. And *see Dodds v. Southern Response Earthquake Services Ltd* [2019] NZHC 216, [2019] 3 NZLR 826.
500. *Goldsboro v. Walker* [1993] 1 NZLR 394 at 401.
501. Fair Trading Act 1986, s. 43.
502. But *see Dungey v. ANZ Banking Group (NZ) Ltd* (1997) 6 NZBLC 102,194.
503. Contract and Commercial Law Act 2017, s. 50: *see* para. 178.
504. Fair Trading Act 1986, ss 5C, 5D; *see* para. 179.

Chapter 2. Conditions of Substantive Validity

§1. CAPACITY OF PARTIES

I. Minors' Contracts

A. Minors' Contracts Legislation

117. At common law, the legal age of majority was 21 years. This was changed by section 4 of the Age of Majority Act 1970, which provides that a minor is a person who has not attained the age of 20. However, as regards contractual capacity, section 85 of the Contract and Commercial Law Act 2017 provides that a minor means a person who is under the age of 18 years.

Certain special rules governing the contractual capacity of minors are found in Part 2, subpart 6 of the Contract and Commercial Law Act 2017, replacing the Minors' Contracts Act 1969. The original Act has been described as constituting a uniquely New Zealand response to the age-old problem of preventing persons taking advantage of youthful inexperience without unduly interfering with the ordinary course of commerce and the rights of innocent adults.[505] As initially provided, the broad scheme of the Act was to divide minors' contracts into separate categories according to the marital status of the minor and whether the minor had attained the age of 18, but with certain qualifications according to the nature of the contract in question. Amendments in 2005 then made significant changes to this structure, by abolishing special provision for married minors and special protection for older minors.

First, married minors originally had full contractual capacity, but this provision was repealed in 2005. So marriage does not affect a minor's contractual capacity.

Second, there is a category of contracts which are presumptively enforceable. By section 92 of the 2017 Act, every contract entered into pursuant to section 66B of the Life Insurance Act 1908 by a minor who has attained the age of 16 years, and a contract of service entered into by a minor, has effect as if the minor were of full age. However, by section 93, if the Court is satisfied that, at the time the contract was entered into, the consideration for the minor's promise or act was so inadequate as to be unconscionable or that any provision imposing an obligation on the minor was harsh or oppressive, it may cancel the contract or decline to enforce it against the minor, or declare that the contract is unenforceable against the minor in whole or in part, and may also make an order as to compensation or restitution of property. Some special types of contracts are excepted from this power of intervention.[506]

Formerly, by section 5(1)(a) of the 1969 Act, contracts made by minors aged 18 and 19 were included within this regime. But with the change in the law in 2005, when the age of majority was reduced from 20 to 18, the need for special protection for older minors disappeared, and paragraph (a) was repealed accordingly.

---

505. *Morrow & Benjamin Ltd v. Whittington* [1989] 3 NZLR 122 at 124 per Thorp J.
506. Contract and Commercial Law Act 2017, s. 94.

It is clear that section 93 has only a relatively narrow field of operation. The focus of the enquiry is solely on the inadequacy of the consideration for the promise or the harshness of the terms. The minor is not protected if the terms are not, objectively, harsh, oppressive, or unconscionable.[507]

Third, a general control upon claims in contract against minors is found in section 85 of the 2017 Act. This provides that every contract entered into by a minor (other than a contract to which section 92 applies) is unenforceable against the minor but otherwise has effect as if the minor were of full age. However, a court may enquire into the fairness and reasonableness of the contract at the time it was entered into and, if satisfied it was fair and reasonable, may enforce it against the minor, declare it to be binding on him in whole or part, make an order entitling the other parties, on such conditions as the court thinks just, to cancel the contract, and make an order as to compensation or restitution of property.[508] If the court finds that the contract was not fair and reasonable, it may cancel the contract, make an order entitling the minor, on such conditions as the court thinks just, to cancel the contract and, again, make a compensation or restitution order.[509] The court has a wide discretion in exercising these powers and must take into account all relevant considerations, including the circumstances surrounding the making of the contract; the subject matter and nature of the contract; in the case of a contract relating to property, the nature and value of the property; and the age and the means (if any) of the minor.[510]

In *Morrow & Benjamin Ltd v. Whittington,*[511] the plaintiff stockbrokers started to buy shares for the defendant when he was a 15-year-old minor. The defendant originally paid for the shares in cash, but over the next two and a half years, the plaintiffs allowed him to purchase on credit to ever-increasing amounts. On 20 October 1987, when the share market collapsed, his total debt was over NZD 35,000. The shares realized about NZD 5,000, and the plaintiffs, seeking to recover the balance, applied for an order under section 6 of the 1969 Act – now section 85 of the 2017 Act – that the contracts be declared enforceable. Thorp J held that the contracts were fair but were not reasonable. The plaintiffs were aware of the defendant's minority, the contracts were for the purchase on credit of highly speculative investments, the plaintiffs knew the minor's means were inadequate and that he was relying on resale to pay for the shares, and they regarded him as unreliable yet failed to implement their normal credit controls.

The 2017 Act contains a number of miscellaneous provisions. Where a court exercises its powers of intervention, it may order compensation or restitution of property.[512] An application may be made to the District Court by or on behalf of a minor for approval of a contract which is to be entered into by a minor. If it is approved,

507. *National Bank of New Zealand Ltd v. Ram* (1992) 4 NZBLC 102,618 (a case concerning the former s. 5(1)(a) of the 1969 Act).
508. Contract and Commercial Law Act 2017, ss 87 and 88.
509. *Ibid.*, s. 89.
510. *Ibid.*, s. 90.
511. [1989] 3 NZLR 122; and *see Wine Country Credit Union v. Raynor* [2008] 2 NZLR 698.
512. Contract and Commercial Law Act 2017, s. 95.

the contract has effect as if the minor were of full age.[513] Persons of full capacity are bound by contracts of guarantee or indemnity entered into by them in respect of a minor's obligations.[514]

B. Tortious Liability of Minors

118. A long-established rule of the common law states that a minor cannot be liable for a tort directly connected with any contract upon which no action will lie.[515] Whether the rule might still apply in New Zealand is uncertain, but almost certainly it can be regarded as obsolete. The legislative protection for minors has undermined its rationale, for there is no longer any question of bypassing a rigid bar on suing in contract. The rule itself is open to criticism, the test of whether the tort is 'directly connected with' or 'really founded upon' contract being vague and unsatisfactory. It is likely, then, that a minor who commits a tort in the course of carrying out a contract can be sued in the ordinary way.

A person's minority is relevant to his or her liability in tort only in so far as it bears upon the state of mind necessary for liability in the particular tort alleged to have been committed. Thus, in torts involving malice or intention or negligence, the question is whether the child could have been malicious or whether he or she could have intended or could have foreseen the consequences of the conduct. This is a question to be determined on the facts of the particular case.[516] Apart from this, it is possible that the parent or guardian of a minor may be personally liable for failing to exercise proper control over his or her child.[517]

II. Trading Corporations

119. Formerly, the contractual capacity of trading corporations was limited by the *ultra vires* doctrine, under which a company created under the Companies Act 1955 could only exercise the powers of the company as set out in its memorandum of association. Everything else was *ultra vires* and void.[518] So a person who made a contract with a company which was outside its powers was unable to enforce the contract, even though that person may have acted in perfect good faith.[519] The *ultra vires* doctrine operated as a trap for the unwary, and was reformed by amendments to the 1955 Act in 1983 and 1985 and by a new Companies Act in 1993. The broad effect of the reforms is not only to allow innocent third parties to make contracts with companies without risk of their being set aside but also to allow members of the company to seek internal redress.

---

513. *Ibid.*, s. 98.
514. *Ibid.*, s. 102.
515. *Burnard v. Haggis* (1863) 14 BNS 45.
516. *See* for example *McHale v. Watson* (1966) 115 CLR 199; *Mullins v. Richards* [1998] 1 WLR 1304.
517. *See* for example *Kenealy v. Karaka* (1906) 26 NZLR 1118 (father).
518. *Attorney-General v. Great Eastern Rly Co* (1880) 5 App Cas 473 at 478.
519. *Ashbury Railway Carriage Co v. Riche* (1875) LR 7 HL 653.

A company has full capacity to undertake any activity, do any act or enter into any transaction, subject to the Act, to any other enactment and to the general law.[520] Further, the company's capacity to contract may be quite unfettered, for there is nothing in the Act requiring the company to state its objects. The company remains at liberty to include objects in its constitution, but if it does so, they will have little effect on contracting parties. Thus, it is provided that no act of a company and no transfer of property are invalid merely because the company did not have the capacity, the right or the power to do it.[521] Further, the fact that an act is not, or would not be, in the best interests of a company does not affect the capacity of the company to perform the act.[522]

The general rule that contracts between companies and outsiders are enforceable in an ordinary way is qualified in two main respects. First, a director or shareholder may apply to prevent the company from contravening its constitution, provided the transaction objected to has not been completed.[523] The Court may grant such consequential relief as it thinks fit, which could include compensation to another contracting party where a transaction is prevented from proceeding. Second, a transaction outside the powers of the company may be upset where the other party knew, or, by reason of his or her position with or relationship to the company, ought to have known, that the constitution had not been complied with or that certain other company rules had been breached.[524] However, a person is not deemed to have knowledge of the contents of a company constitution or company document merely because the constitution or document is registered on the New Zealand register or is available for inspection at the company office.[525]

The making of a contract which is beyond the powers of a company may have internal consequences. Directors and shareholders may bring proceedings in the name of and on behalf of the company against directors who have acted against the rules of the company.[526] Shareholders also may bring personal actions against such directors.[527]

III. Mentally Disordered Persons

A. *Protection of Personal and Property Rights Act 1988*

120. Where a person lacks, wholly or partly, the competence to manage his or her affairs in relation to his or her property, a court acting pursuant to Part III of the Protection of Personal and Property Rights Act 1988 may appoint a suitable person

---

520. Companies Act 1993, s. 16.
521. *Ibid.*, s. 17(1).
522. *Ibid.*, s. 17(3).
523. *Ibid.*, ss 17(2), 164.
524. *Ibid.*, s. 18; and *see Cromwell Corporation Ltd v. Sofrana Immobilier (NZ) Ltd* (1992) 6 NZCLC 67,997; *Bishop Warden Property Holdings Ltd v. Autumn Tree Ltd* [2018] NZCA 285, [2018] 3 NZLR 809 at [31]–[32].
525. *Ibid.*, s. 19.
526. *Ibid.*, ss 17(2), 165.
527. *Ibid.*, ss 17(2), 169.

to act as manager of the property. A person subject to such a 'property order' is incapable of exercising personally any of the powers thus vested in the manager.[528] Any disposition of property and every contract involving property (except for necessaries, as to which *see* below) which is entered into by that person is, unless it is entered into with the leave of the court, avoidable by that person or by his or her manager.[529] If any transaction is so avoided, the court may make such order as it thinks just for adjusting the rights of the parties and of any other person who has received any property or money comprised in the transaction, not being a person who has received the property or money from a person in good faith and for valuable consideration or who claims through such a person.[530] If the person from whom relief is sought received the property or money in good faith and has altered his or her position in reliance on having received an indefeasible interest in it, then the court may deny relief wholly or in part if in its opinion it is inequitable to grant relief.[531]

B. Common Law and Equity

121. A contract made by a person subject to a property order may not be covered by those provisions, as where the contract does not involve property or the order in question does not cover all of that person's property. Again, a person suffering from a mental disorder may not have been made subject to a property order at all. In these cases, the principles of the common law and equity governing contracts made by persons suffering from mental incapacity will apply. A contract entered into by a person of unsound mind is voidable at that person's option if it is proved that the other party knew of the unsoundness of mind when the contract was made.[532] But where a contract is entered into by such a person who is ostensibly sane in circumstances where the other contracting party does not know of his or her lack of capacity, then the contract is to be judged by the same standards as apply to a contract made by a person of sound mind. Such a contract is not, therefore, voidable for 'unfairness' unless such unfairness creates an independent ground for relief in equity, as where undue influence has been exercised or the bargain is unconscionable.[533] Whether a person has contractual capacity in any particular case is related to the transaction. The question is whether the contracting party can understand the general nature, as opposed to the details, of the transaction in which he or she is engaging when it is explained to him or her.[534] Furthermore, there is a distinction between concluding a contract and making a gift. In order to avoid a contract, the

528. Protection of Personal and Property Rights Act 1988, s. 53(1).
529. *Ibid.*, s. 53(2).
530. *Ibid.*, s. 53(6).
531. *Ibid.*, s. 53(8).
532. *O'Connor v. Hart* [1985] 1 NZLR 159.
533. *Ibid. See* paras 137–144.
534. *Scott v. Wise* [1986] 2 NZLR 484.

incapacitated party must show that the other knew of the incapacity, but to avoid a voluntary transaction, the donor need only establish that he or she in fact lacked capacity.[535]

A person of unsound mind can be held liable to pay for the supply of 'necessaries'. This is a term of variable content. Necessaries are not confined to basic necessities or those which are necessary to the support of life, like food, clothing and shelter, but include articles and services fit to maintain the particular person in the station in which he moves.[536] Seemingly, an implied obligation to pay arises because the person of unsound mind has been supplied, not because the person contracted to be supplied.[537] So the obligation is to pay the value of what has been supplied, not the contract price.

In the case of goods, the obligation is founded on statute. By section 124(2) of the Contract and Commercial Law Act 2017, if necessaries are sold and delivered to a person who because of mental incapacity or intoxication is incompetent to contract, he or she must pay a reasonable price for the goods.

IV. Drunken Persons

122. It is likely that the principles which apply in determining the contractual capacity of a person of unsound mind also apply in determining the contractual capacity of a drunken person.[538] In *Peeters v. Schimanski*,[539] Cooke J thought that it might be that extreme intoxication would deprive a person of his reason so as to render his consent void, but where drunkenness deprived a person merely of his or her business sense, the contract was at most voidable. Generally, equity would not interfere either to avoid or to enforce it, but would grant relief to the drunken party if he could show that his condition was known to the other party and that some unfair advantage had been taken of him.

This decision was applied by Priestley J in *Kurth v. McGavin*.[540] K offered to buy McG's property at a time when McG, who was an alcoholic, was too drunk to consider the offer. However, over the next few days, at a time when he appeared to be more sober, he entered some negotiations and concluded a sale. He immediately regretted doing this and refused to perform the agreement. K sought specific performance of the contract, and McG defended the claim on the basis that when he signed the agreement, he was too drunk to have the requisite intention to contract. Priestley J held that at the time when McG entered the contract, the evidence showed that his judgment and business sense were seriously dulled, but he understood what he was doing and was not incapable of forming an intention to contract. Furthermore, neither the plaintiff nor his agent had any knowledge of the nature and extent of the vendor's intoxication. So the agreement was not voidable and was

---

535. *Dark v. Boock* [1991] 1 NZLR 496.
536. *Peters v. Fleming* (1840) 6 M & W 42; *Chapple v. Cooper* (1844) 13 M & W 252; *Proform Sports Management Ltd v. Proactive Sports Management Ltd* [2007] 1 All ER 542.
537. *Nash v. Inman* [1908] 2 KB 1.
538. *See Kurth v. McGavin* [2007] 3 NZLR 614.
539. [1975] 2 NZLR 328.
540. [2007] 3 NZLR 614.

binding. However, in the circumstances, specific performance should be refused and the plaintiff confined to a remedy in damages.

In *154 Ltd v. Bagley*,[541] Associate Judge Gendall held that there was no evidence to suggest that the plaintiff knew of the second defendant's alcohol dependency and mental health problems at the times she executed a lease and signed a personal guarantee. There was no evidence either that the plaintiff acted in an unconscionable manner that would require equity to intervene in the matter.

A drunken person to whom necessaries are sold and delivered must pay a reasonable price for them in the same way as must a person of unsound mind.

§2. Defects of Consent

I. Mistake

123. The common law of mistake was notoriously complex and unsatisfactory. The New Zealand legislature has intervened with the enactment of the Contractual Mistakes Act 1977, a statute in significant part modelled on the regime of discretionary relief pioneered by the Illegal Contracts Act 1970.[542] The Contractual Mistakes Act has been repealed by the Contract and Commercial Law Act 2017, sections 21–32. These provisions form a code[543] which supersedes the common law and equitable rules which could be invoked by the courts to grant relief to any party to a contract which had been affected by mistake. It leaves unaltered the law relating to rectification,[544] *non est factum*,[545] undue influence,[546] fraud and misrepresentation,[547] breach of fiduciary duty, illegality,[548] frustration,[549] recovery of money paid under a mistake of fact,[550] and the discretion to refuse a decree of specific performance.[551] A litigant may in appropriate circumstances seek relief under the mistakes provisions of the Contract and Commercial Law Act 2017 and also bring an action under one or more of these other doctrines.[552]

A. *Scheme of Contractual Mistakes Provisions in the Contract and Commercial Law Act 2017*

124. Sections 21–32 of the Contract and Commercial Law Act 2017 are designed to give the courts a discretionary power to grant relief to persons who have

541. [2012] NZHC 3478.
542. *See* para. 146.
543. Contract and Commercial Law Act 2017, s. 22.
544. *See* para. 132.
545. *See* para. 133.
546. *See* paras 137–143.
547. *See* paras 102–112.
548. *See* paras 146–163.
549. *See* paras 226–232.
550. *See* para. 346.
551. *See* para. 253.
552. *See* for example *Ware v. Johnson* [1984] 2 NZLR 518 (action for misrepresentation as well as for relief under the Contractual Mistakes Act 1977).

been influenced by a mistake of a kind specified by the Act when entering into a contract (or what would have been a contract at common law had it not been for the mistake)[553] and have as a result suffered substantial detriment. The Act does not apply to mistakes made after a contract has been entered into,[554] or to mistakes arising which impact on non-contractual relationships.[555] Relief may be applied for by the mistaken party, or by any person claiming 'through or under' that party.[556]

Persons whose mistakes do not meet the statutory criteria are left without a remedy, as are any persons who enter contracts under a mistake but do not as a result suffer any substantial detriment. Because the power to grant relief is discretionary, there is no guarantee that any relief will be forthcoming, or that it will remedy any detriment suffered.

B. Grounds for Relief

125. Section 24(1) of the Contract and Commercial Law Act 2017 sets out three different matters as to which the Court must be satisfied before an applicant may receive the relief which the Court can dispense. It provides:

> (1) A Court may grant relief under section 28 of this Act to any party to a contract if:
> (a) in entering into that contract:
> (i) that party was influenced in that party's decision to enter into the contract by a mistake that was material to that party, and the existence of the mistake was known to the other party or to 1 or more of the other parties to the contract; or
> (ii) all the parties to the contract were influenced in their respective decisions to enter into the contract by the same mistake; or
> (iii) that party and at least 1 other party were each influenced in their respective decisions to enter into the contract by a different mistake about the same matter of fact or of law; and
> (b) the mistake or mistakes resulted, at the time of the contract:
> (i) in a substantially unequal exchange of values; or
> (ii) in a benefit being conferred, or an obligation being imposed or included, that was, in all the circumstances, a benefit or an obligation substantially disproportionate to the consideration for the benefit or obligation; and
> (c) in a case where the contract expressly or by implication provides for the risk of mistakes, the party seeking relief (or the party through or

553. Contract and Commercial Law Act 2017, s. 23(4). The earlier version of this section was discussed in *Mechenex Pacific Services Ltd v. TCA Airconditioning (New Zealand) Ltd* [1991] 2 NZLR 393 at 397.
554. *N B Hunt & Sons Ltd v. Maori Trustee* [1986] 2 NZLR 641.
555. *National Bank of NZ Ltd v. Waitaki International Processing (NI) Ltd* [1997] 1 NZLR 724.
556. Contract and Commercial Law Act 2017, s. 29. Relief can only be ordered against a person who was a party to the contract or is claiming through or under a party: *Roose v. Duthie* [2015] NZHC 2035.

under whom relief is sought) is not obliged by a term of the contract to assume the risk that that party's belief about the matter in question might be mistaken.

An applicant for relief must therefore show that the applicant entered into the transaction while under a mistake falling within one of the three classes of mistake provided for in subsection (1)(a); that the mistake resulted in a substantial inequality in exchange as required by subsection (1)(b); and that the contract either did not place on any party the obligation to bear any risk of mistake or that any such risk allocation provision did not impose the burden on the applicant.

1. Meaning of 'Mistake' under the Act

126. The legislation provides only a general definition of a mistake, which has left the core concept underlying this part of the Contract and Commercial Law Act 2017 rather less than clearly delimited. Section 23 of the Act provides:

(1) In this subpart, unless the context otherwise requires, mistake means a mistake, whether of law or of fact.
(2) For the purposes of this subpart, a mistake in the interpretation of a document is a mistake of law.
(3) Subsection (2):
   (a) does not limit the meaning of the term mistake of law; but
   (b) is subject to section 25.
(4) There is a contract for the purposes of this Act where a contract would have come into existence but for circumstances of the kind described in section 24(1)(a).

Thus, an applicant may advance a mistake, whether of fact or law.[557] There is one limitation, as provided in subsection (3) by its reference to section 25, in that a mistake in the interpretation of the contractual document itself is not a mistake for which relief can be given.[558] It has been held, albeit somewhat unconvincingly, that a mistaken belief that a particular matter was dealt with in the contractual document was not a mistake in the interpretation of that document.[559]

The courts have not given extensive consideration to the statutory definition. It has been held that a mistake requires actual advertence to some matter and an error regarding it – ignorance or inadvertence do not amount to a 'mistake'.[560] A mistaken belief as to a matter of past or present fact is a mistake of fact.[561] A mistaken

557. A mistaken opinion does not come within the definition: *Prattley Enterprises Ltd v. Vero Insurance New Zealand Ltd* [2016] NZSC 158.
558. The provisions are discussed in *Shotter v. Westpac Banking Corporation* [1988] 2 NZLR 316.
559. *National Bank of NZ v. Murland* [1991] 3 NZLR 86 at 97.
560. *NZ Refining Company v. Attorney-General* (1992) 14 NZTC 9,006 at 9,015; *Ladstone Holdings Ltd v. Leonora Holdings Ltd* [2006] 1 NZLR 211.
561. *Shivas v. Bank of New Zealand* [1990] 2 NZLR 327.

belief can be advanced as a 'mistake' even though the true position was known at some earlier time but has since been forgotten.[562]

2. Classes of Mistake Eligible for Relief

127. Under section 24(1)(a), an applicant for relief must establish that he or she entered the contract 'influenced' by a mistake, and that the mistake alleged came within one of the three classes of mistake provided for in subsection (1)(a)(i), (ii), or (iii). The first two of these classes have proved uncontroversial, but the third has been productive of difficulty. The statutory classes are similar to, but not precisely the same as, the classifications of unilateral, common and mutual mistakes used in common law.

Under section 24(1)(a), an applicant may advance a mistake made by the applicant alone, but only where the other party or parties to the contract knew the applicant was mistaken. While the subsection was primarily intended to deal with cases where the applicant's mistake had been deliberately created by the other party (e.g., the common law 'rogue' cases), it can apply equally well to cases where the applicant's mistake is self-induced, but the other party becomes aware of it and chooses to leave it uncorrected, for example, where a vendor of real estate becomes aware the would-be purchaser is mistaken as to a feature of the property.[563] The subsection requires that the other party have actual knowledge of the applicant's mistake; constructive knowledge is insufficient.[564]

The second form of mistake which may be advanced is that under section 24(1)(a)(ii), where the parties were all mistaken as to the same matter of fact or law. This form of mistake is very similar to 'common' mistake at common law, and has caused no practical or theoretical difficulties.[565]

The last form of 'mistake' coming within section 24(1)(a) is where both parties have made different mistakes as to the same matter of fact or law. It will be rare indeed to find a case coming within this specific wording.[566] The subsection was apparently designed to apply to what at common law were 'mutual mistake' cases, those where the parties had contracted at cross-purposes because the terms of the agreement contained some latent ambiguity so that a difference in the parties' intentions was not revealed prior to entry into the contract.[567] However, the wording of subsection (1)(a)(iii) is not apt to cover that kind of case, as in mutual mistake cases, the problem is not that both parties are mistaken but rather that while one or other party is 'correct' in his or her belief as to what the contract provides, the court cannot tell which party is right and which wrong. The subsection was for some time

562. *Slater Wilmshurst Ltd v. Crown Group Custodian Ltd* [1991] 1 NZLR 344.
563. *King v. Wilkinson* (1994) 2 NZ ConvC 191,828.
564. *Tri-Star Customs and Forwarding Ltd v. Denning* [1999] 1 NZLR 33 at 37.
565. For the operation of the subsection *see Philips v. Philips* [1993] 3 NZLR 159 and *Ware v. Johnson* [1984] 2 NZLR 518.
566. The sole reported case apparently falling within the subsection is *National Bank of NZ v. Murland* [1991] 3 NZLR 86.
567. For example, *Raffles v. Wichelhaus* (1864) 2 H & C 906, 159 ER 375.

applied to cases clearly not coming within the statutory wording, but the courts have now retreated to a literal reading of the section, which confirms its limited application.[568]

3. Requirement of Substantial Inequality of Exchange

128. The requirement in section 24(1)(b) that the mistake should have resulted in an unequal exchange of value has no counterpart at common law, where the focus was on whether there had been a 'fundamental' mistake. In essence, the statute assumes that if there has been no substantial inequality of exchange, a contracting party who has been disappointed as a result of the mistake can simply re-enter the market and seek there to achieve the outcome sought in the mistaken bargain. The subsection has not received any detailed scrutiny in the cases, but it is clear that the critical question is the extent to which the consideration provided by one party is, in the light of the mistake, disproportionate to the consideration furnished by the other.[569] It would appear that in practice the courts will consider a difference of 10%–15% in value as 'significant' and therefore as satisfying the subsection.[570]

4. Provisions Allocating Risk of Mistake

129. Section 24(1)(c) makes it clear that a contractual provision allocating any risk of mistake as to the subject matter of the contract will be effective, and a party who bears the contractual risk cannot get relief under the act. While few if any contracts will specifically allocate risk of mistake, it is common for contracts to require one party or the other to make his or her own enquiries as to some aspect of the subject matter of a contract. A clause of this kind will have effect to allocate the risk of the parties, or one of them, being mistaken as to that matter.[571] Agreements to settle existing disputes may also impliedly allocate to each party a risk that their true position may have been more advantageous than they believed so as to make the settlement a less-than-optimal outcome.[572]

---

568. *See Conlon v. Ozolins* [1984] 1 NZLR 489, a case later described as 'turning on its own facts' in *Paulger v. Butland Industries Ltd* [1989] 3 NZLR 549. *See also Mechenex Pacific Services Ltd v. TCA Airconditioning (New Zealand) Ltd* [1991] 2 NZLR 393.
569. *NZ Refining Company v. Attorney-General* (1992) 14 NZTC 9,006. There is no inequality permitting relief to be given where at the time of the contract each party benefits equally but it is clear that at some later time one or other party will be significantly advantaged and the other disadvantaged: *Gallaway Cook Allan v. Carr* [2013] 1 NZLR 826; [2013] NZCA 11, [57].
570. *Denning v. Tri-Star Customs and Forwarding Ltd* [1996] 3 NZLR 630 at 638 (appeal allowed on other grounds [1999] 1 NZLR 33); compare *Snodgrass v. Hammington* (1994) ANZ Conv R 159, upheld CA 254/93, 22 Dec. 1995 and *Janus Nominees Ltd v. Fairhall* (2008) 23 NZTC 21,978 (difference of 6.5% between price paid and value obtained not sufficiently substantial to come within the statute). In *Prattley Enterprises Ltd v. Vero Insurance New Zealand Ltd* [2016] NZSC 158 a claimed difference in value of 25% would have been material.
571. *Dennis Friedman (Earthmovers) Ltd v. Rodney County Council* [1988] 1 NZLR 184.
572. *See Prattley Enterprises Ltd v. Vero Insurance New Zealand Ltd* [2016] NZSC 158.

C. *Discretion to Grant Relief*

130. The courts are given power by section 28 of the Contract and Commercial Law Act 2017 to grant relief as the court thinks fit. The court may enforce the contract, in whole or in part or for a particular purpose, or it may vary the contract and then enforce it, or it may simply cancel the contract. There is also power to order the restitution of property, or the payment of compensation, or to order the vesting of property in particular persons (not necessarily in the applicant for relief). Any order for relief may be made on such conditions as the court thinks fit. Relief cannot be granted once the mistaken party has affirmed the contract after discovering his or her mistake.[573]

The position of third parties is protected by section 31. The court may not grant relief which would invalidate a disposition to a third party of property which was the subject matter of the mistaken contract, provided the third party has acted without notice of the mistake and has provided consideration for the property received.

The broad discretion conferred by section 28 is not unfettered. The court seized of the matter must consider who caused the mistake[574] and, more broadly, must not exercise the power to grant relief in a manner which will prejudice the general security of contractual relationships.[575]

The courts have generally been prepared to grant relief where a qualifying mistake has been shown, but there has been little discussion of the principles by which the discretion is to be exercised other than to recount the statutory factors. However, it has been said that relief under the legislation should not be granted to an applicant whose conduct has disentitled him or her to similar relief which would otherwise have been available under the general law.[576]

D. *Remedies Preserved by the Contractual Mistakes Legislation*

1. Rectification

131. Rectification is an equitable doctrine whereby the court may change the terms of a written document which does not correspond with the intentions of the maker or makers of the document. If a document which allegedly represents the contractual agreement reached by the parties does not accurately reproduce their common intention, the courts may step in to amend the document so that it does accord with the common contractual intention.[577] The question is whether the document is erroneous, not the nature of the error. Rectification is available for simple

573. Contract and Commercial Law Act 2017, s. 26(1).
574. Contract and Commercial Law Act 2017, s. 27; the predecessor section was applied in *Australian Guarantee Corporation (NZ) Ltd v. Wyness* [1987] 2 NZLR 326.
575. Contract and Commercial Law Act 2017, s. 21(2)(b).
576. *Slater Wilmshurst Ltd v. Crown Group Custodian Ltd* [1991] 1 NZLR 344 at 358.
577. *Dundee Farms v. Bambury Holdings* [1978] 1 NZLR 647; *Wellington City Council v. New Zealand Law Society* [1990] 2 NZLR 22. This logically means that the court must first interpret the document to determine its meaning before considering rectification: *Green Growth No 2 Ltd v. Queen Elizabeth II Trust National Trust* [2018] NZSC 75; [2019] 1 NZLR 161, at [55]. The New Zealand

clerical errors[578] as well as for more substantial matters. The contract can then be given effect to in its corrected form.[579] Rectification will not be needed where the mistake is an error that the court can correct as a part of the process of interpreting the document, but will be needed where an error has occurred that is not repaired through interpretation.[580]

A person who seeks to have a contractual document rectified must show first that the contractual document is incorrect and also that there was a common intention to contract on the terms now contended for.[581] Where the transaction is between corporate entities, the issue will be there was a mutual intention held by the persons or persons within each entity who are taken for these purposes as the 'mind' of the company.[582] Rectification is not available where the document correctly records an agreement which was reached only because the parties were mistaken as to some matter.[583]

The English courts, and some New Zealand judges, have held that rectification is also available in cases where one party was aware that the other's contractual intention is not recorded in the written document, and seeks to take unconscionable advantage of that error.[584] However, in the leading *Tri-Star Customs and Forwarding Ltd v. Denning,*[585] the Court of Appeal considered that rectification on such a basis was inconsistent with the terms of the (then) Contractual Mistakes Act 1977, and so relief for a unilateral mistake could only be granted under the Act and not in

courts have not yet been called on to consider whether the document is to be interpreted solely objectively, an issue which has caused difficulty in England: *see FSHC Group Holding Ltd v. GLAS Trust Corporation Ltd* [2019] EWCA Civ 1361.

578. *Haira v. Burbery Mortgage Finance & Savings Ltd (In Receivership); Koya v. Haira* [1995] 3 NZLR 396, 401–402. In some cases an application for rectification will not be needed as the courts have some power to correct minors errors when interpreting documents: *see Rattray's Wholesale Ltd v. Meredyth-Young & A'Court Ltd* [1997] 2 NZLR 363 at 371–373.

579. A document may in appropriate cases be rectified so as to contain the details required for the document to meet statutory requirements for enforceability: *Whiting v. Diver Plumbing and Heating Ltd* [1992] 1 NZLR 560. As to these requirements, *see* paras 91–93. Rectification of documents which have been registered under the Land Transfer Act 2017 (which provides a state guarantee of the title) is not possible: *Green Growth No 2 Ltd v. Queen Elizabeth II Trust National Trust* [2018] NZSC 75; [2019] 1 NZLR 161.

580. See *Bathurst Resources Ltd v. L & M Coal Holdings Ltd* [2021] NZSC 85, [2021] 1 NZLR 696 at [80].

581. *Joscelyne v. Nissen* [1970] 2 QB 86. Showing such a mistaken recording of a common intention may be difficult where lawyers for the parties have been involved in the drafting, but such involvement does not of itself rule out rectification: *Booth v. Poplar Road Farms Ltd* [2019] NZHC 807, at [39].

582. *Pernod Ricard New Zealand Ltd v. Lion-Beer, Spirits & Wine (NZ) Ltd* [2012] NZHC 2801, at [221].

583. *March Construction Ltd v. Christchurch City Council* (1995) 6 TCLR 394; compare *Frederick E Rose London Ltd v. William H Pim Jnr and Co* [1953] 2 QB 450.

584. *Commission for the New Towns v. Cooper (GB) Ltd* [1995] Ch. 259; *Bates v. Wyndhams* [1981] 1 All ER 1087; *Westland Savings Bank Ltd v. Hancock* [1987] 2 NZLR 21. A contrary view was taken in *Butler v. Countrywide Finance Ltd* [1993] 3 NZLR 623 at 629–630.

585. [1999] 1 NZLR 33 at 39–40.

an action for rectification. The decision has been the subject of convincing criticism,[586] and the Court of Appeal has contemplated that its reconsideration will eventually be necessary.[587]

As rectification is an equitable remedy, the court has a discretion to withhold an order if in all the circumstances the effect of granting relief would be inequitable. Thus, an order for rectification may be refused if there has been unreasonable delay in seeking the order, or if the effect of an order would be unfair to the other party to the contract.[588] Rectification is also not available where it would affect a person who has purchased in good faith property affected by the contract now sought to be rectified.[589]

The evidential burden on the party seeking rectification is generally severe,[590] but may be somewhat relaxed where an employee is alleging an error in the document containing the terms of employment because the employee will be less able to ensure the document accurately reflects the common intention.[591] Evidence of the parties' conduct subsequent to the creation of the document is admissible to prove the intention at the time of the document's creation.[592]

2. *Non Est Factum*

132. It is sometimes, if rarely, possible to plead as a defence to an action based on a written contract *non est factum* – 'this is not my deed'. In essence, the plea is that a written document bearing the defendant's signature is nevertheless not binding on the defendant because the defendant was radically mistaken as to the effect of the document which was signed. The plea developed in medieval times to afford a defence to blind or illiterate persons who were unable to verify the contents of a signed document.[593] In later years, the courts have allowed the plea to become more generally available, but the plea will very rarely be available to a person of full age and competence.[594]

---

586. McLauchlan, *Rectification for Unilateral Mistake* 18 NZULR 360 (1999).
587. *Kaimai Properties Ltd v. Queen Elizabeth the Second National Trust* [2021] NZCA 10 at [57].
588. *Barber v. Barber* [1987] 1 NZLR 426; *Wellington City Council v. New Zealand Law Society* [1990] 2 NZLR 22.
589. *Australian Mutual Provident Society v. Bridgemans Art Deco Ltd* [1996] 2 NZLR 263. However, an order for rectification may be made against a third party who had knowledge of all relevant circumstances including the respective mistakes: *Green Growth No 2 Ltd v. Queen Elizabeth the Second National Trust* [2016] NZCA 308; [2016] 3 NZLR 726 at [97]–[98] (an issue not discussed on appeal to the Supreme Court: *Green Growth No 2 Ltd v. Queen Elizabeth II Trust National Trust* [2018] NZSC 75; [2019] 1 NZLR 161)).
590. *Farmers' Mutual Insurance Ltd v. QBE Insurance International Ltd* [1993] 3 NZLR 305 at 314.
591. *Autoclenz Ltd v. Belcher* [2011] UKSC 41; [2011] 4 All ER 745.
592. *Westland Savings Bank Ltd v. Hancock* [1987] 2 NZLR 21.
593. The most substantial recent discussion of the plea is that in *Gallie v. Lee* [1971] AC 1004 (sub nom *Saunders v. Anglia Building Society*). The defence can also be raised by a person who has, reasonably, signed a document expressed in a language which the signatory does not understand: *Golden Garden Ltd v. Zhao* [2017] NZCA 227.
594. *Conlon v. Ozolins* [1984] 1 NZLR 489; *IFC Securities v. Sewell* [1990] 1 NZLR 177. A rare example is *Radius Residential Care Ltd v. Krishna* [2013] NZHC 2886.

A litigant who seeks to raise the plea of *non est factum* must show that the document actually signed was radically different from the one which was intended to be signed,[595] or that the effect in law of the signature was radically different from that intended.[596] It must also be shown that the litigant was not careless or negligent in regard to the transaction,[597] for example, by failing to read the document in question where this was possible,[598] and that some other person actually misrepresented the contents of the document to the signatory.[599]

These restrictions on the availability of the plea are all based on the necessity to ensure third parties may rely with assurance on the validity of a signed document. If no third party is involved or could be affected, the court may accept the plea despite some lack of care by the party raising it where the party seeking to enforce the contract was at fault in causing the other's mistake.[600]

II. Misrepresentation

133. Misrepresentation can undermine the consent of a contracting party and thus can operate as a vitiating factor affecting the substantive validity of a contract. But misrepresentation also impacts upon the formation of a binding contract and the question of liability for pre-contractual statements and, accordingly, its nature and the available remedies have already been discussed in that context.[601]

III. Improper Pressure

A. *Introduction*

134. A party who lacks free and unfettered consent in the making of a contract may be able to avoid the contract, by arguing that he or she was acting under duress or was subject to undue influence.[602] Again, a contract which is procured not by pressure or influence but by one party taking advantage of another who is in a vulnerable position may similarly be avoided, in this case, on the basis that it amounts

---

595. *Gallie v. Lee* [1971] AC 1004; *Bradley West Solicitors Nominee Co Ltd v. Keeman* [1994] 1 NZLR 111.
596. *Chiswick Investments Ltd v. Pevats* [1990] 1 NZLR 169. The Court of Appeal in *Trotter v. Avonmore Holdings Ltd* (2005) 8 NZBLC 101,646, [32]–[33] indicated the limited scope of the plea in such circumstances.
597. *Gallie v. Lee* [1971] AC 1004; *see also Norwich and Peterborough Building Society v. Steed* [1993] Ch. 116.
598. *Bradley West Solicitors Nominee Co Ltd v. Keeman* [1994] 1 NZLR 111; *Nguyen v. SM & T Homes Limited* [2016] NZCA 581. If a signatory cannot read the language in which the document was expressed, signing it may be reasonable if done on the advice of a person whose description of the contents it was reasonable to trust: *Golden Garden Ltd v. Zhao* [2017] NZCA 227.
599. *Bradley West Solicitors Nominee Co Ltd v. Keeman* [1994] 1 NZLR 111 at 121.
600. *Conlon v. Ozolins* [1984] 1 NZLR 489.
601. *See* paras 102–112.
602. *A-G for England and Wales v. R* [2002] 2 NZLR 91 (affirmed [2004] 2 NZLR 577).

to an unconscionable bargain.[603] Further, a statutory provision prohibiting unconscionable conduct has been added to the Fair Trading Act 1986.[604] In England, attempts have been made to assimilate duress, undue influence and unconscionability under the broad head of inequality of bargaining power.[605] But these have been rejected, on the grounds that the fact of an unequal bargain cannot become an all-embracing basis of principle for transactions 'not to be reasonably accounted for on the ground of friendship, relationship, charity or other ordinary motives on which ordinary men act', and that it is a matter for Parliament to undertake the 'essentially legislative' task of enacting such restrictions upon freedom of contract as are necessary to relieve against the mischief.[606] So also in New Zealand, inequality of bargaining power is not a vitiating factor in its own right, although its existence frequently can assume importance in the application of the established common law and equitable doctrines.

B. Economic Duress

135. Duress at common law initially was confined to actual violence or threats of violence calculated to produce fear of loss of life or bodily harm.[607] It later became clear that there could also be duress of goods and other forms of pressure short of duress to the person.[608] More recent developments show that economic pressure alone can suffice.[609]

Duress involves the illegitimate application of pressure by threats. The illegitimacy of the pressure may lie in the illegality of the actions threatened or, alternatively, may be associated with the illegitimacy of the particular threats in the context in which they were made.[610] A threat to do something unlawful, like a threat to commit a crime, a tort or a breach of contract, is likely to be regarded as illegitimate.[611] So the use of forgery and false evidence in order to put pressure on another to agree to a settlement was illegitimate and rendered the agreement voidable.[612] As for a

603. *Ibid.*
604. *See* para. 145.
605. *See* in particular the judgment of Lord Denning MR in *Lloyds Bank Ltd v. Bundy* [1975] QB 326 at 339.
606. *National Westminster Bank Plc v. Morgan* [1985] AC 686 at 708 per Lord Scarman.
607. *Skeate v. Beale* (1840) 11 Ad & El 983; *Cumming v. Ince* (1847) 11 QB 112.
608. *Maskell v. Horner* [1915] 3 KB 106.
609. *Universe Tankships Inc of Monrovia v. International Transport Workers Federation* [1983] 1 AC 366; *Dimskal Shipping Co SA v. International Transport Workers Federation* [1992] 2 AC 152; *Pharmacy Care Systems Ltd v. Attorney-General* CA 198/03, 16 Aug. 2004, at [92]; *McIntyre v. Nemesis DBK Ltd* [2010] 1 NZLR 463 at [19]–[20]; *Magsons Hardware Ltd v. Concepts 124 Ltd* [2011] NZCA 559 at [20].
610. *Haines v. Carter* [2001] 2 NZLR 167 at 189.
611. *North Ocean Shipping Co Ltd v. Hyundai Construction Co Ltd: The Atlantic Baron* [1979] QB 705 (breach of contract); cp *Willliams v. Roffey Bros* [1991] 1 QB 1; *see* para. 85.
612. *Borrelli v. Ting* [2010] UKPC 21.

threat to do something lawful, this will be illegitimate if the threat is to do gratuitous harm or amounts to the crime of blackmail.[613] But a threat involving lawful conduct in pursuit of a bona fide claim is unlikely to constitute duress. It would introduce a substantial and undesirable element of uncertainty in the commercial bargaining process and would often enable bona fide settled accounts to be reopened when parties to commercial dealings fell out.[614] So the parties to a contract who disputed their liabilities in good faith and then agreed to a compromise were bound and one could not later resile.[615] Again, there was no illegitimate pressure in respect of a threatening demand for extra payment where there was no contractual obligation to sell.[616]

In *Times Travel (UK) Ltd v. Pakistan International Airlines Corp*,[617] the United Kingdom Supreme Court confirmed that there were two circumstances in which a threat of lawful conduct was illegitimate. The first was where a defendant used knowledge of criminal activity by the claimant or the claimant's family to obtain a personal benefit from the claimant by the threat to report the crime. The second was where the defendant, being exposed to a civil claim by the claimant (e.g., for damages for breach of contract), deliberately manoeuvred the claimant into a position of vulnerability by means which the law regarded as illegitimate and thereby forced the claimant to waive his or her claim. Such behaviour amounted to the kind of reprehensible or unconscionable conduct which, in the context of the equitable doctrine of undue influence, had been judged to render the enforcement of a contract unconscionable. In the instant case, the defendant genuinely believed that it was not liable for breach of contract as a result of its failure to pay past commission to the claimant, its agent. Accordingly, the defendant's commercial pressure on the agent to agree to a new contract on terms that included a waiver of the agent's claim for unpaid commission had not been an illegitimate threat, and the claimant could not avoid the new contract.

Whether an illegitimate threat actually constitutes duress must be determined by reference to its coercive effect in the particular case. It is material to enquire whether the person alleged to have been coerced protested, whether he had an alternative course open to him such as an adequate legal remedy, whether he was independently advised and whether after entering the contract he took steps to avoid it.[618] At the very least, a party must show that the duress alleged was an appreciable factor in influencing that party to enter into the bargain in question. The courts look for a significant degree of actual coerciveness, at a level sometimes described as having left the victim with no practical choice but to submit.[619] In another formulation,

613. *Haines v. Carter* [2001] 2 NZLR 167; *Crown Commercial Construction Ltd v. Lee* [2012] NZHC 2473.
614. *CTN Cash and Carry Ltd v. Gallaher Ltd* [1994] 4 All ER 714.
615. *Moyes and Groves Ltd v. Radiation NZ Ltd* [1982] 1 NZLR 368; and *see Dold v. Murphy* [2019] NZHC 1232 (decision to make a payment 'a calculated and considered commercial decision after weighing all the options').
616. *Dold v. Murphy* [2019] NZHC1232 at [87]–[91].
617. *Times Travel (UK) Ltd v. Pakistan International Airlines Corp* [2021] UKSC 40, [2021] 3 WLR 727.
618. *Pao On v. Lau Yiu Long* [1980] AC 614.
619. *Haines v. Carter* [2001] 2 NZLR 167 at 190.

the victim's will must have been overborne by the improper pressure so that his or her free will and judgment have been displaced. The threat or pressure must actually induce the victim's manifestation of assent, and must be sufficiently grave to justify the assent in the sense that it left the victim no reasonable alternative.[620]

The threat need not be the only reason for entering the contract. Once it has been proved that a wrongful threat was made, it is for the threat-maker to show that it was not a reason for the other party contracting.[621] But in a decision in England, it was emphasized that the pressure must actually have caused the making of the agreement, in the sense that it would not otherwise have been made either at all or at least on the terms on which it was made. In that sense, the pressure must have been decisive or clinching.[622]

The elements of illegitimate pressure and coercion are closely related. In *A-G for England and Wales v. R,*[623] Tipping J said that the starting point must be that the law recognizes people generally act under some degree of pressure in making decisions affecting their commercial and other interests. In all duress cases, the Court must consider whether the pressure under which the plaintiff was acting should be regarded as legitimate or illegitimate and, in that respect, the nature of any alternatives reasonably open to the plaintiff will be of major importance.

A right to avoid a contract for economic duress can be lost if the threatened party affirms the contract.[624] A contract induced by duress which has been affirmed cannot be avoided against a person acquiring rights under it for value and without notice of the duress. But it may be avoided against purchasers for value with notice and against volunteers.

In *McIntyre v. Nemesis DBK Ltd,*[625] the issue was whether the trustees of a family trust were acting under duress when they agreed to variations on the terms of a joint venture made with H to subdivide and develop property. H had been appointed to manage the development, and the variation increased the level of his remuneration. The court proceeded on the basis that a threat to break a contract was unlawful and generally illegitimate, although care was needed to distinguish between illegitimate threats and legitimate warnings. Here H's bullying conduct in demanding better terms was reprehensible in many respects, but it did not amount to, and was not construed by the trustees as, a threat to break his management contract by simply stopping work. So it did not cross the line between forceful and illegitimate pressure. Next, the agreement to pay greater remuneration was made because this was seen as the best way to bring the joint venture to completion rather than because the trustees were coerced into agreeing. Finally, the steps taken by the trustees in implementing the variation agreements should be seen as affirming them. Their failure to take steps to avoid the agreements over a four-year period until after H had died pointed inevitably to this conclusion.

---

620. *Pharmacy Care Systems Ltd v. Attorney-General* (2004) 2 NZCCLR 187.
621. *Ibid.*
622. *Huyton SA v. Peter Cremer GmbH & Co* [1999] 1 Lloyds Rep 620.
623. [2002] 2 NZLR 91 (affirmed [2004] 2 NZLR 577).
624. *Haines v. Carter* [2001] 2 NZLR 167; *Pharmacy Care Systems Ltd v. Attorney-General* (2004) 2 NZCCLR 187.
625. [2010] NZLR 463.

C. *Undue Influence*

1. Introduction

136. Undue influence consists in the gaining of an unfair advantage by an unconscientious use of power by a stronger party against a weaker one in the form of some unfair and improper conduct, some coercion from outside, some overreaching, some form of cheating, and generally, though not always, some personal advantage obtained by the stronger party. It is directed at conduct within a relationship which justifies the conclusion that the disposition or agreement was not the result of a free exercise of the disponer's will. The doctrine is founded on the principle that equity will protect the party who is subject to the influence of another from victimization.[626]

The law of undue influence was authoritatively restated in the House of Lords in *Royal Bank of Scotland Plc v. Etridge (No 2)*,[627] which is the leading decision in this area of law and which has been accepted as representing the law in New Zealand.[628] However, before examining the principles it lays down, we need to consider briefly the approach favoured by Lord Browne-Wilkinson in *Barclays Bank Plc v. O'Brien*,[629] for we cannot properly understand *Etridge* without knowing something about the background to the decision.

2. Classes of Undue Influence

137. In *Barclays Bank Plc v. O'Brien*,[630] Lord Browne-Wilkinson divided cases of undue influence into those where undue influence was shown actually to have happened (class 1) and those where it was presumed to have happened (class 2). In the case of actual undue influence, it was necessary for the claimant to prove affirmatively that another person exerted undue influence so as to induce him or her to enter the transaction which was impugned.[631] As regards presumed undue influence, the claimant had to show that there was a special relationship of trust and confidence between the claimant and the other party and that the transaction was manifestly disadvantageous to the claimant.[632] These two factors gave rise to a presumption that undue influence was exerted in bringing about the transaction.

Lord Browne-Wilkinson went on to subdivide presumed undue influence into class 2(A), where undue influence was presumed as a matter of law, and class 2(B), where the necessary relationship of trust and confidence had to be proved on the facts of the case. Class 2(A) relationships that raised the presumption of undue influence as a matter of law included those of solicitor and client, doctor and patient,

---

626. *Contractors Bonding Ltd v. Snee* [1992] 2 NZLR 157 at 165.
627. [2002] 2 AC 773.
628. *R v. Attorney-General for England and Wales* [2004] 2 NZLR 577; *Hogan v. Commercial Factors Ltd* [2006] 3 NZLR 618.
629. [1994] 1 AC 180.
630. *Ibid.*
631. *Contractors Bonding Ltd v. Snee* [1992] 2 NZLR 157.
632. *National Westminster Bank v. Morgan* [1985] AC 686.

trustee and *cestui que* trust, guardian and ward, parent and child, religious adviser and disciple. In these cases, trust and confidence was presumed and did not need to be proved. By contrast, in class 2(B) cases, there should be proof that the particular relationship in question involved trust and confidence. There was no automatic presumption of undue influence as between, say, a husband and a wife, or by an employer over an employee, or by a child over a parent. But it might be shown as a matter of fact that a wife reposed trust and confidence in her husband, an employee in his or her employer, a parent in a son or daughter.

3. Manifest Disadvantage

138. In *National Westminster Bank v. Morgan,*[633] the House of Lords held that for a transaction to be set aside for undue influence, it had also to be shown that the impugned transaction was wrongful in that it constituted a manifest and unfair disadvantage to the person seeking to avoid it. The decision was followed by the Court of Appeal in *Contractors Bonding Ltd v. Snee.*[634] Subsequently, however, in *CIBC Mortgages Plc v. Pitt,*[635] the House of Lords held that the requirement existed only in the case of presumed undue influence. Lord Browne-Wilkinson pointed out that actual undue influence is a species of fraud, and that accordingly the person induced to enter the transaction was entitled as of right to set it aside.

4. Royal Bank of Scotland Plc Etridge (No. 2)

139. In *Royal Bank of Scotland Plc v. Etridge (No. 2),*[636] the House of Lords reviewed and restated the foundations to the law. Lord Nicholls noted at the outset that equity identified broadly two forms of unacceptable conduct. The first form, which overlapped with the principle of duress, comprised overt acts of improper pressure or coercion, such as unlawful threats. The second form arose out of a relationship between two persons where one had acquired over another a measure of influence, or ascendancy, of which the ascendant person took unfair advantage. In cases of this latter nature, the influence one person had over another provided scope for misuse without any specific overt acts of persuasion. The law had long recognized the need to prevent abuse in these 'relationship' cases. The types of relationship could not be listed exhaustively. The question was whether one party had reposed sufficient trust and confidence in the other, rather than whether the relationship between the parties belonged to a particular type.

Lord Nicholls pointed out that whether a transaction was brought about by undue influence was a question of fact. Proof of two key requirements – that the complainant placed trust and confidence in the other party in relation to the management of the complainant's financial affairs, coupled with a transaction which called

633. [1985] AC 686.
634. [1992] 2 NZLR 157 at 166.
635. [1994] 1 AC 200.
636. [2002] 2 AC 773.

for explanation – would normally be sufficient, failing satisfactory evidence to the contrary, to discharge the burden of proof. The court inferred that the defendant abused the influence he acquired in the parties' relationship. The evidential burden shifted to him to counter the inference which would otherwise be drawn. This was conventionally described as a situation in which a presumption of undue influence arose, but when a plaintiff succeeded by this route he did so because he had succeeded in establishing a case of undue influence. Contrasted with this evidential presumption was the different form of presumption which arose out of certain types of relationship in which one party acquired influence over another who was vulnerable and dependent, and where, moreover, substantial gifts by the vulnerable person were not normally to be expected. In these cases, the law presumed, irrebuttably, that one party had influence over the other. The complainant need not prove that he actually reposed trust and confidence in the other. It was sufficient for him to prove the existence of the relationship.

Various factors will be taken into account in determining whether undue influence can be established. One is whether the complainant took independent advice. Lord Nicholls recognized that the weight to be attached to such advice, and whether it had an emancipating effect, depended on all the circumstances. Normally, it would bring home to the complainant a proper understanding of a proposed transaction, yet it did not necessarily show that completion of the transaction was free from the exercise of undue influence. As for the element of manifest disadvantage to the claimant, its relevance should be assessed in the context of the prerequisites to the evidential shift in the burden of proof – trust and confidence in or ascendancy by another and a transaction not readily explicable by the relationship of the parties. Something which called for an explanation was needed. When something more was present, the greater the disadvantage to the vulnerable person, the more cogent the explanation must be before the presumption would be regarded as rebutted.

It follows from this analysis that undue influence should no longer be formally classified as 'presumed' and 'actual', although the expressions may have some descriptive value. In every case, the question is whether undue influence has been established on the facts that have been proved. The legal burden of proof is on the plaintiff. Evidential presumptions assist in reaching the conclusion that there was undue influence in fact. Such presumptions can be rebutted by evidence showing that the weaker party was free from any improper influence.

5. Proof of Undue Influence

140. In any case, the plaintiff may seek to prove the facts which show that undue influence was actually exerted. Examples include: a son prevailing upon his alcoholic and mentally incapable mother to give a guarantee and grant a mortgage over her home by way of security for a loan to the son's company;[637] a son planting materially false impressions in the minds of his parents as to the extent and duration of

637. *Contractors Bonding Ltd v. Snee* [1992] 2 NZLR 157.

the risks they would run in executing a charge over their home;[638] a nephew procuring the resignation of his aged aunt from a family trust when her son was absent and on threat of a dispute affecting the trust having to go to court;[639] a husband persuading his wife to mortgage her interest in the matrimonial home in order to pay his debts, but concealing his affair with another woman which later led to the parties' separation and divorce;[640] an impecunious migrant to Australia told by her rich fiancé that their marriage would not go ahead unless she signed a pre-nuptial agreement making very little financial provision for her;[641] and a wife taking advantage of her husband's acute sense of grief and loneliness shortly after his mother was killed to pressure him into signing a declaration of trust for his infant son.[642]

Alternatively, the plaintiff may seek to prove the circumstances which justify the drawing of an inference of undue influence. Relationships where one person reposes trust and confidence in another and circumstances which call for explanation are both infinitely various. In cases where there is a special presumption of trust and confidence, the focus is on the latter consideration. Otherwise it is on both. Some examples where there was an inference of undue influence include: a chronic alcoholic, shortly before his death and in consideration of a small annuity, transferring a mortgage for practically all his property to his trusted friend and drinking companion;[643] a young and inexperienced musician acting without independent legal advice giving 'bargain basement terms' to his business manager;[644] an 85-year-old farmer granting to a trusted neighbouring farmer a tenancy of, and on his death an option to purchase, his farm, this on terms which were very beneficial to the neighbour;[645] a disabled man of 72 making a very large gift, amounting to over 90% of his liquid assets, to a helpful neighbour;[646] and a frail and elderly husband and his wife using their life savings to enter into two Mudharaba agreements (based on Islamic principles and Sharia law) with an accounting firm, this at the instigation of an old friend who was the sole shareholder and director of the firm.[647] However, the evidence may show no close relationship between the parties, or a close relationship but no special trust or reliance by one towards the other, or no circumstances which call for an explanation. For example, undue influence was not proved where a 'strong-minded, autocratic and eccentric' old man, shortly before his death and without taking legal advice, granted valuable shooting rights over his large estate to the defendant, a local garage proprietor. The evidence showed that the relationship was one of friendship and did not indicate that it was such that the defendant had been in a position of dominance over the deceased.[648] Again, where a husband and wife guaranteed a bank loan to their daughter and son-in-law and gave a mortgage

638. *Greene King plc v. Stanley* [2001] EWCA Civ 1966.
639. *Daniel v. Drew* [2005] EWCA Civ 507.
640. *Hewitt v. First Plus Financial Group Ltd* [2010] EWCA Civ 312.
641. *Thorne v. Kennedy* [2017] HCA 49 (2017) 263 CLR 85.
642. *BOM v. BOK* [2018] SGCA 83.
643. *Brusewitz v. Brown* [1923] NZLR 1106.
644. *O'Sullivan v. Management Agency and Music Ltd* [1985] QB 428.
645. *Goldsworthy v. Brickell* [1987] 1 All ER 853.
646. *Hammond v. Osborn* [2002] WTLR 1125.
647. *Fa'agutu v. Derhamy* [2020] NZHC 404, [2020] 2 NZLR 774.
648. *Re Brocklehurst's Estate* [1978] Ch. 14.

over their house, it was decided that the evidence went no further than to establish a normal family relationship in which parents readily agreed to assist children in their business ventures.[649]

The evidential presumption, where it arises, can be rebutted if the party in whom confidence is reposed can show that the party to whom the duty was owed in fact acted voluntarily, in the sense that he or she was free to make an independent and informed estimate of the expediency of the contract or other transaction.[650] Whether or not independent advice was taken clearly can be a key factor, although it is not always essential.[651]

The Court of Appeal has held that undue influence can be established on the basis that the weaker party did not genuinely consent to the transaction, without clear proof of improper conduct or exploitation by the stronger.[652] But if a transaction can be upset even though the conscience of the person doing the influencing is clear, why exactly should equity intervene? Such cases perhaps ought to be explained on the basis that a failure to give information or to ensure that a person is properly informed can be treated as evidence of abuse.

Some cases of deliberate wrongdoing in relation to a weaker party may not involve undue influence at all. In *Vernon v. Public Trust*,[653] an elderly father had executed an enduring power of attorney in favour of his son and handed him daily control of his banking affairs. The son spent almost the entire estate in circumstances where the father gave no consent, improperly induced or otherwise. After the father died, the estate challenged the payments, and it was held that the plea of undue influence could not succeed. The situation was not one involving improper influence but was one of complete transfer of control of the father's finances. However, the estate's claim could nonetheless be sustained on the basis of a finding of breach of fiduciary duty by the son.

6. Effect of Undue Influence

141. If undue influence is established, the contract or gift in question is voidable. Normally, the parties will be restored to their original position, by transferring back the property and the money paid for it. But a contract procured by undue influence cannot be rescinded after affirmation, express or implied,[654] nor against persons who acquire rights under it for value and without notice of the facts.[655] It may be avoided against purchasers for value with notice[656] and also against volunteers, that is, persons who give no consideration, though they may be unaware of the undue influence.

649. *ASB Bank Ltd v. Harlick* [1996] 1 NZLR 655.
650. *Allcard v. Skinner* (1887) 36 Ch D 145 at 171.
651. *Inche Noriah v. Shaik Allie Bin Omar* [1929] AC 127.
652. *Carey v. Norton* [1998] 1 NZLR 661; *Green v. Green* [2017] 2 NZLR 321; applied in *Fa'agutu v. Derhamy* [2020] NZHC 404, [2020] 2 NZLR 774 at [89].
653. [2016] NZCA 388.
654. *Allcard v. Skinner* (1887) 36 Ch D 145.
655. *Bainbrigge v. Brown* (1881) 18 Ch D 188.
656. *Maitland v. Irving* (1846) 15 Sim 437.

7. Suretyship Transactions

142. It is possible for undue influence to be imputed to a person who did not personally exert the influence. Typical circumstances where the question arises are where parents have unwisely guaranteed advances from a bank or finance company on account of undue influence by their son, or a wife is pressured by her husband to guarantee or give security for advances by a bank to the husband's company. On the son or husband defaulting, the question has been whether the guarantee can be set aside as against the bank.

First, the plea of undue influence can succeed where the person exerting the influence (the wrongdoer) was acting as agent for the bank.[657] The wrongdoer may actually be appointed as agent or may be held out as having authority to act as agent.[658] The question of whether there is a holding out can arise where the bank passes over documents to the wrongdoer to obtain the guarantor's signature. The test is whether a reasonable person in the complainant's position would have concluded that by setting the process in train the principal had held out the wrongdoer as agent in that regard.[659]

Second, a bank or other lender taking a guarantee or security for a loan sometimes may be deemed to have notice of wrongdoing by the principal debtor. The circumstances giving rise to deemed notice to the bank, and the steps which need to be taken by the bank where it has such notice, were explained and clarified in *Etridge*. The principles which apply can be summarized as follows:

(1) A bank or other lender taking a guarantee or security for a loan is put on notice of a risk of undue influence or wrongdoing by the principal debtor in all cases where the relationship between the surety and the principal debtor is non-commercial and the loan is not made to the surety.[660]
(2) The bank is not put on notice where there is a joint loan to the surety and the principal debtor unless the bank knows that the loan is not being used for the surety's purposes.[661] If the loan is made to a company, the bank is put on notice irrespective of any interest of the surety in the company.[662]
(3) A bank which is 'put on notice' or 'put on inquiry' must take reasonable steps to ensure that the surety understands the nature and effect of the transaction and wishes to enter it.[663]
(4) The bank can give appropriate advice itself or can require independent advice.[664]

657. *Barclays Bank Plc v. O'Brien* [1994] 1 AC 180.
658. *Contractors Bonding Ltd v. Snee* [1992] 2 NZLR 157.
659. *Ibid.*
660. *Royal Bank of Scotland Plc v. Etridge (No. 2)* [2002] 2 AC 773.
661. *CIBC Mortgages Plc v. Pitt* [1994] 1 AC 200.
662. *Royal Bank of Scotland Plc v. Etridge (No. 2)* [2002] 2 AC 773.
663. *Barclays Bank Plc v. O'Brien* [1994] 1 AC 180; *Wilkinson v. ASB Bank Ltd* [1998] 1 NZLR 674; *Royal Bank of Scotland Plc v. Etridge (No. 2)* [2002] 2 AC 773.
664. *Wilkinson v. ASB Bank Ltd* [1998] 1 NZLR 674; *Royal Bank of Scotland Plc v. Etridge (No. 2)* [2002] 2 AC 773.

(5) Where the surety is required to take independent advice, the bank must ensure that the surety knows that the solicitor who is giving the advice is in fact acting for the surety. It must communicate directly with the surety informing her of this and telling her that the purpose of the advice is that she should not be able to dispute that she is legally bound on signing the documents. The bank should not proceed until it has had an appropriate response from the surety. Subject to this, the solicitor normally can act for the principal debtor or the bank as well.[665]

(6) If the bank has a particular reason to suspect undue influence or misrepresentation by the principal debtor, it must take reasonable steps to ensure that the surety is giving his or her consent free from the influence or misrepresentation. It must inform the solicitor of the facts giving rise to the suspicion, or it must require that the guarantor be advised by an independent solicitor.[666]

(7) The solicitor must give advice which brings home to the surety the nature and extent of the risks involved in proceeding with the transaction and must give a certificate to this effect to the bank.[667]

(8) Deficiencies in the solicitor's advice do not affect the bank unless it knows or should know that the solicitor has not given proper advice, as where it has not given full information to the solicitor.[668]

(9) If the bank does not take reasonable steps to bring home to the surety the risks he or she is running by standing as surety, it is deemed to have notice of any claim the surety may have that the transaction was procured by undue influence or misrepresentation by the principal debtor.[669]

In *Etridge* itself, the trial judge had found that the wife had not been the victim of any undue influence or misrepresentation by her husband. Accordingly, her case failed *in limine* and none of the other points arose. Again, a father who had guaranteed loans to his son's company and who had played a significant role in running the company was held liable on the guarantee because there was no evidence that he was subjected to undue influence by anyone. The transaction was in every sense 'commercial' from the point of view of the guarantor, and there were no circumstances which could be said to have put the financier relevantly on enquiry.[670] And in a somewhat similar case, where there was a 'weak but arguable' argument that a son unduly influenced his parents to guarantee a loan by a bank to a company to buy certain property, it was held that the bank had taken sufficient steps to insulate itself from that possible influence. It had instructed solicitors to act for it in arranging execution of the relevant documents, and had required the solicitors to explain

665. *Massey v. Midland Bank* [1995] 1 All ER 929; *Banco Exterior v. Mann* [1995] 1 All ER 936; *Royal Bank of Scotland Plc v. Etridge (No. 2)* [2002] 2 AC 773.

666. *Royal Bank of Scotland Plc v. Etridge (No. 2)* [2002] 2 AC 773.

667. *Ibid.*

668. *Wilkinson v. ASB Bank Ltd* [1998] 1 NZLR 674; *Royal Bank of Scotland Plc v. Etridge (No. 2)* [2002] 2 AC 773.

669. *Royal Bank of Scotland Plc v. Etridge (No. 2)* [2002] 2 AC 773.

670. *Hogan v. Commercial Factors Ltd* [2006] 3 NZLR 618; and *see UDC Finance Ltd v. Down* (2009) 9 NZBLC 102,705; *Public Trust v. Ottow* (2010) 10 NZCPR 879; *ANZ National Bank Ltd v. Smith* (2010) 10 NZCPR 898.

the meaning and effect of those documents, to ensure that every guarantor had a full understanding of the obligations being undertaken and to advise the guarantors to seek independent advice. The Court was satisfied that by taking these steps, the bank had met its obligations to the guarantors to ensure they understood the nature and effect of their guarantees.[671] The Court placed no weight on the fact that, contrary to *Etridge*, the bank had no direct communications with the guarantors, but instructed the son's solicitors to act on its behalf and also on behalf of the company and the guarantors.

However, where non-English-speaking parents mortgaged their house to the plaintiff bank as security for a loan to their son, the parents' defence of undue influence by the son was allowed to go to trial. There was a serious question as to whether the solicitor who certified that he had advised the parents was acting for the parents or for the bank, and even if retained by the parents, the bank would not inevitably succeed. It was alleged that the bank was aware that the parents did not speak English and were vulnerable to exploitation, and the letter from the bank to the solicitor did not give any indication of special care that might be needed.[672] In another example, a wife of no economic experience, relying on her husband's and her solicitor's advice, approved a mortgage loan in favour of the Bank of New Zealand (BNZ) to refinance an existing housing loan. However, unknown to the wife and her solicitor, the husband simultaneously obtained further credit for his business, secured in part by mortgage, and the same bank manager handled both loans. The Court held that there was evidence supporting the claim of undue influence, and knowledge of this arguably could be imputed to BNZ. So BNZ's application for summary judgment failed.[673]

D. *Unconscionable Dealings*

143. Equity may also intervene in respect of unconscionable bargains when an unfair advantage is taken of persons who are poor and ignorant or for some other reason are in need of special protection. Undue influence and the doctrine of the unconscionable bargain clearly have much in common, but the first gives protection to a contracting party (or donor) who reposes trust and confidence in the other and who lacks the ability freely to exercise his or her will, whereas the second protects a contracting party who labours under a special disadvantage which the other party is able to exploit.

While most of the cases concern contracts, the doctrine of the unconscionable bargain applies to gifts as well as bargains.[674] The purpose of the remedy is to prevent an unconscionable use of power arising out of the particular circumstances and

671. *Gardiner v. Westpac New Zealand Ltd* [2015] 3 NZLR 1.
672. *National Westminster Bank v. Amin* [2002] 1 FLR 735.
673. *Rutherford v. BNZ* [2007] BCL 261.
674. *Louth v. Diprose* (1992) 175 CLR 621.

conditions affecting the relevant parties. To restrict the operation of the doctrine to contractual dealings would have the potential to exclude those most deserving of its remedial application.[675]

In *Gustav and Co Ltd v. Macfield Ltd,*[676] the Court of Appeal set out the following principles, said to be non-exhaustive but sufficient for the purposes of the case at hand, as summarizing the law concerning unconscionable bargains:

(1) Equity will intervene to relieve a party from the rigours of the common law in respect of an unconscionable bargain.
(2) This equitable jurisdiction is not intended to relieve parties from 'hard' bargains or to save the foolish from their foolishness. Rather, the jurisdiction operates to protect those who enter into bargains when they are under a significant disability or disadvantage from exploitation.
(3) A qualifying disability or disadvantage does not arise simply from an inequality of bargaining power. Rather, it is a condition or characteristic which significantly diminishes a party's ability to assess his or her best interests. Likely characteristics of this kind are ignorance, lack of education, illness, age, mental or physical infirmity, stress or anxiety, but other characteristics may qualify depending on the circumstances of the case.
(4) If one party is under a qualifying disability or disadvantage (the weaker party), the focus shifts to the conduct of the other party (the stronger party). The essential question is whether in the particular circumstances it is unconscionable to permit the stronger party to take the benefit of the bargain.
(5) Before a finding of unconscionability will be made, the stronger party must know of the weaker party's disability or disadvantage and must 'take advantage of' that disability or disadvantage.
(6) The requisite knowledge may be that of the principal or an agent, and may be actual or constructive. Factors associated with the substance of a transaction (e.g., a marked imbalance in consideration) or the way in which a transaction was concluded (e.g., the failure of one party to receive independent advice in relation to a significant transaction) may lead to a finding that the stronger party had constructive knowledge. So, in the particular circumstances, the stronger party may be put on enquiry, and in the absence of such enquiry may be treated as if he or she knew of the disability or disadvantage.
(7) 'Taking advantage of' (or victimization) in this context encompasses both the active extraction and the passive acceptance of a benefit.
(8) If these conditions are met, the burden falls on the stronger party to show that the transaction was a fair and reasonable one and should therefore be upheld.

The court noted that while factors such as a marked imbalance in consideration or procedural impropriety were generally present in unconscionability cases, neither was a prerequisite for relief. However, if there was no significant imbalance in

675. *Willis v. Thompson* [2017] NZHC 645, [2017] NZAR 1448.
676. [2007] NZCA 205; and *see A-G for England and Wales v. R* [2002] 2 NZLR 91 (affirmed [2004] 2 NZLR 577).

consideration or if the weaker party received full independent advice, it was unlikely that any issue of unconscionability would arise.

Ultimately, the question of whether a transaction is or is not unconscionable depends upon the particular facts of the case. Broadly, however, a party needs to show that he or she was in a position of special disadvantage, and that the stronger party knew or ought to have known of this and used his or her knowledge to exploit or victimize the complaining party.[677]

In the *Gustav* decision itself, the sole director (P) of a company (G), when terminally ill with cancer, agreed to purchase development property from M. A joint venture agreement with a partner was needed before the land could be developed, but P died before concluding any such agreement. G failed to proceed with the purchase and sought to recover the deposit. The Court of Appeal held that P's ability to manage his interests was significantly diminished, but while M knew that he had terminal cancer, it did not know that he was disabled from conducting his affairs or of his failure to secure a partner for a joint venture. In all the circumstances, it was not unconscionable for M to insist on its strict legal rights. On appeal,[678] the Supreme Court held, confirming the decision below, that the evidence fell well short of establishing that at that time P had been suffering from a disability which rendered him unable to look after G's interests. M had nominated its price but applied no pressure, and there had been nothing acting on M's conscience requiring it to decline to accept G's acceptance of its price.

Similarly, in *P v. Bridgecorp Ltd*,[679] it was held that a settlement deed made between a debtor and a finance company could not be set aside as an unconscionable bargain. The debtor suffered from post-traumatic stress disorder and depression, but the evidence did not establish that his mental condition was such that he was incapable of understanding the consequences of signing the deed, nor that the company knew of his disability and took advantage of it. So also, in *Blackwell v. Chick*,[680] it was held that an owner who entered a contract while being treated for a brain tumour knew perfectly well what he was doing. He had a close and mutually supportive relationship with the purchasers in which financial considerations in relation to the sale were not paramount. However, *Nichols v. Jessup (No. 1)*[681] goes the other way. In this case, an owner of land who was 'ignorant about property matters' and 'unintelligent and muddle headed' and whose business judgment 'was likely to be swayed by wholly irrelevant considerations' was relieved of her contractual obligation to grant a right-of-way over it to her neighbour. The agreement

677. *Fa'agutu v. Derhamy* [2020] NZHC 404, [2020] 2 NZLR 774 at [88]. In *Uber Technologies Inc v. Heller* [2020] SCC 16, the Supreme Court of Canada did not require knowledge of a claimant's weakness, saying that a weaker party was as disadvantaged by inadvertent exploitation as by deliberate exploitation.
678. [2008] 2 NZLR 735.
679. [2012] NZCA 530.
680. [2015] NZCA 34. For a successful appeal by B's personal representatives against the dismissal of B's concurrent claim for negligence against his solicitors, *see Blackwell v. Edmonds Judd* [2016] NZSC 40, [2016] 1 NZLR 1001.
681. [1986] 1 NZLR 226; and *see Nichols v. Jessup (No. 2)* [1986] 1 NZLR 237.

was of little or no benefit to her yet of very great benefit to the neighbour. The 'glaring' imbalance in the arrangement should have alerted him to the owner's inability to appreciate the consequences of the bargain.

Again, *Willis v. Thompson*[682] determined that a disputed gift was made as a result of unconscionable dealings. It was held here: (i) that an elderly man suffering from a progressive, chronic and terminal illness and other disabilities was labouring under a special disadvantage, and (ii) that his care-giver actively extorted or at the very least passively accepted a substantial gift of money, in circumstances where she had an obligation in equity to decline it in good conscience absent the donor having full and independent advice. Similarly, in *Fa'agutu v. Derhamy*,[683] the claimant was frail and with a terminal illness and the defendant, knowing this, actively arranged all the terms of a high-risk and manifestly detrimental transaction from which he personally gained a substantial benefit. The transaction accordingly was set aside, and the plaintiff was awarded equitable compensation.

The exploitation of the weaker party by the stronger may take the form of either the active extortion of a bargain or the passive acceptance of it in unconscionable circumstances.[684] Suretyship transactions can provide examples of the latter, on the basis that a bank which knows or ought to know of undue influence or other wrongdoing by a principal debtor in procuring a guarantee for a loan, yet which does nothing, has accepted the benefit of the contract of guarantee in unconscionable circumstances.[685] In this case, the principle of notice and the principle of unconscionability both point to the conclusion that the bank cannot rely on the security. But if the bank is merely aware of a risk of undue influence because the relationship between the guarantor and the debtor is non-commercial, and fails to take appropriate steps to see that the guarantor gets independent advice, then it will have constructive notice of any claim by the guarantor, but it is not clear that it can be regarded as having acted unconscionably.[686] So it is doubtful whether there is any need to make resort to the doctrine of unconscionability. The notice principle in *O'Brien* and *Etridge* seems to cover the ground.

E. Statutory Unconscionable Conduct

144. In 2022, a new, statutory, form of unconscionable conduct was added to the Fair Trading Act 1986. Now, by section 7, a person must not, in trade, engage in conduct that is unconscionable. Section 8(1) provides that in determining whether a person's conduct is unconscionable, a court may have regard to, *inter alia*, the relative bargaining power of the trader and the person affected by the conduct concerned, the extent to which the parties acted in good faith, whether the affected person was reasonably able to protect his or her interests, whether the trader used

682. [2017] NZHC 645, [2017] NZAR 1448.
683. [2020] NZHC 404, [2020] 2 NZLR 774, n. 647 above.
684. *O'Connor v. Hart* [1985] 1 NZLR 159 at 171; *Gustav and Co Ltd v. Macfield Ltd* [2007] NZCA 205.
685. *Commercial Bank of Australia Ltd v. Amadio* (1983) 151 CLR 447; *Credit Lyonnais Bank Nederland v. Burch* [1997] 1 All ER 144.
686. *Wilkinson v. ASB Bank Ltd* [1998] 1 NZLR 674 at 689.

unfair pressure or tactics, and whether the trader unreasonably failed to disclose any risks arising from any intended conduct of the trader.

By section 8(2), if the conduct involves a contract between a trader and an affected person, the court may also have regard to various particular matters, including: the circumstances in which the contract was entered into, including any inducement to enter into it and any opportunity to negotiate the terms; whether the affected person obtained independent legal or professional advice; the terms of the contract; the form of the contract and the transparency of its terms; whether the affected person's obligations under the contract were reasonably necessary for the protection of the trader's legitimate interests; the conduct of the trader and affected person in performing the contract; and any other conduct of the trader or affected person, after the contract was entered into, in connection with their relationship.

A range of remedies are available in circumstances where unconscionable conduct in terms of the statute can be established.[687] In the context of a contractual dispute, where section 7 is infringed, they include the various orders that a court may make under section 43 of the 1986 Act, including, in particular, orders for the refund of money, the return of property and the payment of damages.[688]

IV. Illegality

A. General

145. At common law, the courts would not enforce a contract which was contrary to a statute or was regarded as unenforceable because the contract contravened a rule of public policy. The law in this area was complex, and the results of applying it to particular sets of facts were often inconsistent and unsatisfactory. The problems were greatly alleviated by the passing of the Illegal Contracts Act 1970, which introduced a regime whereby the courts could grant relief, including relief by way of enforcement of the contract, to parties whose agreements were invalid at common law or in equity. Its success did much to encourage the adoption of similar discretionary regimes in other areas[689] and, more generally, to create acceptance of statutory alteration to contractual principle. If the court becomes aware that an issue of illegality of a contract has arisen, the issue must be enquired into and dealt with, whether or not either party has pleaded the illegality or sought to rely on it.[690] The Illegal Contracts Act 1970 was repealed by the Contract and Commercial Law Act 2017, but its provisions reappear as sections 70–84 of the new Act.

---

687. *See* paras 114-115 where the remedies for misleading and deceptive conduct are examined.
688. Fair Trading Act 1986, s. 43(3)(e),(f).
689. The former Contractual Mistakes Act 1977, replaced by the Contract and Commercial Law Act 2017, ss 21–32 (as to which *see* para. 125) and the former Contractual Remedies Act 1979, replaced by the Contract and Commercial Law Act 2017, ss 33–59 (as to which *see* paras 210–220).
690. *Duncan v. McDonald* [1997] 3 NZLR 669 at 676–677.

B. Definition of an Illegal Contract

146. Section 71(1) of the Contract and Commercial Law Act 2017 provides:

> In this subpart **illegal contract**:
>
> (a) means a contract governed by New Zealand law that is illegal at law or in equity, whether the illegality arises from the creation or the performance of the contract; and
>
> (b) includes a contract that contains an illegal provision, whether that provision is severable or not.[691]

Section 71(1) is however subject to section 72, which provides that a contract which has been lawfully entered into does not become illegal or unenforceable by any party to it because its performance is in breach of an enactment, unless that enactment expressly provides for illegality as a consequence or its object clearly requires that consequence. This means that contracts in breach of a statute are not necessarily thereby rendered illegal, although they might well have been at common law.[692] It is therefore necessary to consider both the common law heads of illegality as they apply in New Zealand and section 72 in relation to contracts in breach of a statute to determine whether any agreement falls to be classed as an illegal contract.

A preliminary question sometimes arises as to the status of a contract which is contrary to a statute or to a rule. The illegal contracts provisions of the Contract and Commercial Law Act 2017 can only apply where the contract is rendered 'illegal' by a rule of the common law or by statute.

Where the contract is challenged on the basis of contravention of, or non-compliance with, a statute, regard must first be had to the wording of the statute. While modern New Zealand statutes will usually clearly reveal whether or not a contract contravening the statute is illegal, the position is more difficult with statutes enacted before 1970. It is not uncommon to find references to contracts contravening the statute as being 'void', although in some contexts, the word 'void' appears to be used in a sense akin to 'voidable' – that is, that the contract only ceased to have effect if a party opted to use the breach of the legislation as a basis for bringing the contract to an end.[693] In the majority of cases, however, the word 'void' means simply that any contract in breach of the statute has no legal effect.

In cases where the contract is rendered void and ineffective, the courts must then consider whether the enactment in question requires that the contract be not just

691. The reference to severability of a provision refers to a common law doctrine whereby a court might in some instances be able to sever inessential parts of a contract which rendered it illegal, thus rescuing the remainder of the agreement. In New Zealand the doctrine of severance as regards provisions in an illegal contract is restricted to the statutorily modified form in s. 83 Contract and Commercial Law Act 2017 in relation to restraint of trade cases. *See also* para. 163.

692. *See* below.

693. *See* for example Contract and Commercial Law Act 2017, s. 128; Marine Insurance Act 1908, s. 5; Mutual Insurance Act 1955, ss 20 and 21.

void but also illegal.[694] In the era before the Illegal Contracts Act allowed relief for illegality, courts tended to lean away from finding illegality so as to avoid the harsh consequences of such a finding at common law. They may now be more ready to find illegality established, so that the possibility of relief under the Contract and Commercial Law Act is open.

A similar question may arise where the contract is impugned as being void as contrary to public policy. The common law recognized certain classes of contract as being void, but not illegal, on such grounds. These were contracts ousting the courts' jurisdiction and contracts affecting the freedom and security of marriage. These are discussed below. The Courts will be reluctant to add further categories of contracts which are void on such public policy grounds; *see Landco Albany Ltd v. Fu Hao Construction Ltd.*[695]

C. Contracts Which Are Void Rather than Illegal

1. Contracts Ousting the Jurisdiction of the Courts

147. Section 84(1)(b) of the Contract and Commercial Law Act preserves the common law rule that a contractual provision which purports to prevent a party from initiating legal proceedings in relation to a matter of dispute is unlawful and of no effect.[696] The common law prohibition also attached to contractual provisions which imposed upon the party having recourse to the courts some penalty or detriment for doing so.[697] Section 84(1)(b) does not in its terms apply to such contracts, but they may well be illegal under the general rule prohibiting contractual arrangements from interfering with the course of justice.[698] But neither the common law rule nor the statute treats as objectionable contractual provisions which require the parties to go through specific arbitration or mediation procedures prior to resorting to litigation,[699] or which impose a time limit for any proceedings to challenge an arbitrator's award.[700]

2. Contracts Affecting the Freedom or Security of Marriage

148. At common law, a contract which sought to prevent a person from marriage, or which significantly limited potential marriage partners, was 'invalid',

694. For a recent discussion of the issues *see Gallaway Cook Allan v. Carr* [2013] 1 NZLR 826; [2013] NZCA 11 where it was held that a contractual provision which purported to grant rights greater than those permitted by statute was void but not illegal.
695. [2006] 2 NZLR 174.
696. As to the common law rule *see Lee v. Showmen's Guild of Great Britain* [1952] 2 QB 329.
697. *Novamaze Pty Ltd v. Cut Price Deli Pty Ltd* (1995) 128 ALR 540.
698. *See* para. 146.
699. *Scott v. Avery* (1865) 5 HL Cas 811. It appears that provisions which allow factual matters to be conclusively determined by a specified third party may also be valid: *Jones v. Sherwood Computer Services plc* [1992] 1 WLR 277.
700. *Webb v. Queensland Insurance Co Ltd* [1920] NZLR 118.

which in this context meant 'void' rather than illegal.[701] A similar result is attached to agreements – such as agreements between an unmarried person and a married person for their future marriage[702] – which would have the effect of breaking up a subsisting and functioning marriage.[703] There was no such consequence if the marriage was in reality at an end.[704]

The exact scope of the rule, and indeed its continued existence, are uncertain. Legislative policy has encouraged the delineation by married persons of their respective rights in the event of a subsequent termination of their marriage,[705] and it may be thought such changes in social policy remove any basis for the rule.

D. Illegality at Common Law

149. A number of heads of illegality were and are recognized at common law and are discussed below. It was said many years ago in England[706] that only these established heads gave rise to illegality, but the New Zealand courts have been more adventurous and have in recent times recognized as illegal at common law a contractual provision not apparently covered by the English authorities.[707]

1. Contracts to Commit a Criminal Offence, a Fraud or a Tort

150. At common law, an agreement to do any act which was a criminal offence was illegal.[708] In New Zealand, this rule is modified by section 72 of the Contract and Commercial Law Act so that it is possible that a contractual provision which entails conduct which is technically an offence might nevertheless not be seen as illegal. An agreement to commit a crime against a friendly foreign government is illegal.[709] Less difficulty attaches to agreements to commit a fraud or a tort on a third party; such agreements are always illegal contracts.[710]

2. Contracts Interfering with the Course of Justice

151. Contracts interfering with the course of justice are illegal under a broad common law rule. At the core of this prohibition is a rule making illegal any

701. *Snell v. Potter* [1953] NZLR 696 at 714, 720; compare *Lowe v. Peers* (1768) 4 Burr 2225.
702. New Zealand has abolished any right to sue for breach of promise to marry (Domestic Actions Act 1975, s. 8), but the issue could conceivably arise as an incident of other proceedings.
703. *Dobersek v. Petrizza* [1968] NZLR 211.
704. *Fender v. St. John Mildmay* [1938] AC 1.
705. *See* for example Property (Relationships) Act 1976 (passed in 2001 as part of a major amendment to the relevant law).
706. *Fender v. St. John Mildmay* [1938] AC 1.
707. *Peters v. Collinge* [1993] 2 NZLR 554.
708. *Belvoir Finance Co v. Stapleton* [1971] 1 QB 210; compare *Bigos v. Bousted* [1951] 1 All ER 92.
709. *Duncan v. McDonald* [1997] 3 NZLR 669.
710. *Ted Jones Ltd v. Donselaar* [1969] NZLR 537; *Silver v. Mitchell* [1932] NZLR 882; *Barnett Glass Rubber Co Ltd v. McDonald* [1922] NZLR 767; *Duncan v. McDonald* [1997] 3 NZLR 669 at 672; compare *Mallalieu v. Hodgson* (1851) 16 QB 689.

agreement intended to prevent the reporting, investigation, or prosecution of a criminal offence.[711] The rule applies to agreements not to bring private prosecutions as well as those dealing with prosecutions by police or other agencies of the state.[712] There are overseas authorities which indicate an agreement to settle or discontinue proceedings which in form are a criminal prosecution but which are in fact concerned with a matter of private rights is lawful,[713] but this rule was questioned in a recent New Zealand case.[714] The general prohibition, however, reaches further than simple agreements to stifle a prosecution, and makes illegal ancillary contracts such as agreements to recompense defendants for penalties imposed by the courts[715] or contracts of loan where moneys lent were intended to be used to induce victims not to report offending.[716] Further, a contractual provision, such as a confidentiality clause, which operates to hinder investigation of a reported offence will become illegal once it operates in that manner.[717] The rule also comprehends agreements which are tainted by maintenance or champerty (i.e., giving assistance with litigation where one has no interest justifying involvement, or where one's involvement is prompted by a promise of a share of any proceeds).[718] These rules have caused significant discussion in England in the context of contingent fee agreements between lawyers and their clients.[719] The point is resolved in New Zealand by a recent statute which declares conditional fee arrangements coming within the statute not to be illegal.[720]

3. Contracts to Defraud the Revenue

152. Contracts to defraud the revenue by evasion of taxes (national or local) which are properly due are illegal.[721] The purpose of the agreement must be that such taxes be evaded; it is not sufficient for one party to take advantage of the agreement to attempt such evasion.[722]

---

711. *Osborne v. WorkSafe New Zealand* [2017] NZSC 175; [2018] 1 NZLR 447, at [1].
712. *Polymer Developments Group Ltd v. Tilialo* [2002] 3 NZLR 258.
713. *Kerridge v. Simmonds* (1906) 4 CLR 253; *Fisher & Co v. Apollinaris Co* (1875) 10 Ch App 297.
714. *Polymer Developments Group Ltd v. Tilialo* [2002] 3 NZLR 258 at 271.
715. *Machinery Movers Ltd v. Auckland Regional Council* [1994] 1 NZLR 493; compare *McGregor Koch v. Barrett* HC Invercargill CIV-2007-425-236, 19 Dec. 2008. An agreement for indemnity against civil liability for illegal acts made after the relevant acts were performed will not necessarily be illegal: *Mulcaire v. News Group Newspapers Ltd* [2012] Ch. 435; [2011] EWHC 3469(Ch), [43]–[45].
716. *Barsdell v. Kerr* [1979] 2 NZLR 731.
717. *A v. Hayden* (1985) 56 ALR 82; *Wyatt & Co Ltd v. Queenstown-Lakes District Council* [1991] 2 NZLR 180.
718. *See Sievwright v. Ward* [1935] NZLR 43 and *Body Corporate 326421 v. Auckland Council* [2015] NZHC 862.
719. The authorities are canvassed in *Awwad v. Geraghty & Co* [2001] QB 570.
720. Lawyers and Conveyancers Act 2006, s. 334. For discussion of the area *see Wynn Williams & Co v. Kain* [2012] NZCA 563; [2013] 1 NZLR 498; leave to appeal to the Supreme Court was refused: *Kain v. Wynn Williams & Co* [2013] NZSC 26.
721. *Herbison v. Papakura Video Ltd (No. 2)* [1987] 2 NZLR 720; *TRA Case 91/125* (1993) 15 NZTC 5,180; sub nom *TRA case 23* (1993) 17 TRNZ 870.
722. *Phillips v. Foster* [1991] 3 NZLR 263. Such contracts will generally also be illegal as being in breach of a statute: *Horsfall v. Potter* [2017] NZSC 196, at [57].

4. Contracts Which Are Prejudicial to Good Government

153. There is a broad public policy interest in having a freely operating democratic state with an effective government free from corruption. A wide range of contracts which in some way run counter to this policy interest have been struck down as illegal. A contract which purported to prevent an eligible person from standing for election to the House of Representatives has been held illegal.[723] A different aspect of the policy interest has led the courts to hold illegal contracts to procure the conferment of a title or other public honour.[724] More broadly, any contract which interferes with the conduct of the government's relations with other governments may be illegal. At its simplest, this rule renders illegal contracts with enemy entities in time of war,[725] but the rule extends to contracts which require the performance of some act which is illegal in the country in which it is to be performed.[726]

5. Contracts Promoting Sexual Immorality

154. At common law, the courts held illegal not only any contract which provided for benefits to be conferred in return for sexual intercourse outside marriage but also any agreement collateral to any such intercourse.[727] Thus, a contract for the sale of sexual services (prostitution) was illegal, and so also was a contract providing facilities or accommodation for persons engaging in sexual intercourse outside marriage.[728] Public morality and legislative policy have significantly altered over recent years, and the New Zealand parliament has not only removed or minimized most legal distinctions between married persons and those living together outside marriage[729] but also abolished the core element of the rule so that a contract of prostitution is not illegal and unenforceable.[730] It is probable that the common law rule has effectively been abolished.

---

723. *Peters v. Collinge* [1993] 2 NZLR 554. As to contracts injurious to these public policy interests in another country *see Lemenda Trading Co Ltd v. African Middle East Petroleum Ltd* [1988] QB 448.
724. *Parkinson v. College of Ambulance Ltd and Harrison* [1925] 2 KB 1.
725. *Branigan v. Saba* [1924] NZLR 481; *Husheer v. New Zealand Tobacco Co Ltd* [1921] NZLR 304. During both World Wars statutory regulations extended the common law rule: War Regulations 1916; Enemy Trading Emergency Regulations 1939.
726. *Duncan v. McDonald* [1997] 3 NZLR 669; compare *Regazzoni v. KC Sethia (1944) Ltd* [1958] AC 301. There may be cases where other policy considerations override the 'comity of nations' basis for this part of the rule; *see* for example *Controller and Auditor-General v. Davison* [1996] 2 NZLR 278. Difficulty arises where the act required to be done is not illegal in the country in which it is to be performed, but is seen there as contrary to that state's public policy: *see Lemenda Trading Co Ltd v. African Middle East Petroleum Ltd* [1988] QB 448; *Westacre Investments Inc v. Jugoimport-SDPR Holding Co Ltd* [1999] 3 All ER 864.
727. *Hutchinson v. Davis* [1940] NZLR 490; *Franco v. Bolton* (1797) 3 Wes 368.
728. *Pearce v. Brooks* (1866) LR 1 Ex 213; *Upfill v. Wright* [1911] 1 KB 506. Contrast the very different view in *Ashton v. Pratt* (2015) 318 ALR 260; [2015] NSWCA 12.
729. *See* for example Property (Relationships) Act 1976, s. 21; Human Rights Act 1993, s. 21; Property Law Act 1952, s. 40A and Domestic Protection Act 1982, s. 13(2).
730. Prostitution Law Reform Act 2003, s. 7.

E. Contracts in Breach of a Statute and the Illegality Provisions of the Contract and Commercial Law Act 2017

155. Section 72 of the Contract and Commercial Law Act provides that a contract lawfully entered into does not become an illegal contract as a result of the performance of the contract being in breach of a statute unless either the statute in question expressly provides for such a result or the object of the statute clearly requires that contracts performed in breach of the statute be illegal. Where the issue of statutory illegality arises, the first question to be asked is whether the statute in question renders the contract illegal at inception, or whether the statute would allow the contract to be lawfully entered into. If the contract is illegal at inception, there is neither need nor ability to apply the ameliorative provision in section 72. If, however, the contract is lawfully entered into, the section must be considered to determine whether the contract has become illegal.

There are relatively few statutes which specifically state that contracts which contravene the Act's provisions will be illegal,[731] but there are many more where the statute makes unlawful certain conduct in terms which give rise to a clear implication that contracts providing for such conduct must be illegal.[732] There are also cases where an enactment specifically provides for the lawfulness of certain contracts in terms which imply that non-complying contracts will be illegal. An example is *Lower Hutt City Council v. Martin*,[733] where a statutory authorization for the payment by local government agencies of retirement gratuities to staff of ten years' service was held to render illegal contractual provisions promising such gratuities to staff whose service had been for a shorter period. Illegality of this type is not dependent on whether the parties, or any of them, were aware the contract sought to be entered would be illegal.[734] It should be noted that a contract designed to assist or encourage one or both of its parties to enter into a further contract which is illegal as being in breach of a statute will itself be considered to be an illegal contract.[735]

We may now turn to cases where a contract may have become illegal because some aspect of its performance involves a breach of an enactment. Section 72 of the Contract and Commercial Law Act means that an illegality in performance only renders the contract illegal if the statute so provides or its object clearly so requires. It will be rare indeed for a statute to make specific provision of this kind, so the issue will normally be determined by consideration of the parliamentary intention in enacting the statute, and whether that intention would be frustrated if contracts

731. *See* for example Companies Act 1993, s. 40; Human Rights Act 1993, s. 86; Gambling Act 2003, s. 14.
732. So statutes such as the Arms Act 1983 and the Misuse of Drugs Act 1978, which make illegal the sale of prohibited substances or items, must by implication render agreements for the sale of such substances or items illegal.
733. [1987] 1 NZLR 321.
734. *National Westminster Finance New Zealand Ltd v. South Pacific Rent-a-Car Ltd* [1985] 1 NZLR 646.
735. *Equiticorp Industries Group (In Statutory Management) v. The Crown* [1996] 3 NZLR 586; compare *Portland Holdings Ltd v. Cameo Motors Ltd* [1966] NZLR 571.

performed in breach of the act were not held illegal.[736] The impact of a finding of illegality on third parties to the contract may be considered in determining whether the parliamentary intention would be frustrated.[737]

F. Consequences of Illegality of a Contract

156. An illegal contract is of no effect, and no person becomes entitled to any property under a disposition made by or pursuant to any such contract.[738] However, there is an important exception to protect third parties. A disposition of property by a party to an illegal contract for valuable consideration to a person who is not a party to the illegal contract and acts in good faith without knowledge of the illegality of the contract in question (or a disposition by or through such an innocent third party) is effective.[739]

G. Relief under the Contract and Commercial Law Act 2017

1. Power to Grant Relief Where Contract Is Illegal

157. The Contract and Commercial Law Act confers upon the courts wide discretionary powers to grant relief from the consequences of the contract being illegal and ineffective. The powers are set out in section 76 of the Act, whereby relief may be granted 'by way of restitution, compensation, variation of the contract, validation of the contract in whole or in part or for any particular purpose howsoever as the Court in its discretion thinks just'. Relief may be sought not only by a party to the illegal contract but also by a person claiming 'through or under' such a party.[740] The court may make orders vesting any property which was the subject of, or all or part of the consideration for, the illegal contract in any party to the proceedings, or may order a party to the proceedings to transfer or assign the relevant property to another party to the proceedings.[741] Any order granting relief may be made on such terms or conditions as the court sees fit to impose.[742]

---

736. For discussion of the relevant principles in particular cases *see Brown v. NZ Basing Ltd* [2017] NZSC 139; [2018] 1 NZLR 245, at [87]-[90]; *Low Volume Vehicle Technical Association Inc v. Brett* [2019] NZCA 67, at [35] and [40], and *Xiao v. Sun* [2018] NZHC 536 at [441].
737. *National Australia Finance Ltd v. Fahey* [1990] 2 NZLR 482; *DFC Financial Services Ltd v. Abel* [1991] 2 NZLR 619; *Abbott v. UDC Finance Ltd* [1992] 1 NZLR 405.
738. Contract and Commercial Law Act 2017, s. 73.
739. Contract and Commercial Law Act 2017, s. 74; and *see Begley Industries Ltd v. Cramp* [1977] 2 NZLR 207 at 221–222. It has been held that both actual and constructive knowledge of the illegality will remove the protection afforded by the proviso: *Equiticorp Industries Group (In Statutory Management) v. The Crown* [1996] 3 NZLR 586.
740. Contract and Commercial Law Act 2017 75. The power to grant compensation has rarely been used; for an example of its use *see Bevin v. Smith* [1994] 3 NZLR 648.
741. Contract and Commercial Law Act 2017, s. 76(4).
742. Contract and Commercial Law Act 2017, s. 77.

2. Jurisdiction to Grant Discretionary Relief

158. The jurisdiction of the courts to grant discretionary relief is 'subject to the express provisions of any other enactment'.[743] This limitation has rarely proved a significant obstacle to judicial willingness to provide relief to parties seen as deserving. The courts quickly held that a statute which provided for a contract in breach of its terms to be illegal or to be of no effect did no more than establish the precondition for relief to be granted.[744] Next to arise for consideration were cases where a statute not only provided for certain contracts to be illegal but also provided for specific consequences to follow upon such illegality, such as the purchaser's right under an illegal hire-purchase contract to recover all monies paid. Such a provision was held to bar the grant of discretionary relief if the contract remained illegal, but not to prevent the court from granting relief by way of validation of the contract. Once the contract was validated, the statute's provision for the consequence of illegality ceased to have effect, and there was no longer a bar on relief in addition to the validation being granted.[745]

Any privative provisions declaring an inability to grant relief are narrowly construed.[746] Further, if an enactment expressly forbids relief by way of validation of the contract, without barring the grant of other forms of relief, the courts retain the capacity to give other forms of relief, which capacity has in some cases been exercised in such a manner as to produce a result identical to the validation which parliament had forbidden.[747] It appears the jurisdiction to grant relief will only be unavailable where the statute in question contains words to the effect that relief under the Contract and Commercial Law Act is not to be granted, and few statutes contain such specific wording.[748]

3. Factors Relevant to the Exercise of the Discretion to Grant Relief

159. The Courts are required to consider a number of matters in determining whether and how to exercise the discretionary power to grant relief. Principal among these matters is the general element of the conduct of the parties.[749] The subsection also makes relevant post-contractual conduct, in particular, any delay in seeking relief where that delay has prejudiced the other party to the contract.[750] The court must also consider whether or not the party to whom it is considering granting relief entered into the contract, or committed an unlawful act, with knowledge of

---

743. Contract and Commercial Law Act 2017, s. 76(3)(b).
744. *Harding v. Coburn* [1976] 2 NZLR 577 at 582–584.
745. *National Westminster Finance New Zealand Ltd v. South Pacific Rent-a-car Ltd* [1985] 1 NZLR 646.
746. *Edwards v. O'Connor* [1989] 3 NZLR 448.
747. *See* for example *Re AIC Merchant Finance Ltd* [1990] 2 NZLR 385; *Duncan v. McDonald* [1997] 3 NZLR 669.
748. For an example, *see* Gaming and Lotteries Act 1977, s. 128(3).
749. Contract and Commercial Law Act 2017, s. 78(a).
750. *House v. Jones* [1985] 2 NZLR 288; compare *Williams v. Gibbons* [1994] 1 NZLR 273 where the delay was not held to have caused prejudice.

the facts or law giving rise to the illegality of the conduct or the contract.[751] It has proved rare for relief to be granted to a party who deliberately breached a statute,[752] while a mistaken belief that the contractual provision or the conduct it required was lawful is a factor favouring relief.[753] In cases involving illegality by breach of a statute, the court must have regard to the object of the enactment in question and the severity of any penalty provided for a breach of the relevant provision.[754] Lastly, the court may consider such other matters as it sees fit.[755]

While most of the reported cases have dealt with breaches of statute, the diversity of outcomes which can result from the application of the discretion is shown by three cases involving agreements interfering with the course of justice, where relief was denied in two cases but granted by way of variation and validation in the third.[756]

In most cases, the courts have started from the premise that the purpose of the legislation is to mitigate unfairness which results from the invalidity of the contract. Relief will not therefore be granted where it would result in increased unfairness.[757] In a small number of cases, the courts have found that the object of a statute is such that relief cannot be given without the statutory purpose being frustrated,[758] but it has been much more common for the courts to determine that the granting of relief will, on the specific facts of the case, not be objectionable on that ground.[759] Where the illegality in question is that the parties have not obtained a licence or approval needed by statute and the courts cannot be certain the licence or approval would be forthcoming, relief has been granted by validating the contract after variation to make it conditional on the licence or approval being obtained.[760] In some cases, there has been an evident tension between providing relief to parties on whom illegality has impacted particularly harshly and observing the policy aims of statutes which have limited the forms of relief which the courts may grant; the courts' resolutions have favoured the former over the latter.[761]

---

751. Contract and Commercial Law Act 2017, s. 80.
752. *Leith v. Gould* [1986] 1 NZLR 760. If confronted by a case similar to *Patel v. Mirza* [2016] UKSC 42; [2016] 3 WLR 399 where both parties had intended to take part in an illegal scheme, the court would need to apply the illegality provisions of the Contract and Commercial Law Act 2017: *Horsfall v. Potter* [2017] NZSC 196, at [58].
753. *National Westminster Finance New Zealand Ltd v. South Pacific Rent-a-car Ltd* [1985] 1 NZLR 646.
754. Contract and Commercial Law Act 2017, s. 78(b).
755. Contract and Commercial Law Act 2017, s. 78(c).
756. *See Slater v. Mall Finance and Investment Ltd* [1976] 2 NZLR 685; *Barsdell v. Kerr* [1979] 2 NZLR 731 (relief denied); compare *Polymer Developments Group Ltd v. Tilialo* [2002] 3 NZLR 258 (agreement varied and validated).
757. *Broadlands Rentals Ltd v. RD Bull Ltd* [1976] 2 NZLR 595; *House v. Jones* [1985] 2 NZLR 288.
758. *See* for example *Lower Hutt City Council v. Martin* [1987] 1 NZLR 321; *Edwards v. O'Connor* [1989] 3 NZLR 448; contrast *Mercurius Ventures Ltd v. Waitakere CC* [1996] 2 NZLR 495.
759. *See* for example *Hurrell v. Townend* [1982] 1 NZLR 536, *Catley v. Herbert* [1988] 1 NZLR 606, *Re AIC Merchant Finance Ltd* [1990] 2 NZLR 385, *Euro-National Corporation v. NZI Bank Ltd* [1992] 3 NZLR 528; *Duncan v. McDonald* [1997] 3 NZLR 669.
760. *McLachlan v. Taylor* [1985] 2 NZLR 277; *Combined Taxis Co-operative Society Ltd v. Slobbe* [1973] 2 NZLR 651.
761. *See* in particular *Re AIC Merchant Finance Ltd* [1990] 2 NZLR 385; *Duncan v. McDonald* [1997] 3 NZLR 669.

H. Contracts in Restraint of Trade

1. General

160. A contract in restraint of trade is a contract, or a contractual provision, in which one or both parties agree to some restriction of greater or lesser severity upon the party's freedom to carry on his or her trade, profession or employment. A classic example is that of the vendor of a business who agrees not to set up a fresh business in competition with the one sold. Restraints of trade also operate in other areas, as in the case of provisions of a contract of employment which limit the freedom of employees later to work for the employer's trade rival.

At common law, contracts in restraint of trade were prima facie void as being contrary to public policy. It was assumed that market competition was for the public benefit; agreements which restricted such competition were therefore generally suspect. However, it was also recognized that there were cases where some restraint could be seen as necessary or desirable to encourage investment or employment. An employer who could not prevent employees from using the knowledge or customer connections acquired while in his or her employment to set up as a trade rival, or indeed for the benefit of an existing trade rival, would be reluctant to hire employees or to entrust them with significant knowledge, and so the expansion of business would be hindered. Equally, a purchaser of a business would want to be sure the vendor would not compete with the business sold, and in the absence of binding restraints the flow of new investment would be seriously affected. Thus the courts came to uphold those restraints which could be shown by the party seeking to enforce them to be reasonable.

The restraint of trade doctrine is now recognized as applying to a range of relationships falling outside the traditional categories of vendor and purchaser of a business or employer and employee. It will apply also to so-called solus agreements whereby a retailer agrees to sell only the products of a particular supplier, to franchise agreements, and to rules of professional or trade bodies which determine the right to carry out a particular trade or business nationally. This last aspect has led to a number of cases involving contracts or rules relating to participation in professional sports.[762]

2. Reasonable Restraints

161. Before a restraint of trade agreement can be held to be valid, a number of conditions must be satisfied:

762. For the history of the restraint of trade doctrine *see Nordenfeldt v. Maxim Nordenfeldt Guns and Ammunition Co* [1894] AC 535; *Esso Petroleum Co Ltd v. Harpers Garage (Stourport) Ltd* [1968] AC 269. For restraints on vendors of businesses *see Brown v. Brown* [1980] 1 NZLR 484; for restrictions on employees *see H and R Block Ltd v. Sanott* [1976] 1 NZLR 213; for regulation of a profession *see Dickson v. Pharmaceutical Society of Great Britain* [1967] Ch. 708; as to sport *see* for example *Kemp v. NZRFL* [1989] 3 NZLR 463.

(1) The covenantee (the person to whom the restraining promise is made, and who seeks to enforce it) must have a genuine interest which is protected by the restraint of trade provision. The interest to be protected may be customer goodwill of a business, the confidentiality of information or the investment of capital in the design, production and marketing of novel products.[763]

(2) The restraint must be no wider than is reasonably needed to protect the covenantee's interest. Here, the court must consider a number or matters which affect the reasonableness or otherwise of the interest. The court must look at the geographical extent of any restraint, as a restraint which applies to geographical areas in which the covenantee does not trade or in which he or she has no goodwill will not be reasonable. Thus a restraint which prohibits competition within a very limited area may be valid where the covenantee's business is very localized, but in extreme cases, a worldwide restraint may be valid.[764] Again, the court will look at the duration of the covenant or restraint. It should be for no greater period than is necessary to protect the covenantee's interest. A purchaser of a business may receive protection for a period sufficient to attract to the new owner any customer goodwill purchased with the business; an employer may protect the confidentiality of information for the period it is of value; the likely consumer goodwill attaching to an employee can be protected for as long as it is significant, but no longer.[765]

(3) The restraint must be reasonable as between the parties to the contract in restraint of trade.[766] Here, the court will have regard to the relative bargaining strengths of the parties. While the courts will generally consider that vendors and purchasers are likely to be able to achieve a reasonable balance of their competing interests, the inequality of bargaining power usually found in employment relationships means that it is less likely that a restrictive covenant in a contract between an employer and employees, particularly youthful employees, will be couched in fair and reasonable terms.[767] Franchising contracts may fall somewhere between the vendor/purchaser and the employer/employee cases.[768]

763. *Fletcher Aluminium Ltd v. O'Sullivan* [2001] 2 NZLR 731; *Brown v. Brown* [1980] 1 NZLR 484; *H and R Block Ltd v. Sanott* [1976] 1 NZLR 213; *Vancouver Malt and Sake Brewing Co v. Vancouver Breweries Ltd* [1934] AC 1.

764. Compare *Brown v. Brown* [1980] 1 NZLR 484 and *Anderson v. Davies* [1997] 1 NZLR 616 with *Gallagher Group Ltd v. Walley* [1999] 1 ERNZ 490.

765. *Gallagher Group Ltd v. Walley* [1999] 1 ERNZ 490; *Fletcher Aluminium Ltd v. O'Sullivan* [2001] 2 NZLR 731; compare *Anderson v. Davies* [1997] 1 NZLR 616; *Helsby v. Oliver* [1999] 1 NZLR 77, 85–87.

766. Reasonableness is to be assessed by reference to the circumstances at the time it is entered into, rather than in the light of subsequent events: *BYOF Holdings Pty Ltd v. Bencho Ltd* [2014] NZHC 1560.

767. *Brown v. Brown* [1980] 1 NZLR 484; *H and R Block Ltd v. Sanott* [1976] 1 NZLR 213; *Landzeal Group Ltd v. Kyne* [1990] 3 NZLR 574. The adequacy of the consideration, if any, for the restraint of trade clause is relevant to its reasonableness: *Fuel Espresso Ltd v. Hsieh* [2007] 2 NZLR 651; *see also Tillman v. Egon Zehnder Ltd* [2019] UKSC 32.

768. *Dymocks Franchise Systems (NSW) Pty Ltd v. Bilgola Enterprises Ltd* (1999) 8 TCLR 612.

(4) It is also necessary to consider the way the covenant is drafted. If it gives the covenantee the power to operate it unfairly, the provision may be unreasonable even though its actual exercise has not been unreasonable.[769]

(5) The restraint must contain nothing to make it unreasonable when the public interest is considered. In particular, the courts will consider the impact of the restraint on third parties. For example, if two employers each agree not to hire persons formerly employed by the other, the impact on such former employees must be considered to determine whether there is a public interest which is being unreasonably infringed.[770]

3. Impact of Illegal Contracts Legislation

162. The Contract and Commercial Law Act 2017 gives the courts rather less wide-reaching powers than are given in relation to truly illegal contracts. Where the court is satisfied a contractual provision is an unreasonable restraint of trade, it is given power to delete the provision and enforce the remainder of the contract or to modify the objectionable provision so that it would have been reasonable at the time the contract was entered into and then to enforce the contract. If deletion or variation does not make the provision reasonable, the courts must decline to enforce the restraint of trade.[771]

In practice, the court has rarely used the option simply to delete a restraint of trade provision. This is in accord with the general principle that severance should not be ordered if it would alter the nature of the contract or destroy the main purpose and substance of what has been agreed.[772] In the vast majority of those cases in which a restraint has been found to be unreasonable, the critical question for the court has been whether variation of the restrictive provision would provide a sufficient solution. In many cases, the courts have varied either the duration of the restraint or the area of its geographical operation,[773] but sometimes a more creative solution has been found. A prime example is *Cooney v. Welsh,*[774] where the Court of Appeal modified a geographical restraint on the area in which a solicitor could practice to a conduct-based restraint which prohibited the covenantor from acting for any clients of the former employer for the period of the restraint.

Experience has shown that the conferral on the courts of the discretionary power of modification has for the most part been a very great success. There may, however, be some occasions where knowledge that an overly wide restraint might be redrawn but enforced by the courts has encouraged employers, in particular, to draft

---

769. *Kemp v. NZRFL* [1989] 3 NZLR 463.

770. *Mutual Leasing Ltd v. Fleetlease Ltd* (2000) 9 TCLR 412; compare *Kores Manufacturing Co Ltd v. Kolak Manufacturing Co Ltd* [1959] 1 Ch. 108. *See also Harcus Sinclair llp v. Your Lawyers Ltd* [2019] EWCA Civ 335; [2019] 4 WLR 81 where the restraint affected the ability of members of the public to engage particular lawyers.

771. *See* Contract and Commercial Law Act 2017, s. 83; *C E Elley Ltd v. Burgess* (1997) 7 TCLR 582.

772. *Carr v. Gallaway Cook Allan* [2014] NZSC 75; [2014] 1 NZLR 792.

773. *See* for example *Brown v. Brown* [1980] 1 NZLR 484; *Gallagher Group Ltd v. Walley* [1999] 1 ERNZ 490; *Dhanapala v. Jackson* (1999) 9 TCLR 67.

774. [1993] 1 ERNZ 407.

clauses that are unnecessarily broad in the hope of discouraging potentially legitimate competition.

Chapter 3. The Contents of a Contract

§1. The Different Clauses

I. Ascertaining of Express Terms

A. The Parol Evidence Rule

163. If the contract is entirely by word of mouth, the court must ascertain its express terms by evidence. By their very nature, oral contracts usually contain little more than the bare necessities, and will need to be supplemented by implied terms.

If the contract is in writing, the parol evidence rule in theory excludes extrinsic evidence to 'add to, vary or contradict' the writing. This rule has always been subject to exceptions, and has less impact than in past years. However, it does still operate to prevent a party to a contract giving oral evidence directly contradicting the written contract.[775] The law in New Zealand does allow oral evidence to show the written agreement should not be treated as conclusive.

First, evidence may be adduced to show that the writing does not properly record the agreement of the parties: they may have reached an oral agreement which has been written down wrongly in the document. In such cases, the remedy of rectification is available.[776]

Second, evidence may be adduced to show that the parties did not intend their written contract to be binding until some condition, such as the approval of a third party, is satisfied.[777]

Third, evidence may be adduced to show that the contract comprises not just one, but several connected documents.[778]

Fourth, and most importantly, the exclusion of oral evidence is inappropriate where the written document was never intended to be the whole contract – where, in other words, the parties intended their contract to be partly in writing and partly by word of mouth. This situation is so common as greatly to weaken the supposed prohibition on adducing evidence to *add* to a written contract. The present position can best be put by saying it will be presumed that a document which looks like a contract is to be treated as the whole contract. Thus, in *Tak and Co Inc v. AEL Corporation,*[779] an invoice for the sale of animals was held to constitute the entire contract; the document looked like a contract, and set out all the necessary terms.[780] But that presumption is rebuttable, and it can often be shown that the writing is but part of the contract, and must be set alongside a set of complementary oral terms. Thus in one case it was held that a tenancy agreement was supplemented by an oral agreement that the tenant, in addition to the leased part of the building, was to have the

---

775. *Krukziener v. Hanover Finance Ltd* (2008) 19 PRNZ 162; [2008] NZCA 187.
776. *See* para. 132.
777. *Pym v. Campbell* (1856) 6 E & B 370.
778. *Masport Ltd v. Morrison Industries Ltd* CA 362/92, 31 Aug. 1993.
779. (1995) 5 NZBLC 103,887.
780. The New Zealand courts have yet to consider the view taken in *Rock Advertising Ltd v. MWB Business Exchange Centres Limited* [2018] UKSC 24, [2019] AC 119 that a term in a contract precluding oral variations to the written contractual terms was invalid.

use of two other rooms for storage, and also the use of the garden.[781] Again, in *AM Bisley & Co Ltd v. Thompson,*[782] a written contract for the sale of farming machinery specified that it would be delivered 'ASAP'. Evidence was admitted of an oral agreement that delivery would take place before the harvest season. An oral statement which directly contradicts a written term will more rarely be accepted, but in appropriate cases, oral evidence may be received to show the true nature of a written transaction, for example, that a transfer of ownership of property was intended only to amount to a security for money owed.[783]

In *ANZ Bank New Zealand Ltd v. Bushline Trustees Ltd,*[784] the Supreme Court recognized that ascertaining whether an oral contract (or a partly oral and partly written contract) was entered into and, if so, what its terms were was a question of fact. This meant that all evidence to assist that task was admissible, including evidence of the parties' subjective intentions and subsequent conduct.

Finally, there are cases where clear oral assurances have been held to override exclusion clauses in contracts,[785] and the doctrine of promissory estoppel has been prayed in aid to enforce pre-contract assurances that a particular written term of the contract will not be enforced.[786]

B. Collateral Contracts

164. Sometimes, an oral statement or promise will be held not to be a term of a single contract, but to constitute a separate contract by itself which stands alongside the written contract. The statement or promise is given in consideration of the entry into the written contract. A court is more likely to find an oral statement or promise is a collateral contract when the main contract is of a kind which by law is required to have all its terms in writing. In *Kenneth Williams & Co Ltd v. Thomas,*[787] a prospective purchaser of a section was told there would be 'no state rentals' in the subdivision. That oral assurance was held to be enforceable as a collateral contract. An oral collateral contract will not be found where it would contradict the provisions of the main contract, but as already seen, there have been indications of a liberalization of what amounts to a 'contradiction' for this purpose.[788]

C. Representations and Terms

165. The common law distinction between representations and terms is of greatly reduced importance in New Zealand. Section 35 of the Contract and Commercial Law Act 2017 provides that a misrepresentation which induces a contract is

781. *Walker Property Investments (Brighton) Ltd v. Walker* (1947) 177 LT 204.
782. [1982] 2 NZLR 696.
783. *McKay v. Collins Paper Haulage Ltd* (2007) 7 NZCPR 954, at [7].
784. [2020] NZSC 71, [2020] 1 NZLR 145 at [65].
785. For example *Couchman v. Hill* [1947] KB 554; *Evans v. Andrea Merzario Ltd* [1976] 1 WLR 1078.
786. *Harris v. Harris* (1989) 1 NZ Conv C 190,406.
787. (1990) 1 NZ ConvC 190,583; *see also Helsby v. Oliver* [1999] 1 NZLR 77.
788. *See* para. 164.

redressable in damages as if it were a term which has been broken. Nevertheless, the distinction may still have relevance in a very restricted set of circumstances:

(1) If the statement is a representation, a party claiming damages under section 35 will have to show it induced the contract. If the statement is a contractual term that will not be necessary: its binding force derives not from the inducement but simply from its contractual nature.
(2) An exclusion clause which expressly covers one may be interpreted so as not to cover the other.[789]
(3) If the contract is for the sale of goods, the distinction between term and representation may still be relevant for determining the question of cancellation or rescission for breach. The old rule in *Riddiford v. Warren*[790] provides that if a contract for the sale of goods has been induced by an innocent misrepresentation, there can be rescission only if there has been a total failure of consideration.

II. Implied Terms

166. There are several ways in which terms may be implied in a contract.

A. *Custom*

167. Some trades and professions have developed customs or usages which are known to all who practise in them. A contract may be subject to terms that are sanctioned by such customs, even though they have not been expressly mentioned by the parties. In such a case, 'the parties did not mean to express in writing the whole of the contract by which they intended to be bound, but to contract with reference to those known usages'.[791]

In *Woods v. NJ Ellingham & Co Ltd,*[792] Henry J summarized the criteria for implying a customary term. First, the custom must have acquired such notoriety that the parties must be taken to have known of it and intended it should form part of the contract. Second, the custom must be certain. Third, in addition to being certain, it may be reasonable. If it is 'in high degree unreasonable', this is of weight in considering whether it exists or not. Fourth, until the courts take judicial notice of a custom, it must be proved by clear and convincing evidence. Finally, the custom must not be inconsistent with the express contract.

The principles enunciated in this case were applied by Tipping J in *Everist v. McEvedy.*[793] His Honour held that there can be a custom that one party will not

789. For example *Wilsons (NZ) Portland Cement Ltd v. Gatx-Fuller Australia Pty Ltd (No. 2)* [1985] 2 NZLR 33 at 37.
790. (1901) 20 NZLR 572; *see also Cutelli v. Brian Cotter Motors Ltd* (1993) 5 TCLR 520.
791. *Hutton v. Warren* (1836) 1 M & W 466 at 475 per Parke P.
792. [1977] 1 NZLR 218.
793. [1996] 3 NZLR 348.

exercise rights that the law otherwise gives him or her; he found that it was a custom in New Zealand that a legal practitioner employer would indemnify an employee in terms of his or her vicarious liability. By contrast, in *Forivermor v. ANZ Bank New Zealand Ltd*, the court held that terms of an industry code of practice were not sufficiently 'notorious' to be treated as implied terms of a contract between a bank and a customer.[794]

B. *Statute*

168. Many statutes prescribe that certain terms will be implied in various classes of contract. Part 3 of the Contract and Commercial Law Act 2017, for example, implies conditions and warranties of quality, title, etc., in contracts for the sale of goods, as does the Credit Contracts and Consumer Finance Act 2003 in relation to consumer credit contracts in relation to rights to cancel the contract. Some of these are genuine implied terms in that the parties can exclude them by express argument, but others are more in the nature of mandatory rules of law in that they cannot be excluded: those in the Credit Contracts and Consumer Finance Act are of this latter kind. Some of the most recent consumer protection statutes have abandoned the terminology of implied terms. The Consumer Guarantees Act 1993, for instance, prescribes a set of statutory guarantees whenever a consumer buys goods or contracts for the supply of services; these guarantees are mandatory, and are nowhere described as implied terms.

C. *The Courts*

1. Implied by Law

169. Sometimes, the courts imply a term as a matter of course into all contracts of a particular class. These are often called 'terms implied by law'.

So, if a person contracts to sell land and to build, or to complete the building of, a house upon the land, there is a standard implied term that the house when completed will be reasonably fit for habitation, and that the work remaining to be done will be done in a proper and workmanlike manner.[795]

Likewise, a solicitor impliedly promises his or her client a duty of care;[796] a person hiring goods to another impliedly promises that they are as fit for their purpose as reasonable care and skill can make them;[797] a contract to sell land contains

794. [2014] NZCA 129.
795. *McKey v. Rorison* [1953] NZLR 498; *Miller Construction Ltd v. Olsen* [1973] 1 NZLR 265.
796. *Clark v. Kirby-Smith* [1964] 2 All ER 385.
797. *Fowler v. Lock* (1872) LR 7 CP 272.

implied terms that a reasonable time will be allowed for settlement and that the vendor can deliver good title to the land;[798] an employee impliedly promises the employer to 'serve with good faith and fidelity'.[799]

These terms are implied in all contracts of the relevant class unless they are inconsistent with the parties' express contract.

Most of these terms are well settled, and all the court needs to do is follow established precedent. But sometimes a court has to decide whether a new term of this kind should be created. In such a case, the test applied is whether the proposed term is 'necessary for the reasonable operation of the type of contract concerned', or whether 'the nature of the contract itself implicitly requires' such a term.[800]

2. Implied in Fact

170. In addition to terms thus implied in contracts of a class, the courts will sometimes imply a term into a particular contract in order to repair an intrinsic failure of expression. The New Zealand Court of Appeal has subdivided this sort of implication into two types.[801] '[There] are … terms deduced by implication or interpretation from the express terms of the contract; and terms held to be implied to give business efficacy to the contract.' Even this is probably too simple. It has also been said in the Court of Appeal that implied terms are 'categories or shades in a continuous spectrum' and that 'it may be doubted whether tabulated legalism will ever produce an exhaustive or rigidly discrete classification'.[802]

It is possible to isolate at least three 'categories or shades'.

First, if the contract is informal (even oral) and contains only the bare essentials, the courts will readily enough imply other terms to render it workable. In such cases, '… what the law desires to effect by the implication is to give such business efficacy to the transaction as must have been intended at all events by both parties who are business men'.[803] Thus, in *The Moorcock*,[804] the case from which this quotation was taken, the court implied in a contract to moor a vessel at a wharf an undertaking by the proprietors of the wharf that the river bottom was, as far as reasonable care could provide, in such a condition as not to endanger the vessel.

Second, sometimes in a written contract, one can discover from simply reading it that the parties clearly intended a certain consequence. One is here simply drawing out a meaning implicit in the words themselves. The process can best be described as construction rather than implication:

The conclusion merely involves the consideration of the contract as a whole, and the construction of its language, according to its natural measure, in such a way as

798. *Barrett v. IBC International Ltd* [1995] 3 NZLR 170 and *Armstrong v. Mitchell* [2018] NZHC 2353, at [22], respectively.
799. *Robb v. Green* [1895] 2QB 315.
800. *Liverpool City Council v. Irwin* [1977] AC 239.
801. *Rod Milner Motors Ltd v. Attorney-General* [1999] 2 NZLR 568 at 579.
802. *Vickery v. Waitaki International Ltd* [1992] 2 NZLR 58 at 64.
803. *The Moorcock* (1889) 14 PD 64 at 68 per Bowen LJ.
804. *The Moorcock* (1889) 14 PD 64. *See also Byrne v. Australian Airlines Ltd* (1995) 185 CLR 411.

will best reconcile its provisions one with the other and carry out the intention of the parties as disclosed by the language they have used.[805]

Third, addition unexpressed terms may be able to be added to a written contract, even a *detailed* written contract, if stringent criteria are met. The law in this regard is not entirely settled. For many years, the New Zealand courts approached the implication of terms of this kind by applying the criteria formulated by the Privy Council in *BP Refinery (Westernport) Pty Ltd v. Shire of Hastings* ('*BP Westernport*'):[806]

> In [their Lordships'] view, for a term to be implied, the following conditions (which may overlap) must be satisfied: (1) it must be reasonable and equitable: (2) it must be necessary to give business efficacy to the contract, so that no term will be implied if the contract is effective without it; (3) it must be so obvious that 'it goes without saying'; (4) it must be capable of clear expression; (5) it must not contradict any express term of the contract.

However, some decades later in *Attorney General of Belize v. Belize Telecom Ltd*,[807] ('*Belize Telecom*') the Privy Council took a somewhat different view, holding that the question of implication of a term will only arise where some event has occurred for which the contract has not provided expressly, and in such cases normally the lack of any express provision indicates that the event was not to alter the contractual relationship, so that any loss flowing from the event would lie where it fell. However, this would not always be so. If the court was satisfied that a reasonable person having all the background knowledge which was reasonably available to the parties would think there was a common intention of the parties that the occurrence of the event would affect the rights of the parties in a particular way not inconsistent with the written contract, the court would imply a term to that effect. On that basis, the five points to be proved in the extract cited above were not cumulative requirements but different ways of expressing the same test. The New Zealand Supreme Court cited *Belize Telecom* with approval in one case[808] but later noted that there was some doubt whether that approach should be applied in an 'undiluted' form.[809]

The question accordingly was addressed again in *Bathurst Resources Ltd v. L & M Coal Holdings Ltd*,[810] where Winkelmann CJ and Ellen France J set out six 'principal points' governing the implications of terms into contracts:

---

805. *Brodie v. Cardiff Corporation* [1919] AC 337 at 358–359 per Lord Atkinson.
806. *BP Refinery (Westernport) Pty Ltd v. Shire of Hastings* (1977) 16 ALR 363 at 376.
807. *Attorney General of Belize v. Belize Telecom Ltd* [2009] UKPC 11, [2009] 1 WLR 1988, at [16]–[27].
808. *Nielsen v. Dysart Timbers Ltd* [2009] 3 NZLR 160, [2009] NZSC 43, at [25] and footnote 12.
809. *Mobil Oil NZ Ltd v. Development Auckland Ltd* [2016] NZSC 89 at [81], citing comments made by members of the United Kingdom Supreme Court in *Marks & Spencer plc v. BNP Paribas Securities Services Trust Co (Jersey) Ltd* [2015] UKSC 72, [2016] AC 742. The Court of Appeal has applied the *BP Refinery (Westernport)* test without treating the issue as settled: *The Malthouse Ltd v. Rangatira Ltd* [2018] NZCA 621, at [59].
810. [2021] NZSC 85, [2021] 1 NZLR 696 at [106]–[117], [232].

(i) The legal test for the implication of a term is a standard of strict necessity, a high hurdle to overcome.

(ii) The starting point is the words of the contract. If a contract does not provide for an eventuality, the usual inference is that no contractual provision was made for it.

(iii) While the task of implication only begins when the court finds that the text of the contract does not provide for the eventuality, the implication of a term is nevertheless part of the construction of the written contract as a whole. An unexpressed term can only be implied if the court finds that the term would spell out what the contract, read against the relevant background, must be understood to mean.

(iv) As with the task of interpreting a contract, the enquiry for the court when considering the implication of a term is an objective enquiry – it is the understanding of the notional reasonable person with all of the background knowledge reasonably available to the parties at the time of contract that is the focus of this assessment. The court is tasked with the role of constructing the understanding of that reasonable person.

(v) Thus, the implication of a term does not depend upon proof of the parties' actual intentions, nor does it require the court to speculate on how the actual parties would have wanted the contract to regulate the eventuality if confronted with it prior to contracting.

(vi) The *BP Refinery* conditions are a useful tool to test whether the proposed implied term is strictly necessary to spell out what the contract, read against the relevant background, must be understood to mean. While conditions (4) and (5) must always be met before a term will be implied, conditions (1)–(3) can be viewed as analytical tools which overlap and are not cumulative. The business efficacy and the 'so obvious that "it goes without saying"' conditions are both ways, useful in their own right, of testing whether the implication of a term is strictly necessary to give effect to what the contract, objectively interpreted by the court, must be understood to mean.

Their Honours saw this approach to the implication of terms as aligning with the objective theory of contractual interpretation. It promoted the primacy of the words of the contract while also seeking to reach a complete understanding of what the contract, read against the relevant background, should be understood to mean. By excluding speculation as to how the actual parties would have wanted the contract to regulate an unforeseen eventuality, this approach treated as irrelevant (and unreliable) any evidence of subjective intent, given with the benefit of hindsight. It thereby promoted the efficient and just conduct of proceedings.

III. Exclusion Clauses

A. *Introduction*

171. A term in a contract may seek to exclude or limit any liabilities which might otherwise arise if there is a breach of, or a failure to perform, the contract. A term of this kind can take various forms. It may, for example, deny that a promise was made, or deny responsibility for a promise, or exclude all or some part of a potential liability for breach of the promise, or limit the damage payable for such breach, or limit the time for making any claim. Our concern is with the impact of all such clauses.

The issues which are raised by the use and operation of exclusion clauses overlap with those caused by two other emergent themes of modern contract law, the increased use of standard form contracts and the development of special rules for the protection of consumers. Exclusion clauses often are contained in standard form contracts made between a business and a private person in circumstances where any element of genuine bargaining between the parties as to the terms of the contract is likely to be absent. The courts have sought to alleviate the harsh or unjust consequences that can follow if exclusion clauses are left to operate without any controls or fetters, but this common law protection is of very limited scope. Certainly, the courts have found it difficult to develop doctrines that can be applied equally appropriately to both consumer and commercial transactions, giving a measure of protection to the private person yet not interfering unduly with freedom of contract or the commercial expectations of the parties. However, as will be explained, Parliament has stepped in to alleviate possible hardship in consumer-related cases. So, the common law is now only of real significance in commercial cases where statute does not apply. Accordingly, the significance of the discussion of the common law principles which follows is confined primarily to non-consumer cases.

B. Incorporation into the Contract

172. An exclusion clause must have been incorporated into a contract in order for it to have contractual force. A document relied on as containing an exclusion clause must have been intended as a contractual document and not as a mere acknowledgement of payment or as having some other purpose.[811]

Where a contractual document containing an exclusion clause is signed by a party, then the view in England and Australia is that that party is bound even if he or she did not read the document,[812] unless the effect of signing is nullified by fraud,[813] or misrepresentation.[814] But authority in Canada holds that whether an exclusion clause is part of a contract turns on the rules about notice, to be considered below, irrespective of whether the contract has been signed.[815] As for the position in New Zealand, in *Nalder & Biddle (Nelson) Ltd v. C & F Fishing Ltd*,[816] the Court of Appeal said about *Toll* that it restated the well-settled principle that the

811. *Holmes v. Burgess* [1975] 2 NZLR 311; *Vance v. Huhtamaki New Zealand Ltd* [2011] NZCA 602.
812. *L'Estrange v. Graucob* [1934] 2 KB 394 and *Toll (FGCT) Pty Ltd v. Alphapharm Pty Ltd* (2005) 219 CLR 165 respectively.
813. *HIH Casualty and General Insurance Ltd v. Chase Manhattan Bank* [2003] 1 All ER (Comm) 349. *See also Dodds v. Southern Response Earthquake Services Ltd* [2019] NZHC 2016, [2019] 3 NZLR 826 at [194]–[198].
814. *Curtis v. Chemical Cleaning & Dyeing Co* [1951] 1 KB 805.
815. *Crocker v. Sundance Northwest Resorts Ltd* (1989) 51 DLR (4th) 321.
816. [2007] 1 NZLR 721.

meaning of a contract is to be construed objectively, not according to the parties' subjective views. But the decision did not assist on the instant facts, where certain signed documents (job cards signifying approval to start the work described on the cards, some containing limiting terms) were not themselves contractual documents. So the case does not authoritatively determine the matter. However, the *Toll* rule has been accepted in the Court of Appeal in *BBX Financial Solutions Pty Ltd v. Wallace*[817] and in decisions at first instance.[818]

An exclusion clause may be incorporated into a contract by giving reasonable notice of its existence to the party adversely affected by it. This may be done orally, but normally, it will be by giving a document or putting up a sign stating liability is excluded. The notice must be given before or at the time of making the contract. A belated notice is of no effect.[819] In addition, the steps taken to bring the notice to the attention of the other party must be reasonably sufficient in all the circumstances.[820] Ultimately this is a question of fact. It is relevant to take into account such factors as the size and prominence of the clause or notice, its position in relation to other clauses or words, and whether it has specifically been brought to the attention of the other contracting party. It may be sufficient to refer to a clause contained in another document.[821] And notice can be inferred from a previous consistent course of dealing between the parties.[822] If a clause is unusual, unexpected or of especially far-reaching effect, a higher degree of notice may be required.[823] But in all cases, as with signed documents, it is not necessary that the party affected should have actually read and understood the clause.[824]

In the case of online contracts, purchasers may be required to click that they are accepting the terms before they can proceed. It is likely that this will constitute adequate notice so that the purchaser is bound by the terms.[825]

---

817. [2011] NZCA 667.
818. *Nightingale v. Barfoot & Thompson Ltd* HC, Auckland, Venning J, CIV 2009-404-4073, 22 Oct. 2009; *George Grant Engineering Ltd v. Fabrication and Pipe Services Ltd* [2021] NZHC 1281 at [49].
819. *Olley v. Marlborough Court Ltd* [1949] 1 KB 532; *Thornton v. Shoe Lane Parking Ltd* [1971] 2 QB 163.
820. *Harvey v. Ascot Dry Cleaning Co Ltd* [1953] NZLR 549.
821. *Thompson v. LM and S Railway* [1930] 1 KB 41.
822. *Henry Kendall and Sons v. William Lillico and Sons Ltd* [1969] 2 AC 31; compare *Engineering Dynamics Ltd v. Norgren Matonair (NZ) Ltd* unreported, CA 105/96, 29 Oct. 1996; *Steel Co Ltd v. Pipes NZ Ltd* [2015] NZCA 175.
823. *J Spurling Ltd v. Bradshaw* [1956] 1 WLR 461; *Interfoto Picture Library Ltd v. Stiletto Visual Programmes Ltd* [1989] QB 433.
824. Even where there is no contract between disputing parties, a potential liability in tort for negligence may similarly be excluded by a non-contractual notice: *Hedley Byrne & Co Ltd v. Heller & Partners Ltd* [1964] AC 465 (HL); *Rolls-Royce New Zealand Ltd v. Carter Holt Harvey Ltd* [2005] 1 NZLR 324 (CA); *Taberna Europe CDO II plc v. Selskapet AF1* [2016] EWCA Civ 1262, [2017] 2 WLR 803. *See* generally *Todd on Torts* paras [4.8.8], [20.5.2] (9th ed, 2023).
825. *Feldman v. Google Inc* 513 F Supp 2d 229 (ED Pa 2007).

C. Interpretation

173. Inequalities of bargaining power between contracting parties can allow the stronger party to impose an exclusion clause on the weaker. So, the courts have sought to provide a measure of protection from the operation of harsh exclusion clauses by adopting a rule of strict construction. If there is any doubt as to the meaning and scope of the excluding or limiting term, the ambiguity will be resolved against the party who had inserted it and who is now relying on it. This is known as the rule of construction *contra proferentem.* The onus is on the person seeking the protection of the clause to show that the words clearly and aptly describe the contingency that has in fact arisen.[826] The relationship between this rule of strict construction and the ordinary approach towards the construction of contracts, where the court seeks to ascertain the meaning of contractual provisions in accordance with the true intention of the parties,[827] is somewhat mysterious. Several recent cases show a degree of tension between the two approaches.[828] Indeed, in *Ledcor Construction Ltd v. Northbridge Indemnity Insurance Co,*[829] the Supreme Court of Canada (SCC) looked simply to the intention of the parties in determining the meaning of an ambiguous exclusion clause.

The strict approach retains vitality in New Zealand, although the need for it has been alleviated in cases governed by consumer legislation.[830] In commercial cases, moreover, the courts are not astute to upset clauses which represent a negotiated allocation of risk between the parties.[831] They have also emphasized that clauses should not be given unrealistic, strained and tortured meanings.[832] While exclusion clauses are to be narrowly construed, a court should adopt an interpretation that correlates with the presumed mutual intention of the parties.[833]

There is no call to rely on the *contra proferentem* rule if the words in their ordinary meaning do not cover the events which have happened.[834] For example, a clause disclaiming liability in respect of 'goods delivered' did not apply where there was delivery of a short quantity, for the complaint was of goods *not* delivered:[835] and a clause which excluded liability for loss arising out of any defect 'in the said

826. *Ailsa Craig Fishing Co Ltd v. Malvern Fishing Co Ltd* [1983] 1 All ER 101; *DHL International (NZ) Ltd v. Richmond Ltd* [1993] 3 NZLR 10; *Vance v. Huhtamaki New Zealand Ltd* [2011] NZCA 602; *Nobahar-Cookson v. The Hut Group Ltd* [2016] EWCA Civ 128.
827. *Vector Gas Ltd v. Bay of Plenty Energy Ltd* [2010] 2 NZLR 444.
828. For example, *DA Constable Syndicate v. Auckland District Law Society* [2010] 3 NZLR 23; *i-Health Ltd v. iSoft NZ Ltd* [2012] 1 NZLR 379, at [45]; *Dorchester Finance Ltd v. Deloitte* [2012] NZAR 226 at [33].
829. [2016] SCC 37.
830. *See* paras 176–181.
831. *Photo Production Ltd v. Securicor Transport Ltd* [1980] AC 827; *DHL International (NZ) Ltd v. Richmond Ltd* [1993] 3 NZLR 10; *Arrow International Ltd v. QBE Insurance (International) Ltd* [2009] 3 NZLR 650, at [73]; *Taberna Europe CDO II plc v. Selskapet AF1* [2016] EWCA Civ 1262, [2017] 2 WLR 803, at [24].
832. *George Mitchell Ltd v. Finney Lock Seeds Ltd* [1983] 2 AC 803; *Lumley General Insurance (NZ) Ltd v. Body Corporate No 205963* [2010] NZCA 316, at [27].
833. *Trustees Executors Ltd v. QBE Insurance (International) Ltd* [2010] NZCA 608, at [40]; but *see The Mercini Lady* [2010] EWCA Civ 1145.
834. *Lumley General Insurance (NZ) Ltd v. Body Corporate No 205963* [2010] NZCA 316, at [31].
835. *Beck & Co v. Szymanowski* [1924] AC 43.

[contract goods]' referred to the goods as described in the contract and did not apply to goods not within the contractual specification.[836] The line between determining an ordinary meaning and giving a strict construction to an ambiguous meaning frequently is blurred, and certainly if more than one interpretation is reasonably open, then construing the words *contra proferentem* can justify choosing the narrower meaning.[837]

One application of the *contra proferentem* rule is seen in the requirement that clear words must be used before a party will be held to be exempt from liability in negligence.[838] For example, where a clause in a contract for processing meat at a freezing works stated that 'the wool, meat and skins are uninsured and are held at the owner's risk', it was held that these words simply gave notice to the owner that the meat was held at the owner's risk in respect of accidental loss or damage and did not prevent the owner suing the processor in negligence.[839] However, it is not necessary for the word 'negligence' to be mentioned expressly if the defendant makes it clear that the exemption is from any conceivable liability.[840] So it could not be inferred that a clause which referred to 'no liability of any kind whatsoever' really meant 'no liability of any kind whatsoever other than a claim in negligence'.[841] Again, a notice which stated 'All Care Taken – No Responsibility' was held to convey 'the very antithesis of acceptance of a legal obligation to take care'.[842]

Some types of clauses may be construed more strictly than others. It has been held in England that a clause limiting rather than excluding liability should be clearly and unambiguously expressed and construed *contra proferentem* but was not to be construed as rigidly and strictly as an exclusion clause since a limitation clause was more likely to accord with the true intention of the parties.[843] In New Zealand, Cooke P, in like vein, observed that a court should be especially slow to interpret a clause as in effect totally negating contractual liability.[844] But his Honour also was attracted by the view of the High Court of Australia (HCA)[845] that a clause ostensibly of limitation but in effect of virtual exclusion should be approached for what it really is.

D. Fundamental Breach of Contract

174. In certain special cases, the courts go beyond questions of interpretation and recognize that exclusion clauses may be ineffective as a matter of law. It is well

836. *MacDonald v. NZ Forestry Corporation Ltd* (High Court, Christchurch CP 220/88, 28 Jun. 1989).
837. *H C Senior & Co Ltd v. Body Corporate 52655* unreported, CA 175/90, 27 Sep. 1991.
838. *AM Bisley and Co Ltd v. Thompson* [1982] 2 NZLR 696; *Hepburn v. Cunningham Contracts Ltd* [2013] NZHC 210 at [83].
839. *Producer Meats Ltd v. Thomas Borthwick and Sons Ltd* [1964] NZLR 700.
840. *George Mitchell Ltd v. Finney Lock Seeds Ltd* [1983] 2 AC 803.
841. *Kaniere Gold Dredging Ltd v. Dunedin Engineering and Steel Co Ltd* (1985) 1 NZBLC 102,223.
842. *Shipbuilders Ltd v. Benson* [1993] 3 NZLR 549; cp *Livingstone v. Roskilly* [1992] 3 NZLR 230.
843. *Ailsa Craig Fishing Co Ltd v. Malvern Fishing Co Ltd* [1983] 1 All ER 101.
844. *SGS (NZ) Ltd v. Quirke Export Ltd* [1988] 1 NZLR 52.
845. In *Darlington Futures Ltd v. Delco Australia Pty Ltd* (1986) 161 CLR 500.

established that a shipowner who deviates from the agreed or usual route thereby loses the benefit of an exemption clause in the contract of carriage.[846] A bailee who stores goods in a place other than agreed or who without authority parts with possession of the goods similarly is unable to rely on such a clause.[847] The shipowner or bailee is regarded as having performed something fundamentally different from that which was agreed, and as having thereby 'stepped out of the contract'.

These 'deviation' cases probably should be considered as a body of authority sui generis, with special rules derived from historical and commercial reasons.[848] However, they underlay the development in England of the so-called doctrine of fundamental breach of contract, which held that no excluding or limiting term could operate to protect a party whose breach was so serious as to be termed 'fundamental'. The doctrine was largely the creation of the English Court of Appeal,[849] but it was consistently rejected by the House of Lords. In particular, in *Suisse Atlantique*,[850] the Lords laid down that there was no blanket rule that an exclusion clause would not apply in the case of a fundamental breach of contract. It was simply a matter of construction of the contract, and an appropriately worded clause could cover such a breach. And in *Photo Production Ltd v. Securicor Transport Ltd*,[851] following attempts by the Court of Appeal to resurrect the doctrine in the guise of a rule of construction,[852] Lord Wilberforce affirmed that the question of whether, and to what extent, an exclusion clause is to be applied to a fundamental breach, or a breach of a fundamental term, or indeed to any breach of contract, is a matter of construction of the contract. In this case, the defendants' security patrolman lit a fire in the plaintiff's factory, which burned to the ground. The defendants relied on a clause in the contract for their security service which exempted them from liability for unforeseeable conduct by their employees. Their Lordships were satisfied that the wording of the clause was clear and unambiguous and perfectly adequate to cover the defendants' position. There was certainly no adequate reason why the court should interfere with the parties' negotiated allocation of the risk.

The New Zealand Court of Appeal has confirmed that the application of an exclusion clause to a 'fundamental' breach of contract is a question of construction of the contract. In *DHL International (NZ) Ltd v. Richmond Ltd*,[853] a carrier contracted with a seller of goods to deliver shipping documents to a bank, and limited its liability to NZD 100. It was held that the carriers could rely on the limitation clause in defence of a claim alleging misdelivery of the documents. Richardson J said that in international commercial arrangements of this kind, it would be unsafe to regard standard terms and limitation provisions as somehow suspect and so give them a strained construction to protect the shipper. The limiting terms were unqualified and clearly expressed. To read down the unqualified breadth of the exclusion clause

846. *Joseph Thorley Ltd v. Orchis SS Co Ltd* [1907] 1 KB 660.
847. *Lilley v. Doubleday* (1881) 7 QBD 510.
848. *Photo Production Ltd v. Securicor Transport Ltd* [1980] AC 827 at 845.
849. *See* for example *Alexander v. Railway Executive* [1951] 2 KB 882; *Karsales (Harrow) Ltd v. Wallis* [1956] 2 All ER 866.
850. [1967] 1 AC 361.
851. [1980] AC 827.
852. *See* especially *Harbutt's Plasticine Ltd v. Wayne Tank and Pump Co Ltd* [1970] 1 QB 447.
853. [1993] 3 NZLR 10.

would involve rewriting the contract and transferring to the defendant what was properly a commercial risk accepted by the plaintiff.

There can be little doubt that the application of an exclusion clause to the facts of a particular case is a question of construction. However, it remains possible for general words of exclusion to be construed as not to cover a serious or 'fundamental' breach. The more serious the breach of contract, or the more important the term, the less likely it may be for the parties to the contract to have intended an exclusion clause to apply.[854] Further, such a clause cannot absolve a party from total non-performance or totally different performance of the contract. Suppose, for example, a contract is to sell beans, and peas are delivered and the contract contains an exclusion clause so widely drafted as to cover even such gross misperformance. In *Suisse Atlantique,* Lord Reid suggested that a court might refuse to give effect to a clause if it would 'lead to an absurdity' or 'defeat the main object of the contract'. Lord Wilberforce thought likewise if it would 'deprive one party's stipulation of all contractual force' and 'reduce the contract to a mere declaration of intent'. In *Photo Productions*, Lord Diplock confirmed that the agreement must 'retain the legal characteristics of a contract'. It is clear, then, that ultimately there are limits to the efficacy of wide-ranging clauses, for they cannot be used to avoid coming under any contractual obligations at all.

The preceding discussion demonstrates that the notion of fundamental breach is outmoded. Yet the underlying policy involved in determining how far to take the notion of freedom of contract remains a matter for debate. In *Tercon Contractors Ltd v. British Columbia (Ministry of Transport and Highways)*,[855] the SCC held that a court may need to ask whether an overriding public policy could justify a refusal to enforce the terms of a contract.[856]

E. Statutory Control

175. The application of common law principles to control exclusion clauses has diminished in importance in the light of various statutory interventions in the field. There has been no all-embracing reform, but in their totality, the relevant statutes go a substantial way along a path towards a general legislative control of exclusion clauses.

It is not possible to contract out of the terms of a number of statutes governing the operation of certain particular types of contracts. Examples are the Insurance Law Reform Act 1977 and the Credit Contracts and Consumer Finance Act 2003.[857] Other statutes are of wider significance. The most significant of these are set out below.

---

854. Compare *Clark v. Rural Livestock Ltd* [2019] NZHC 671 with *George Grant Engineering Ltd v. Fabrication and Pipe Services Ltd* [2021] NZHC 1281.

855. [2010] 1 SCR 69.

856. A possible example is *HIH Casualty and General Insurance Ltd v. Chase Manhattan Bank* [2003] 1 All ER (Comm) 349 (contracting party cannot exclude liability for his or her own fraud).

857. Insurance Law Reform Act 1977, s. 15; Credit Contracts and Consumer Finance Act 2003, s. 135.

1. Disputes Tribunal Act 1988

176. Disputes Tribunals have jurisdiction to hear claims in contract, quasi-contract or for property damage in tort for sums up to NZD 30,000.[858] Tribunals are required to determine a dispute according to the substantial merits and justice of the case and in doing so must have regard to the law, but they are not bound to give effect to strict legal rights or obligations.[859] In particular, they may disregard any limiting or excluding provisions in an agreement or document bearing upon the dispute between the parties.[860] So in the case of relatively small disputes, exclusion clauses may be held to be of no effect.

2. Contract and Commercial Law Act 2017, Section 50

177. A special statutory regime applies in the case of statements made in the course of pre-contract negotiations. Broadly, where a provision in a contract denies that any pre-contract representations were made, or that they were terms of the contract, or that they were relied on by the other party, a court is not precluded by any such provision from enquiring into the truth of the matter and from determining whether it is fair and reasonable to treat the clause as conclusive between the parties.[861] In the case of a contract between commercial parties, each with separate legal advice, the court is likely to uphold the conclusiveness of a provision of this kind, at least in the absence of any fraud.[862] But where there has been a deliberate misrepresentation, or one party is peculiarly in possession of relevant facts, or there is a disparity of bargaining power, the court is more likely to set the clause aside.[863]

3. Fair Trading Act 1986

178. Persons who suffer loss or damage caused by conduct in breach of the Fair Trading Act 1986 may institute civil proceedings for the amount of the loss or damage.[864] It is not generally possible to contract out of the operation of the Act. Section 5C(1) provides that the provisions of the Act have effect despite anything to the contrary in any agreement. Again, by section 5C(2), a provision in an agreement that has the effect of overriding a provision of the Act (whether directly or indirectly) is

858. Disputes Tribunal Act 1988, s. 10.
859. Disputes Tribunal Act 1988, s. 18(6).
860. *Ibid.*, s. 18(7).
861. Contract and Commercial Law Act 2017, s. 50 (formerly Contractual Remedies Act 1979, s. 4(1)). In *ANZ Bank New Zealand Ltd v. Bushline Trustees Ltd* [2020] NZSC 71, [2020] 1 NZLR 145 at [132], O'Regan J said that s. 50 did not mandate a general empowerment to determine the 'true bargain' between the parties.
862. For example, *Herbison v. Papakura Video Ltd* [1987] 2 NZLR 527; *Brownlie v. Shotover Mining Ltd* unreported, CA 187/87, 21 Feb. 1992; *PAE (New Zealand) Ltd v. Brosnahan* (2009) 10 TCLR 626.
863. For example, *M E Torbett Ltd v. Keirlor Motels Ltd* (1984) 1 NZBLC 102,079; *Snodgrass v. Hammington* (1995) 10 PRNZ 672.
864. Fair Trading Act 1986, s. 43(3)(f). For the ambit of the Act *see* paras 109–118.

unenforceable. However, there is a limited exception to these rules in section 5D, which allows parties in trade to contract out of the provisions concerning misleading or deceptive conduct in sections 9–14, provided that the agreement is in writing and it is fair and reasonable that they be bound by the excluding provision.

The words of the Act are mandatory, and so, quite apart from section 5C, any term in a contract purporting to contract out of the provisions of the Act can be of no effect. A court cannot allow anyone simply to opt out of a statute decreeing fair trading in the public interest.[865]

It is possible for a disclaimer to negative the otherwise misleading effect of a statement, so the defendant's overall conduct then is not misleading at all.[866] In *Body Corporate 202254 v. Taylor*,[867] certain brochures prepared by the vendor, and distributed by the selling agents, of a leaky building development contained statements about the quality of the building that were arguably misleading and deceptive, and also contained a disclaimer stating that neither the vendor nor the vendor's agent warranted the correctness of the information. The Court of Appeal accepted that an appropriately worded disclaimer might be material to the nature of the alleged misleading and deceptive conduct. So if it was made clear that the agent was merely acting as a conduit, then a court would likely conclude that the agent's conduct was not itself misleading. But the present case was well removed from the conduit line of cases. In particular, it seemed likely that most or all of the information came from the vendor, so he could not sensibly be regarded as a conduit.

4. Unfair Terms in Consumer Contracts

179. By amendment made in 2013, the Fair Trading Act 1986 now makes provision for a court, on the application of the Commerce Commission, to declare that a term in a standard form consumer contract is an unfair contract term.[868] On such an application being made, the court may make the declaration if satisfied, *inter alia*, that the term is in a 'consumer contract', the contract is a 'standard form contract', and the term is relevantly 'unfair'.[869]

'Consumer' has the same meaning as in the Consumer Guarantees Act 1993, that is, a person who acquires from a supplier goods or services of a kind ordinarily acquired for personal, domestic, or household use or consumption, and not for the purpose of resupplying them in trade, or consuming them in the course of a process of production or manufacture, or, in the case of goods, repairing or treating in trade other goods or fixtures on land.[870] A court may determine that any contract in which the terms have not been subject to effective negotiation between the parties is a

865. *Smythe v. Bayley's Real Estate Ltd* (1993) 5 TCLR 454.
866. *Butcher v. Lachlan Elder Realty Ltd* (2005) 79 ALJR 308, where a real estate agent passed on information supplied by another and disclaimed any guarantee as to its accuracy.
867. [2009] 2 NZLR 17; *and see David v. TFAC Ltd* [2009] 2 NZLR 239; *PAE (New Zealand) Ltd v. Brosnahan* (2009) 10 TCLR 626.
868. Fair Trading Act 1986, s. 46H.
869. *Ibid.*, s. 46I(2).
870. *Ibid.*, s. 2(1).

'standard form contract'.[871] In judging this question, various factors directed primarily at aspects of the parties' bargaining power must be taken into account.[872] And finally, there is the question of whether the term is 'unfair'. The core definition requires that the court be satisfied that the term: (a) would cause a significant imbalance in the parties' rights and obligations arising under the contract; (b) is not reasonably necessary in order to protect the legitimate interests of the party who would be advantaged by the term; and (c) would cause detriment (whether financial or otherwise) to a party if it were applied, enforced, or relied on.[873] The court may take into account any matters it thinks relevant, and must take into account: (a) the extent to which the term is transparent; and (b) the contract as a whole. Further guidance is provided by a list of non-limiting examples of terms that may be unfair.[874] These include various forms of exclusion clauses.

If a court has declared that a term in a consumer contract is an unfair contract term, a person must not include that unfair contract term in a standard form contract or apply, enforce or rely on the unfair contract term, and the term cannot be enforced against the consumer.[875] Furthermore, by contravening this requirement, the trader will have committed an offence under Part 1 of the Fair Trading Act and will be subject to the ordinary regime concerning enforcement of the Act and remedies for its breach.

5. Consumer Guarantees Act 1993

180. The Consumer Guarantees Act 1993 provides for an extended regime of rights and remedies in circumstances where goods or services are supplied in trade to consumers.[876] And subject to certain exceptions, the provisions of the Act have effect notwithstanding any provision to the contrary in any agreement.[877] So there is now a general legislative control on exclusion clauses in consumer cases where the plaintiff seeks to rely on one of the statutory guarantees. The Act does not apply, and the common law rules can still operate, in the case of sales of non-consumer goods or services, or sales between businesses, or purely private agreements.

IV. Penalty Clauses

181. The parties to a contract may agree beforehand what sum shall be payable by way of liquidated damages in the event of breach. A provision of this kind may be advantageous to both parties, for it enables them to envisage the financial consequences of a breach and to avoid the difficulty and the costs of proving what loss

871. *Ibid.*, s. 46J(1).
872. *Ibid.*, s. 46J(2).
873. *Ibid.*, s. 46L.
874. *Ibid.*, s. 46M.
875. *Ibid.*, s. 26A.
876. *See* Part II, Specific Contracts, Ch. 5.
877. Consumer Guarantees Act 1993, s. 43(1).

has in fact been suffered by the innocent party.[878] However, it cannot be used in effect as a means of forcing the offending party to perform the contract. If the clause is in the nature of a threat held over the other party *in terrorem* – a security to the promisee that the contract will be performed – the sum in question is called a penalty and is unenforceable. In such a case, the promisee is entitled to be indemnified only for his or her actual loss.

A test for determining whether a clause fixing the damages in the event of breach was valid as a liquidated damages clause or unenforceable as a penalty was laid down by Lord Dunedin in *Dunlop Pneumatic Tyre Co Ltd v. New Garage and Motor Co Ltd.*[879] His Lordship stated here a number of propositions drawn from the cases which turned ultimately on the question of whether the clause could be seen as a genuine pre-estimate of the loss that would be caused to one party if the contract was broken by the other. The *Dunlop* rules formerly were highly influential in common law countries, and certainly in New Zealand,[880] but a major reassessment came with the decision of the UK Supreme Court in *Cavendish Square Holding BV v. Makdessi*,[881] where a different test was propounded. A provision was penal if it was a secondary obligation by way of a remedy for a breach which imposed a detriment on the contract-breaker which was out of all proportion to any legitimate interest of the innocent party in the enforcement of the primary obligation to perform the contractual obligation. The rule could apply not only to provisions requiring the payment of money on breach of contract but also to clauses providing for the withholding of payments or the transfer of property. But the fact that a provision did not provide for a pre-estimate of loss, or that it was deterrent, did not necessarily mean that it was penal since the legitimate interest of the innocent party might extend well beyond the recovery of compensation for his loss.

The agreement in this case concerned the sale of an advertising and marketing company for up to USD 147 million, depending on a calculation of profits in instalments and with a large amount reflecting goodwill. It provided in particular that for a period after the sale the defendant was not to compete with his old business and that, if he did, he would not be entitled to any further payments and the claimant would acquire an option to purchase his remaining shares at a price which disregarded goodwill. The defendant did in fact breach the non-competition provisions, but claimed they were penal and unenforceable. The court recognized that the relevant provisions had no relationship with the measure of loss attributable to the breach, but the claimant had a legitimate interest in the observance of the provisions which extended beyond the recovery of that loss since the goodwill of the business was critical to its value and the loyalty of the defendant was critical to that goodwill. In all the circumstances, it was right to conclude that the non-competition clauses were enforceable.

---

878. *Robophone Facilities Ltd v. Blank* [1966] 1 WLR 1428 at 1447 per Diplock LJ.
879. [1915] AC 79.
880. See *Amaltal Corp Ltd v. Maruha (NZ) Corp Ltd* [2004] 2 NZLR 614 at 630 (CA), referring to the 'classic statement' of Lord Dunedin in *Dunlop*.
881. [2015] UKSC 67, [2016] AC 1172.

In *ParkingEye Ltd v. Beavis*, a second case decided together with *Cavendish Square*, a driver who left his car in a car park beyond the time limit stated in prominent notices in the park was obliged to pay the sum of GBP 85 stipulated in the notices. Their Lordships recognized that both parties had a legitimate interest in the efficient use of the parking spaces for the benefit of users of the shopping centre, which interest could only be served by deterring drivers from occupying parking spaces for long periods of time. Since the charge was no greater than was necessary to achieve that result and was not unreasonable, the charge was not a penalty at common law.

In *127 Hobson Street Ltd v. Honey Bees Preschool Ltd*,[882] the Supreme Court accepted that *Cavendish Square* provided a more flexible and permissive test than that in *Dunlop* and that it should apply in New Zealand. Winkelmann CJ said that its features could be found in the following propositions.[883]

(i) A clause stipulating a consequence for breach of a term of the contract will be an unenforceable penalty if the consequence is out of all proportion to the legitimate interests of the innocent party in performance of the primary obligation.
(ii) Determining whether or not the impugned clause is an unenforceable penalty requires an objective exercise of construction, notionally undertaken at the time of contract formation, and by reference to the terms and circumstances of the contract.
(iii) A contractual clause which provides for consequences on breach may provide for consequences designed to protect the legitimate interests of the party in performance of the primary contractual term which has been breached.
(iv) A party's legitimate interests may extend beyond the loss caused by the breach as conventionally measured, and extend to the impact of non-performance on the broader commercial interests of the parties.
(v) While legitimate interests will not include objectives unrelated to the performance interest, such as punishment, deterring breach can be a legitimate objective of a clause.
(vi) The bargaining power of the parties will be relevant to the courts' enquiry as to the nature and extent of the innocent party's interest in performance of the primary obligation. The fact that a party was legally advised as to the nature and effect of the transaction will also weigh in favour of upholding the bargain.
(vii) It is not necessary in all cases for the court to assess the damages that would have been awarded at common law for breach, but there may be cases where such calculation is the measure of the performance interest. That is likely where the impugned clause purports to provide a pre-estimate of damage.

In the case at hand, a term of a lease of a commercial building required the lessor to instal a second lift, and a collateral deed provided that if the lift was not fully

882. [2020] NZSC 53, [2020] 1 NZLR 179; and *see also Wilaci Pty Ltd v. Torchlight Fund No 1 LP* [2017] NZCA 152.
883. *Ibid.*, at [91].

operational by a specified date, the lessor was required to indemnify the lessee, by giving relief against the obligation to pay rent and outgoings from the date of default to the expiry of the initial term of the lease. The lift was not installed by that date, and the lessee sought to enforce the indemnity. It was held that the clause did not offend against the penalty rule and was enforceable. Honey Bees wanted the second lift because of the impact the limited existing access would have on the development of its new business. A single lift could involve lengthy wait times for children and parents in competition with other users of a busy high-rise building. While there was no attempt to secure proportionality between the extent of the delay and the consequence, the lessor had been given ample opportunity to comply with the obligation before the due date. Further, the lessor had insisted that the obligation to complete the installation was contained in a collateral document rather than in a covenant in the lease, and this was disadvantageous to Honey Bees. Its rights under the collateral deed did not include a right to cancel the lease, and it would have to enforce the indemnity while its obligation to pay rent continued, exposing it to unmatched timing and credit risks. Accordingly, the consequences of the indemnity clause being triggered were not out of all proportion to Honey Bees' legitimate interests in performance.

Another example of the operation of the rules as to penalties is where a party in breach of contract seeks to recover a deposit. The provision for the payment by the purchaser of land of a reasonable amount as a deposit, to be forfeited if the party fails to complete, is not an unlawful penalty provided that, viewed objectively, it operates as an earnest for the performance of the contract. So a conventional deposit of 10% on the purchase price of land was payable in full on the purchaser's default.[884] But a vendor could not retain a deposit of 25% where it had failed to show that the greater sum was to encourage performance of the contract or that it should be regarded as reasonable in the circumstances.[885]

Sometimes, a defendant's breach, say, in supplying defective goods, causes a plaintiff to breach a contract by failing to supply the goods to another party within the agreed time or at all. Whether such consequential loss will be recoverable from the defendant will depend on the defendant's knowledge of the second contract and the reasonably contemplated consequences of its breach.[886] Suppose now that the plaintiff is liable to pay liquidated damages fixed by the second contract to the other party. The Court of Appeal has said that there was force in the submission that if party A sought to recover damages from party B equating to the liquidated damages party A had paid to a third party C, then party A had to prove the reasonableness of the damages it had paid.[887]

In *Andrews v. Australia & New Zealand Banking Group Ltd*,[888] the HCA held that the rule against contractual penalties could apply even though the triggering event was not a breach of contract. But in *Cavendish Square*, the UK Supreme Court declined to follow this decision. Rather, it affirmed the earlier decision of the House

884. *Garratt v. Ikeda* [2002] 1 NZLR 577.
885. *Workers Trust & Merchant Bank Ltd v. Dojap Investments Ltd* [1993] AC 573.
886. *Steel Co Ltd v. Pipes NZ Ltd* [2015] NZCA 175 at [76], [77]; *see* para. 244 below.
887. *Ibid.*, at [81], although the question was not finally decided.
888. [2012] HCA 30; and *see also Paciocco v. Australia and New Zealand Banking Group Ltd* [2016] HCA 28, which in other respects is consistent with *Cavendish Square*.

of Lords in *Export Credits Guarantee Department v. Universal Oil Products Co*[889] and held that the penalties rule should not be extended to cover clauses which imposed onerous obligations on a party on contingencies which did not involve a breach of contract. Lord Neuberger and Lord Sumption said that there was a fundamental difference between a jurisdiction to review the fairness of a contractual obligation and a jurisdiction to regulate the remedy for its breach. The courts did not review the fairness of men's bargains – the primary obligations themselves – either at law or in equity. This also is the position in New Zealand. The question was not discussed in *Honey Bees* in the Supreme Court, but in the Court of Appeal, it was accepted that the penalty doctrine applied only to contingent obligations operating upon breach.[890]

Although the *Dunlop* test has been replaced and no longer governs, this is not to say that it has lost all significance. In *Cavendish Square*,[891] Lord Neuberger and Lord Sumption recognized that in the case of a straightforward damages clause, the interest of the innocent party would rarely extend beyond compensation for the breach, and the *Dunlop* test would usually be perfectly adequate to determine its validity.

V. Arbitration Clauses

182. Arbitration is a process for the private resolution of matters in dispute between two or more parties whereby the parties agree to accept a decision of another person (or persons) as to matters of fact and/or law in dispute. The person or persons selected to make this decision are the arbitrators; the decision rendered is referred to as the 'award'. Arbitration is seen as generally both speedier and cheaper than resort to the normal court system, as long as neither party then seeks by litigation to upset the arbitrator's award. The ability to avoid publicity may also be an advantage. In New Zealand, most arbitrators will be qualified as members of the Institute of Arbitrators and Mediators Institute of New Zealand; most but not all will have legal qualifications.

The law relating to arbitration is largely contained in the Arbitration Act 1996, a statute which was modelled on the UNCITRAL Model Law on International Commercial Arbitration of 1985. The Schedules to that Act provide a set of rules which will apply to arbitrations unless the parties have agreed otherwise.

While it is commonplace for large-scale commercial contracts to contain an express provision requiring disputes as to the subject matter of the contract or its performance to be subject to arbitration – something commonly referred to as an arbitration clause – an agreement that a matter go to arbitration may be separate

889. [1983] 1 WLR 399.
890. [2019] NZCA 122 at [42].
891. [2015] UKSC 67, [2016] AC 1172 at [32]; *see Matapiro Olives (2008) Ltd v. The Olive Press Ltd* [2020] NZHC 1394.

from, and indeed entered into after, the main contract. An agreement to have a matter settled by arbitration may normally be made orally or in writing, but as a consumer protection measure, a provision in a consumer contract which provides for arbitration must be in writing, and the consumer must specifically indicate his or her acceptance of the provision.[892]

As long as the arbitration clause provides an opportunity for matters to be referred to the courts should disputes not be resolved by the arbitration, it is not objectionable as being a contract to oust the jurisdiction of the courts, and may therefore be enforced.[893] Indeed, if one party to a contract seeks to bring before the courts a matter which by the contract is required to go to arbitration, the other party may apply to the court for an order staying those proceedings.[894]

§2. Interpretation

I. The Rules of Interpretation

A. *Introduction*

183. The rules for the interpretation of contracts, as stated by Lord Hoffmann in *Investors Compensation Scheme Ltd v. West Bromwich Building Society,*[895] have been adopted in New Zealand.[896] They have been much cited. Lord Hoffmann's rules may be summarized as follows:

(1) Interpretation is the ascertainment of the meaning which the document would convey to a reasonable person having all the background knowledge which would reasonably have been available to the parties in the situation in which they were at the time of the contract.
(2) The background is often called the 'matrix of fact'. It includes anything which would have affected the way in which the language of the document would have been understood by a reasonable person.
(3) The law excludes from the admissible background the previous negotiations of the parties and their declarations of subjective intent. They are admissible only in an action for rectification.
(4) The meaning which a document (or any other utterance) would convey to a reasonable person is not the same thing as the meaning of its words. The meaning of words is a matter of dictionaries and grammar; the meaning of the document is what the parties using those words against the relevant background would reasonably have been understood to mean. In particular, when trying to discover the objective meaning of a contract, the court may disregard

892. Arbitration Act 1996, Sch. 1, Art. 6(1) and s. 11.
893. *Scott v. Avery* (1856) 5 HL Cas 81; *Webb v. Queensland Insurance Co Ltd* [1920] NZLR 118.
894. Arbitration Act 1996, Sch. 1, Art. 8; s. 5(1).
895. [1998] 1 WLR 896 at 912–913.
896. *Boat Park Ltd v. Hutchinson* [1999] 2 NZLR 74 at 81–82.

or give less emphasis to standard form or 'boilerplate' provisions if otherwise the clear intention of the parties would be distorted.[897]

(5) The 'rule' that words should be given their 'natural and ordinary meaning' reflects the common sense proposition that we do not easily accept that people have made linguistic mistakes, particularly in formal documents. However, if one would nevertheless conclude from the background that something must have gone wrong with the language, the law does not require judges to attribute to the parties an intention which they plainly could not have had.

B. The Matrix of Fact

184. The words of a contract should be read in their context. This includes the factual setting and background known to the parties:

> In a commercial contract it is certainly right that the court should know the commercial purpose of the contract and this in turn presupposes knowledge of the genesis of the transaction, the background, the context, the market in which the parties are operating.[898]

Whereas in the past, the New Zealand courts have declined to consider the factual matrix if the words of the contract were plain,[899] they have now accepted that recourse to that matrix is desirable in all cases, whether or not the terms of the contract are ambiguous.[900] Commonly recourse to the matrix of fact is of value as a 'cross-check':[901]

> The best start to understanding a document is to read the words used, and to ascertain their natural and ordinary meaning in the context of the document as a whole. One then looks to the background – to 'surrounding circumstances' – to cross-check whether some other or modified meaning was intended.

In *Firm PI 1 Ltd v. Zurich Australian Insurance Ltd*,[902] Arnold J said that the proper approach was an objective one, the aim being to ascertain the meaning which the document would convey to a reasonable person having all the background knowledge which would reasonably have been available to the parties in the situation in which they were at the time of the contract.

897. *Totara Investments Ltd v. Crismac Ltd* [2010] 3 NZLR 285; [2010] NZSC 36.
898. *Reardon-Smith Ltd v. Yngvar Hansen-Tangen* [1976] 1 WLR 989 at 995–996 per Lord Wilberforce.
899. *Benjamin Developments Ltd v. Robt Jones (Pacific) Ltd* [1994] 23 NZLR 189.
900. *Vector Gas Ltd v. Bay of Plenty Energy Ltd* [2010] 2 NZLR 444; [2010] NZSC 5.
901. *Pyne Gould Guinness Ltd v. Montgomery Watson (NZ) Ltd* [2001] NZAR 789; *Starrenburg v. Mortre Holdings Ltd* (2004) 6 NZCPR 193.
902. *Firm PI 1 Ltd v. Zurich Australian Insurance Ltd* [2014] NZSC 147, [2015] 1 NZLR 432 at [60]; and *see Bathurst Resources Ltd v. L & M Coal Holdings Ltd* [2021] NZSC 85, [2021] 1 NZLR 696 at [54]-[90].

Sometimes recourse to such extrinsic material will be unproductive, and may indeed provide ammunition for each of the opposing views of the parties.[903] Quite often, the material will fail to persuade the court that the apparently clear meaning of the words as they stand is the wrong one. Thus, in one case the Privy Council held, after hearing argument based on factual matrix, that a requirement that all necessary consents be *obtained* within a year was not capable of being satisfied by the fact that at the end of that year a certain consent was *highly likely to be obtained*.[904]

C. Pre-contract Negotiations, Subsequent Conduct

185. Although in *Investors Compensation*, Lord Hoffmann repeated the traditional view that the law excludes previous negotiations and declarations of subjective intent because contract interpretation is an objective exercise,[905] that no longer represents the law in New Zealand. A majority of the Supreme Court in *Vector Gas Ltd v. Bay of Plenty Energy Ltd*[906] held that the court may have regard to evidence about pre-contractual negotiations to see what an objective observer would consider had been mutually agreed by the parties.

186. Formerly it was accepted that evidence of the conduct of the parties after the making of a contract was not admissible to construe it. This was because the subjective intentions of the parties, whether evidenced by pre- or post-contractual behaviour, are irrelevant, and because the contract has to be construed as at the date it was made.[907]

However, this 'rule' was reviewed by the Supreme Court in *Wholesale Distributors Ltd v. Gibbons Holdings Ltd*,[908] where the Court held that in appropriate cases, which will not be common, a Court could when determining the meaning of a contractual provision have regard to *mutual or shared* conduct of the parties after the contract was entered into. The words emphasized provide an important limitation. To have regard to the conduct of one party which did not involve the other would, in the words of Tipping J,[909] 'make a significant inroad into the need to ascertain objectively the shared intention of the parties' as to the meaning of the terms of their agreement.

903. *Pyne Gould Guinness Ltd v. Montgomery Watson (NZ) Ltd* [2001] NZAR 789.
904. *Canterbury Golf International Ltd v. Yoshimoto* [2004] 1 NZLR 1. *See also WEL Energy Group Ltd v. Electricity Corporation of New Zealand Ltd* [2001] 2 NZLR 1 at 4 and 19; *Astra Pharmaceuticals (NZ) Ltd v. Pharmaceutical Management Agency Ltd* [2001] 1 NZLR 415 at 426.
905. [1998] 1 WLR 896 at 912. That view was followed in *Chartbrook Ltd v. Persimmon Homes Ltd* [2009] 1 AC 1101.
906. [2010] NZSC 5, [2010] 2 NZLR 444 (*see* the judgments of Tipping, McGrath and Wilson JJ).
907. *Superior Refrigeration & Air Conditioning v. Hoverd Industries Ltd* [1994] 3 NZLR 350; *New Zealand Post Ltd v. ASB Bank Ltd* [1995] 2 NZLR 508.
908. [2008] 1 NZLR 277; [2007] NZSC 37.
909. *Ibid.*, at [53] per Tipping J; approved in *Bathurst Resources Ltd v. L & M Coal Holdings Ltd* [2021] NZSC 85, [2021] 1 NZLR 696 at [89].

D. Business Common Sense

187. The Courts have consistently held that 'if detailed semantic and syntactical analysis of words in a commercial contract is going to lead to a conclusion that flouts business common sense, it must be made to yield to business common sense'.[910] This is an injunction not to be tied to dictionaries and grammar, but to interpret contextually to attain the purpose of the contract. Thus, an interpretation which produces illogical commercial results 'is to be avoided where possible'.[911] The court is, however, not permitted to rewrite a contract to accord with its view of what is reasonable. As it was put in a recent Court of Appeal case, it is 'unprincipled to interpret a contract so as to avoid a bad outcome for one party'.[912] A court can only do violence to language if it is clear what the parties' intention was and 'something has gone wrong with the language'.[913]

E. Evidential Issues

188. In *Bathurst Resources Ltd v. L & M Coal Holdings Ltd*,[914] the Supreme Court adopted a broad approach to what extrinsic material could be relevant, including that of prior negotiations and subsequent conduct, but drew attention to the use of the general rules of evidence to control the admissibility of such material. Winkelmann CJ and Ellen France J, with the agreement of the other judges, stated that the approach to be taken to contractual interpretation was governed by the law of contract, but it was the law of evidence that ensured the trial court's enquiry focused only on evidence that would materially assist in applying that test. The rules of evidence did not operate independently of the law of contractual interpretation. Rather, the law of evidence served the law of contract. However, it was the law governing the interpretation of contracts which fundamentally shaped what was relevant, and what was therefore admissible, extrinsic evidence.

The relevant principles of evidence are laid down in the Evidence Act 2006, as the judges recognized. Section 7 sets out the 'fundamental principle' that all relevant evidence is admissible except if it is inadmissible or excluded under an Act, and that evidence that is not relevant is not admissible. Further, it says that evidence is relevant if it 'has a tendency to prove or disprove anything that is of consequence to the determination of the proceeding'. Section 8 states that a judge may

---

910. *See Antaios Cia Naviera SA v. Salen Rederierna AB* [1985] AC 191 at 201, cited in the *Investors' Compensation Case* by Lord Hoffmann. This preference for a purposive rather than a literal construction was shown in *Vector Gas Ltd v. Bay of Plenty Energy Ltd* [2010] 2 NZLR 444; [2010] NZSC 5 where the Court unanimously adopted a construction of the contract which departed from a literal reading of the contract because such a literal reading made no commercial sense.

911. *Capital + Merchant Finance Ltd (in liq and rec) v. Vision Securities Ltd (in rec)* [2011] NZCA 371, [2011] NZCCLR 28, [39].

912. *Air New Zealand Ltd v. New Zealand Air Line Pilots' Association Inc* [2016] 2 NZLR 829 at [75].

913. For recent examples of interpreting contracts, taking into account 'business common sense', *see Malthouse Ltd v. Rangatira Ltd* [2018] NZCA 621; *Forsgren NZ Ltd v. Restaurant Brands Ltd* [2020] NZCA 254; *Bathurst Resources Ltd v. L & M Coal Holdings Ltd* [2021] NZSC 85; [2021] 1 NZLR 696.

914. [2021] NZSC 85, [2021] 1 NZLR 696 at [54]–[90].

exclude evidence if its probative value is outweighed by the risk that the evidence will have an unfairly prejudicial effect on the proceeding or will needlessly prolong the proceeding. Accordingly, these matters have to be weighed in determining the admissibility of evidence in any particular case.

Chapter 4. Privity of Contract

§1. The Doctrine of Privity of Contract

189. There are two limbs to the common law doctrine of privity of contract. One is that a contract cannot impose liabilities on a stranger to it. The other is that a contract cannot confer enforceable rights on a stranger. The first limb usually is seen as unobjectionable. The second is more controversial, and as a consequence it has been heavily modified by statute.

I. The Imposition of Contractual Liabilities upon Third Parties

190. The general rule is that two persons cannot, by any contract into which they enter, impose liabilities on a third person not a party to the contract. The reason for the rule is simply that a person should not be subjected to contractual obligations without his or her consent. The rule is nonetheless capable of causing injustice or inconvenience in practice and is subject to certain exceptions. So, in the context of leases and restrictive covenants over land, the rule does not apply. The benefit and burden of covenants which 'touch and concern' land bind third parties on meeting certain qualifying conditions.[915] Again, in the case of a charterparty, a purchaser or mortgagee who acquires a ship knowing of the charter is bound.[916] In addition, a person who acquires a chattel with knowledge of an existing covenant affecting its use may be liable in tort for wrongfully interfering with the contractual rights of the covenantee.[917]

II. The Acquisition of Contractual Rights by Third Parties

A. *Introduction*

191. The rule of the common law rule is that no one except a party can acquire rights under a contract.[918] The inability of a third party to enforce a contract made for his or her benefit means, for example, that a simple contract to pay money to a third person is unenforceable by the third person,[919] or a widow may be unable to

915. The exception is founded on *Tulk v. Moxhay* (1848) 2 Ph 774, holding that the purchaser of land was bound by a restrictive covenant affecting the land of which he had notice at the time of purchase. The position at common law and in equity has been supplemented by statute: *see* Property Law Act 2007, ss 301–307.
916. *De Mattos v. Gibson* (1858) 4 De G & J 276; *Lord Strathcona SS Co v. Dominion Coal Co* [1926] AC 108. But damages cannot be awarded, and the only remedy is by way of injunction, to restrain the third party from doing acts which would be inconsistent with performance of the contract by the original contracting party: *Law Debenture Trust Corporation v. Ural Caspian Oil Corporation Ltd* [1993] 1 WLR 138, not discussed on appeal [1994] 3 WLR 1221.
917. *British Motor Trade Association v. Salvadori* [1949] Ch. 556.
918. *Dunlop Pneumatic Tyre Co Ltd v. Selfridge and Co Ltd* [1915] AC 847.
919. *Tweddle v. Atkinson* (1861) 1 B &S 393.

enforce a contract between her husband and his employer for the payment of an annuity to her after the husband's death.[920] Cases such as these led to sustained criticism of the rule, both in the courts and elsewhere, on the grounds that it was unjust and out of step with common experience and that it was not supported by any compelling considerations of policy. Eventually, its shortcomings were addressed by legislation, viz., the Contracts (Privity) Act 1982, the provisions of which are now found in Part 2, subpart 1 of the Contract and Commercial Law Act 2017.[921] But, before examining this legislation, the ambit of the privity rule needs to be examined, for it is qualified in a number of respects.

B. Remedies of the Promisee

192. A third party may receive a promised benefit if the promisee personally takes action to enforce the promise. So the promisee may seek an order requiring the promisor specifically to perform the contract.[922] Again, the promisee may obtain a declaration that the promise is binding on the promisor, effectively preventing the promisor from suing the third party.[923] An order for specific performance or a declaration will provide the third party with a complete remedy, but they are only available at the discretion of the court.[924]

A promisee may also seek to recover damages. This raises two questions. One is whether or in what circumstances the promisee can recover in respect of the loss suffered by the third party. The other is whether the promisee's own loss is nominal or substantial.

First, the general rule is that a contracting party cannot recover damages in respect of a loss suffered by another.[925] But there are exceptions to the rule. One of these is the principle of 'transferred loss', which was reviewed recently by the UK Supreme Court in *Swynson Ltd v. Lowick Rose LLP*.[926] Lord Sumption said that the principle applied where the known object of a transaction was to benefit a third party or a class of persons to which the third party belonged, and the anticipated effect of a breach of duty would be to cause loss to that third party. It had hitherto been recognized only in cases where the third party suffered loss as the intended transferee of the property affected by the breach.

The paradigm example is that of a commercial contract concerning goods where it is in the contemplation of the parties that the proprietary interest in the goods may be transferred to another before any breach causing damage to the goods. In this

920. *Re Schebsman* [1944] Ch. 83.
921. In *Reid v. Castelton-Reid* [2020] NZHC 2313 at [105], n. 19, Gordon J recognized that the two Acts did not differ in any material respect, so there was no difference in the analysis or the outcome.
922. *Beswick v. Beswick* [1968] AC 58; *Rattrays Wholesale Ltd v. Meredyth-Young & A'Court Ltd* [1997] 2 NZLR 363.
923. *Snelling v. John Snelling Ltd* [1973] QB 87.
924. Below para. 252.
925. *Woodar Investment Development Co Ltd v. Wimpey Construction (UK) Ltd* [1980] 1 WLR 270.
926. [2018] AC 313; applied in *BV Nederlandse Industrie v. Rembrandt Enterprises Inc* [2019] EWCA Civ 596, [2019] 3 WLR 1113.

case, an original party to the contract is to be treated as having entered into the contract for the benefit of the other person and may recover the actual loss suffered by that person.[927] A similar principle has been applied in the context of building contracts. So where a building development was, to the knowledge of the parties, likely to be acquired by third parties, who would foreseeably suffer loss from defective performance of the contract but who would be unable personally to sue on the contract, the contracting party could recover in respect of the third party's loss.[928] But the principle does not apply if it was no part of the object of the transaction in question to benefit the third party.[929] There is no justification for applying the exception if the third party has a direct remedy, as where a contracting party entered a duty of care deed accepting liability to a third party purchaser for negligence.[930] Seemingly, this qualification can apply in New Zealand in circumstances where a third party has a direct cause of action against a contracting party pursuant to a deed or under the Contract and Commercial Law Act. Whether a right of action in tort[931] could operate as a bar is not clear, but the different basis for liability and, maybe, a different measure of damages suggests it would not.

Second, the promisee may personally suffer loss if the third party does not receive the promised benefit, certainly where the promisee has paid for alternative performance or would account to the third party for the damages.[932] Once again, it is probable that no action lies if the third party has a direct right of action against the promisor. There is little inducement for the courts to extend the law so as to give both the promisee and the third party concurrent rights of enforcement.[933] So if the third party can sue, as above, the promisee's interest in the performance of the contract is satisfied. This solution avoids any risk of the defendant being potentially liable to pay damages twice over.

C. *Trusts of Contractual Rights*

193. A promisee under a contract may constitute a trust of the right to which he or she is entitled in favour of a third party. The property which is the subject matter of the trust is here the contractual right, and the beneficiary can enforce the trust

927. *The Albazero* [1977] AC 774.
928. *Linden Gardens Trust Ltd v. Lenesta Sludge Disposals Ltd* [1994] AC 85.
929. *Swynson Ltd v. Lowick Rose LLP* [2018] AC 313.
930. *Alfred McAlpine Construction Ltd v. Panatown Ltd* [2000] 3 WLR 946; *Swynson Ltd v. Lowick Rose LLP* [2018] AC 313.
931. *See North Shore City Council v. Body Corporate 188529 (Sunset Terraces)* [2011] 2 NZLR 289; *North Shore City Council v. Body Corporate 207624 (Spencer on Byron)* [2013] 2 NZLR 297.
932. *Linden Gardens Trust Ltd v. Lenesta Sludge Disposals Ltd* [1994] AC 85 per Lord Griffiths; *Alfred McAlpine Construction Ltd v. Panatown Ltd* [2000] 3 WLR 946 per Lord Clyde and Lord Jauncey. However, in *McKinlay Hendry Ltd v. Tonkin & Taylor* HC, Wellington, CIV 1999-485-78, 22 Mar. 2004 Miller J preferred not to follow the wider approach of Lord Griffiths (in *McKinlay Hendry Ltd v. Tonkin & Taylor* CA 81/04, 9 Dec. 2005 the Court Appeal dismissed an appeal on another issue).
933. *Alfred McAlpine Construction Ltd v. Panatown Ltd* [2000] 3 WLR 946 per Lord Browne-Wilkinson.

just as can a beneficiary under a trust of tangible property.[934] However, there must be clear evidence that the promisee intended to create a trust of the promise.[935] The parties must be shown to have intended to create a property right in the beneficiary, which prevents them from rescinding or varying the contract so as to deprive the beneficiary of that right. This intention can rarely be shown to the court's satisfaction.[936]

D. Exclusion Clauses and Third Parties

194. Whether a clause in a contract between A and B limiting or excluding the liability of C can be relied on by C in an action by A may involve questions of privity, of agency, and of possible defences to actions in tort. In some of the cases, it has been thought that to allow the third person to rely on the clause would be to ignore the basic rule of privity. The solution has been to look for a second contract with that person made by an original contracting party as his or her agent under which he or she gets the benefit of the clause.[937] Part 2 subpart 1 of the Contract and Commercial Law Act may apply where there is no such contract, and the third person seeks to claim the benefit as a non-party.[938] In other cases, the doctrine of privity has not been thought to be relevant. The liability of the third person being in tort, the question has been whether as a matter of tort law the plaintiff has consented to the risk or whether liability has been excluded by a non-contractual notice.[939] The principle can still apply where the excluding notice happens to be in a contract made between the plaintiff and another.[940] There is support in Canada for extending the benefit of an exclusion clause to a third party in circumstances where the contracting parties intended this, and the activities performed by the third party were the very activities contemplated as coming within the scope of the contract or of the particular provision in the contract.[941] Probably, this principle is subsumed by the broader principles of the privity legislation.[942]

---

934. *Tomlinson v. Gill* (1756) Amb 330; 27 ER 221.
935. *See Swain v. Law Society* [1983] 1 AC 598.
936. By s. 75A(2) of the Life Insurance Act 1908, a life insurance policy expressed to be for the benefit of the spouse or children of the policyholder creates a trust in favour of the named beneficiaries.
937. *Scruttons Ltd v. Midland Silicones Ltd* [1962] AC 446; *New Zealand Shipping Co Ltd v. AM Satterthwaite and Co Ltd* [1974] 1 NZLR 505; *Herrick v. Leonard and Dingley Ltd* [1975] 2 NZLR 566.
938. *See* para. 195.
939. *Smith v. Eric S Bush* [1990] 1 AC 831; *Pacific Associates Inc v. Baxter* [1990] 1 QB 993.
940. *Rolls Royce New Zealand Ltd v. Carter Holt Harvey Ltd* [2005] 1 NZLR 324.
941. *Fraser River Pile & Dredge Ltd v. Can-Dive Services Ltd* (1999) 176 DLR (4th) 257; applied in *Adventurer Hobson Ltd v. Cockery* [2020] NZHC 675, [2020] 2 NZLR 554.
942. However, in *Sheehan v. Watson* [2011] 1 NZLR 314, the Court of Appeal applied a directly analogous principle to a claim by a third party for the benefit of a statutory cause of action under the Property Law Act 2007 rather than a contractual cause of action.

E. Privity Legislation

1. Right of Enforcement to Third Parties

195. The purpose of the reform achieved by the Contracts (Privity) Act 1982, and now contained in Part 2, subpart 1 of the Contract and Commercial Law Act 2017, is to allow an intended beneficiary of a contract between others to enforce the benefit conferred by the contract, yet not to interfere too much with the autonomy of the contracting parties. Section 4 of the 1982 Act was the key provision, and its terms now are found in sections 12 and 13 of the 2017 Act. They state:

> 12 (1) This section applies to a promise contained in a deed or contract that confers, or purports to confer, a benefit on a person, designated by name, description or reference to a class, who is not a party to the deed or contract.
> (2) The promisor is under an obligation, enforceable by the beneficiary, to perform the promise
> (3) This section applies whether or not the person referred to in subsection (1) is in existence when the deed or contract is made.
> 13. Section 12 does not apply to a promise that, on the proper construction of the deed or contract, is not intended to create, in respect of the benefit, an obligation enforceable by the beneficiary.[943]

First, there needs to be a promise contained in a deed or contract which confers or purports to confer a 'benefit' on a third person. So one of the purposes of the bargain (rather than one of its incidental effects if performed) should be to benefit the third party.[944] A benefit includes any advantage, any immunity and any limitation or other qualification of rights or obligations.[945] Normally, the third party is likely to claim the benefit of any 'advantage', in the sense of a positive benefit conferred by the contract on that party. The benefit may be money or property or some other form of financial advantage.[946] It is apparent also that the benefit may be by way of an exclusion or limitation of any liability of the third party to one of the contracting parties, or by way of a release from such liability.[947] A contractual promise to

943. Section 12 is complemented by s. 17, which provides that the obligation imposed on the promisor by s. 12 can be enforced at the suit of the beneficiary as if he or she were a party to the deed or contract.

944. *Dolphin Maritime & Aviation Services Ltd v. Sveriges Angfartygs Assurans Forening* [2009] 2 Lloyd's Rep 123 at [74], interpreting the words in similar UK legislation.

945. Contract and Commercial Law Act 2017, s. 11.

946. *See* for example *Wellington AHA v. Wellington Hotel, Hospital, Restaurant and Related Trades Union* [1992] 3 NZLR 658 at 662.

947. *Allison v. KPMG Peat Marwick* [2000] 1 NZLR 560; *Nightingale v. Barfoot & Thompson Ltd* HC Auckland CIV-2009-404-4073, 22 Oct. 2009 at [34]; *CBL Insurance Ltd v. Harris* [2021] NZHC 1393.

relinquish all claims against a third party is a benefit enforceable by that party,[948] as is an indemnity in respect of the repayment of a debt.[949]

Second, the promise upon which the third-party beneficiary wishes to sue must be contained in a deed or contract made between the promisor and the promisee. Seemingly, then, the promise must be a term of the contract, and a misrepresentation inducing the contract which gives a benefit to a third party is not covered. However, it has been held, contrary to this view, that the purpose of the legislation in allowing a third party to enforce a contract between others simply would not be met if a party who should benefit from a representation inducing entry into the contract was left without a remedy.[950] On the other hand, in *Closurepac NZ Ltd v. WS 2014 Ltd*,[951] Thomas J affirmed that the words of the statute did not include an inducing misrepresentation. The benefit also must be conferred or purport to be conferred by the promise. Early authority held that a nominee to a contract made with a contracting party 'or nominee' could not enforce under section 4 of the 1982 Act because the benefit arose by virtue of the nomination, not the contractual promise.[952] However, the accepted view now is that the nominee gets the benefit from both the contract and the nomination. It is the contract which allows the nomination, and the nomination is the process by which the contract beneficiary is identified.[953]

Third, the beneficiary must be designated by 'name, description or reference to a class'. The onus is on the third party to show that he or she has been designated in these terms.[954] 'Designation is a strong word, a positive word, and means something more than a mere contemplation or possibility.'[955] Most judicial discussion of the requirement has been concerned with the position of nominees. In *Field v. Fitton*,[956] Bisson J said that if the nominee is not named, the word 'nominee' in the contract should be qualified by the addition of a descriptive phrase or the addition of the particular class within which the nominee falls so as to specify or identify the nominee in the manner required by the statute. But Tipping J in *Rattrays Wholesale Ltd v. Meredyth-Young & A'Court Ltd*[957] preferred a wider view. He thought that the purpose of the designation requirement was to enable the promisor to know with sufficient certainty who could claim the benefit of the promise, and that once nominated that person was identified with certainty. It did not matter that until then the person could be anyone at all. In *Ballance Agri-Nutrients (Kapuni) Ltd v. The Gama Foundation*,[958] William Young J in the Court of Appeal agreed with this view. Any

948. *Reid v. Castelton-Reid* [2020] NZHC 2313 at [108].
949. *Provident Insurance Corporation Ltd v. Commissioner of Inland Revenue* [2019] NZHC 995 at [125].
950. *Pragma Holdings Ltd v. Great South 507 Ltd* (HC, Auckland CIV 2005-404-1931, 30 Aug. 2006).
951. [2015] NZHC 1587 at [148]–[164]; and *see Do Yay Ltd v. Wei* [2020] NZHC 759 at [54]–[57].
952. *Karangahape Road International Village Ltd v. Holloway* [1989] 1 NZLR 83.
953. *Rattray's Wholesale Ltd v. Meredyth-Young & A'Court Ltd* [1997] 2 NZLR 363, affirmed in *Laidlaw v. Parsonage* [2010] 1 NZLR 286.
954. It is not a requirement that the beneficiary should have been aware of the contract and its terms: *Chudley v. Clydesdale Bank plc* [2019] EWCA Civ 344, [2020] QB 284, interpreting similar UK legislation.
955. *Cross v. Aurora Group Ltd* (1989) 4 NZCLC 64,909 per Wylie J at 64,913.
956. [1988] 1 NZLR 482.
957. [1997] 2 NZLR 363.
958. [2006] 2 NZLR 319.

doubt about which view should be preferred was put to rest in *Laidlaw v. Parsonage*,[959] where *Rattrays* and *Ballance* were both thought to have been correctly decided.

Subsequent purchasers of buildings generally will not be designated in the building contract as beneficiaries, in which case they cannot sue the builder by virtue of section 12. But if the building contract states that building warranties extend for the benefit of purchasers, they will have a cause of action. Third-party purchasers may in any event be able to sue a builder or council in tort, for negligence.[960]

Fourth, an otherwise qualifying beneficiary does not actually have to be in existence at the time the deed or contract is made. In principle, then, section 12 can apply in the case of a contract purportedly made for the benefit of a company before the company has been incorporated.[961] But where a contract is made *on behalf of* a proposed company, it being intended that the contract should be with the company after it has been incorporated, section 12 does not apply. The company can enforce only if it ratifies the contract after its incorporation.[962]

Finally, by section 13, either of the contracting parties may seek to show that it was not intended that the promise should create an obligation enforceable at the suit of the beneficiary. An express agreement about enforceability is conclusive of the matter. Otherwise, the courts will look for some clear evidence suggesting that enforcement by the beneficiary was in fact contemplated.[963]

2. Variation or Discharge of the Contract

196. Giving a right of action to a third party beneficiary necessarily must restrict to some extent the ability of the contracting parties to vary or cancel the contract. A balance is achieved by allowing variation or cancellation:

(1) until the third party materially alters his position in reliance on the promise or obtains judgment or the award of an arbitrator against the promisor;[964]
(2) at any time by agreement between the parties and the beneficiary or pursuant to express provisions in the contract which are known to the beneficiary;[965] or
(3) pursuant to a court order.[966]

959. [2010] 1 NZLR 286.
960. *North Shore City Council v. Body Corporate 188529 (Sunset Terraces)* [2011] 2 NZLR 289; *North Shore City Council v. Body Corporate 207624 (Spencer on Byron)* [2013] 2 NZLR 297.
961. *Speedy v. Nylex New Zealand Ltd* unreported, High Court, Auckland CL 29/87, 3 Feb. 1989; *McKinlay Hendry Ltd v. Tonkin & Taylor* HC, Wellington, CIV 1999-485-78, 22 Mar. 2004 (appeal dismissed CA 81/04, 9 Dec. 2005).
962. Companies Act 1993, s. 182.
963. *See* for example *Saunders v. BNZ* [2002] 2 NZLR 270; *Hoare v. Heidelberg Graphic Equipment Ltd* (HC, Wellington, CIV 2006-485-233, 9 Nov. 2006); *Robins v. Fusion Electronics Ltd* [2012] NZHC 656; *Body Corporate 207715 v. McNish* [2016] 2 NZLR 429.
964. Contract and Commercial Law Act 2017, s. 14.
965. *Ibid.*, s. 15.
966. *Ibid.*, s. 16.

3. Defences

197. In a claim by a beneficiary against a promisor, the promisor may rely on any defence, counterclaim, setoff or otherwise which would have been available to him or her if the beneficiary had been a party or if the beneficiary were the promisee.[967] The defences of setoff or counterclaim can only be utilized if the subject matter of the setoff or counterclaim arises out of or in connection with the deed or contract in which the promise is contained.[968] The beneficiary is liable on a counterclaim only if he or she elects with full knowledge of the counterclaim to proceed with his or her claim against the promisor, and his or her liability is limited to the value of the benefit conferred on him or her by the promise.[969]

§2. The Transfer of Contractual Rights

I. Voluntary Assignment

A. *Introduction*

198. Personal rights to property which can only be claimed or enforced by action (in the sense of litigation) and not by taking physical possession are known as choses or things in action. A chose in action may be legal or equitable. A legal chose is one which is enforceable at common law and this includes, in particular, a debt or other right under a contract. Further examples of legal choses are company shares, bills of exchange, insurance policies and intellectual property. An equitable chose is one which originally was enforceable only in equity, examples being a share in a trust fund or a legacy.

Both legal and equitable choses may be assigned to another person on meeting certain qualifying conditions.[970] Assignment involves the transfer of the benefit of the chose in action by the party entitled to that benefit (the creditor or assignor) to a third party (the assignee) as a result of which the assignee becomes entitled to sue the person liable under the contract (the debtor). At common law, a legal chose, such as a debt due under a contract, could not be assigned. However, Parliament intervened to provide generally for the assignment of legal rights,[971] and on a number of occasions make specific provision for certain particular cases.[972] In equity, there may be a valid assignment even where the statutory formalities are not met.[973]

---

967. *Ibid.*, s. 18(2).
968. *Ibid.*, s. 18(3).
969. *Ibid.*, s. 18(4).
970. 'It is long-established in New Zealand that legal and equitable assignments of a thing in action in New Zealand are lawful and effective': *FTG Securities Ltd v. Bank of New Zealand* [2019] NZCA 16, [2019] 3 NZLR 607 at [22].
971. Property Law Act 1952, s. 130; *see* para. 199; Property Law Act 2007, ss 50, 51; *see* para. 204.
972. *See* for example the Bill of Exchange Act 1908, s. 31 (negotiable instruments); Companies Act 1993, s. 84 (company shares).
973. *See* para. 200.

The Property Law Act 2007 has reformed the law governing assignments which are made on or after 1 January 2008. We will consider first the law governing assignments made prior to that date, and then consider the new law and the changes it has made.

B. Assignment under the Property Law Act 1952

199. A statutory method of assignment is provided for in section 130(1) of the Property Law Act 1952. This governs assignments made up to and including 31 December 2007:

> Any absolute assignment by writing under the hand of the assignor (not purporting to be by way of charge only) of any debt or other legal or equitable thing in action, of which express notice in writing has been given to the debtor, trustee, or other person from whom the assignor would have been entitled to receive or claim that debt or thing in action, shall be and be deemed to have been effectual in law (subject to all equities that would have been entitled to priority over the right of the assignee if this Act had not been passed) to pass and transfer the legal or equitable right to that debt or thing in action from the date of the notice, and all legal or equitable and other remedies for the same, and the power to give a good discharge for the same, without the concurrence of the assignor.

It may be seen that there are three conditions which must be satisfied to make a valid assignment under the statute: it must be absolute, it must be written, and written notice must be given to the debtor.

As regards the first of these, an absolute assignment is one by which the entire interest of the assignor in the chose in action is for the time being transferred unconditionally to the assignee. It is not necessary that the assignment should take the form of an out-and-out transfer which deprives the assignor forever of all further interest in the subject matter. It is well settled that a mortgage in the ordinary form is an absolute assignment. In such a case, the whole right of the mortgagor in the subject matter passes for the time being to the mortgagee, and the fact that there is an express or implied right to reassignment upon redemption does not destroy the absolute character of the transfer.[974] But an assignment of a purchaser's interest in a contract to buy land was not absolute where the terms were inconsistent with the notion that the purchaser's contractual rights against the vendor had been absolutely vested in the lender, subject only to a right of redemption.[975]

The requirement of writing needs no further comment. The requirement of notice is considered further below.[976]

---

974. *Hughes v. Pump House Hotel Co* [1902] 2 KB 190; *In Re Kirton* [1919] NZLR 138; *HEB Contractors Ltd v. Verrissimo* [1990] 3 NZLR 754.
975. *Gibbston Valley Estate Ltd v. Owen* (1999) 4 NZ ConvC 193,024.
976. *See* para. 202.

C. Assignment in Equity

200. Section 130(1) does not forbid or impair the efficacy of equitable assignments, and these may be made with a minimum of formality and restriction. Thus, an assignment which fails to meet the conditions laid down by the statute may nonetheless be good in equity.[977] First, as regards form, writing is not essential. All that is required is that the assignor should have made clear his or her intention to make the assignment.[978] By statute, however, the disposition of an existing legal or equitable interest in land must be in writing and signed by the person making the disposition.[979] So, apart from the disposition of an interest in land, the oral assignment of a legal or equitable chose in action is valid. Second, if an assignment is not of an absolute character, then something will remain to be done to complete the title of the assignee. In this case, the assignment is enforceable only if it is supported by consideration.[980]

D. Consideration

201. Consideration is not necessary to the validity of a statutory assignment. An assignment which satisfies the requirements of section 130 transfers the chose in action by virtue of the section itself and consideration is irrelevant.[981]

The equitable assignment of a chose in action, if completed, need not be supported by consideration. The gift is both valid and irrevocable in the same way as is the gift of a money note by delivery of possession.[982] If, however, the assignment is incomplete, the assignor can change his or her mind and revoke it. The assignee cannot enlist the aid of equity in such a case for it is well settled that equity will not assist a volunteer (i.e., a person who has not given consideration). Whether a gift has been 'completed' hinges on whether any act remains to be done by the assignor in order to perfect the assignment, and this in turn depends on the requirements, if any, for the transfer of the particular chose at law. For example, the voluntary assignment of a debt may be achieved simply on the creditor clearly expressing an intention to make the assignment there and then, for nothing else needs to be done on his or her part. However, if a creditor only promises to assign in the future an existing debt, he or she has not done everything necessary to transfer the chose to the assignee and the promise can only operate as a contract to assign, which requires consideration like any other contract.[983] A purported assignment of a right which does not yet exist, such as a future debt, must likewise be supported by consideration.

---

977. *Mountain Road (No. 9) Ltd v. Michael Edgley Corporation Pty Ltd* [1999] 1 NZLR 335 at 340.
978. *Peacocke Land Co Ltd v. Hamilton Milk Producers Co Ltd* [1963] NZLR 576.
979. Property Law Act 2007, s. 25(1).
980. *See* para. 201.
981. *Re Westerton, Public Trustee v. Gray* [1919] 2 Ch. 104 at 112–113.
982. *Re McArdle* [1951] Ch. 669; *Pennington v. Waine* [2002] 1 WLR 2075.
983. *Pulley v. Public Trustee* [1956] NZLR 771.

E. Notice

202. Written notice to the debtor or other person from whom the right assigned is due is necessary to complete the title of a statutory assignee under the Property Law Act 1952. It becomes effective on the date when it is received by or on behalf of the debtor.[984] By contrast, notice is not necessary to perfect an equitable assignment, at least as between assignor and assignee. Even without notice to the debtor, the title of the assignee is complete as against the assignor personally, and also against persons who stand in the same position as the assignor, for example, his or her trustee in bankruptcy.[985] But it has been held by the Court of Appeal that notice must be given to the debtor before an equitable assignee can bring an action against the debtor.[986] A contrary view, upheld in Australia, is that the consequences of failure to give notice do not go to the validity of the assignment.[987] Rather, an assignee should give notice in order to ensure that his or her rights under the assignment are protected. In the first place, if the debtor pays the assignor before receiving notice of the assignment, he or she cannot be compelled to make a second payment to the assignee.[988] Second, an assignee who first gives notice to the debtor of the assignment has priority over other assignees, provided he or she was unaware of any prior assignments when the assignment was made.[989]

F. Assignment Subject to Equities

203. An assignee under both a statutory and an equitable assignment is said to take 'subject to equities'. What this means is that the debtor can plead against the assignee any defences that he or she could have pleaded against the assignor. The assignee cannot take more than the assignor has to give.[990] Any defects in the title of the assignor, as may arise, for example, by reason of mistake, illegality, misrepresentation or non-performance by the assignor, may all be pleaded by the debtor in answer to a claim by the assignee.[991] The debtor can also set off against the assignee a claim for unliquidated damages for breach of the contract by the assignor, whether the breach occurred before or after notice of the assignment had been given.[992] Again, where the debtor has a claim arising out of a transaction other than the contract assigned, it can be set off against the assignee if the claim accrued before the

984. *Holt v. Heatherfield Trust Ltd* [1942] 2 KB 1.
985. *See Gorringe v. Irwell India Rubber Works* (1886) 34 Ch D 128.
986. *Mountain Road (No. 9) Ltd v. Michael Edgley Corporation Pty Ltd* [1999] 1 NZLR 335 at 342.
987. *Thomas v. National Australia Bank Ltd* [2000] 2 Qd R 448.
988. *Stocks v. Dobson* (1853) 4 De GM & G 11.
989. *Dearle v. Hall* (1828) 3 Russ 1.
990. For a recent statement of the rule, *see Savvy Vineyards 3552 Ltd v. Kakara Estate Ltd* [2014] NZSC 121, [2015] 1 NZLR 281 at [86].
991. *See* for example *Field v. Fitton* [1988] 1 NZLR 482; *Isaac Construction Co Ltd v. McDonald* (1998) 3 NZ ConvC 192,707; *HEB Contractors Ltd v. Verrissimo* [1990] 3 NZLR 754 at 761–762.
992. *Young v. Kitchin* (1878) 3 Ex D 127.

debtor had notice of the assignment.[993] But a personal claim by the debtor against the assignor which is unconnected with the contract cannot defeat the claim of the assignee.[994]

The 'subject to equities' rule also means that the assignee cannot recover more from the debtor than the assignor could have done had there been no assignment.[995] However, the rule has caused difficulty in relation to claims arising out of the sale of land. It has been argued in this context that a purchaser to whom the vendor has later assigned a right to sue a third party in respect of damage to the land cannot recover damages because the assignor has ceased to own the land at the time of the damage and of the assignment and, accordingly, has suffered no loss. In response, it has been held that the rule should be amended so that it states that an assignee can recover no more damages than the assignor could have recovered if there had been no assignment *and if the property had not been transferred to the assignee*. The damages rule was not designed to allow a party to escape liability for breach but to ensure that he did not have to meet a bigger liability than he would have been under to the assignor.[996]

G. Assignment under the Property Law Act 2007

204. Section 50 of the Property Law Act 2007 provides as follows:

(1) The absolute assignment in writing of a legal or equitable thing in action, signed by the assignor, passes to the assignee:
  (a) all the rights of the assignor in relation to the thing in action; and
  (b) all the remedies of the assignor in relation to the thing in action; and
  (c) the power to give a good discharge to the debtor.
(2) Subsection (1) applies whether or not the assignment is given for valuable consideration.
(3) Subsection (1) applies subject to:
  (a) section 51; and
  (b) any equities in relation to the thing in action that arise before the debtor has actual notice of the assignment and would, but for subsection (1), have priority over the rights of the assignee.
(4) The priority of an assignment to which subsection (1) applies and which is not given for valuable consideration is to be determined as if the assignment had been given for valuable consideration.
(5) A legal or equitable thing in action is to be treated as having been assigned in equity (whether the assignment is oral or in writing) if:
  (a) the assignee has given valuable consideration for the assignment; or
  (b) the assignment is complete.
(6) Subsection (5):
  (a) prevails over any rule of equity to the contrary; but

993. *Business Computers Ltd v. Anglo African Leasing Ltd* [1977] 1 WLR 578.
994. *Stoddart v. Union Trust Ltd* [1912] 1 KB 181.
995. *Dawson v. Great Northern and City Railway Co* [1905] 1 KB 260.
996. *Offer-Hoare v. Larkstore Ltd* [2006] 1 WLR 2926.

(b) applies subject to sections 24 and 25.[997]

(7) An assignment to which subsection (5) applies is complete when the assignor has done everything that needs to be done by the assignor to transfer to the assignee (whether absolutely, conditionally, or by way of charge) the rights of the assignor in relation to the thing in action.

(8) Subsection (7) applies even though some other thing may remain to be done, without the intervention or assistance of the assignor, in order to confer title to the rights on the assignee.

Section 51 provides for some further consequences of the assignment of things in action:

(1) This section applies to a thing in action assigned in accordance with section 50(1) or in equity.

(2) Payment of all or part of the debt to the assignor by a debtor who does not have actual notice of the assignment discharges the debtor to the extent of the payment.

(3) The debt owing by a debtor who has actual notice of the assignment is payable to the assignee.

(4) However, the debt is payable to another assignee if:
  (a) before discharge, the debtor receives actual notice of the assignment of the same thing in action to another assignee; and
  (b) the rights of the other assignee in relation to the thing in action have priority over the rights of the first assignee.[998]

It is apparent that sections 50 and 51 have clarified the law and have reformed it in terms that confirm certain of the principles laid down in the existing case law. A number of particular points need to be made: (i) no consideration is needed for a valid assignment under the statute (section 51(2)); (ii) an equitable assignment is enforceable if consideration is given or if the assignor has done everything that needs to be done by the assignor to transfer his or her rights to the assignee, irrespective of whether something remains to be done by someone else (section 51(5), (7)); (iii) the view taken in Australia[999] is adopted, in that notice does not determine the validity of a statutory assignment, but is necessary to ensure that the debt is paid to the assignee and that his or her position is fully protected (section 51(2), (3)); (iv) the assignee takes subject to equities (section 50(3)(b)); (v) a valid assignment can continue to be made either under the statute or in equity; (vi) the Act addresses the assignment of debts (including the right to performance of obligations), but not the assignment of the burden of obligations.[1000]

Furthermore, any assignment operates subject to the overriding principle that equity will not allow a party to take advantage of its own wrongdoing. So where it was alleged that certain assignments made in settlement of a dispute were procured by misrepresentation, the assignor could still bring proceedings in its own name to

997. These sections govern contracts concerning land; *see* para. 200.
998. Section 51(5) makes provision for the debtor to interplead where there are disputed claims.
999. *See* para. 202.
1000. *Savvy Vineyards 3552 Ltd v. Kakara Estate Ltd* [2015] 1 NZLR 281 at [85].

set aside the underlying agreement, notwithstanding that formal effect had been given to the transaction and that this in its terms prevented the assignor's claim.[1001]

H. Limits on Assignability

1. Bare Right to Litigate

205. The right to claim unliquidated damages for breach of contract cannot usually be assigned after the contract has been broken, and a purported attempt to do so is without effect.[1002] This is because a bare right to litigate smacks of the tort of 'maintenance', which is the improper stirring up of legal proceedings by a stranger not directly concerned with them. However, the assignment of a right to sue may validly be made where the assignee has a 'genuine commercial interest' in the subject matter of the action.[1003] Examples are where the assignee is a creditor of the assignor,[1004] or where the assignee acquires a property interest to which any cause of action is ancillary.[1005]

There are contrasting decisions where a Council has settled a claim against it for negligence in approving the construction of defective residences and has taken an assignment of the original plaintiffs' causes of action against the remaining defendants. On the one hand, it was held that the Council had a genuine commercial interest in completing the settlement and taking the assignment: the settlement was advantageous to the Council in limiting its liability and to the plaintiffs in receiving funds and removing the costs and risks of proceeding to trial.[1006] On the other hand, it was held that such an assignment was void as being contrary to public policy, for it undermined both the law of maintenance and champerty and also the purpose of section 17(1)(c) of the Law Reform Act 1936 in achieving just and equitable contribution between tortfeasors.[1007]

Recent decisions have examined the lawfulness of litigation funding agreements. In *Waterhouse v. Contractors Bonding Ltd*,[1008] the Supreme Court held: (i) it was not the role of the courts to act as general regulators of litigation funding arrangements; (ii) funding arrangements that amounted to an assignment of a cause of action to a third party where this was not permissible would be an abuse of process; and (iii) on an application for a stay on the grounds of abuse of process (or any other

1001. *Telecom New Zealand Ltd v. Sintel-Com Ltd* [2008] 1 NZLR 730.
1002. *Trendtex Trading Co Ltd v. Credit Suisse* [1982] AC 679; *PricewaterhouseCoopers v. Walker* [2017] NZSC 151, [2018] 1 NZLR 735.
1003. *Trendtex Trading Co Ltd v. Credit Suisse* [1982] AC 679.
1004. *Ibid.*
1005. *First City Corporation v. Downsview Nominees Ltd* [1989] 3 NZLR 710 (on appeal [1990] 3 NZLR 265, [1993] 1 NZLR 513).
1006. *Auckland CC as Assignee of Body Corporate 16113 v. Auckland CC* [2008] 1 NZLR 838.
1007. *Body Corporate 160361 (Fleetwood Apartments) v. BC 2004 Ltd and BC 2009 Ltd* [2014] NZHC 1514, [2014] 3 NZLR 758.
1008. [2014] 1 NZLR 91; *and see Saunders v. Houghton* [2010] 3 NZLR 331 (and for later developments *see Saunders v. Houghton* [2012] NZCA 545, [2013] 2 NZLR 652, *Credit Suisse Private Equity LLC v. v. Houghton* [2014] 1 NZLR 541); *PricewaterhouseCoopers v. Walker* [2017] NZSC 151, [2018] 1 NZLR 735.

application where the terms of the agreement might be relevant) the court could order disclosure, subject to redactions concerning confidentiality and litigation-sensitive and privileged matters.

The assignment of a debt raises no question of maintenance even if the necessity for litigation to recover it is contemplated. It is an essential element of modern life that debts are bought and sold, and such transactions cannot be impugned where the debt is bona fide and maintenance is not the object.[1009] Again, there may be an assignment of the fruits of litigation, as opposed to the right to sue for those fruits.[1010]

2. Contracts Involving Personal Skill or Confidence

206. The benefit of a contract of a 'personal' nature cannot be assigned. Contracts where one party relies on the particular skills and qualifications of the other or which otherwise involve a relation of special confidence fall into this category. Thus, a contract of employment cannot be assigned by the employer so as to oblige the employee to work for another.[1011] However, contracts for the sale of land normally are capable of assignment because personal considerations are not important.[1012]

3. Prohibitions on Assignment

207. The parties to a contract are free to make it a term of their contract that the rights under it shall not be assignable.[1013] The Court of Appeal has held that an agreement not to assign contractual rights or other rights in personam should generally be specifically enforced as between the parties unless there is some strong reason why that course should not be adopted.[1014] Tipping J explained that a non-assignability clause has a clear commercial purpose. The parties do not wish, without consent, to be obliged to deal with a party not of their own choosing. If the law did not enforce such an agreement, the legitimate commercial expectations of the parties would be defeated.[1015]

If a clause prohibits assignment of the benefit of a contract, and a third party suffers a loss due to defective performance but cannot sue directly, the assignor may be able to recover damages for the benefit of the third party.[1016]

1009. *Camdex International Ltd v. Bank of Zambia* [1996] 3 WLR 759.
1010. *Glegg v. Bromley* [1912] 3 KB 474.
1011. *Nokes v. Doncaster Amalgamated Collieries Ltd* [1940] AC 1014.
1012. *HEB Contractors Ltd v. Verrissimo* [1990] 3 NZLR 754.
1013. *Linden Gardens Trust Ltd v. Lenesta Sludge Disposals Ltd* [1994] AC 85.
1014. *New Zealand Payroll Software Systems Ltd v. Advanced Management Systems Ltd* [2003] 3 NZLR 1; *FTG Securities Ltd v. Bank of New Zealand* [2019] NZCA 16, [2019] 3 NZLR 607.
1015. A provision that consent 'shall not be unreasonably withheld' is irrelevant if the process of seeking approval is never undertaken: *FTG Securities Ltd v. Bank of New Zealand* [2019] NZCA 16 at [43]–[46].
1016. *Linden Gardens Trust Ltd v. Lenesta Sludge Disposals Ltd* [1994] AC 85; *see* para. 192.

I. The Transfer of Contractual Liabilities

208. Assignment is the transfer of a right to a third person. Contractual liabilities cannot normally be transferred save by novation.[1017] Under an assignment, the assignor is not relieved of the burden of a contract as regards the other original contracting party, and the assignment can take place by agreement between the assignor and the assignee without the consent of the other contracting party, unless the terms of the original contract provide otherwise.[1018] In contrast to this, a novation is a transaction that creates a new contract that is substituted for the original contract, and the consent of all the parties to the original contract is required.[1019] Where novation takes place, the debt owed by the debtor is henceforth owed to the third party. Frequently, this happens in the context of the amalgamation or restructuring of companies.[1020] Rights as well as duties may be transferred by novation, but it is a simpler matter for a creditor who wishes to transfer a contractual right to proceed by way of assignment as he or she need not then seek the consent of the debtor.

In *Savvy Vineyards 3552 Ltd v. Kakara Estate Ltd*,[1021] it was held by the Supreme Court that it was conceptually possible for a party to a contract to have a contractual right to novate by nominating a successor, who, by accepting the novation, became a party to the contract in succession to the novating party. On the facts, it was held that this had occurred, for while the agreement concerned used the language of assignment, it clearly contemplated novation. So where consent is given by way of contractual provision, no further consent is needed when a contracting party later exercises that contractual right.

To say that a contracting party cannot, save by novation, transfer his or her liabilities to another does not mean that that party cannot engage another to perform the contract on his or her behalf. A creditor cannot object to vicarious performance unless the contract forbids it or unless the contract is 'personal' in the sense that one party has contracted for the particular skill, expertise or personal qualification of the other.[1022] Vicarious performance is, however, quite different from assignment or novation, for one debtor is not thereby substituted for another. The original debtor remains liable to the other contracting party for the due performance of the contract, and the third party is not liable to that contracting party for non-performance or defective performance, although he or she may be liable on a separate contract with the debtor.

1017. For exceptions, *see* subpart 8 of Part 3 of the Property Law Act 2007, as confirmed in the Contract and Commercial Law Act 2017, s. 57(1)(a); Consumer Guarantees Act 1993, s. 46(1)–(3), as confirmed in the Contract and Commercial Law Act 2017, s. 57(1)(b).
1018. *Savvy Vineyards 3552 Ltd v. Kakara Estate Ltd* [2014] NZSC 121, [2015] 1 NZLR 281 at [85].
1019. *ALH Group Property Holdings Pty Ltd v. Chief Commissioner of State Revenue* [2012] HCA 6 at [12].
1020. *Hela Pharma AB v. Hela Pharma Australasian Ltd* CA165/03, CA 206/03, 17 Feb. 2005.
1021. [2014] NZSC 121, [2015] 1 NZLR 281.
1022. *Robson and Sharpe v. Drummond* (1831) 2 B & Ad 303.

Where the contractual remedies regime in the Contract and Commercial Law Act 2017 applies,[1023] an assignee of the burden of a contract may become personally liable in an action by the other contracting party. Section 54(1) and (2) of the 2017 Act provide:

> (1) If a contract, or the benefit or burden of a contract, is assigned, the remedies of damages and cancellation shall, except to the extent that it is otherwise provided in the assigned contract, be enforceable by or against the assignee (except to the extent that it is otherwise provided in the assigned contract).
> (2) This section is subject to sections 55 to 57.

Section 54(1) re-enacts section 11(1) of the Contractual Remedies Act 1979, and the following cases refer to section 11 and the 1979 Act.

In *SB Properties Ltd v. Holdgate,*[1024] the Court of Appeal accepted that as a matter of general principle, a simple burden could not be shifted off the assignor's shoulders without the consent of the other contracting party other than by novation, by which the non-assigning party consented to the release of the assignor and the substitution of the assignor by the assignee. However, section 11(1) (now section 54(1)) added to the continuing liability on the assignor a new liability on the assignee to the non-assigning party.

It is apparent, then, that what is now section 54 does not alter the obligations of the parties to the contract, nor does it make the assignee a party to the contract. That can occur only through novation. However, as recognized in *SB Properties Ltd*, a new liability arises under section 54 where there has been an assignment of the benefit of the contract. In *Gibbston Valley Estate Ltd v. Owen*[1025] Henry and Blanchard JJ noted that the former section 11(1) appeared to provide that where the benefit of a contract was assigned, the other party to the contract had a remedy in damages against the assignee if there was a breach of the assignor's obligations under the contract.

If the assignee becomes liable for the assignor's breach in this way then, subject to any agreement or provision in the contract to the contrary, the assignee's obligations are limited to the value of the performance of the assigned contract to which the assignee is entitled by virtue of the agreement.[1026] Any excess has to be recovered from the assignor, who remains fully liable on the assigned contract.[1027]

In *Gibbston*, Tipping J went further than Henry and Blanchard JJ and contemplated assignment of the contract as a whole with its benefits and burdens, and in *SB Properties Ltd*, the Court of Appeal expressed its agreement with Tipping J's approach. Baragwanath J said that to the extent that the rules of the common law

1023. *See* para. 222.
1024. (2009) 9 NZBLC 102,697.
1025. (1999) 4 NZ ConvC 193,024.
1026. Contract and Commercial Law Act 2017, s. 55 (formerly Contractual Remedies Act 1979, s. 11(2)); *Gray v. UDC Finance Ltd* [2000] 3 NZLR 192. The assignee is entitled to be indemnified by the assignor in respect of undisclosed terms or representations: Contract and Commercial Law Act 2017, s. 56.
1027. *S B Properties Ltd v. Holdgate* (2009) 24 NZBLC 102,697.

did not impose a burden on the assignee, that could not withstand the pressure placed on it by the emphatic language of (the former) section 11(1). But this wide view has been rejected by the Supreme Court. In *Savvy Vineyards 3552 Ltd v. Kakara Estate Ltd*,[1028] William Young J said that the Contractual Remedies Act was an unlikely vehicle for the making of a change to the law of personal property as radical as that postulated in *SB Properties*. There was no suggestion in its legislative history that such a change to the law was the purpose of the Act. Its purpose was to clarify and simplify the law in relation to remedies for misrepresentation and breach of contract. There was also no indication in the Property Law Act 2007 that such a change had occurred. The text of section 11(1) did not provide that the burden of a contract might be assigned, and when construed in light of its purpose, it was clear that it did not have that effect. So whatever the explanation for the opening words of section 11(1), they did not operate so as to provide for the assignment of the burden of a contract.

Savvy Vineyards has clarified the law. And, certainly, William Young J's words apply equally to section 54 of the 2017 Act.

II. Assignment by Operation of Law

209. On the death of a contracting party, all causes of action subsisting against or vested in that party survive against or for the benefit of the estate.[1029] The personal representatives may thus sue or be sued on the deceased's contracts, although in the latter case, their liability is limited to the value of the assets in their hands.[1030] The general rule does not apply to contracts of a personal nature, where the death of either party brings the contract to an end.[1031]

Any right of action for breach of contract possessed by a bankrupt which relates to his or her property and which, if enforced, will swell his or her assets, passes to the trustee in bankruptcy.[1032] Instances are a contract by a third person to deliver goods or to pay money to the bankrupt. On the other hand, the right to sue for an injury to the character, feelings or reputation of a bankrupt, though arising from a breach of contract, does not vest in the trustee.[1033]

1028. [2014] NZSC 121, [2015] 1 NZLR 281 at [92]; *and see Water Guard NZ Ltd v. Cynortic Water Systems Ltd* [2016] NZCA 291.
1029. Law Reform Act 1936, s. 3.
1030. *Cooper v. Jarman* (1866) LR 3 Eq 98.
1031. *Farrow v. Wilson* (1869) LR 4 CP 744.
1032. Insolvency Act 2006, s. 64(1)(e).
1033. *Wilson v. United Counties Bank* [1920] AC 102.

Chapter 5. The Termination of the Contract

§1. Performance and Breach

I. Cancellation for Breach

210. By virtue of section 37 of the Contract and Commercial Law Act 2017, a party to a contract may cancel if the other has committed a substantial breach of the contract. There are several types of breaches which justify cancellation.

A. *The Types of Breach*

1. Repudiation

211. Section 36(1) of the Contract and Commercial Law Act 2017 provides:

> A party to a contract may cancel the contract if, by words or conduct, another party (B) repudiates the contract by making it clear that B does not intend to-perform B's obligations under the contract; or complete the performance of B's obligations under the contract.

Repudiation can occur before performance is due, or in the course of performance. In the former case, it is sometimes called anticipatory repudiation. The wording of section 36 contemplates both a refusal to perform any obligations under the contract and 'partial repudiation', a refusal to perform only some of those obligations.[1034]

While repudiation is normally constituted by words, it can be by conduct such as lengthy delay or acting inconsistently with the contract.[1035] Repudiation may be inferred from conduct if a reasonable person would believe the actions evidenced an intention not to perform the obligations of the contract.[1036] An example is where the owner of a building entered it and changed the locks, thus denying the tenant access to the building.[1037]

It can also be repudiation to make clear an intention to perform only in a way which departs substantially from the true contract obligation, but only where the party doing so is asserting an unwillingness to comply with the contractual terms as

1034. *Kumar v. Station Properties Ltd* [2015] NZSC 34; [2016] 1 NZLR 99, at [57]; and *see Jade Residential Ltd v. Paul* [2020] NZCA 477 at [40]–[45].
1035. For example *Cameron v. Worboys* [1952] NZLR 962.
1036. *Bromley Industries Ltd v. Martin and Judith Fitzsimons Ltd* (2009) 19 PRNZ 850; [2009] NZCA 382.
1037. *Ingram v. Patcroft Properties Ltd* [2011] 3 NZLR 433.

they might be ultimately determined to be.[1038] Thus, a party who accepts the contract is binding but, mistakenly, argues that he or she is entitled to perform the contract in a particular way does not repudiate the contract.[1039]

A wrongful attempt to cancel can amount to a repudiation which itself places the cancelling party in breach. *Ingram v. Patcroft Properties Ltd*[1040] provides an example. A tenant (I) was in arrears of rent and accordingly in breach of contract. The lease required punctual payment and allowed re-entry by the landlord (PPL) if the rent was in arrears for fourteen days. PPL re-entered one day early, changed the locks, posted a notice saying that the lease was terminated and distrained I's chattels. The Supreme Court held that PPL had unlawfully excluded I by reason of its premature re-entry and that this was a breach of the lease contract giving rise to the immediate right of cancellation by I under the predecessor to section 37(2)(b) of the Contract and Commercial Law Act 2017.[1041] While PPL's repudiatory stance remained unchanged, there was a continuing breach capable of acceptance by I. PPL intimated that that payment of the balance of the rent would be futile as it would not lead to reinstatement of possession, and therefore PPL was precluded from cancelling for non-payment. And PPL's repudiation was accepted when I issued proceedings.

2. Breach of Term

212. Section 37(1) of the Contract and Commercial Law Act 2017 provides that the innocent party can cancel if one of the following has occurred, provided in each case that the breach is of the level of gravity defined in section 37(2):

> (a) the party has been induced to enter into it [the contract] by a misrepresentation, whether innocent or fraudulent, made by or on behalf of another party to the contract; or
> (b) a term in the contract is breached by another party to the contract; or
> (c) It is clear that a term in the contract will be breached by another party to that contract.

This provision applies the same cancellation regime to misrepresentation as it does to breach. Paragraph (c) envisages an anticipated breach. It goes wider than repudiation, for it could cover a case where the party still intends to perform, but it is clear to a reasonable onlooker that that is not going to happen. In *Brooklands*

1038. *Kumar v. Station Properties Ltd* [2015] NZSC 34; [2016] 1 NZLR 99 at [63].
1039. *Kumar v. Station Properties Ltd* [2015] NZSC 34; [2016] 1 NZLR 99 at [63]; *see also Starlight Enterprises Ltd v. Lapco Enterprises Ltd* [1979] 2 NZLR 744; *Oxborough v. North Harbour Builders Ltd* [2002] 1 NZLR 145.
1040. [2011] 3 NZLR 433.
1041. *See* para. 214 below.

Motor Co Ltd v. Bridge Wholesale Acceptance Corp (Australia) Ltd, Blanchard J said of section 7(3)(c) Contractual Remedies Act 1979, the predecessor to 37(2):[1042]

> The test is whether a reasonable bystander, aware of all relevant existing and future facts, would have believed that by the time of the purported cancellation it was clear that there would be a breach of the requisite essentiality or seriousness.

But he forewarned that:[1043] '... the court will err on the side of caution: the risk of unexpected performance by the non-cancelling party should lie of the party who elects to give notice of cancellation'.

B. The Substantiality of Breach

1. Essential Term

213. By virtue of section 37(2)(a) of the Contract and Commercial Law Act 2017, a party may cancel in the case of a breach or misrepresentation if:

(a) The parties have expressly or impliedly agreed that the truth of the representation, or as the case may require, the performance of the term, is essential to the cancelling party.

This provision has been interpreted by the Supreme Court as extending to a particular combination of terms which collectively may be essential to one or both parties, even if no single one of the terms is in itself essential.[1044]

The parties may expressly provide in their contract that a particular term or combination of terms is of the essence.[1045] In *Mana Property Trustee Ltd v. James Developments Ltd*,[1046] for instance, the parties agreed that the vendor of land had to deliver title to land of not less than a stipulated area. The requirement was seen as essential, the court emphasizing that the parties could agree that a term was essential even though the consequences of breach might be relatively minor. And even if not express, essentiality may be implied. But if the parties intend a stipulation as to time to be essential, they must state this as the Courts will not imply essentiality on that point.[1047] Further, where the term is 'essential', the slightest deviation from the

1042. (1994) 7 NZCLC 260,449. *See also NZ Automobile Association Inc v. McKay* [1996] 2 ERNZ 622 at 644–645; *Eastern Pacific Trading Ltd v. International Primary Products Ltd* [2014] NZHC 3225.
1043. (1994) NZ CLC at 260,461.
1044. *Kumar v. Station Properties Ltd* [2015] NZSC 34; [2016] 1 NZLR 99 at [93].
1045. For example *New Zealand Tenancy Bonds Ltd v. Mooney* [1986] 1 NZLR 280: time for payment of a deposit was 'strictly of the essence of the contract'.
1046. [2010] 3 NZLR 805.
1047. *Mana Property Trustee Ltd v. James Developments Ltd* [2010] 3 NZLR 805 at [31].

contract provides a basis for cancellation. In one case, for example, the receipt of a fax seven minutes after the stipulated time was too late.[1048]

In the case of misrepresentations, a test often applied is whether the party would have entered the contract at all had it not been for the misrepresentation. In *Progeni Systems Ltd v. Hampton Studios Ltd*, Tipping J put it this way:[1049]

> the truth of a representation will be essential when the representation is of such fundamental importance to the representee in his consideration whether to enter into the proposed contractual relationship that without it he would not have contracted with the representor either at all or on those particular terms.

The essentiality of a term or combination of terms may be express or implied. An example of the latter is *Kumar v. Station Properties Ltd.*[1050] In that case, the appellant had contracted to purchase apartments in a building under development in a resort area, where both parties contemplated the apartments would ultimately be let out on short-term rentals to visiting tourists. The respondent had promised to supply a furniture package and a property management agreement but failed to do so. The Supreme Court held that given the common expectation the apartments would be used for short-term rentals, these failures were as to impliedly essential matters.

2. Substantial Breach

214. Many terms in many contracts are not essential in the sense that any breach of them will justify cancellation. However, a breach of any term will justify cancellation if the effects of the breach are substantial. Section 37(2)(b)of the Contract and Commercial Law Act 2017 provides that a party may cancel if:

> (b) The effect of the misrepresentation or breach is, or, in the case of an anticipated breach, will be:
>   (i) substantially to reduce the benefit of the contract to the cancelling party; or
>   (ii) substantially to increase the burden of the cancelling party under the contract; or
>   (iii) in relation to the cancelling party, to make the benefit or burden of the contract substantially different from that represented or contracted for.

Again misrepresentation and breach are equated for this purpose.

Whether the effects of a breach are substantial enough to justify cancellation depends on the facts of the particular case. The courts have declined to define 'substantial', saying it is a matter of fact, degree and impression. It is incapable of any

---

1048. *Larsen v. Rick Dees Ltd* [2007] NZSC 39, [2007] 3 NZLR 577.
1049. *Progeni Systems Ltd v. Hampton Studios Ltd* HC Christchurch, CP 105/86, 11 Aug. 1987. *See also Wilson v. Hines* (1994) 6 TCLR 163.
1050. [2015] NZSC 34; [2016] 1 NZLR 99. *See also Pegasus Town Ltd v. Draper* [2011] NZCA 140.

kind of arithmetical analysis. An individual determination must be made in each case having regard to the nature of the contract and its subject matter and all the circumstances of the case.[1051] For example, in *Ingram v. Patcroft Properties Ltd*,[1052] the unlawful exclusion of the lessee by the landlord was held to give rise to the right to cancel under the predecessor to section 37(2)(b). It prevented the lessees from carrying on their businesses, which was the very purpose of the lease. Again, a misrepresentation that a property would produce a net return of 9% when it produced only 2% was substantial enough to justify cancellation, for the former would have been sufficient to service the borrowings, whereas the latter would require a substantial subsidy.[1053]

Although some dicta suggest that the question of substantiality must be determined objectively,[1054] others suggest that subjective factors may sometimes enter into the equation.[1055]

It is important for an innocent party not to be too ready to cancel. If he or she makes an incorrect judgment that a breach is substantial enough to justify cancellation, the innocent party may himself or herself be held in breach.

C. Election

215. The innocent party is not obliged to cancel for even the most serious breach, although in many cases it will be the sensible, practical option. The party has an election whether to cancel or to keep the contract on foot. This was so at common law as well as under the Contractual Remedies Act 1979 and the current Contract and Commercial Law Act 2017. In *White and Carter (Councils) Ltd v. McGregor*,[1056] the defendant repudiated an advertising contract almost immediately after it was made. The repudiation was not accepted by the company, which continued to display the defendant's advertisement contrary to his wishes. The company was held to be entitled to do so, and to recover the agreed contract price.

It has been said in England that an unaccepted repudiation does not affect the rights of either party to the contract,[1057] but a different view has prevailed in New Zealand. In *Ingram v. Patcroft Properties Ltd*,[1058] the issue was whether the tenant of a building was able to bring an action for repudiation of a lease by the landlord when the tenant had not paid rent as required by the lease. The Supreme Court held that the party who makes an unaccepted repudiation of the contract (in this case the landlord) cannot later claim to be able to cancel the contract because the non-repudiating party has not performed his or her obligations under the contract if the

1051. *MacIndoe v. Mainzeal Group Ltd* [1991] 3 NZLR 273 at 284–285; *Jolly v. Palmer* [1985] 1 NZLR 658 at 662; *Oxborough v. North Harbour Builders* [2002] 1 NZLR 145 at 152–153.
1052. [2011] 3 NZLR 433; *see* para. 211 above.
1053. *JB Aubin Realty Ltd v. Hinton* [2011] NZCA 465.
1054. *MacIndoe v. Mainzeal Group Ltd* [1991] 3 NZLR 273, at 284.
1055. *Sharplin v. Henderson* [1990] 2 NZLR 134 at 137; *Jolly v. Palmer* [1985] 1 NZLR 658 at 662, and *see Tinnock v. Birkenhead* (2004) NZCPR 1.
1056. [1962] AC 413.
1057. *Howard v. Pickford Tool Co Ltd* [1951] 1 KB 417, 421.
1058. [2011] 3 NZLR 433; *see* para. 211 above.

repudiation makes it clear that attempting to perform would be futile. In effect, the unaccepted repudiation can be seen as waiving the requirement of the innocent party perform his or her obligations. So here the non-payment of the rent did not bar the tenants from later cancelling in their turn because they were willing to pay, but the landlord had made it clear that they would not be allowed back into possession.

The decision may be compared with that in *Messenger v. Goodman.*[1059] An agreement was made for the sale of property, but the parties disputed about the settlement date and settlement never occurred. Eventually, the vendors cancelled, resold at a lower price and sued for damages. They argued that accepting they were wrong about the settlement date, the purchasers had not tendered settlement on the date they contended for or at any time thereafter. The question in issue was whether a tender of payment on that date would have been futile. The Court thought that there was a real doubt about what would have happened, that the purchasers were in breach of contract in not tendering payment and that the vendors thus were not in breach in failing to give title on that date. So the contract remained on foot until it was validly cancelled by the vendors for non-payment of the price and their claim accordingly succeeded.

D. *Affirmation*

216. If the party elects to affirm the contract, it remains in force for all purposes. A subsequent event rendering further performance impossible will frustrate the contract,[1060] and the party who committed the original breach or repudiation will itself be able to cancel if the other party, who has elected to affirm, then itself commits a substantial breach.[1061]

Section 38 of the Contract and Commercial Law Act 2017 provides that a party shall not be entitled to cancel the contract if, with full knowledge of the repudiation or misrepresentation or breach, that party has affirmed the contract. Thus, an election to affirm the contract is final, and the innocent party cannot then change its mind and cancel in respect of the same breach. What conduct will be sufficient to amount to affirmation depends on the facts of the case. In *Mana Property Trustee Ltd v. James Developments Ltd,*[1062] the Supreme Court held that where one party to a contract for sale of land was in breach of the terms of the contract, the other party would not affirm the contract by issuing a settlement notice, but rather would by doing so only be making clear that that party was entitled to cancel if the settlement notice was not complied with. In other cases, affirmation has been established on the basis of continued performance of contractual obligations with knowledge of a basis for cancellation.[1063]

1059. (2012) 13 NZCPR 535.
1060. *Avery v. Bowden* (1855) 5 E & B 714.
1061. *Fercometal SARL v. Mediterranean Shipping Co SA* [1989] AC 788.
1062. [2010] 3 NZLR 805; [2010] NZSC 90.
1063. *Catley v. Herbert* [1988] 1 NZLR 606 at 619; *New Zealand Public Service Association v. Department of Survey* [1992] 2 ERNZ 869.

However, the courts are not ready to find affirmation, such is the finality of its consequences unless it is clear that that is what the party intended. As Gallen J has said, in the end, the question is always one of fact – has there been a real and genuine affirmation in the circumstances of the case?[1064] So, delay alone will usually not amount to affirmation,[1065] and even the issue of proceedings for specific performance may not be conclusive.[1066]

Affirmation only bars cancellation in respect of the breach in question. If there is a further breach or repudiation after the affirmation, cancellation will lie for that. A repudiation which continues after the affirmation can for this purpose be regarded as having been renewed.[1067]

E. Cancellation

217. Section 41 of the Contract and Commercial Law Act 2017 provides as follows:

> (1) The cancellation of a contract by a party does not take effect:
> a. Before the time at which the cancellation is made known to the other party; or
> b. Before the time at which the party cancelling the contract shows, by some clear means that is reasonable in the circumstances, an intention to cancel the contract, if:
> (i) it is not reasonably practicable for the cancelling party to communicate with the other party; or
> (ii) the other party cannot reasonably expect to receive notice of the cancellation because of that other party's conduct in relation to the contract.
>
> (2) The cancellation may be made known by words, or by conduct showing an intention to cancel, or both. It shall not be necessary to use any particular form of words, so long as the intention to cancel is made known.

The cancellation may be made known by words or conduct. Thus, a lease may be cancelled by a tenant moving out and returning the key;[1068] and a contract of loan by stopping the cheque for the loan payment.[1069]

The words or conduct must evince an intention to cancel; equivocal conduct will not be enough. Once the contract has been cancelled, any subsequent conduct which

1064. *Hughes v. Huppert* [1991] 1 NZLR 474 at 478.
1065. *New Zealand Tenancy Bonds Ltd v. Mooney* [1986] 1 NZLR 280. *See also Westpac Merchant Finance Ltd v. Winstone Industries Ltd* [1993] 2 NZLR 247.
1066. *Oxborough v. North Harbour Builders Ltd* [2002] 1 NZLR 145 at 149.
1067. *Jolly v. Palmer* [1985] 1 NZLR 658; the *Oxborough* case above.
1068. *Cash Handling Systems Ltd v. Augustus Terrace Ltd* (1996) 3 NZ Conv C 192 400.
1069. *Auckland Waterbed Co v. Progressive Finance Ltd* HC Christchurch A 31/84, 11 Apr. and 24 May 1984.

might be construed as an affirmation will be ineffective; a cancelled contract can only be revived by agreement between the parties.[1070]

There is no clear authority on what constitutes 'making known', for example, in what circumstances notice to an agent will be sufficient, or whether it is enough that the other party hears via an indirect source.[1071]

Section 41(2) was first enacted in 2002 to meet a difficulty which arose from the rule that a cancellation does not take effect until it is made known. That difficulty manifested itself in cases where a vendor of property resold after the original purchaser had repudiated, without informing that purchaser of the resale. The matter was initially resolved by the Court of Appeal in *Chatfield v. Jones,*[1072] by saying that the resale was in fact a cancellation, and it was sufficient that the original purchaser found out later, perhaps when he or she received a statement of claim claiming damages. This separation of the cancellation from the notice of it sat uneasily with the words of the section.

Paragraph (b)(ii) now provides that a party in breach need not be notified of the cancellation if the conduct of that party has been such that he or she cannot reasonably expect to receive notice. In such a case, it is sufficient for the cancelling party to evince by some overt means reasonable in the circumstances an intention to cancel. The same is true if it is not reasonably possible for the cancelling party to communicate with the other.

There is one further matter which may be of importance in some cases. The party seeking to cancel the contract must not be gaining a benefit from the cancellation, as where that party would not have been able to perform his or her own obligations under the contract.[1073]

F. The Effect of Cancellation

218. Cancellation, whether for breach or misrepresentation, is not rescission *ab initio*: it does not avoid the contract as though it had never existed, but operates for the future only. With regard to misrepresentation, this differs from the position at law prior to the Contractual Remedies Act 1979, now replaced by the Contract and Commercial Law Act 2017. The effect of cancellation is defined in section 42 of the Contract and Commercial Law Act 2017:

> (1) When a contract is cancelled the following provisions apply:
> a. To the extent that the contract remains unperformed at the time of the cancellation, no party is obliged or entitled to perform it further;
> b. To the extent that the contract has been performed at the time of the cancellation, no party is, by reason only of the cancellation, divested of any property transferred or money paid pursuant to the contract.
>
> ...

1070. The *Auckland Waterbed* case, *ibid.*
1071. *See Kauri Developments Ltd v. Nicholson* (1986) 2 NZCPR 532 at 540.
1072. [1990] 3 NZLR 285.
1073. *Noble Investments Ltd v. Keenan* (2005) 6NZCPR 43, [47]–[48].

(3) Nothing in this section affects the right of a party to recover damages in respect of a misrepresentation or the repudiation or breach of the contract by another party.

A literal reading of subsection (1)(a) might suggest that claims in a contract regulating secondary obligations, such as arbitration clauses and liquidated damages claims, cease to have effect on cancellation. However, that is unlikely. At common law, cancellation (rescission) affected only the primary obligations, and it is likely that a similar finding would be made under the Contract and Commercial Law Act.[1074] It has also been held that a restraint of trade clause survives cancellation because that must have been the intention of the parties when they agreed on its inclusion in the contract.[1075]

It has also been held that cancellation does not affect the enforceability of obligations which have unconditionally accrued due before cancellation. Thus a deposit, or periodic payments such as rent or franchise fees, which fall due before cancellation can be recovered afterwards.[1076] In *Garratt v. Ikeda*, the Court of Appeal said:[1077]

> The better view is to say that Section [42(1)] does not have the effect of divesting unconditionally accrued rights. … We are here using the word 'unconditionally' in the … sense … that (i) there must be no impediment, by unfulfilled condition or otherwise, to the enforcement of the right at the point of cancellation; and (ii) enforcement must not be subject to any reciprocal obligation on the part of the enforcing party.

In *Simanke v. Liu,*[1078] it was held that a 'deposit' of NZD 300,000 on the purchase of a house for NZD 650,000 was not a true deposit at all, and payment of it was dependent on the vendor's giving title to the purchaser. When the contract was cancelled, therefore, the vendor's right to it ceased.

Section 42(1)(b) provides that money and property which have changed hands before cancellation are not divested by the cancellation.[1079] So if a deposit or part payment has been paid before cancellation, the payee remains the owner of it; and if the assets of a business have been acquired by the purchaser, the property in them remains with that purchaser even if the contract is cancelled. However, if injustice is thus caused, there is a discretionary power in the court under section 43 of the Contract and Commercial Law Act 2017 to grant relief.

Section 42(3) provides, as was the case at common law, that nothing in the section affects the right of a party to recover damages. That is to say, cancellation of a contract under the Contract and Commercial Law Act 2017 does not avoid the contract *ab initio*; the innocent party can still recover damages for any repudiation,

1074. *Grain Processors Ltd v. Bluebird Foods Ltd* [1999] 9 TCLR 385; *Brown v. Langwoods Photo Stores Ltd* [1991] 1 NZLR 173 at 176.
1075. *Broadcasting Corporation of New Zealand v. Neilsen* (1988) 2 NZELC 96,040.
1076. *Brown v. Langwoods Photo Stores Ltd* [1991] 1 NZLR 173; *Garratt v. Ikeda* [2002] 1 NZLR 577.
1077. [2002] 1 NZLR 577 at 584.
1078. (1994) 2 NZ ConvC 191,888.
1079. *See Mayall v. Weal* [1982] 2 NZLR 385.

breach or misrepresentation committed before the cancellation took place. This point is re-emphasized by section 49 of the Act which provides:

> (1) A party to a contract is not prevented by the cancellation of the contract, or by the granting of relief under section 43, from recovering damages for a misrepresentation or the repudiation or breach of the contract by another party to the contract.
> (2) However the value of any relief granted under section 43 must be taken into account in assessing those damages.
> (3) Subsection (1) is subject to sections 34, 35, and 50 to 53.
> (4) Any sum ordered to be paid by any party to the contract to any other party under section 43(3) may be set off against any damages payable by the party to that other party.

G. Relief under Section 43

219. Section 43 of the Contract and Commercial Law Act 2017 gives a court power to make orders granting relief after cancellation. Such an order may be made 'if it is just and practicable to do so'. Such an order may:

(a) direct that property be vested in a party, or transferred from one party to another;
(b) direct one party to pay the other such sum as the Court thinks just;
(c) direct one party to do in relation to the other any act or thing the court thinks just.

Such an order can be made on terms and conditions. In considering whether to make an order, the Court must have regard to a variety of matters such as the terms of the contract, any expenditure incurred by a party, the value of work or services performed by a party, and any benefit or advantage obtained by a party. Most of the cases have involved orders for monetary payments which are restitutionary in nature. In one case, the purchaser of a house was granted recovery of the whole purchase price plus interest.[1080] But a defaulting purchaser will not be allowed to recover a deposit paid because the very nature of a deposit is that the parties have agreed that it be forfeited on breach by the purchaser; it would be different if the 'deposit' was excessive in amount.[1081] The courts have also held that an award under section 43 may be compensatory in nature. As such it can be an alternative to common law damages, but 'need not be trammelled' by common law restrictions.[1082]

1080. *Gallagher v. Young* [1981] 1 NZLR 734.
1081. *Garratt v. Ikeda* [2002] 1 NZLR 577.
1082. *Coxhead v. Newmans Tours Ltd* (1993) 6 TCLR 1; *Thomson v. Rankin* [1993] 1 NZLR 408 at 410; *Burch v. Willoughby Consultants Ltd* (1990) 3 NZELC 78.

No order may be made which deprives a person, not being a party to the contract, of property acquired by him or her in good faith and for valuable consideration;[1083] nor may an order be made in respect of property if a party to the contract has so altered his or her position that it would be inequitable to make such an order.[1084]

H. Cancellation for a Bad Reason When a Good Reason Also Exists

220. At common law, a party's cancellation was held justified if a valid reason for it existed even though that reason was unknown to the cancelling party at the time of the cancellation.[1085] The question most commonly arose where a party purported to cancel in reliance on an insufficient ground (e.g., an inessential breach) and subsequently discovered that a sufficient ground (e.g., a serious misrepresentation) did exist, albeit unknown to the canceller. Although the Contractual Remedies Act (CRA) and the Contract and Commercial Law Act make no reference to this issue, it has now been settled that a purported cancellation relying on an invalid ground is nevertheless effective if a good reason existed, even if it was not known by the cancelling party at the time.[1086]

II. Contracting Out of the Contract and Commercial Law Act 2017

221. Section 34 of the Contract and Commercial Law Act provides:

> 34. If a contract expressly provides for a remedy in respect of misrepresentation or repudiation or breach of contract or makes express provision for any of the other matters to which sections 35 to 49 relate, those sections have effect subject to that provision.

It is thus open to the parties expressly to provide in the contract for their own remedies for breach, or their own variations of remedies such as cancellation. If they do so, their express contractual provisions will prevail over the Contract and Commercial Law Act 2017 in so far as they are inconsistent with it. The form of agreement for sale and purchase drawn up by the New Zealand Law Society in conjunction with the Real Estate Institute lays down a special procedure (the serving of a settlement notice and consequent cancellation) if a purchaser of land does not settle on due date; a party may rely on this to the exclusion of the Contract and Commercial Law Act if he or she wishes, in the event of such a failure to settle. But this clause is limited in scope. It does not, for instance, cover matters such as repudiation, misrepresentation or indeed any type of breach other than a failure to settle on due date; to those things, the general law, that is, the Act, applies. An innocent party may be able to elect whether to proceed under the Act or under the express

1083. Contract and Commercial Law Act 2017, s. 46.
1084. Contract and Commercial Law Act 2017, s. 47.
1085. *Pearce v. Stevens* (1904) 24 NZLR 357.
1086. *Kumar v. Station Properties Ltd* [2015] NZSC 34; [2016] 1 NZLR 99.

contractual provisions.[1087] The Courts have been unwilling to find that remedies clauses exclude the predecessor to the Contract and Commercial Law Act entirely; where possible, they find that they merely supplement or modify its provisions.[1088]

The former section 5 of the Contractual Remedies Act, section 34's predecessor, has been relied upon to hold that a restraint of trade clause survived after cancellation of the contract because the intention of the parties in including the clause in the contract clearly was that it would continue after termination.[1089] It has also been held that the parties' description of a payment as a 'deposit' means that it is forfeited on breach by the purchaser and that relief under section 43 of the Act is thereby excluded.[1090] And a clause contracting out of liability for misrepresentation has been treated as a clause making provision for a remedy, so section 5 or section 34 can apply.[1091]

III. Savings

222. Section 59(1) of the Contract and Commercial Law Act 2017 provides:

> Nothing in this subpart affects:
>
> (a) the law relating to specific performance or injunction;
> (b) the law relating to mistake, duress, or undue influence;
> (c) the doctrine of non est factum (it is not my deed);
> (d) subpart 4 (frustrated contracts);
> (e) Part 3 (sale of goods);
> (f) sections 253–260 of the Property Law Act 2007 (which relate to relief against cancellation of leases for breach of a covenant or a condition);
> (g) the Consumer Guarantees Act 1993;
> (h) any other enactment so far as it prescribes or governs terms of contracts or remedies available in respect of contracts, or governs the enforcement of contracts.

A. *Sale of Goods Act Provisions of the Contract and Commercial Law Act 2017*

223. The most important of these savings is paragraph (e). The Contract and Commercial Law Act 2017 governs the 'cancellation' of contracts for the sale of

---

1087. *MacIndoe v. Mainzeal Group Ltd* [1991] 3 NZLR 273.
1088. For example *Cash Handling Systems Ltd v. Augustus Terrace Ltd* (1996) 3 NZConvC 192,400; *Kauri Developments Ltd v. Nicholson* (1986) 2 NZCPR 532; *Morris v. Robert Jones Investments Ltd* [1994] 2 NZLR 275. By contrast it was held that the standard REINZ-ADLS contract for sale and purchase of land limited a buyer's right to cancel if a defect in the title to the land is discovered, *see Armstrong v. Mitchell* [2018] NZHC 3431, at [25].
1089. *Broadcasting Corporation of New Zealand v. Neilsen* (1988) 2 NZELC 96,040.
1090. *Garratt v. Ikeda* [2002] 1 NZLR 577.
1091. *McKenzie Institute International v. ARCIC* (1997) 8 TCLR 329; *Cygnet Farms Ltd v. ANZ Bank of New Zealand Ltd* [2017] 2 NZLR 538.

goods. Basically, in such a contract, if there is breach of a 'condition', as opposed to a 'warranty', the party may 'treat the contract as repudiated' and reject the goods. Once goods have been 'accepted', they cannot be rejected. Where the Act is silent, the common law is preserved.[1092] This is a matter of great significance. It means that what is probably the most common type of contract is treated differently with regard to cancellation for breach.[1093] The New Zealand Law Commission recommended amendments to the Sale of Goods Act to bring that Act into line with the Contractual Remedies Act.[1094] But this has not occurred. Instead, the Sale of Goods Act provisions have been essentially re-enacted as Part 3 of the Contract and Commercial Law Act 2017.

B. Consumer Guarantees Act 1993

224. Paragraph (g) of section 59 of the Contract and Commercial Law Act 2017 saves the Consumer Guarantees Act 1993. This latter Act provides remedies for consumers of goods and services where those goods or services do not live up to the guarantees of quality which are implied by the Act.[1095] Some of those remedies are in the nature of cancellation. With regard to goods, if the failure cannot be remedied, or is of a substantial character, as defined in the Act, the consumer may reject the goods, and choose to have either a refund of the price or replacement goods. The right to reject is lost if not exercised within a reasonable time, or if the goods have been damaged.[1096]

With regard to services, the consumer may cancel the contract if the failure cannot be remedied or is substantial. The rules about cancellation are closely analogous to those in the Contract and Commercial Law Act 2017. Notice of cancellation is required;[1097] so far as the contract remains unperformed, no party is obliged or entitled to perform it further;[1098] and so far as it has been performed, no party is divested of money paid or property transferred with the important exception that, subject to the discretion of the Court, the consumer is entitled to a refund of any money paid.[1099]

It should be noted that this Act applies only to consumer contracts, and not commercial contracts, for goods and services, and that even then the remedies are available only to consumers; sellers of goods and providers of services must look to the Contract and Commercial Law Act 2017.

Moreover, the Consumer Guarantees Act provides that the rights and remedies provided in it are in addition to any other right or remedy under any other Act unless the Consumer Guarantees Act expressly or impliedly repeals or modifies that other

1092. Contract and Commercial Law Act 2017, s. 60.
1093. *See* further para. 305.
1094. NZLC R25 *Contract Statutes Review* (1993).
1095. *See* further paras 318–321, where the remedies under the 1993 Act are considered in more detail.
1096. Consumer Guarantees Act 1993, ss 18–28.
1097. Section 37.
1098. Section 38(1)(c).
1099. Section 38(1)(a)(b).

right or remedy.[1100] Thus, even a consumer may be entitled to protection under the Contract and Commercial Law Act 2017 as an alternative to the Consumer Guarantees Act (CGA) except insofar as the latter repeals or modifies the former.

C. Fair Trading Act 1986

225. Paragraph (h) of section 59 of the Contract and Commercial Law Act 2017 provides that nothing in the CRA affects any other enactment relating to contracts. The Fair Trading Act 1986 is such an enactment. The FTA likewise provides that nothing in it affects any other enactment.[1101] Thus in some cases a plaintiff might have a choice of cancelling under the Contract and Commercial Law Act or applying to the Court for the discretionary remedy of avoidance of the contract under the FTA. But this will apply only in the limited situation where there has been misleading conduct in trade by the other party. Cancellation under the Contract and Commercial Law Act 2017 will normally be the more attractive simply because the party can effect it himself or herself without the necessity for a court order; that is not so under the FTA.

§2. Impossibility, Frustration, and Hardship: The Unforeseen

I. Definition

226. New Zealand law follows English law in regarding a contractual promise as absolute unless the contract is frustrated by an external event which renders further performance of the contract impossible, or a totally different thing from that which was promised. The dictum of Lord Radcliffe that frustration occurs where 'the circumstances in which performance is called for would render it a thing radically different from that which was undertaken by the contract'[1102] has been applied in New Zealand.[1103] In a recent New Zealand case, it was said there must have been a change of circumstances so significant as to destroy a basic assumption which the parties had made when they entered into the contract.[1104]

Thus, a contract is frustrated if, due to some extraneous cause, property the subject of the contract is destroyed,[1105] or a person essential to its performance dies or becomes unavailable through illness. The same is true where the very basis of the contract disappears because of the non-occurrence of some event on which it

---

1100. Section 4.
1101. Fair Trading Act 1986, s. 50(1).
1102. *Davis Contractors Ltd v. Fareham* [1956] AC 696 at 728–729.
1103. *Roberts v. Independent Publishers Ltd* [1974] 1 NZLR 459 at 472.
1104. *Neilson v. Dysart Timbers Limited* [2009] 3 NZLR 160 [2009] NZSC 43, at [30], per Tipping J.
1105. *See* the discussion in *Planet Kids Ltd v. Auckland Council* [2013] NZSC 137, which is now New Zealand's leading case on frustration.

depended: the cancellation of the King's coronation in 1903 resulted in the frustration of a number of contracts to rent rooms along the route of the proposed coronation procession.[1106] Government intervention in the form of war, or the requisition of property such as a ship,[1107] is another cause, as is supervening illegality.[1108]

II. The Threshold

227. The interruption caused by the external event must be extreme, to the extent that performance would be a different thing because of it. The fact that the contract has become more difficult, or more expensive, to perform is not enough. While a change in the value of money over the years which is outside the realm of reasonable speculation may possibly frustrate a contract, this is very unlikely. In *The Power Co Ltd v. Gore District Council,*[1109] a contract to supply electricity at one penny per unit entered into in 1927 was held not to be frustrated when over seventy years later the market price had risen to NZD 0.102 per unit. Likewise in *Wilkins & Davies Construction Ltd v. Geraldine Borough,*[1110] a building contract was held not to be frustrated even though unanticipated ground conditions caused a massive rise in costs. In *Roberts v. Independent Publishers Ltd,*[1111] the fact that takeovers had changed the nature of a company did not frustrate a contract giving an option to take shares in it; and in *Des Forges v. Wright,*[1112] a contract to sell a small goods distribution business was not frustrated by the closure of one of the supplier's plants.

The question of whether an interruption to performance is enough to frustrate the contract is a matter of degree and judgment. In *Karelybflot Ao v. Udovenko,*[1113] chartered fishing vessels were forfeited when the contracts of the crew members had five weeks to run out of a total term of nine months. The Court of Appeal held that the crew's contracts were not frustrated. Five weeks was a small proportion of nine months. There was, moreover, a possibility under the relevant legislation, and in fact, that a return of the vessels might be able to be negotiated. The issue has also arisen in the context of events which affect the ability of a lessee to use land for a portion of the lease, although the courts have been slow to find any such interruption frustrates the lease.[1114]

1106. For example *Krell v. Henry* [1903] 2 KB 740.
1107. *Metropolitan Water Board v. Dick Kerr & Co* [1918] AC 119.
1108. *Denny Mott and Dickson Ltd v. James B. Fraser & Co Ltd* [1944] AC 265; *Scott v. Bank of New South Wales* [1940] NZLR 922.
1109. [1997] 1 NZLR 537.
1110. [1958] NZLR 985.
1111. [1974] 1 NZLR 459.
1112. [1996] 2 NZLR 758.
1113. [2000] 2 NZLR 24.
1114. *National Carriers Ltd v. Panalpina (Northern) Ltd* [1981] AC 675; and *see Roman Catholic Bishop of Christchurch v. RFD Investments Ltd* [2015] NZHC 2647.

In the case of an interruption such as war or requisition, it may be unclear at the outset how long it is to last. The law requires that the judgment of whether the contract is frustrated or not be made at the outset by looking at the circumstances and probabilities which then exist. But it is permissible to wait a short time to see how things turn out.[1115]

III. Express Provision

228. If the parties have expressly provided in their contract for the contingency which has occurred, or for a procedure for handling contingencies of this kind,[1116] the contractual provision will govern. Many contracts contain force majeure clauses to cover potentially frustrating events. But it is a question of construction whether the form of words used covers the event which has occurred, and the exact consequence it attributes to it. A Court may sometimes hold that although the type of risk is contemplated by the clause, it is not widely enough drafted to cover an event of the catastrophic kind which has in fact occurred.[1117] 'It is possible for a risk to be covered by an express provision, but for the contract to be frustrated when that risk materializes in overwhelming form.'[1118] Force majeure clauses require much care in their drafting.

IV. Foreseeability

229. There has been debate as to whether the fact that the event was foreseen by the parties at the time of entry into the contract precludes the doctrine of frustration. In other words, the question is whether unforeseeability is an essential ingredient. The issue was considered in *Planet Kids Ltd v. Auckland Council*,[1119] where the majority held that a foreseen event will generally exclude the doctrine of frustration, but a foreseeable but unforeseen one will only do so if the event is obviously likely to occur and its consequences are foreseeable.[1120]

However, too much should not be made of these cases. The question is not so much whether the risk was foreseeable as whether one party or the other should be deemed to have taken the risk of its occurrence. The *Borthwick* depended as much on the construction of the contract as on any question of foreseeability. It has been held that one of the fundamental features of a 'hedge' contract in the electricity industry is that it is specifically designed to give security of pricing by sharing the risk of electricity price fluctuations which are clearly foreseeable.[1121] However, in

1115. *Pioneer Shipping Ltd v. BTP Tioxide Ltd* [1981] 2 All ER 1030 at 1047.
1116. *A Worker v. A Farmer* [2010] NZCA 547; (2011) 9 NZELC 93,694 (employment contract not frustrated by event because contract made provision for dealing with issues of that kind).
1117. For example *Jackson v. Union Marine Insurance Co Ltd* (1974) LR 10 CP 125.
1118. *The Safeer* [1994] 1 Lloyd's Rep 637 at 643 per Rix J.
1119. [2013] NZSC 137.
1120. At [158]–[159].
1121. *Pacific Energy Ltd v. Electricity Corporation of New Zealand* (1999) 9 TCLR 227.

some contracts, the true inference in all the circumstances may be that while the parties foresaw the event, they were not allocating that risk to either party, but preferred to leave it to the law of frustration to sort it out.[1122]

V. Self-Induced Frustration

230. A party cannot claim frustration when he or she has brought about the impossibility. Thus, a party cannot claim frustration by reason of the fact that it has put itself into voluntary liquidation.[1123] Likewise, where a party was granted fewer fishing licences than it had applied for, it was held unable to rely on the doctrine of frustration when it allocated the licences to its own vessels rather than to one it had chartered.[1124]

The onus lies on the party who alleges that the frustration was self-induced to prove it. What is applied in such a case is a pragmatic judgment as to responsibility: it is not every degree of fault, however minor, which can be said to 'cause' the frustration.[1125]

VI. The Effect of Frustration and the Contract and Commercial Law Act 2017

231. The occurrence of the frustrating event 'brings the contract to an end forthwith, without more and automatically'.[1126] It does not depend on an election by either party. Moreover, the whole contract is discharged, not just the promises of one of the parties, and the termination is *de futuro.* At common law, this could lead to injustice, in relation to expenses incurred and benefits gained before the frustrating event occurred. The Frustrated Contracts Act 1944, a direct copy of the United Kingdom Act of 1943, was enacted to give the court power to grant relief in such a case. That Act has been replaced by sections 60–69 of the Contract and Commercial Law Act 2017; section 61 provides that after the discharge of the contract, money paid before the discharge can be recovered, and that money payable ceases to be so payable. However, if the other party had incurred expenses before the time of discharge in or for the purpose of performance of the contract, the court may, if it considers just to do so, allow him or her to retain or recover the whole or part of those expenses, *see* section 62. There is no presumption of total reimbursement, and it is up to the defendant to establish the claim to expenses.[1127]

By section 63 the court may order that such sum as it considers just be paid by one party to the other in return for a valuable benefit received by that party as a result of the other's performance of the contract. The court must consider all the circumstances of the case, especially whether any expenses have been incurred by the

1122. *The Eugenia* [1964] 2 QB 226 at 234.
1123. *Wooden Boat Workshop Ltd (in liq) v. Thompson* [2000] DCR 820.
1124. *Maritime National Fish Ltd v. Ocean Trawlers Ltd* [1935] AC 524.
1125. *Joseph Constantine Steamship Line Ltd v. Imperial Smelting Corporation Ltd* [1942] AC 154.
1126. *Hirji Mulji v. Cheong Yue SS Co* [1926] AC 497 at 505 per Lord Sumner.
1127. *Gamerco SA v. ICM/Fair Warning (Agency) Ltd* [1995] 1 WLR 1226.

benefited party, and also whether the circumstances causing the frustration have affected the value of the benefit. The amount to be awarded is in the court's discretion, and an appeal court will not interfere with the exercise of that discretion unless it is based on a wrong principle, or has not taken proper account of relevant considerations, or is 'plainly wrong'.[1128]

VII. Exclusions from the Frustrated Contracts Provisions of the Contract and Commercial Law Act 2017

232. Several types of contracts are excluded from the operation of the Contract and Commercial Law Act 2017. They include a contract for the carriage of goods by sea, a charterparty (except a time charterparty or a charterparty by way of demise) and contracts of insurance).[1129] But the most important category of excluded contract is:[1130]

> Any contract to which section 128 applies, or any other contract for the sale, or for the sale and delivery, of specific goods, where the contract is frustrated because the goods have perished.

Section 128 of the Contract and Commercial Law Act 2017 provides that where there is an agreement to sell specific goods and subsequently the goods, without the fault of either seller or buyer, perish before the risk passes to the buyer, the agreement is avoided. This section requires four things. First, there must be an agreement to sell rather than a sale. Second, the risk must not have passed to the buyer. Third, the goods must be specific. Fourth, the goods must have perished. The concept of 'perishing' includes the case where the goods have been so badly damaged that they have ceased to have those qualities which led to the parties entering the contract.[1131] In such a case, the contract is 'avoided'. This will involve that the seller is not liable for non-delivery, but bears the loss; the risk is with the seller.

Contracts for the sale of specific goods which do not fall within section 128 of the Contract and Commercial Law Act 2017 are excluded from the operation of the frustration provisions of that act too: they will be mainly contracts where the risk remains with the buyer.

1128. *BP Exploration Co (Libya) Ltd v. Hunt (No. 2)* [1983] 2 AC 352.
1129. Contract and Commercial Law Act 2017, s. 69(a) and (b).
1130. Contract and Commercial Law Act 2017, s. 69(c).
1131. *Oldfield Asphalts Ltd v. Grovedale Coolstores (1994) Ltd* [1998] 3 NZLR 479.

§3. Discharge by Agreement

I. Termination by Virtue of Term in Contract

233. A contract may contain a term to the effect that it may be terminated by one or either party upon a certain eventuality, or upon a certain period of notice.[1132] Sometimes, the court will be able to imply a term that a contract, particularly a long-term contract, is terminable by reasonable notice. That was held to be so in *Minister of Education v. De Luxe Motor Services (1972) Ltd,*[1133] where school bus contracts, not in writing, were held to be terminable on reasonable notice. The Court of Appeal said one would expect to find cogent reasons in the nature or terms of the particular contract before placing on it the interpretation that it was not to be terminable. In cases of an implied term allowing termination, the calculation of the appropriate period may be difficult.[1134]

However, everything depends on the construction of the particular contract, and its true construction may be that it is not terminable. Thus, in *The Power Co Ltd v. Gore District Council,*[1135] the Court of Appeal found that a contract to supply electricity for a nominal price could not be ended by notice because, among other things, it was expressed to be 'binding for all time hereafter'. A term cannot be implied which is inconsistent with the express terms of the contract.

Per *contra* in *Anchor Butter Co Ltd v. Tui Foods Ltd,*[1136] the court found that a contract for the use of a trademark was terminable on notice despite the fact that it was expressed to be 'without limit of period': that expression did not convey permanence, rather that there was no *fixed* term.

In *South Taranaki District Council v. Burke,*[1137] the Court of Appeal found that a contract to supply a ratepayer with free water was only intended to run so long as the original water main existed: it was not meant to be perpetual.

II. Bilateral Discharge by Agreement

234. A contract which is still executory on both sides can be discharged by the agreement of both parties. The contract of discharge is supported by consideration in that each side is releasing the other from the whole or part of their obligation. It is now established that even a contract by deed can be extinguished by a simple contract.[1138]

Difficult questions can arise about the discharge by agreement of a contract which is required by law to be in writing. Three situations need to be distinguished. First,

1132. Unless the contract expressly provides otherwise, a right to terminate may be expressed orally or in writing: *Prophecy Networks Ltd v. Revera Ltd* [2015] NZHC 215.
1133. [1990] 1 NZLR 27.
1134. *See* for example *Paper Reclaim Ltd v. Aotearoa International Ltd* [2007] 3 NZLR 169.
1135. [1997] 1 NZLR 537. *See also Bobux Marketing Ltd v. Raynor Marketing Ltd* [2002] 1 NZLR 506.
1136. [1997] 3 NZLR 107.
1137. (1995) 3 NZ ConvC 192 172.
1138. *Berry v. Berry* [1929] 2 KB 316; *Buckland v. Commissioner of Stamp Duties* [1954] NZLR 1194.

if the agreement is a partial discharge or variation of the original, it will be ineffective unless it also meets the requirement of writing.[1139] Second, if the agreement totally discharges the contract, it can be oral, and need not meet the requirements of the law requiring writing.[1140] Third, if the agreement extinguishes the original contract and replaces it by a new one, an oral agreement will be effective to discharge the old one but not to create its replacement.[1141] There can be difficult questions as to which of these alternatives the parties intended. It depends on the construction of their agreement.[1142]

III. Waiver

235. If one party agrees to modify, or not to insist on strict performance of, one contractual term to suit the convenience of the other, this may be treated by the court as a *waiver* rather than a variation. An example might be an assurance by one party that he or she will not insist on the strict observance of a time limit by the other.

A waiver is effective, and the party granting it cannot resile from it without at least giving the other side fair notice.[1143] Unlike a variation, an oral waiver can be effective even if it is of a term in a contract required to be in writing.[1144] There can sometimes be difficulty distinguishing a waiver from a variation. Woodhouse J has defined the distinction as follows:[1145]

> [A]t least I think it can be said that where the modified version of the original contract involves such changes in the contractual obligations of the parties that its structure is clearly affected, then the changes goes beyond any question of waiver and must be regarded as a variation.

New Zealand authority has established the following propositions about waiver.

First, a waiver requires a clear unequivocal representation, whether by words or conduct.[1146] Second, a waiver can be retracted by clear notice, provided this does not cause injustice to the other party.[1147] Third, waiver normally occurs *before* the other party has departed from the contractual term in question; indeed the departure is in reliance on the waiver. But sometimes the term is loosely used to describe the

---

1139. *Morris v. Baron & Co* [1918] AC 1 at 31; *Hall v. Goldstone* [1923] NZLR 916; *Scully v. South* [1931] NZLR 1187; *Watson v. Healy Lands Ltd* [1965] NZLR 511 at 513. However an oral variation may be enforceable by specific performance if it is part performed: *Boviard v. Brown* [1975] 2 NZLR 694.
1140. *Morris v. Baron & Co* [1918] AC 1 at 12 and 26; *Booth McDonald & Co Ltd v. Hall* [1931] NZLR 1086.
1141. *Morris v. Baron & Co* [1918] AC 1.
1142. *See Robert Jones Investments Ltd v. Instrument Supplies Ltd* (1991) 1 NZ Conv C 190 746.
1143. For example *Panoutsos v. Raymond Hadley Corporation of New York* [1917] 2 KB 473; *Hartley v. Hymans* [1920] 3 KB 475.
1144. *Boviard v. Brown* [1975] 2 NZLR 694 at 699.
1145. *Watson v. Healy Lands Ltd* [1965] NZLR 511 at 513.
1146. *Connor v. Pukerau Store Ltd* [1981] 1 NZLR 384; *Neylon v. Dickens* [1978] 2 NZLR 35.
1147. *Connor v. Pukerau Store Ltd* [1981] 1 NZLR 384.

situation where the first party has condoned the other's departure from a contractual term *after* that departure has happened. In this situation, one should not confuse waiver with the doctrine of election.[1148]

It will be apparent that the doctrine of waiver bears close similarities to promissory estoppel, and the modern tendency is to rationalize the cases on the basis of the latter doctrine.[1149]

IV. Accord and Satisfaction

236. If an obligation of only one party to a contract remains outstanding, the other cannot effectively release that party from the obligation unless the release is by deed or there is consideration for it. The rule in *Foakes v. Beer*[1150] – that the release of the whole or part of a debt without consideration is ineffective – is the best-known example. But if such a release takes place for good consideration, it is effective, and is known as an 'accord and satisfaction'.[1151]

Accord and satisfaction can operate where the existence of the debt, or the amount owing under it, is in dispute. An agreement by the creditor to accept a lesser amount than he or she is claiming 'in full settlement' is binding because each side is making a concession. The arrangement effectively amounts to a compromise of suit.[1152]

In New Zealand, there have been a number of cases where this question has arisen in the form of a debtor, in response to a disputed amount, sending a cheque for a lesser amount 'in full settlement'. The courts regard this as an offer of a compromise which the creditor can accept by words or conduct. It was once held that if the creditor banks such a cheque that is conclusive of acceptance,[1153] but later authority has held that that is not so. It is a question of fact in each case whether the creditor's words or conduct evince an intention to accept, or lead the other party to believe there has been an acceptance.[1154] Thus if the creditor banks the cheque but contemporaneously notifies the debtor that he or she does not assent to the 'full

1148. *See* the judgment of Richmond P in *Barton v. Russell* (1975) 1 NZCPR 616; also *Miller v. Elston* [1983] ANZ Conv R 486; *Prisk v. McKenzie* (1985) 2 NZCPR 334; *Cycle Manufacturing Co v. Williamson* [1993] 1 NZLR 455.
1149. For example *Boviard v. Brown* [1975] 2 NZLR 694.
1150. *See* para. 86.
1151. *British Russian Gazette Ltd v. Associated Newspapers Ltd* [1933] 2 KB 616.
1152. *See* para. 86.
1153. *Homeguard Products (NZ) Ltd v. Kiwi Packaging Ltd* [1981] 2 NZLR 322.
1154. *HBF Dalgety Ltd v. Morton* [1987] 1 NZLR 411; *Turner's Horticultural Supplies Ltd v. Waitui Holdings* (1990) 3 NZBLC 102,485; *Magnum Photo Supplies Ltd v. Viko NZ Ltd* [1999] 1 NZLR 395.

settlement' proposed, there is no acceptance.[1155] Nevertheless, the banking of the cheque without any communication will often be taken as presumptive evidence of acceptance.[1156]

Sometimes, a debtor accompanies the cheque with a note to the effect that it may only be banked if the offer of full settlement is accepted. Although the effect of such a condition is less than absolutely clear, it is likely that while a banking in contravention of the condition may amount to a conversion of the cheque, it will still not constitute an acceptance if the creditor manifests a contrary intention.[1157]

1155. *HBF Dalgety Ltd v. Morton* [1987] 1 NZLR 411; *Magnum Photo Supplies Ltd v. Viko NZ Ltd* [1999] 1 NZLR 395.

1156. *Haines House Haulage Co Ltd v. Gamble* [1989] 3 NZLR 221; *Dunrae Manufacturing Ltd v. CL North & Co Ltd* [1988] 2 NZLR 602; *Turner's Horticultural Supplies Ltd v. Waitui Holdings* (1990) 3 NZBLC 102485.

1157. *McMahon's (Transport) Pty Ltd v. Ebbage* [1999] 1 Qd R 185. Compare *Magnum Photo Supplies Ltd v. Viko NZ Ltd* [1999] 1 NZLR 395 at 400.

Chapter 6. Remedies

§1. DAMAGES

I. Measure of Damages

A. Expectation Loss

237. The plaintiff's primary entitlement is to be compensated for loss of his or her expectation or bargain and thus get the benefit of what was promised. An award of damages on this basis puts the plaintiff in the position he or she would have enjoyed if the contract had been performed.[1158] For example, the measure of damages in the case of breach of a contract to supply goods prima facie is the difference between the contract price and the market price on the day appointed for delivery.[1159] The buyer's loss is the higher price he or she has to pay in the market for similar goods. Damages will be nominal if the market price is lower than the contract price. Conversely, in the case of breach of a contract to buy goods, the measure of damages prima facie is the difference between the contract price and the lower price obtainable for the goods when reselling them in the market.[1160] Where the plaintiff is a dealer in the particular goods sold, his or her loss is the profit that would have been made had the sale gone through. It is no answer to a claim to say that the goods have been or may be sold to another if the plaintiff has profited from only one sale instead of from two.[1161]

The cost to the plaintiff who has lost the benefit of a bargain may be measured in different ways. So where building work done under a contract is defective, the loss may be represented by the difference in value between what was promised and what was supplied, the cost of rectifying the breach or the loss of amenity caused by the breach. The courts take a pragmatic attitude and adopt whichever seems a reasonable solution.[1162] In *Ruxley Electronics Ltd v. Forsyth,*[1163] the builders of a swimming pool constructed it to a depth which did not satisfy the contractual specifications, but the shortfall did not affect the value of the property where it was situated, and the pool could still be used for diving. It was held that the cost of rectification was out of all proportion to the advantage conferred on the innocent party, so the damages should be awarded on a difference in value basis which in this case was nil. However, a modest sum for loss of amenity by reason of the pool being too shallow could still be awarded.

1158. *Stirling v. Poulgrain* [1980] 2 NZLR 402 at 419; *Bloxham v. Robinson* (1996) 7 TCLR 122 at 133; *One Step (Support) Ltd v. Morris-Garner* [2018] UKSC 20, [2018] 2 WLR 1353, at [31]-[32].

1159. Contract and Commercial Law Act 2017, s. 193(3).

1160. *Ibid.*, s. 192(3).

1161. *W L Thompson Ltd v. Robinson (Gunmakers) Ltd* [1955] Ch. 177; and *see Charter v. Sullivan* [1957] QB 117; *Lazenby Garages Ltd v. Wright* [1976] 2 All ER 770; *Hughes v. Pendragon Sabre Ltd T/A Porsche Centre Bolton* [2016] EWCA Civ 18.

1162. *Bevan Investments Ltd v. Blackhall and Struthers (No. 2)* [1978] 2 NZLR 97.

1163. [1996] 1 AC 344.

The quantification issue arose in a different context in *Marlborough District Council v. Altimarloch Joint Venture Ltd.*[1164] Here, the purchasers of land sought damages in respect of the loss they suffered in acquiring land without the water rights attached to the land that had been represented by agents for the vendors, and one of the questions in issue was whether the damages should be quantified by reference to the difference in the value of the land with and without those water rights or by reference to the full cost of providing the water. It was held by the Supreme Court, in a majority decision, that only by building a dam could the purchasers be reasonably assured of having the full quantity of water which the vendors had contracted to supply. Tipping J said that there was nothing to suggest that simply because the performance measure was substantially more than the compensation measure (NZD 1.055,907 as opposed to NZD 125,000), the former was an unreasonable response to the vendors' breach, nor that the performance measure was disproportionate to the benefit to be obtained.

Sometimes, the bargain that has been lost will be very difficult to quantify, but the courts will make an assessment as best they can. In *One Step (Support) Ltd v. Morris-Garner*,[1165] the question in issue was the value of the claimant's right to prevent the defendants, a former director and a former employee, from competing with the claimant's business in breach of restrictive covenants made with the claimant. The UK Supreme Court held that 'negotiating damages' could be awarded for breach of contract resulting in a loss equivalent to the economic value of the right, considered as an asset. There should be a hearing on quantum, not for an assessment of a hypothetical 'release fee' which the parties would have agreed, but to measure the financial loss actually sustained. If evidence were led in relation to such a fee, it would be a matter for the judge to determine its relevance and weight, if any.

In the case of future possibilities and hypotheses, the damages may be quantified by reference to the value of the chance or opportunity that has been lost.[1166] Examples of successful claims include a lost chance of success in a beauty contest;[1167] a lost commercial opportunity;[1168] the loss of the chance of avoiding entry into a guarantee of a liability which the plaintiff ultimately had to assume;[1169] and the loss of a chance of a better property arrangement for a spouse on the break-up of a marriage.[1170]

In *Strack v. Grey*,[1171] Miller J accepted that damages for loss of a chance could be awarded when a future outcome depended, or a past hypothetical outcome would have depended, on the independent decision of a third party. The Court would adopt

1164. [2012] 2 NZLR 726.
1165. [2018] UKSC 20, [2018] 2 WLR 1353; and *see Turf Club Auto Emporium Pte Ltd v. Yeo Boong Hua* [2018] SGCA 44.
1166. *Benton v. Miller & Poulgrain* [2005] 1 NZLR 66; *Wagner v. Gill* [2014] NZCA 336, [2015] 3 NZLR 157 at [108]–[120].
1167. *Chaplin v. Hicks* [1911] 2 KB 786.
1168. *Allied Maples Group Ltd v. Simmons & Simmons* [1995] 1 WLR 1602.
1169. *Gilbert v. Shanahan* [1998] 3 NZLR 528.
1170. *Benton v. Miller & Poulgrain* [2005] 1 NZLR 66.
1171. *Strack v. Grey* [2019] NZCA 432 at [46]–[53].

a lost chance analysis where it characterized the third party's decision as unknowable. Here, a contract was made conditional on the purchaser obtaining finance, and this was contingent on the decision of the purchaser's financiers which was a hypothetical past event. However, a person's eligibility for obtaining finance was verifiable and could be proven on the balance of probabilities. Here, the burden was on the purchaser to show that his reasonable efforts to secure an offer of finance would have failed, but he had never prepared a loan application and it was far from clear that a bank would have refused one. The vendor accordingly could recover damages for a wrongful cancellation of the contract.

B. Reliance Loss

238. The plaintiff may claim for expenses incurred in reliance on the contract, and here he or she is put in the position as if the contract had never been made. This head of loss is likely to be asserted where the plaintiff's bargain turns out to be unprofitable, or where the plaintiff cannot prove the value of his or her expectations. In *McRae v. Commonwealth Disposals Commission,*[1172] the plaintiffs contracted to buy from the defendants an oil tanker said to be wrecked on a reef north of Samarai. It turned out that no such tanker existed. Anticipated profits could not have been recovered as they would have been too speculative. The court held that the plaintiffs could recover as damages for breach of contract the agreed purchase price and the costs incurred in fitting out a salvage expedition, being expenditure wasted in reliance on the promise that there was a tanker at the locality given.

C. Restoration of Benefits

239. A plaintiff who has paid money or given other benefits under the contract may seek restoration of the money or benefits. So a seller who has received payment but who has failed to deliver the promised goods is liable to restore the sum that has been paid. The restitutionary remedy is founded on there having been a total failure of consideration. But if there has only been a partial failure, the orthodox view is that the plaintiff cannot recover this in a restitutionary claim and that he or she must seek damages.[1173] The requirement that the failure of consideration must be total has been widely criticized, and it may be modified in some circumstances. In particular, where counter-restitution can easily be made, it has been effectively abandoned.[1174] And where cancellation is sought under the Contract and Commercial Law Act 2017, the prima facie position is that property already transferred under the contract remains transferred,[1175] but the court has a discretion to make an order for restitution.[1176]

1172. (1951) 84 CLR 377.
1173. *White Arrow Express Ltd v. Lamey's Distribution Ltd* [1996] Trad LR 69.
1174. *Goss v. Chilcott* [1996] AC 788 at 798.
1175. Contract and Commercial Law Act 2017, s. 42.
1176. *Ibid.*, ss 43–48: *see* para. 219.

A second form of restitutionary remedy is where the defendant has gained a benefit from his or her wrongdoing, as opposed to from the plaintiff. Normally, the aim of an action in contract is to compensate the plaintiff, not to require the defendant to disgorge a benefit. But sometimes a victim may not be able to show any loss. Whether an action in respect of a gain made by a defendant could be maintainable was considered by the House of Lords in *Attorney-General v. Blake*.[1177] The defendant was a former member of the Secret Intelligence Service (SIS) who had signed an undertaking not to divulge any official information gained as a result of his employment. He subsequently was convicted of spying and sentenced to imprisonment, but escaped and went to live in Moscow. He then wrote an autobiography, substantial parts of which were based on information he had acquired in the course of his duties. The Crown sought damages representing all the profits of the book which the publisher had not yet paid and an injunction to restrain the defendant from receiving any payment or other benefit resulting from his criminal conduct. The House of Lords held that the injunction was in substance a confiscatory order, and the court had no common law or statutory power to confiscate property without compensation. Accordingly, there was no jurisdiction to grant the injunction. However, there was a remedy in private law, even though the plaintiff could show no loss. Lord Nicholls said that there is no reason in principle to rule out an account of profits when, exceptionally, it is a just response to a breach. The main argument against it is the fear that it will have an unsettling effect on commercial contracts where certainty is important. But normally the remedies of damages, specific performance and injunction, coupled with the characterization of some contractual obligations as fiduciary, will provide an adequate response to a breach of contract. Only in exceptional circumstances will any question of accounting for profits arise:

> No fixed rules can be prescribed. The court will have regard to all the circumstances, including the subject matter of the contract, the purpose of the contractual provision which has been breached, the circumstances in which the breach occurred, the consequences of the breach and the circumstances in which relief is being sought. A useful general guide, although not exhaustive, is whether the plaintiff had a legitimate interest in preventing the defendant's profit-making activity and, hence, in depriving him of his profit.[1178]

It was decided that the instant case was indeed exceptional. The Crown did have a legitimate interest in preventing the defendant from profiting from the disclosure of official information.

D. Consequential Loss

240. A breach of contract may in addition involve the innocent party in extra expenses or cause further harm such as damage to property, and these losses also

---

1177. [2000] 3 WLR 625; applied in *Experience Hendrix LLC v. PPX Enterprises Inc* [2003] 1 All ER (Comm) 830.
1178. *Ibid.*, at 639.

are recoverable. So a pig farmer recovered damages for loss of his pigs from the supplier of a hopper which in breach of contract had not been properly ventilated, causing the pignuts stored in it to go mouldy and the pigs which ate the nuts to die.[1179] Again, an insurance agent was liable for substantial business losses suffered by an underwriter after the agent failed to warn of the dangers of joining high-risk syndicates.[1180]

E. Relationship Between Different Heads of Loss

241. The plaintiff has a free choice as to the basis for quantifying the loss that has been suffered.[1181] Indeed, there is no objection to combining the various types of claim but not so as to recover more than once for the same loss.[1182] It might, for example, be necessary to expend money in reliance on a contract in order to earn the anticipated profits; both losses cannot then be recovered. Again, a plaintiff who is compensated for loss of goodwill cannot in addition claim the loss of the income which is the reason for the lesser value of the goodwill.[1183]

In a decision in England,[1184] Teare J emphasized that expectation losses and reliance losses were not in some way separate and that their award did not somehow reflect discrete and independent rights. Both were simply emanations of the fundamental rule that contract damages existed to replicate the claimant's would-be position had the contract been kept. Neither licensed the claimant to recover more than he had actually lost. In the case at hand, a charterer's repudiation of a five-year charter allowed the owners to charter elsewhere at much higher rates, and this gain far exceeded the amount wasted by the owners in fitting out the vessel for the initial charter. So the owners had suffered no loss and were confined to nominal damages.

As a general rule, the plaintiff's expectation of a benefit puts a ceiling on recovery under the other heads.[1185] However, the burden is on the defendant to show that a venture would have been unprofitable, and as the defendant probably will lack information on the issue, it is likely to be difficult to discharge.[1186] Furthermore, where restitution is sought, it seems the plaintiff can recover irrespective of whether or not the contract would have been profitable.[1187]

F. Date of Quantification

242. The date of the breach of the contract is usually taken as the starting point for quantifying the damage. Thus, on a refusal to accept or deliver goods, the

1179. *Parsons Ltd v. Uttley Ingham Ltd* [1978] QB 791.
1180. *Brown v. KMR Services Ltd* [1995] 4 All ER 598.
1181. *Ti Leaf Productions Ltd v. Baikie* (2001) 7 NZBLC 103,464.
1182. *Herbison v. Papakura Video Ltd (No. 2)* [1987] 2 NZLR 720.
1183. *Bloxham v. Robinson* (1996) 7 TCLR 122.
1184. *The Mamola Challenger* [2011] 1 Lloyd's Rep 47.
1185. *C & P Haulage Ltd v. Middleton* [1983] 3 All ER 94.
1186. *Commonwealth of Australia v. Amann Aviation Pty Ltd* (1991) 61 ALJR 23; cp *Ti Leaf Productions Ltd v. Baikie* (2001) 7 NZBLC 103,464.
1187. *Slodder v. Lowey* (1901) 20 NZLR 321; [1904] AC 442.

damages are prima facie measured by the difference between the contract and the market price at the time when the goods ought to have been accepted or delivered.[1188] The general rule may, however, yield to the Court's power in the interests of justice to fix such other date as may be appropriate in all the circumstances.[1189] Relaxation of the general rule typically occurs when fixing another date is required to achieve the objective of contractual damages – that is, to place the injured party in the position it would have been in if the contract had been performed.[1190]

One purpose of the breach-date rule is that of achieving certainty in commercial contracts. But in *Golden Strait Corporation v. Nippon Yusen Kubishika Kaisa,*[1191] the House of Lords held that this was subject to the overriding compensatory principle that the damages awarded should represent no more than the value of the contractual benefits of which the plaintiff had been deprived. So if at the date of breach there had been a real possibility that an event would happen terminating the contract or reducing the contractual benefits, the quantum of damages might need to be reduced proportionately to reflect the estimated likelihood of the possibility materializing. But where such an event had already happened by the time damages were assessed, the court should have regard to what had actually occurred. In the instant case, charterers had repudiated the charter, and subsequently a war broke out between certain countries which would have entitled the charterers to terminate the charterparty. It was held that the owners' right to the hire rate and profit share under the charterparty would have been brought to an end, and the owners were not entitled to damages after that time.

If the innocent party, acting reasonably, only discovers the breach sometime after it has been committed and then acts with reasonable promptitude, for example, by doing necessary repairs to a defective building, he or she is not limited to claiming the cost of repair at the time of the breach but may be compensated for the actual costs incurred.[1192] Further, the innocent party may know of a breach but be unable to act on it, for example, by making a substitute contract or putting right a defect, because he or she lacks the means to do so or because it would not make sense, from a commercial point of view, to incur further expense while issues of both liability and quantum remain in dispute. Damages may then be assessed as at the date of trial.[1193]

G. Exemplary Damages

243. Exemplary or punitive damages are designed to punish a wrongdoer rather than compensate a victim. They can be awarded in tort actions where the defendant is guilty of outrageous and contumelious misconduct.[1194] Orthodox authority holds

1188. Contract and Commercial Law Act 2017, ss 192(3), 193(3).
1189. *Stirling v. Poulgrain* [1980] 2 NZLR 402 at 420.
1190. *OHL Ltd v. Johns* [2021] NZHC 77 at [34].
1191. [2007] 2 WLR 690; applied in *Bunge SA v. Nidera BV* [2015] UKSC 43.
1192. *Bevan Investments Ltd v. Blackhall and Struthers (No. 2)* [1978] 2 NZLR 97.
1193. *Alcoa Minerals of Jamaica Inc v. Broderick* [2002] 1 AC 371 (a tort case).
1194. *Taylor v. Beere* [1982] 1 NZLR 81.

that damages for breach of contract are compensatory only and that exemplary damages cannot be awarded.[1195] In recent years, some New Zealand cases at first instance challenged this view,[1196] but in the Court of Appeal in *Paper Reclaim Ltd v. Aotearoa International Ltd,*[1197] exemplary damages for breach of contract were decisively rejected. There was no gap in the range of compensatory damages needing to be filled, and no reason to add yet another remedy that would give a contracting party a windfall profit. However, the court did not rule out the possibility that exemplary damages might be available in circumstances where the breach of contract also constituted a tort for which exemplary damages were recoverable. This was left for another day.

II. Remoteness of Damage

A. *The Rule in Hadley v. Baxendale*

244. A defendant is not liable for damage caused by his or her breach of contract but which nonetheless is too remote a consequence of it. The leading case is *Hadley v. Baxendale.*[1198] The plaintiffs, who were mill owners in Gloucestershire, engaged the defendant carriers to take a broken mill shaft to Greenwich as a pattern for a new one. The defendants promised to deliver the shaft at Greenwich the following day, but due to their neglect it was delayed in transit so that there was a stoppage of several days at the mill. The plaintiffs claimed damages for loss of profit caused by the delay, and the question rose whether the damage was too remote. The test to be applied was laid down by Alderson B:[1199]

> Where two parties have made a contract which one of them has broken, the damages which the other party ought to receive in respect of such breach of contract should be such as may fairly and reasonably be considered either arising naturally, i.e., according to the usual course of things, from such breach of contract itself, or such as may reasonably be supposed to have been in the contemplation of both parties, at the time they made the contract, as the probable result of the breach of it.

Here, the stoppage was not the 'natural' consequence of the delay: it could not have been foreseen by the carrier that delay would keep the mill idle. The plaintiffs might have had a spare shaft or been able to get one. Nor could the stoppage have been contemplated by both parties as the probable result of the breach, for the defendants were not told that any delay would keep the mill idle.

1195. *Addis v. Gramophone Co Ltd* [1909] AC 488.
1196. For example, *Tak and Co Inc v. AEL Corporation Ltd* (1995) 5 NZBLC 103,887.
1197. [2006] 3 NZLR 188. The decision was taken on appeal to the Supreme Court on a different point: *see Paper Reclaim Ltd v. Aotearoa International Ltd* [2007] 3 NZLR 169.
1198. (1854) 9 Exch 341.
1199. *Ibid.*, at 354.

In *Victoria Laundry (Windsor) Ltd v. Newman Industries Ltd*,[1200] Asquith LJ reformulated Alderson B's test in terms of whether the loss was 'reasonably foreseeable as liable to result from the breach'. This gave rise to the view that the same test governed remoteness of damage in both contract and tort, but the House of Lords held in *The Heron II; Koufos v. C Czarnikow Ltd*[1201] that liability in tort was wider than in contract. Lord Upjohn observed that a tortfeasor was liable for any damage which he could reasonably foresee may happen as a result of a breach of duty, however unlikely it might be, unless it could be brushed aside as far-fetched.[1202] A tortfeasor usually was a stranger to the innocent party but was a neighbour for the purposes of the law and was bound to act with due regard for his neighbour's rights. If the tortfeasor failed in such a duty, the law had rightly laid down a stringent test for the assessment of damages. In contract, however, the parties had only to consider the consequences of the breach to the other; it was fair that the assessment of damages should depend on their assumed common knowledge and contemplation and not on a foreseeable but most unlikely consequence.[1203]

The decision of the Privy Council in *Attorney-General of the Virgin Islands v. Global Water Associates Ltd*[1204] has given an overview of the application of the *Hadley v. Baxendale* test. Their Lordships determined that the party whose rights had been breached was entitled to recover only such part of the loss actually resulting as was, at the time the contract was made, reasonably contemplated as a serious possibility as liable to result from the breach. The test was an objective one, which involved asking what the defendant had to be taken as contemplating as a result of the breach of contract, rather than only what he or she actually contemplated. In other words, one assumed that the defendant at the time the contract was made had thought about the consequences of its breach.

The principle of *Hadley v. Baxendale* usually is accepted as representing the law in New Zealand.[1205] However, in *McElroy Milne v. Commercial Electronics Ltd*,[1206] Cooke P took a different approach to this whole issue. His Honour doubted whether references to *Hadley v. Baxendale* amounted to more than ritual incantation in discussions of remoteness problems. Rather than applying a fixed rule, he favoured a multi-factor discretionary approach. Factors including directness, 'naturalness', as distinct from freak combinations of foreseeable circumstances, even perhaps the

---

1200. [1949] 2 KB 528.
1201. [1969] 1 AC 350.
1202. *The Wagon Mound (No 1)* [1961] AC 388; *The Wagon Mound (No 2)* [1967] 1 AC 617.
1203. In *Wellesley Partners LLP v. Withers LLP* [2015] EWCA Civ 1146, [2016] 2 WLR 1351 at [80], the court held that a contracting party could not rely on the tort test in circumstances where the other party was liable under both heads. The parties were assumed to be contracting on the basis that liability would be confined to damage of the kind which was in their reasonable contemplation, and it made no sense for the existence of the concurrent duty in tort to upset this consensus.
1204. [2020] UKPC 18, [2021] AC 23.
1205. *See* for example *Inder Lynch Devoy & Co v. Subritzky* [1979] 1 NZLR 87; *Isaac Naylor & Sons Ltd v. NZ Co-operative Wool Marketing Association Ltd* [1981] 1 NZLR 361.
1206. [1993] 1 NZLR 39.

magnitude of the claim and the degree of the defendant's culpability, were not necessarily to be ignored in seeking a just balance between the parties. But the other members of the court did not adopt Cooke P's stance, and it has not attracted significant support.[1207]

B. The Scope of the Defendant's Duty

245. Sometimes, the question of whether damage is too remote does not require answer, on the basis that the damage suffered is not within the scope of the defendant's duty. Such an analysis may be needed in relation to claims in contract in the same way as in relation to claims in tort, and many of the cases involve claims under both heads.

246. In *South Australia Asset Management Co v. York Montague (SAAMCO)*,[1208] the question at issue was the extent of liability of valuers who made negligent over-valuations of property offered as security for a loan. The borrowers later defaulted, but in the meantime the property market had fallen, greatly increasing the losses suffered by the plaintiff lenders. The Court of Appeal held that the valuers were fully liable, on the ground that a fall in the market was foreseeable and but for the valuers' negligence the lenders would not have entered the transactions at all. However, in the House of Lords, the valuers were held liable only for the foreseeable consequences of the information being wrong. What this meant was that the valuers' liability was subject to a ceiling represented by the difference between the valuation given and what the valuation should have been. So loss that was equal to or less than that difference was recoverable, but any greater loss was borne by the lender. The latter was seen as outside the scope of the defendant's duty.

Their Lordships in *SAAMCO* focused on the nature of the duty that the valuers owed to the lenders. The question was whether the duty was to advise the lenders as to a course of conduct – whether they should lend money – or whether it was simply to provide the lenders with information on which they could make their own decision. If the former, the valuers would be liable for all reasonably foreseeable losses suffered as a result of their lending, but if the latter, the claim would be limited to the value of the lost security interest. The duty being held to be of the latter type, damages were based on the difference between the amount of the valuation provided and the amount of a proper and careful valuation. So whether loss stemming from the fall in the property market was too remote did not need to be determined because the valuer did not owe any duty to avoid a loss caused in that way.

In *Hughes-Holland v. BPE Solicitors*,[1209] the UK Supreme Court held that where a defendant supplied information which was only one of the factors relevant to the

1207. In this case, the defendant solicitors negligently omitted to include a guarantor of the lessee's obligations in preparing a lease of the plaintiff's property, making it hard to resell, and by the time of the trial the market for commercial property had collapsed and the property still had not been sold. The Court held that the plaintiff's loss should include the impact of the downturn in the property market, as part of the very purpose of the guarantee was to protect against market deterioration.
1208. [1997] AC 191.
1209. [2017] UKSC 21, [2018] AC 599; applied in *Khan v. MNX* [2018] EWCA Civ 2609.

decision whether to proceed with a transaction, the claimant could only recover that part of his loss which was within the scope of the defendant's duty of care and would have been avoided had the defendant not breached that duty. If the defendant's contribution had been to supply material which the client would take into account in making his own decision based upon a broader assessment of the risks, the defendant had no legal responsibility for the client's decision. On the facts, the defendant solicitors had not assumed responsibility for their client's decision to lend money, their instructions having been only to draft the relevant documentation, and they were only responsible for mistakenly confirming the client's assumption about one of a number of factors in his assessment of the project concerned. No loss had resulted from that incorrect assessment since the claimant would have lost his money anyway as the development would have failed. The loss was not within the scope of the solicitors' duty but had arisen from commercial misjudgements which were not their concern.

The 'scope of duty' approach was applied in New Zealand in *Sherwin Chan & Walshe Ltd v. Jones*.[1210] SCWL gave negligent tax advice to J, with the result that J became potentially liable to pay a large tax bill. After discovery of the problem, J's new accountants advised that a voluntary disclosure be made to the Inland Revenue Department (IRD). This was done, and J then accepted the IRD's amended assessments and made a significant tax payment. It was held by the Court of Appeal that SCWL was liable to J in respect of that payment. If SCWL's duty was simply to provide information to enable J to determine how to structure his tax affairs, then the decision to disclose or to accept the amended assessments might have limited or extinguished SCWL's liability. However, SCWL's duty here was to advise on a course of conduct, and they were therefore responsible for all foreseeable consequences of that advice being wrong, including the foreseeable and reasonable actions taken by J in response to the problem.

A further illustration of the operation of the scope of the duty principle is found in the decision of the UK Supreme Court in *Khan v. Meadows*.[1211] The claimant was wrongly advised by her doctor that any child she might have would not have haemophilia. She later became pregnant and gave birth to a son, who was found to suffer from haemophilia and also was autistic. The claimant sought damages in respect of her son's disabilities, and the Supreme Court held that the defendant doctor was liable to compensate her for the additional costs associated with the child's haemophilia but not for those associated with his autism. The medical advice she was given was concerned only with the risk of a child having haemophilia, and the law did not impose on her doctor any duty in relation to unrelated risks (such as autism) which might arise in any pregnancy.

The scope of duty enquiry sometimes may be seen as overlapping with an enquiry into the remoteness of the damage. In *Transfield Shipping Inc v. Mercator Shipping Inc (The Achilleas)*,[1212] Lord Hoffmann and Lord Hope considered that the ordinary *Hadley v. Baxendale* rule represented only a prima facie assumption about what the

1210. [2013] 1 NZLR 166.
1211. [2021] UKSC 21, [2021] 3 WLR 147; and *see also Manchester Building Society v. Grant Thornton UK LLP* [2021] UKSC 20, [2021] 3 WLR 81.
1212. [2009] 1 AC 61.

parties might be taken to have intended, and this could be rebutted in cases in which the context, surrounding circumstances or general understanding of the relevant market showed that a party would not reasonably have been regarded as assuming responsibility for the loss in question. And on the facts, they considered that a charterer of a ship who was late in redelivering the ship at the end of the charter could not reasonably be regarded as having assumed responsibility for the shipowners' loss of profit on a following charter, as such a risk was completely unquantifiable: the charterers would have had no idea when the owners would make a forward fixture or what its length and terms might be.

On this view, even if the kind of loss was within the parties' reasonable contemplation as quite likely or not unlikely, it will be too remote if it cannot reasonably be inferred that the defendant accepted responsibility for that loss. Particular factors which may suggest that a promisor did not assume responsibility for a loss, even if foreseeable, may include an established industry custom or well-understood insurance arrangements indicating the risk was something the promisee was expected to bear, and a substantial disproportion between the amount of the foreseeable loss and the consideration received by the promisor indicating that full recovery would be an unfair allocation of the risk.

Lord Hoffmann recognized that departure from the ordinary foreseeability rule would be unusual, but seemingly, it could sometimes lead to a different result from that mandated by *Hadley v. Baxendale*. However, in *The Achilleas* itself, other members of the court applied orthodox reasoning in deciding that the loss could not reasonably have been foreseen as being likely to arise out of the delay, so the claim failed on either approach. Further, *The Achilleas* has had a limited impact even in the United Kingdom, and subsequent cases broadly have favoured the conventional approach to remoteness.[1213] The New Zealand courts also have continued to rely on the tried and tested two-limb test in *Hadley v. Baxendale*, and there is little evidence of any desire for making a change.

It is apparent from the preceding decisions that the enquiry into the scope of the duty sometimes can cover much the same ground as the enquiry into remoteness. So how should we decide which question should be asked? The duty analysis seems appropriate in the case of professional advisers, where one asks what kind of risk was assumed by that adviser in giving the advice, and in any other case where the essence of the enquiry lies in determining what the defendant has assumed a responsibility to do. In other cases involving intervening conduct or events or different kinds of loss, an enquiry into the cause of the damage or the remoteness of the damage covers the ground.

1213. *See*, for example, *Siemens Building Technologies Ltd v. Supershield Ltd* [2010] EWCA Civ 7; *John Grimes Partnership Ltd v. Gubbins* [2013] EWCA Civ 37; *SC Confectia SA v. Miss Mania Wholesale Ltd* [2014] EWCA Civ 1484.

C. Upset and Distress

247. Claims for compensation in respect of vexation, annoyance and distress caused by a breach of contract are subject to a special restriction. In *Addis v. Gramophone Co Ltd,*[1214] the House of Lords held that a manager who had been wrongfully dismissed by his employer in a harsh and humiliating way could recover damages for loss of salary and commission but not for injured feelings. The *Addis* rule applies in New Zealand, but is subject to a number of qualifications or exceptions.

First, it is apparent that injury to reputation causing financial loss can be recoverable. For example, where a bank collapsed after being involved in fraudulent activities, which constituted a breach of an implied obligation owed to its employees that it would not carry on a dishonest business, the employees who had lost their jobs could recover damages for the loss stemming from the stigma attaching to them as former employees of the bank and their inability to obtain subsequent employment.[1215]

Second, it has been recognized in a number of cases that the *Addis* rule does not apply in the case of contracts to provide enjoyment or prevent distress. Applying this principle, damages have been awarded for loss of enjoyment of the amenities of a social club;[1216] disappointment and loss of a pleasurable holiday;[1217] upset on the cremated remains of the plaintiff's parents being lost;[1218] and loss of pleasurable enjoyment of property due to excessive aircraft noise.[1219]

Third, claims for wrongful dismissal are governed by statute. Under the Employment Relations Act 2000, the damages which can be awarded to an employee under the personal grievance procedure contained in Part 9 of the Act include compensation for 'humiliation, loss of dignity and injury to the feelings of the employee'.[1220] The statute provides the only remedy.[1221] So, common law actions for wrongful dismissal can no longer be maintained.

Lastly, the question remains whether, instead of formulating exceptions to a general rule of non-recovery, the courts might take the further step and apply ordinary rules of remoteness. In England, the courts have not been persuaded,[1222] but the SCC has taken the view that the 'peace of mind' class of cases should not be viewed as an exception to the general rule of the non-availability of damages for mental distress in contract law, but rather as an application of the reasonable contemplation or

1214. [1909] AC 499.
1215. *Mahmud v. Bank of Credit and Commerce International SA* [1998] AC 20; compare *James-Bowen v. Commissioner of Police of the Metropolis* [2018] UKSC 40, [2018] 1 WLR 4021 (no duty of care to protect employee from reputational loss caused by the employer's conduct of litigation).
1216. *Byrne v. Auckland Irish Society* [1979] 1 NZLR 351.
1217. *Jarvis v. Swan's Tours Ltd* [1973] 2 QB 233.
1218. *Mason v. Westside Cemeteries Ltd* (1996) 135 DLR (4th) 361.
1219. *Farley v. Skinner* [2001] 3 WLR 899.
1220. Employment Relations Act 2000, s. 123(c)(i).
1221. *Ibid.*, s. 113.
1222. *Hayes v. James and Charles Dodd* [1990] 2 All ER 815; *Watts v. Morrow* [1991] 4 All ER 937; *Johnson v. Gore Wood & Co* [2002] 2 AC 1 at 49–50.

foreseeability principle that applies generally to determine the availability of damages for breach of contract.[1223] In New Zealand, both approaches can be seen. In *Mouat v. Clark Boyce*,[1224] the Court of Appeal held that damages were recoverable where stress could be said to have been within the reasonable contemplation of the parties at the time of the contract, subject to an exception in the case of ordinary commercial contracts. However, in *Bloxham v. Robinson*,[1225] a majority in the Court of Appeal reverted to the English view. So a contract-breaker is not as a general rule liable for causing mental upset even if foreseeable, but may be in certain types of cases, in particular where one of the objects of the contract is to safeguard the innocent party from loss of this kind.

D. Failure to Pay Money

248. The common law said that if the defendant's breach consisted of a failure to pay money, the plaintiff's loss consisted only of that sum.[1226] This is clearly not an application of the ordinary rules of remoteness since a defendant often can contemplate that his or her failure to pay money on time will prevent the plaintiff from completing a profitable transaction. Further, a secondary rule stated that debts did not as a rule carry interest.[1227] This rule was hard on creditors, particularly in times of high rates of interest and inflation. However, in *Sempra Metals Ltd v. Inland Revenue Commissioners*,[1228] the House of Lords abandoned the old rules, holding that interest could be claimed as damages under either limb of *Hadley v. Baxendale*. Lord Nicholls recognized that English law had developed to the point that interest could be recovered as damages where there was special knowledge under the second limb of *Hadley v. Baxendale*, but not under the first,[1229] and was satisfied that the House should erase the remains of this blot on English common law jurisprudence. It should always be open to a claimant to plead and prove his actual interest losses caused by late payment of a debt. These losses would be recoverable, subject to the principles governing all claims for damages for breach of contract, such as remoteness, failure to mitigate and so forth. Even so, an unparticularized and unproved claim simply for 'damages' would not suffice. The common law did not assume that delay in payment of a debt would of itself cause damage. Loss always had to be proved. Lord Mance considered that it was still fair to assume that loss of interest was not within the parties' contemplation under many everyday contracts.

1223. *Fidler v. Sun Life Assurance Co of Canada* [2006] 2 SCR 3; and *see Honda Canada Inc v. Keays* [2008] 2 SCR 362.
1224. [1992] 2 NZLR 559.
1225. (1996) 7 TCLR 122.
1226. *William v. Reynolds* (1865) 6 B & S 495. Cf. *Wallis v. Smith* (1882) 21 Ch D 243.
1227. *London Chatham and Dover Rly Co v. South Eastern Rly Co* [1893] AC 429.
1228. [2008] AC 561.
1229. *Wadsworth v. Lydall* [1981] 2 All ER 401; *President of India v. La Pintada Cia Navegacion SA (No 2)* [1985] 1 AC 104.

Before loss by way of interest was recoverable as damages, the threshold of reasonable contemplation had to be crossed.[1230]

Sempra Metals brought the law in the UK into line with that in Australia[1231] and Canada.[1232] In New Zealand, the question arose for decision in *Clarkson v. Whangamata Metal Supplies Ltd*,[1233] and here the Court of Appeal considered that it was time for the same clarity and certainty as was achieved in *Sempra* to be brought to New Zealand law. The case made for the rejection of an 'unprincipled remnant of an unprincipled rule' was compelling, and there was no authority preventing that course. So, in an appropriate case, interest, including compound interest, could be awarded as damages for breach of contract under either limb. However, the claim for interest failed on the facts, for the loss had not been pleaded and the evidence had not established loss.

Quite apart from the position at common law, in every money judgment, a court must award interest as compensation for a delay in the payment of money, unless the Act expressly provides otherwise.[1234] The period during which interest is payable begins on the day on which the cause of action arose and ends on the day on which the judgment debt is paid in full, unless the court specifies any shorter period in accordance with the Act.[1235] The rate of interest is calculated on a daily basis using an Internet site calculator established pursuant to the Act.[1236]

III. Mitigation of Damage

249. A plaintiff should take reasonable steps to mitigate or reduce the loss caused by a breach of contract.[1237] The burden is on the defendant to prove that there has been a failure to mitigate, but if the defendant succeeds in showing this, the plaintiff cannot recover compensation for loss flowing from that failure. For example, an employee who has been dismissed in breach of contract must seek other employment and so reduce the loss caused by the breach.[1238] Where a buyer refuses to accept the contract goods, the seller must use his or her best efforts to sell to other purchasers.[1239]

It is implicit in the principle of mitigation that if mitigating steps are in fact reasonably taken, and additional loss or damage results notwithstanding the reasonable

1230. Compare *Prudential Assurance Co Ltd v. Revenue and Customs Commissioners* [2018] UKSC 39, [2018] 3 WLR 652, where the UK Supreme Court departed from *Sempra Metals* in holding that there was no right to interest in the context of a claim by a taxpayer that the Revenue had been unjustly enriched by its payment of tax.
1231. *Hungerfords v. Walker* (1989) 171 CLR 125.
1232. *Bank of America Canada v. Mutual Trust Co* [2002] 2 SCR 601.
1233. [2008] 3 NZLR 31; applied in *Cockburn v. CS Developments No 2 Ltd* [2013] 2 NZLR 413.
1234. Interest on Money Claims Act 2016, s. 10 (1) and (2). The payment of interest formerly was governed by the Judicature Act 1908, s. 87, as to which *see Worldwide NZ LLC v. NZ Venue and Event Management Ltd* [2015] 1 NZLR 1.
1235. *Ibid*., s. 9(1) and (2).
1236. *Ibid*., ss 12, 13.
1237. *Sullivan v. Darkin* [1986] 1 NZLR 214.
1238. *Brace v. Calder* [1895] 2 QB 253.
1239. *Pacific Overseas Corporation Ltd v. Watkins Browne and Co (NZ) Ltd* [1954] NZLR 459.

decision to take those steps, then that extra loss is recoverable in addition to any other loss.[1240] So, it was reasonable in all the circumstances to repair a helicopter, notwithstanding that, in hindsight, losses would have been minimized by selling it for parts.[1241]

Loss may also be said to be mitigated if some collateral benefit in fact accrues to the plaintiff as a result of the breach. In *British Westinghouse Co v. Underground Electric Rys Co of London,*[1242] the plaintiffs were supplied by the defendants with turbines which did not meet the contractual specifications. They accepted and used the machines but later replaced them with turbines which were far more efficient than those supplied by the defendants would have been even if they had complied with the contract. It was held that in calculating the damages, the consequential gain in profits and saved expenses from acquiring the new machines had to be brought into account.

For the *British Westinghouse* principle to apply, there must be a collateral benefit which arose out of the circumstances giving rise to a loss. In *Swynson Ltd v. Lowick Rose LLP*,[1243] the claimant made loans to a borrower relying on the defendant accountants' negligently prepared report. The borrower failed to repay the loans, and the claimant sought damages from the defendant. However, at the time when the damages came to be assessed, the borrower had repaid the loans by using money lent to it by H, who owned the claimant company. It was held that this transaction could not be regarded as collateral as it discharged the very liability the existence of which represented the claimant's loss. Further, the consequences of refinancing the borrower could not be recoverable as the costs of mitigation because H's loan was not an act of the claimant and was not attributable to the defendant's breach of duty. So, the claimant had no claim which could be maintained against the defendant.

If a collateral benefit accrues to a plaintiff, its value has to be determined. In *J & B Caldwell Ltd v. Logan House Retirement Home Ltd,*[1244] Fisher J thought that giving a full indemnity for a new and improved substitute over-compensated the plaintiff, but allowing only the depreciated value of the original item under-compensated, by overlooking the economic burdens associated with immediate or more expensive replacement. The middle way was to allow a deduction for betterment, after making allowance for the disadvantages associated with making an additional involuntary investment.

For the *British Westinghouse* principle to apply, the gain must arise directly out of the conduct aimed at lessening the consequences of the breach. If the benefit arises out of an independent or disconnected transaction, such as a payment under an insurance policy,[1245] it is not taken into account. In *Fulton Shipping Inc of Panama v. Globalia Business Travel SAU of Spain (The New Flamenco)*,[1246] a time charter was repudiated by the charterers with still two years to run. The owners

1240. *Pipes NZ Ltd v. Steel Co Ltd* [2014] NZHC 1216 at [103] (appeal dismissed in *Steel Co Ltd v. Pipes NZ Ltd* [2015] NZCA 175).
1241. *Gunton v. Aviation Classics Ltd* [2004] 3 NZLR 836.
1242. [1912] AC 673.
1243. [2018] AC 313.
1244. [1999] 2 NZLR 99; *Gunton v. Aviation Classics Ltd* [2004] 3 NZLR 836.
1245. *Bradburn v. Great Western Railway Co* (1974) LR 10 Exch 1.
1246. [2017] UKSC 43, [2017] 1 WLR 2581.

accepted the repudiation, but they were unable to arrange a substitute charter, and they sold the ship for NZD 23.7 million. When their claim for lost profits came to be quantified, the evidence showed that the value of the ship at the end of the charter would have been NZD 7 million. The UK Supreme Court held that the repudiation had resulted in a prospective loss of income to the owners, and any relevant mitigation was the acquisition of an alternative income stream. The sale of the vessel was not an act of successful mitigation because it was incapable of mitigating the loss of income stream, and was irrelevant.

IV. Contributory Negligence

250. The Contributory Negligence Act 1947 gives a power to the Court to apportion responsibility between the plaintiff and the defendant where both of them are at fault.[1247] 'Fault' is defined as 'negligence, breach of statutory duty or other act or omission which gives rise to a liability in tort or would, apart from the Act, give rise to the defence of contributory negligence'.[1248] The definition is made up of two limbs. The first is directed to fault as it relates to the conduct of the defendant or, in other words, as it relates to the plaintiff's cause of action. The second is concerned with and is referable only to the conduct of the plaintiff.[1249]

In *Mouat v. Clark Boyce,*[1250] Cooke P held that the first part of the definition is satisfied whenever negligence is an essential ingredient of the plaintiff's cause of action. The Act was not confined to cases of tort liability and could apply to cases of a purely contractual duty of care and to cases of a duty of care arising from tort and contract concurrently. Furthermore, if a liability in negligence exists, it makes no difference that the plaintiff may have chosen to frame his or her action in contract.[1251] But where there is a breach by the defendant of a strict contractual duty arising independently of negligence, so there is no liability in negligence or in tort at all, this does not constitute fault, as defined, and accordingly the 1947 Act does not apply.[1252] In *Vining Realty Group Ltd v. Moorhouse*,[1253] where purchasers sued the vendors of land for misrepresentation in breach of section 6 of the Contractual Remedies Act 1979 (now the Contract and Commercial Law Act 2017, section 35), the Court of Appeal held that since liability under section 6 did not depend on negligence, contributory negligence was not available as a defence.[1254]

Where there is no power to apportion, arguments about contributory negligence are likely to be resolved on an all-or-nothing basis in terms of whether the conduct

1247. Contributory Negligence Act 1947, s. 3.
1248. *Ibid.*, s. 2.
1249. *Rowe v. Turner Hopkins & Partners* [1980] 2 NZLR 550; *Standard Chartered Bank v. Pakistan National Shipping Corporation* [2002] 3 WLR 1547; cp *Dairy Containers Ltd v. NZI Bank Ltd* [1995] 2 NZLR 30 at 112.
1250. [1992] 2 NZLR 559.
1251. *Forsikrings Vesta v. Butcher* [1989] AC 852 at 867.
1252. *Barclays Bank plc v. Fairclough Building Ltd* [1994] 3 WLR 1057.
1253. [2010] NZCA 104.
1254. The case was taken on appeal (*Marlborough District Council v. Altimarloch Joint Venture Ltd* [2012] 2 NZLR 726, above para. 237), where the issue of contributory negligence was not considered.

of the plaintiff or of the defendant was the cause of the loss. Again, the plaintiff's conduct after the breach may raise the question of whether he or she has taken reasonable steps to mitigate the loss.

In cases where the Act does apply, the plaintiff also must be at 'fault'. The second limb of the definition is relevant here. It must be shown that the plaintiff's conduct 'would, apart from the Act, give rise to the defence of contributory negligence'. This requires the defendant to prove simply that the injured party did not in his or her own interest take reasonable care of himself or herself and contributed, by this want of care, to his or her own injury.[1255] The question of whether conduct constitutes contributory negligence in any particular case essentially is one of fact. Merely relying on the other party to perform a contract cannot in itself amount to contributory negligence.

Once each party has been shown to be at fault, the plaintiff's damages are to be reduced 'to such extent as the Court thinks just and equitable having regard to the claimant's share in the responsibility for the damage'.[1256] The main emphasis is on the comparative culpability or blameworthiness of the parties,[1257] but the 'causative potency' of their conduct is also taken into account.[1258]

V. Damages Fixed by the Contract

251. The courts will not enforce a clause which seeks to force a party in breach to perform the contract. The distinction between a clause which protects a contracting party's legitimate interests, which is perfectly valid, and a clause which imposes a penalty on the other party for breach, which is not, was discussed in Chapter 3.[1259]

§2. Cancellation of Contract

252. In addition to damages, the innocent party has the right to cancel the contract or withhold his or her performance where the other party has repudiated before performance is due or before it has been fully performed, or where the other has committed a substantial breach of the contract. This is a 'self-help' remedy which can be exercised without going to court. However, if the evidence of repudiation is not sufficient or the breach is not sufficiently serious, the exercise of the remedy will itself be a breach of contract by the cancelling party.[1260]

1255. *Nance v. British Columbia Electric Railway* [1951] AC 601 at 611.
1256. Contributory Negligence Act 1947, s. 3.
1257. *See Blackmore v. Department for Communities and Local Government* [2017] EWCA Civ 1136, [2018] QB 471.
1258. *Helson v. McKenzies Ltd* [1950] NZLR 878.
1259. *See* para. 182.
1260. The right to cancel a contract has already been discussed at paras 210–220.

§3. SPECIFIC PERFORMANCE AND INJUNCTION

253. The usual remedy for breach of contract is the recovery of damages. But sometimes a mere award of damages may defeat the just and reasonable expectations of the innocent party, in which case the courts may make an order for specific performance of the contract. So also, the performance of a contract may be enforced by the grant of an injunction, which may be prohibitory or mandatory. A prohibitory injunction may be granted in the case of a negative promise requiring the defendant to refrain from doing what he or she has promised not to do. A mandatory injunction is restorative and orders an existing breach of contract to be undone.

Long-standing authority, recently affirmed in the Court of Appeal, holds that these equitable remedies will normally be granted when damages or other financial relief would be inadequate and, conversely, they will not ordinarily be granted in cases where financial relief constitutes an adequate remedy.[1261] But it has been suggested that an equitable remedy should not be treated as a secondary alternative to damages, and the court should simply make a context-specific evaluation of which remedy is the most appropriate in the circumstances of a given case.[1262]

It is clear that the exercise of the equitable jurisdiction to grant specific performance or an injunction is a matter within the discretion of the court. But the discretion involved is a judicial discretion and must be exercised in a principled way.[1263] Factors which are commonly taken into account include the following considerations.

First, the loss which the defendant may suffer through having to comply with an order may be far greater than the plaintiff would suffer from the contract being broken. So hardship to the defendant was a factor militating against an order to carry out contracts with about 240 applicants to hold a ballot for the sale of land.[1264] And it was inequitable to order specific performance of a contract to sell land where the vendor had entered the contract at a time when his judgment was seriously dulled by drink.[1265] But it was not a good reason to refuse specific performance where there was a delay in the completion of a contract for the exchange of farmland (for which the plaintiff was not responsible), and during this time one of the farms suffered a substantial fall in value.[1266]

Second, it is generally seen as undesirable and unworkable to attempt to force upon an unwilling party the performance of a contract for personal services.[1267] So an injunction will not be issued if its effect is to oblige the defendant to perform a contract which is not otherwise specifically enforceable. In *Lumley v. Wagner*,[1268]

1261. *Attorney-General for England and Wales v. R* [2002] 2 NZLR 9 (affirmed [2004] 2 NZLR 577); and *see Co-operative Insurance Society Ltd v. Argyll Stores (Holdings) Ltd* [1998] AC 1.
1262. *Butler v. Countrywide Finance Ltd* [1993] 3 NZLR 623; and *see Kurth v. McGavin* [2007] 3 NZLR 614.
1263. *Attorney-General for England and Wales v. R* [2002] 2 NZLR 9 (affirmed [2004] 2 NZLR 577).
1264. *Markholm Construction Co Ltd v. Wellington City Council* [1985] 2 NZLR 520.
1265. *Kurth v. McGavin* [2007] 3 NZLR 614.
1266. *Hutton v. Palmer* [1990] 2 NZLR 260.
1267. *Rigby v. Connol* (1880) 14 Ch D 482; cp *Thomas Borthwick & Sons (Australasia) Ltd v. South Otago Freezing Co Ltd* [1978] 1 NZLR 538.
1268. (1852) 1 De GM & G 604.

Mlle Wagner was engaged to sing exclusively at Mr Lumley's theatre. During the currency of the contract, she agreed to sing for a competitor and refused to sing for Mr Lumley. The court granted an injunction restraining Mlle Wagner from singing elsewhere during the term of her contract with Mr Lumley. This operated as an inducement to carry out her contract but did not compel it for she could have taken other employment which did not involve singing. But an injunction was refused where the effect would have been either to render the defendant idle and without employment or to force him to return to the employment of the plaintiff.[1269]

Third, specific performance will not be decreed if constant supervision is needed to ensure obedience to the order.[1270] So there is a 'settled practice' not to grant specific performance of an obligation to carry on a business because of the difficulty of drawing up a sufficiently precise order and because the defendant might suffer far greater loss by having to comply with such an order than the plaintiff would suffer from the contract being broken.[1271] But where there was a dispute between parties to a joint venture, from which neither party sought to withdraw, the court was prepared to grant injunctive relief against a threatened breach of contract by one of the parties. This was not a case where the injunction would yoke the parties together in a continuing hostile relationship.[1272]

Fourth, it is relevant to take into account whether specific performance would be available to both parties. So where an employer sought to enforce an employee's promise of confidentiality in relation to his employment, and the employee could not enforce any promise of continuing employment, the lack of mutuality of remedy pointed away from the grant of an injunction against the employee.[1273]

§4. Damages in Substitution for Specific Performance or Injunction

254. Section 13 of the Senior Courts Act 2016 (formerly section 16A of the Judicature Act 1908) gives power to the High Court to order damages in addition to or in substitution for an injunction or specific performance.[1274] Damages can be awarded under the Act even where they would not be available at common law, for example, where an injunction lies but damage has not yet happened.[1275]

In *New Zealand Land Development Co Ltd v. Porter*,[1276] Tipping J said that there was no longer any value, except for historical purposes, in seeking to distinguish or keep conceptually separate common law damages or damages in equity. The court should award such damages as were a proper and fair reflection of what the plaintiff had lost by reason of the failure of the defendant to perform the contract.

1269. *McBean and Pope Ltd v. Coley* [1965] NZLR 966.
1270. *Ryan v. Mutual Tontine Westminster Chambers Association* [1893] 1 Ch. 116.
1271. *Co-operative Insurance Society Ltd v. Argyll Stores (Holdings) Ltd* [1998] AC 1.
1272. *Shell (Petroleum Mining) Co Ltd v. Todd Petroleum Mining Co Ltd* [2008] 2 NZLR 418.
1273. *Attorney-General for England and Wales v. R* [2002] 2 NZLR 9 (affirmed [2003] UKPC 22).
1274. *See generally One Step (Support) Ltd v. Morris-Garner* [2018] UKSC 20, [2019] AC 649 at [41]-[47].
1275. *Neylon v. Dickens* [1987] 1 NZLR 402; *One Step (Support) Ltd v. Morris-Garner* [2018] UKSC 20, [2018] 2 WLR 1353, at [41]-[47].
1276. [1992] 2 NZLR 462 at 468–469.

Tipping J's approach is reflected in the decision of the Court of Appeal in *Cockburn v. CS Developments No 2 Ltd.*[1277] The vendors of commercial land gave a tax invoice with nil Goods and Services Tax (GST), but the purchasers alleged GST was payable and sought damages under the former section 16A. The Court held that it would have been within the reasonable contemplation of the parties that, if the vendors were required and failed to provide an accurate GST tax invoice, this would 'necessarily' mean that the purchasers could not receive a tax credit and would be out of pocket. So there was a proper basis for the award of interest as damages.

§5. Account of Profits

255. The normal remedies for breach of contract are damages, specific performance and injunction. But sometimes, these remedies may be inadequate. A victim of a breach of contract may not be able to show a loss, yet may seek to recover a gain made by the defendant. Whether such an action might sometimes be maintainable was considered in the earlier discussion of the measurement of damages.[1278]

§6. Limitation of Actions

I. Introduction

256. The limitation of actions is entirely a creature of statute. At common law, there was no particular time by which an action had to be commenced. However, the practical need for some temporal restriction on the bringing of claims was recognized by the legislature as early as 1623, when the first limitation statute was enacted.[1279] This Act governed the matter in New Zealand until 1952, when it was repealed and replaced by the Limitation Act 1950. Yet over the years, it became increasingly apparent both that the impact of the 1950 Act was uncertain in some critical aspects and also that it could in some cases cause serious injustice, in particular where a victim did not at first know of some wrongdoing or its consequences. The Law Commission made recommendations for reform in two separate reports,[1280] but Parliament largely ignored them. The courts made their own attempts to mitigate some of the harsher consequences of the law, but recognized that they could not resolve all the difficulties and on a number of occasions called for parliamentary intervention. Indeed, in *Murray v. Morel & Co Ltd,*[1281] Tipping J

1277. [2013] 2 NZLR 413.
1278. *See* para. 239.
1279. Statute of James I, 21 Jac 1, c 16.
1280. *Limitation Defences in Civil Proceedings*, Report No. 6, Wellington, 1988; *Tidying the Limitation Act*, Report No. 61, Wellington, 2000). In 2007 a Miscellaneous Paper made recommendations for the enactment of a new Limitation Defences Act, taking account of the earlier recommendations and of later developments (*Limitation Defences in Civil Cases: Update Report for the Law Commission*, by C Corry, NZLC MP 16, 2007).
1281. [2007] 3 NZLR 721, at [76].

remarked that what was required in New Zealand was a complete legislative overhaul. Piecemeal attempts at reform by the Courts produced their own difficulties, and the surgery required was beyond the proper province of the courts.

Wide-ranging reform was achieved with the passing of the Limitation Act 2010, which came into force on 1 January 2011.[1282] The 1950 Act continues to apply to claims based on acts or omissions before that date, but these must be brought by the later of fifteen years after the date of the relevant act or omission or five years after the date of commencement of the new Act.[1283] We will consider both Acts, although in nearly all cases, the 2010 Act is now going to apply. As regards both Acts, our concern is only with those provisions that apply to or may involve actions for breach of contract.

II. Actions Subject to the Limitation Act 1950

257. An action founded on simple contract cannot be brought after the expiration of six years from the date on which the cause of action accrued.[1284] In the case of contracts under seal, the period is twelve years.[1285] A cause of action accrues in contract not when the damage is suffered but on the date when the breach takes place.[1286] So an action founded on contract where the breach occurs before 1 January 2011 normally can no longer be brought because the six-year period would have expired at the latest on 31 December 2016. However, sometimes, there may be extended periods during which late claims may be made.

If on the date of accrual the person to whom the right of action accrued was under a disability, the action may be brought within six years from the date when the person ceases to be under the disability or dies.[1287] 'Disability' includes infancy or unsoundness of mind.[1288] An infant is a person under the age of 18.[1289] A person is of unsound mind if he or she is detained under any provision of the Mental Health (Compulsory Assessment and Treatment) Act 1992,[1290] or if the person is incapable of managing his or her affairs at the relevant time.[1291] A person may be capable of managing his or her affairs in some respects but not others, in which case he or she can be regarded as being of unsound mind in the latter respects.[1292]

When an action is based on the fraud of the defendant, or the right of action has been concealed by fraud, or when an action is for relief from the consequences of a mistake, the period does not begin to run until the plaintiff has discovered the

1282. Limitation Act 2011, s. 2.
1283. Limitation Act 1950, s. 23B.
1284. *Ibid.*, s. 4(1).
1285. *Ibid.*, s. 4(3).
1286. *White v. Taupo Totara Timber Co* [1960] NZLR 547.
1287. Limitation Act 1950, s. 24.
1288. *Ibid.*, s. 2(2).
1289. Contract and Commercial Law Act 2017, s. 85.
1290. Limitation Act 1950, s. 2(3).
1291. *Millar v. Wellington Hospital Board* unreported, CA 15/86, 4 Oct. 1988.
1292. *T v. H* [1995] 3 NZLR 37 at 49, 59–61.

fraud or mistake or could with reasonable diligence have discovered it.[1293] In *Inca Ltd v. Autoscript (NZ) Ltd*,[1294] Mahon J thought that concealment of a right of action by 'fraud' meant wilful concealment in breach of either a fiduciary duty or a special duty of disclosure inherent in the contract made by the parties, or in some other legal relationship to which they had become committed. In this case, a supplier agreed to sell goods to a purchaser at current wholesale prices less 'the usual trade discount', and the supplier failed to keep the purchaser informed of its discount rates. It was held that the purchaser's action for breach of contract had been 'concealed by fraud' in the relevant sense.

Where a son with an enduring power of attorney over his aged father's property set about forestalling the possibility under the father's will of him receiving only half the estate, and his nephew receiving the other half, by transferring almost its entirety to himself, the Court was satisfied that the son must have known that his actions were dishonest and that in the circumstances section 28(a) applied. The son was not absolved simply by asserting in his own mind he was acting honestly.[1295]

In the case of a claim to a debt or other liquidated sum an acknowledgement of liability or a part payment by the debtor starts time running afresh.[1296] The policy is to allow a creditor to give time to negotiate for the payment of an admitted indebtedness without fear that the claim will become statute barred.[1297] This is so even though the acknowledgement or part payment is not given or made until after the period of limitation has expired. The acknowledgement must be in writing and be signed by the person making it.[1298] It must admit legal liability to pay the sum claimed by the creditor. A statement by a debtor that did not dispute money was owing but said that he was unable to make payment was treated as an admission, notwithstanding that it did not explicitly acknowledge the quantum of the outstanding debt.[1299] An acknowledgement of a debt or other liquidated claim binds only the person making the acknowledgement and his or her successors, whereas a part payment binds co-debtors as well, unless it is made after the expiration of the limitation period when it binds the payer alone.[1300]

III. Actions Subject to the Limitation Act 2010

258. The purpose of the Limitation Act 2010 is to encourage claimants to make claims for monetary or other relief without undue delay by providing defendants

1293. Limitation Act 1950, s. 28.
1294. [1979] 2 NZLR 700.
1295. *Vernon v. Public Trust* [2016] NZCA 388.
1296. Limitation Act 1950, s. 25(4).
1297. *Bradford & Bingley plc v. Rashid* [2006] 1 WLR 2066.
1298. Limitation Act 1950, s. 26(1).
1299. *Bradford & Bingley plc v. Rashid* [2006] 1 WLR 2066; and *see Phillips & Co v. Bath Housing Co-operative Ltd* [2013] 2 All ER 475 at [49]–[53] (letter expressing concern about the amount of a claim but not about the fact of there being a claim at all an acknowledgement).
1300. Limitation Act 1950, s. 27(5), (6).

with defences to stale claims.[1301] Our concern is with the limitation defence to money claims and in particular a claim for breach of contract.[1302]

It is a defence to a money claim if the defendant proves that the date on which the claim is filed is at least six years after the date of the act or omission on which the claim is based.[1303] This is the claim's primary period. However, it is subject to both a late knowledge period and a longstop period.

Where a claimant has late knowledge of a claim and so the claim has a late knowledge date, and the claim is made after its primary period, it is a defence if the defendant proves that the date on which the claim is filed is at least three years after the late knowledge date.[1304] This is the date on which the claimant gained or ought reasonably to have gained knowledge of all of: (a) the fact that the act or omission on which the claim is based had occurred; (b) the fact that the act or omission was attributable (wholly or in part) to, or involved, the defendant; (c) if the alleged liability is dependent on the claimant suffering damage or loss, the fact that the claimant had suffered damage or loss; (d) if the alleged liability is dependent on the claimant not having consented to the act or omission, the fact that the claimant did not consent to that act or omission; (e) if the alleged liability is dependent on the act or omission having been induced by fraud or a mistaken belief, the fact that the act or omission is one that was induced by fraud or mistaken belief.[1305] The onus is on the claimant to prove that at the close of the start date of the primary period he or she neither knew nor ought reasonably to have known of these matters.[1306] The claimant's lack of knowledge may be attributable to causes that include fraud or mistake of fact or law.[1307]

A claimant thus may have three years from when he or she discovers the basis for a claim to bring proceedings. In order to prevent indefinite liability, there is in addition a longstop defence. A defendant can argue that a claim which is brought more than fifteen years after the date of the act or omission on which the claim is based is barred even if the claimant was not aware of the claim at any earlier time.[1308] However, there is no bar on contracting out of a defence under the Act.[1309]

There are a number of exceptions or modifications to the statutory periods and start dates. In the case of a minor, the primary or longstop period does not start to run until the claimant turns 18.[1310] A claimant who was incapacitated at the start of or during the primary or longstop period may apply for a discretionary extension of the periods.[1311] In deciding whether to make an order extending one of the periods,

1301. Limitation Act 2010, s. 3.
1302. A money claim means a claim for monetary relief at common law, in equity, or under an enactment: *ibid.*, s. 12(1).
1303. *Ibid.*, s. 11(1).
1304. *Ibid.*, s. 11(2),(3)(a).
1305. *Ibid.*, s. 14(1).
1306. *Ibid.*, s. 14(2).
1307. *Ibid.*, s. 14(3).
1308. *Ibid.*, s. 11(3)(b).
1309. *Ibid.*, s. 41.
1310. *Ibid.*, s. 44.
1311. *Ibid.*, s. 45(1),(2). 'Incapacitated' means that a claimant or personal representative is not capable of understanding the relevant issues, or is unable to give instructions to issue, defend or compromise proceedings, because of, *inter alia*, physical, intellectual or mental impairment: *ibid.*, s. 46.

the court must take into account, *inter alia*, whether a litigation guardian was managing the claimant's affairs with respect to the act or omission concerned, the effects of the delay on the defendant's ability to defend the claim and on the cogency of the evidence, the defendant's conduct in responding to reasonable requests for information, the extent to which prompt and reasonable steps were taken after the claimant became aware that he or she was entitled to make the claim, any steps taken to obtain relevant medical, legal or other expert advice and the nature of any such advice, and any other matters considered relevant.[1312]

If after the start of a primary or longstop period a defendant acknowledges in writing a liability to the claimant, or makes a payment in respect of that liability, the claimant is deemed to have a fresh claim on the day after the date of the acknowledgement or part payment.[1313] The acknowledgement or part payment binds the defendant's successors, and may be given or made by the defendant or his or her agent and to the claimant or his or her agent.[1314]

A claim's longstop period does not apply if the claimant proves that, because of fraud by or on behalf of the defendant, the claimant neither knew nor ought reasonably to have known of those various facts that are relevant in determining a claimant's knowledge date.[1315] 'Fraud' includes dishonest or fraudulent concealment and fraudulent breach of trust.[1316]

Some comments. First, the 1950 Act and the 2010 Act are going to be operating side by side for up to fifteen years (and, it may be, in some exceptional cases for even longer). So we cannot ignore the old law for a long time to come. Second, the application of the provision for a date of knowledge will lead to a degree of uncertainty, but this inevitably must follow from the introduction of a provision of this kind. Third, the provision in the Building Act 2004 for a ten-year longstop period remains,[1317] so in a field which tends to attract a large number of old claims, the cut-off date is appreciably shorter.

IV. Equitable Relief

259. Under the 1950 Act, the periods of limitation prescribed in the Act do not apply to claims for purely equitable relief, but these may be barred by analogy with the statute or by the equitable doctrine of laches, whereby equitable remedies such as claims for rectification, specific performance or injunction are barred by reason of undue delay in asserting them.[1318] The 2010 Act is similar in that it is provided that nothing in the Act limits or affects any equitable or other jurisdiction to refuse relief, whether on the ground of acquiescence or delay or any other ground.[1319]

1312. *Ibid.*, s. 45(3).
1313. *Ibid.*, s. 47(1),(2).
1314. *Ibid.*, s. 47(3).
1315. *Ibid.*, s. 48.
1316. *Ibid.*, s. 4.
1317. Building Act 2004, s. 393(2).
1318. Limitation Act 1950, s. 4(9).
1319. Limitation Act 2010, s. 8.

Again, nothing in the Act prevents it from being applied by analogy to a claim in equity to which no defence prescribed by the Act applies.[1320]

There will be a bar by analogy only when the fiduciary claim parallels the statute-barred claim so closely that it would be inequitable to allow the statutory bar to be outflanked by the fiduciary claim. The court must examine the underlying facts, the nature of the relationship between the parties, and the policy and purpose of the different causes of action.[1321]

The laches doctrine applies to equitable claims that are not otherwise subject to any time limit, whether under the statute or by analogy with it. The length of the delay and the parties' actions during the interval are important factors in deciding whether it would be inequitable to allow a claim to proceed.[1322] For example, a delay of twenty-five years in bringing an action to enforce an agreement to grant a registered right-of-way over land did not bar an order for specific performance.[1323] The right-of-way was an impediment to the profitable development of the land, but there was no evidence of there being any change in the way it was used during that period that could be attributed to the belief that the right-of-way was not required. Its impact on the land could not be seen as a detriment that was due to the delay in bringing the action.

The doctrine of laches is notably flexible in its application. It has been said that ultimately the enquiry involves a balancing of equities in relation to the broad span of human conduct.[1324]

1320. *Ibid.*, s. 9.
1321. *Johns v. Johns* [2004] 3 NZLR 202.
1322. *Neylon v. Dickens* [1987] 1 NZLR 402.
1323. *No. 68 Ltd v. Eastern Services Ltd* [2006] 2 NZLR 43, affirmed in *Eastern Services Ltd v. No. 68 Ltd* [2006] 3 NZLR 335; and *see Zhang v. Zhou* [2014] 3 NZLR 69 (specific performance of contract for the purchase of property ordered notwithstanding nine-year delay); *Willis v. Thompson* [2017] NZHC 1645, [2017] NZAR 1448 (no prejudice caused by 15 year delay in asserting unconscionable dealings by donee of gift).
1324. *Proprietors of Wakatū v. Attorney-General* [2017] NZSC 17, [2017] 1 NZLR 423 at [696].

Part II. Specific Contracts

Chapter 1. Agency

§1. Introduction

260. An agent is a person who is engaged for the purpose of bringing his or her principal into contractual relations with third persons. An agency agreement is one by which the agent is authorized to establish privity of contract between his or her principal and a third party. Whether a relationship of this kind can be shown turns ultimately on the particular facts of the case. It may coexist with some other legal relationship between the parties. For example, employees and independent contractors may also be agents if the tasks they are engaged to perform include acts which alter the legal relations of employers with third parties.[1325] But the relationship of agency sometimes may be irreconcilable with another relationship. For example, if the parties are in reality buyer and seller, their conflicting interests exclude any possibility of agency.[1326]

The relationship of principal and agent produces effects of two quite different kinds. First, it creates an obligation between the principal and the agent, under which each acquires in regard to the other certain rights and liabilities. Second, when acted upon by the agent, it leads to the creation of privity of contract between the principal and the third party. A contract made with a third party by the agent in the exercise of his or her authority is enforceable both by and against the principal. Thus, an agent may make a contract for the principal which has the same consequences as if the latter personally had made it.

§2. Types of Agents

261. Agency may be of varying kinds. An agent may have unrestricted power to contract on behalf of his or her principal for any purpose, or to contract in the usual course of a particular business, trade or profession, or simply to represent the principal for a specific purpose. The descriptions 'agent' or 'agency' also tend to be used loosely simply to denote the circumstances in which one person acts in some way for the benefit of another. We are not concerned here with this broader meaning.

1325. For a comparison of agents and independent contractors *see Lower Hutt City v. Attorney-General* [1965] NZLR 65; and *see Challenge Realty v. CIR* [1990] 3 NZLR 43.
1326. *Fraser-Robinson (NZ) Ltd v. De Renzy* (1912) 32 NZLR 553.

Some special types of agent require particular mention.

I. Mercantile Agents

262. The Contract and Commercial Law Act 2017 defines a mercantile agent as an agent who has, in the customary course of the agent's business as an agent, authority to sell goods, or to consign goods for the purpose of sale, or to buy goods, or to raise money on the security of goods.[1327] Despite the use of the words 'in the customary course of the agent's business', to be a mercantile agent it is not necessary to carry on business normally as such. What is needed is that authority is given to deal with the goods in the manner described.[1328]

II. Brokers

263. A broker is a person employed to make contracts between persons in matters of trade and commerce. He or she is a negotiator between other parties. Unlike mercantile agents, a broker does not take possession of goods, nor does he or she determine their destination.[1329] Examples include stockbrokers and insurance brokers.

III. *Del Credere* Agents

264. Del credere agents, in return for an extra commission, promise that they will indemnify the principal if the third party with whom they contract in respect of goods fails to pay what is due under the contract. The *del credere* agent acts as a surety for the person with whom he or she dealt, and is only secondarily liable to the principal.[1330] The agent will only be liable to the principal for the other party's failure to pay what is due under the contract, and for no other breach on that party's part.[1331]

IV. Auctioneers

265. Auctioneers are agents whose ordinary course of business is to sell by public auction. If given possession of goods, they will be mercantile agents within the Contract and Commercial Law Act 2017. Auctioneers occupy an unusual position in that they are agents for both parties to the sale which they negotiate. They may

1327. Contract and Commercial Law Act 2017, s. 296. This definition reflects earlier decisions of the courts on the definition of the term 'factor'; *see Dexter Motors Ltd v. Mitcalfe* [1938] NZLR 804.
1328. *Hayman v. Flewker* (1863) 13 CBNS 519.
1329. *Fowler v. Hollins* (1872) LR 7 QB 616.
1330. *Morris v. Cleasby* (1816) 4 M & S 566.
1331. *Thomas Gabriel and Sons v. Churchill and Sim* [1914] 3 KB 1272.

personally sue for the price of goods sold by them as auctioneer.[1332] If they sell goods to which the vendor had no title, they will be liable to the true owner even though they acted innocently and merely as agent.[1333] But an auctioneer who merely returns unsold goods to a consignor who does not own them will not be liable in conversion.[1334] The Auctioneers Act 2013 provides for the licensing of auctioneers and creates various offences arising out of non-compliance with the Act.[1335]

V. Estate Agents

266. The Real Estate Agents Act 2008 sets up a new regulatory framework for the real estate industry. The Act seeks to raise industry standards, by regulating agents, managers and salespersons and ensuring that real estate agency services are offered only by licensed persons, and by providing for accountability through a disciplinary process that is independent and transparent.[1336] A Real Estate Agents Authority oversees the processes of licensing, discipline and complaints, and also develops practice rules and provides consumer information. There is also a Complaints Assessment Committee to deal with complaints and a new Disciplinary Tribunal. The Act makes provision for, *inter alia*, the duty to account for money received and the audit of accounts;[1337] the performance of real estate agency work pursuant to a written agency agreement signed by the client and the agent, without which an agent cannot claim commission or expenses;[1338] and the disclosure of information as to a transaction and possible conflicts of interest.[1339]

§3. Formation of Agency

I. Express or Implied Appointment

267. As a general rule, the appointment of an agent requires no particular formality. Writing is not needed and an appointment may be made orally. However, an

1332. *Chelmsford Auctions Ltd v. Poole* [1973] 1 All ER 810.
1333. *RH Willis & Son v. British Car Auctions Ltd* [1978] 1 WLR 438.
1334. *Marcq v. Christie, Manson & Woods Ltd* [2004] QB 286.
1335. The concept of 'auction' is redefined and clarified, and the rules applying to it set out in detail, in the Fair Trading Act 1986, Part 4A, subpart 4.
1336. Real Estate Agents Act 2008, Part 4; *see Wyatt v. Real Estate Agents Authority* [2012] NZHC 2550; *House v. Real Estate Agents Authority* [2013] NZHC 1619; *Brown v. Real Estate Agents Authority* [2013] NZHC 3309; *Barfoot and Thompson Ltd v. Real Estate Agents Authority* [2015] 2 NZLR 254.
1337. *Ibid.*, ss 122–125.
1338. *Ibid.*, ss 126–131.
1339. *Ibid.*, ss 132–137.

attorney who executes a deed must be appointed by deed.[1340] In certain special cases, there is a statutory requirement that the appointment of the agent be in writing.[1341]

An agency relationship also may be impliedly created by the conduct of the parties, without any express agreement. The circumstances must raise the implication that one person has given authority to another to act on his or her behalf. In this case, the principal is estopped from disputing the agency.[1342]

II. Ratification

268. A person may purport to contract for and on behalf of another, but without any authority to do so. If the 'principal' ratifies or adopts the act of the 'agent', the effect is the same as if there had been a prior authorization by the principal. The ratification relates back to the moment when the contract between the agent and the other contracting party was made.

The requirements for a valid ratification are as follows.

First, the person who makes the contract must profess at the time of making it to be acting on behalf of, and intending to bind, the person who subsequently ratifies the contract.[1343] The principal must be ascertained or at least 'be capable of being ascertained' at the time of the contract.[1344] If the 'agent' makes no allusion to agency, but gives the appearance of contracting in his or her own right, the contract cannot later be adopted by another person.

Second, at the time when the contract was made, the agent must have had a principal who was competent to act in law as the agent did. Formerly this principle meant that a company which was not incorporated at the time of the contract could not be bound by or take a benefit under the contract, and nor could it ratify the contract.[1345] However, under the Companies Act 1993, a company may ratify a contract made in its name or on its behalf within such period as may be specified in the contract, or if no time is specified, within a reasonable time after incorporation.[1346] A contract so ratified is valid and enforceable as if the company had been a party to the contract when it was made.[1347] These provisions operate to the exclusion of the privity provisions of Part 2, subpart 1 of the Contract and Commercial Law Act 2017.[1348] Accordingly, the company must ratify under the Companies Act in order to be able to enforce the contract. Where, however, a contract is made not in the

1340. Property Law Act 2007, 12.

1341. For example, a real estate agent seeking to enforce payment of his or her commission must produce an appointment in writing: Real Estate Agents Act 2008, s. 126.

1342. *Pole v. Leask* (1863) 33 LJ Ch. 155 at 161–162.

1343. *Keighley, Maxsted & Co v. Durant* [1901] AC 240.

1344. *Watson v. Swann* (1862) 11 CBNS 756 at 771 per Willes J.

1345. *Kelner v. Baxter* (1866) LR 2 CP 174.

1346. Companies Act 1993, s. 182(2).

1347. *Ibid.*, s. 182(3). The provisions of the Act cannot apply if the contract was not made on behalf of the particular company now seeking to ratify: *Cross v. Aurora Group Ltd* (1989) 4 NZCLC 64,909; *Taylor v. Todd* [2004] 3 NZLR 76.

1348. *Ibid.*, s. 182(5); applied in *Dargaville Farms Ltd v. Webster* [2017] NZHC 1790 at [33]–[34].

name of or on behalf of, but simply for the benefit of, a company to be formed, those provisions can still apply. In this case, the company can get the benefit of the contract without being bound by it.[1349]

Third, the principal must be aware of all the material facts.[1350] So a principal who purports to ratify a transaction may not be bound if, unknown to the principal, the transaction was invalid.[1351] However, the circumstances may warrant the inference that the principal was adopting the acts of the agent, whatever their nature or culpability.[1352] There can be no ratification of a legal nullity, such as a forgery.[1353]

III. Agency of Necessity

269. There is a limited class of case in which, on the ground of urgent necessity, one person may be bound by a contract made by another on his or her behalf but without that person's authority. In *China Pacific SA v. Food Corporation of India*,[1354] Lord Simon gave this example:

> One of the ways in which an agency of necessity can arise is where A is in possession of goods the property of B, and an emergency arises which places those goods in imminent jeopardy. If A cannot obtain instructions from B as to how he should act in such circumstances, A is bound to take without authority such action in relation to the goods as B, as a prudent owner, would himself have taken in the circumstances.

A person who seeks to bind a principal on these grounds bears the onus of proving that the course adopted by the person in possession was reasonably necessary in the circumstances, and also that it was practically impossible to communicate with the owners. In earlier times, the forced sale of cargo was a common occurrence, but in the light of modern methods of communication, it seems unlikely that circumstances giving rise to an agency of this nature will arise very often.

Probably, the doctrine applies only where there is already some existing contractual relationship between the principal and the person who acts on his or her behalf.[1355] It is extremely doubtful whether a person can be bound by the act of a complete stranger.[1356]

1349. *McKinlay Hendry Ltd v. Tonkin & Taylor Ltd* (HC, Wellington, CIV 1999-485-78, 22 Mar. 2004) (appeal dismissed on another point CA 81/04, 22 Mar. 2004): *see* paras 195–197.
1350. *The Roofing Specialists Ltd v. BLM Engineering Co Ltd* [2012] NZHC 3391 at [57].
1351. *Savery v. King* (1856) 5 HL Cas 627.
1352. *Marsh v. Joseph* [1897] 1 Ch. 213.
1353. *Brook v. Hook* (1871) LR 6 Exch 89.
1354. *See generally China Pacific SA v. Food Corporation of India* [1982] AC 939.
1355. But *see Croskery v. Gee* [1957] NZLR 586.
1356. *Jebara v. Ottoman Bank* [1927] 2 KB 254 at 271.

§4. AUTHORITY OF AGENTS

270. The nature of the agent's authority to bind his or her principal is the central feature of the agency relationship. As a general rule, the principal is only bound by acts of the agent that are within the agent's authority. Furthermore, an agent acting beyond his or her authority may be liable to his or her principal for breach of contract, or to the third party for breach of warranty of authority.

I. Express or Implied Actual Authority

271. Actual authority is that which has actually been conferred on the agent in terms of his or her contract with the principal. Actual authority exists when the principal confers specific authority on the agent to bind the principal to a particular transaction, or when the principal confers a general authority on the agent which covers the particular transaction in issue.[1357] Such authority may be express or implied.[1358] It is *express* when it is given by express words, such as when a board of directors pass a resolution which authorizes two of their number to sign cheques. It is *implied* when it is inferred from the conduct of the parties and the circumstances of the case, such as where the board of directors appoint one of their number to be managing director. They thereby impliedly authorize him to do all such things as fall within the usual scope of that office.[1359] The extent of an agent's implied or usual authority will vary with the nature, customs and usages of the business or trade in which he or she is employed. The burden of proving the existence of actual authority falls on the person alleging it.[1360]

II. Apparent Authority

272. Apparent or ostensible authority is the authority of the agent as it appears to others. There may be an agency of this kind where the agent has no actual authority at all, but the more usual situation is for there to be an agency relationship, but the authority of the agent is limited by agreement between the parties. In this case, the apparent authority of the agent supplements his or her actual authority. It is created by a representation, made by the principal to the contractor, intended to be and in fact acted upon by the contractor, that the agent has authority to enter on behalf of the principal into a contract of a kind within the scope of the apparent authority. The representation, when acted upon by the contractor by entering into a contract with the agent, operates as an estoppel, preventing the principal from asserting that

1357. *Lim v. Ward McCulloch Solicitors Nominees Ltd* (1998) 8 NZCLC 261,922 at 261,929.
1358. *Giltrap City Ltd v. Commerce Commission* [2004] 1 NZLR 608 at [40].
1359. *Hely-Hutchinson v. Brayhead Ltd* [1968] 1 QB 549 at 583; *Cromwell Corporation Ltd v. Sofrana Immobilier (NZ) Ltd* (1992) 6 NZCLC 67,997 at 68,005.
1360. *The Roofing Specialists Ltd v. BLM Engineering Co Ltd* [2012] NZHC 3391.

he is not bound by the contract.[1361] Reliance by the representee to his or her detriment generally makes it unjust to permit the principal to resile from the position as he or she has represented it to be.[1362]

Whether there has been a representation by the principal, express or implied, that the agent has the authority to enter into the transaction is determined objectively. The matter is judged from the viewpoint of a reasonable person dealing with the alleged agent.[1363] The normal practices of the trade or business in question will be taken into account.[1364] For example, a solicitor giving an undertaking to a bank as security for a loan had ostensible authority to bind his partners and his principal, because it would have appeared to the bank that the undertaking was given within the ordinary business of the solicitor;[1365] a solicitor's nominee company was bound in circumstances where, through its solicitor and director, it made it appear to a guarantor that a legal executive employed by the solicitor had authority to bind it in agreeing to a release of the guarantor;[1366] a bank officer who was authorized only to verify customers' signatures on letters of indemnity nonetheless bound the bank as an indemnifying party, because the bank had placed the officer in a position to stamp and sign letters of indemnity without any internal check on their final form or any qualification of the capacity in which the bank was participating in the transaction;[1367] a foreign exchange dealer who forbade its employees from engaging in major foreign exchange transactions, but who gave an employee the trappings of authority to do so, was bound by a fraudulent transaction brokered by the employee apparently on the dealer's behalf;[1368] and an agent for the purchaser of land had the apparent authority to send a fax giving notice that a contract to buy the land was at an end, thereby binding the purchaser.[1369] However, a real estate agent did not have apparent authority to receive a deposit on behalf of the vendor of a house.[1370] Nor was there any evidence that the general manager of a timber treatment company had ostensible authority to sign an agreement to license the use of its product, and the existence of such authority was in any event inconsistent with the terms of the contract concerning the formalities of execution.[1371]

The agent cannot himself or herself enlarge the scope of his or her apparent authority. It is the principal's representation that creates the authority, not the agent's

1361. *Freeman and Lockyer v. Buckhurst Park Properties (Magnal) Ltd* [1964] 2 QB 480 at 503; *Broadlands Finance Ltd v. Gisborne Aero Club* [1975] 2 NZLR 496; *Pascoe Properties Ltd v. Attorney-General* [2014] NZCA 616; *Bishop Warden Property Holdings Ltd v. Autumn Tree Ltd* [2018] NZCA 285 at [29]-[30].
1362. *Kelly v. Fraser* [2013] 1 AC 415.
1363. *Credit Services Investments Ltd v. Evans* [1974] 2 NZLR 683; *Contractors Bonding Ltd v. Snee* [1992] 2 NZLR 157 at 167; *Clark v. Rural Supplies Ltd* [2019] NZHC 671 at [70]; *East Asia Company Ltd v. PT Satria Tirtatama Energindo* [2019] UKPC 30.
1364. *Pascoe Properties Ltd v. Attorney-General* [2014] NZCA 616 at [21].
1365. *United Bank* of *Kuwait v. Hammoud* [1988] 3 All ER 418.
1366. *Lim v. Ward McCulloch Solicitors Nominees Ltd* (1998) 8 NZCLC 261,922.
1367. *Pacific Carriers Ltd v. BNP Paribas* (2004) 218 CLR 451.
1368. *Moneyworld NZ 2000 Ltd v. Lee* (2005) 8 NZBLC 101,638.
1369. *BS Developments No. 12 Ltd v. PB & SF Properties Ltd* CA 73/05, 30 Jun. 2006.
1370. *Sorrell v. Finch* [1977] AC 728.
1371. *Kop-Cote New Zealand Ltd v. Incodo Ltd* [2018] NZCA 430.

assertion that he or she has that authority.[1372] So a real estate agent with authority to accept payment of a deposit could not exceed the limits laid down by the express terms of the contract by asserting to the purchaser that he was entitled to accept late payment.[1373]

§5. Duties of the Parties to the Agency Relationship

I. Duties of the Agent

273. The more important duties of the agent which arise out of the relationship of principal and agent may be summarized as follows:

(1) Where the agency is contractual, the agent must perform what he or she has agreed to perform. Where the agency is gratuitous, the agent is not liable for non-performance but may be liable for negligence in performance.
(2) The agent must act in accordance with the authority conferred by the principal. He or she must act within his or her express or implied authority or within the bounds of prevailing trade customs or usages.
(3) The agent must perform his or her undertaking with due care and skill. In the case of a contractual agency, the agent must exhibit such care and skill as an agent would normally possess and exercise, taking into account the nature of the agent's business.[1374] A gratuitous agent must exercise the care that a reasonable person would exercise in respect of his or her own affairs or, if the agent has held himself or herself out as possessing the skill necessary for a particular undertaking, the care which is reasonably necessary for that undertaking.[1375]
(4) Generally speaking, an agent must act personally. However, the agent may delegate if this is provided for expressly or impliedly in the agreement. Consent to delegation will be implied where it is obvious that performance of the agent's undertaking requires that he or she employ subordinates, for example, where the agent is a company, or where delegation is within the usual authority of the agent, or where it may reasonably be presumed that the parties intended that the power to delegate must exist.[1376] Delegation also is permissible if the function delegated is purely ministerial and does not involve confidence or the exercise of discretion.[1377]
(5) The agent must avoid any conflict with the interest of the principal. The agent must, therefore, disclose any personal interest which may affect the performance of his duty to the principal. In the absence of proper disclosure, the

1372. *Armagas Ltd v. Mundogas SA* [1986] AC 717; *Savill v. Chase Holdings (Wellington) Ltd* [1989] 1 NZLR 257; *Kop-Cote New Zealand Ltd v. Incodo Ltd* [2018] NZCA 430.
1373. *New Zealand Tenancy Bonds Ltd v. Mooney* [1986] 1 NZLR 280.
1374. *See* for example *Hooker v. Stewart* [1989] 3 NZLR 543 (real estate agent); *Cee Bee Marine Ltd v. Lombard Insurance Co Ltd* [1990] 2 NZLR 1 (insurance broker).
1375. *See* for example *Chaudry v. Prabhakar* [1989] 1 WLR 29.
1376. *Nathan v. Dollars & Sense Ltd* [2008] 2 NZLR 557.
1377. *Parkin v. Williams* [1986] 1 NZLR 294; *Herman v. Tournament Railways Ltd* [2007] DCR 823.

principal may set aside the transaction and claim any profits made from it. It is immaterial that the contract was a fair one if the principal was ignorant of the agent's interest.[1378]

(6) An agent cannot act for two principals unless the agent ensures that he or she fully discloses all material facts to both parties and obtains their informed consent.[1379] However, an agent who acts for a number of different clients in different transactions may acquire information in the course of one transaction which is of relevance in another. In one case, it was held that an agent with numerous principals who inevitably would acquire information concerning some which might be material to the interests of another had no duty to disclose the information to the other.[1380] But there was a duty of disclosure where an agent knew certain facts about a purchaser of property which would have been of interest to her principals and which were not confidential and were a matter of public record.[1381] The court observed, obiter, that an agent should not continue to act for a second vendor of land unless and until the first vendor had released the agent from any obligation to maintain confidentiality, or alternatively the agent should disclose the existence of the conflict of interest to the second vendor.

(7) The agent must account to his or her principal for all money received on behalf of the principal. In order for this duty to be properly performed, the agent should keep proper accounts and normally should keep the principal's property and money separate from his or her own property and money.[1382] However, this general rule may be displaced, depending on the particular terms of the agency.[1383] Sometimes, there is a statutory obligation to keep separate accounts.[1384]

(8) The agent must not disclose confidential information of the principal.[1385] The agent may be accountable for profits obtained from the use of the information even if the agent obtained the information otherwise than while acting as agent.[1386]

(9) An agent may not make a secret profit from the performance of his or her duties as agent, and must account for all such profits even without any fraud.[1387] A secret profit extends to any secret financial advantage gained by

---

1378. *Christie v. Harcourt* [1973] NZLR 139.
1379. *McDonnell v. Barton Realty Ltd* [1992] 3 NZLR 418.
1380. *Kelly v. Cooper* [1993] AC 205.
1381. *Stevens v. Premium Real Estate* [2009] 2 NZLR 384.
1382. *North Shore City Council v. Stiassny* [2008] NZCA 522.
1383. *Westpac Banking Corporation v. Savin* [1985] 2 NZLR 41 (overruled on another point by *US International Marketing v. National Bank of New Zealand* [2004] 1 NZLR 589).
1384. *See* for example Real Estate Agents Act 2008, ss 122–125; Lawyers and Conveyancers Act 2006, s. 110.
1385. *SSC and B Lintas NZ Ltd v. Murphy* [1986] 2 NZLR 436; *Peninsular Real Estate Ltd v. Harris* [1992] 2 NZLR 216.
1386. *Regal (Hastings) Ltd v. Gulliver* [1967] 2 AC 134.
1387. *Boardman v. Phipps* [1967] 2 AC 46; and *see Strother v. 3464920 Canada Inc* (2007) 281 DLR (4th) 640.

the agent from the exercise of his or her authority, and includes bribes.[1388] In such a case, the financial advantage is owned by the principal, who has a proprietary as well as a personal remedy against the agent.[1389]

II. Duties of the Principal

274. The duties of the principal are as follows:

(1) The principal must remunerate the agent in terms of the express or implied contract between the parties. If nothing is said about remuneration, but the circumstances indicate that it is to be paid, the appropriate payment will be what is reasonable in the circumstances or what is customary in the particular trade, profession or business.

(2) Whether an agent is entitled to commission depends on whether, on the proper interpretation of the contract between the principal and the agent, the event has happened upon which the commission is to be paid.[1390] For example, in the case of a real estate agent, the intention which as a matter of probability the court will impute to the parties is that if no sale in fact results from the agent's efforts, no commission shall be payable. This is the normal expectation of the vendor. Where, therefore, there is a simple authority to sell, without any special term making commission payable only upon completion of the purchase or upon performance of some other specified condition, the agent is prima facie entitled to commission, provided that there has been no breach of his or her duty as agent, as soon as the agent has procured a person approved by the vendor to enter into a binding contract to purchase on terms warranted by his or her authority.[1391] Where, however, the contract is subject to conditions, no such right arises if the conditions have not been fulfilled.[1392] And where the circumstances giving rise to the right to commission have been described in general or ambiguous terms, the courts have been ready to attribute to the parties an intention that a sale should actually be achieved.[1393] Again, an agent with an undisclosed conflict of interest will not normally be entitled to any payment for work performed for the principal.[1394]

(3) The principal must indemnify the agent against losses, liabilities and expenses incurred in the performance of the undertaking. The extent of this indemnity depends on the agreement between the parties, the kind of business in which

---

1388. *Mahesan v. Malaysia Government Officers Co-operative Housing Society Ltd* [1978] 2 All ER 405.

1389. *FHR European Ventures LLP v. Cedar Capital Partners LLC* [2014] UKSC 45, [2015] AC 250.

1390. *Luxor (Eastbourne) Ltd v. Cooper* [1941] AC 108; *Devani v. Wells* [2017] 2 WLR 1391.

1391. *Latter v. Parsons* (1907) 26 NZLR 645; *Christie v. Harcourt & Co* [1973] 2 NZLR 139; *Pemberton v. Action Realty Ltd* [1986] 1 NZLR 286.

1392. *McKean v. Brice* (1912) 31 NZLR 759; *Progressive Agency v. Bennett* [1928] NZLR 100; *Herdman v. Dickinson* [1929] NZLR 432; *Columbus v. Williamson & Co Ltd* [1969] NZLR 608; *Phillipson v. Indus Realty Pty Ltd* (2004) 8 VR 446.

1393. *Midgley Estates Ltd v. Hand* [1952] 2 QB 432; *A L Wilkinson Ltd v. Brown* [1966] 1 All ER 509.

1394. *Stevens v. Premium Real Estate* [2009] 2 NZLR 384.

the agent is employed and the nature of the authority granted to the agent. There is no duty to indemnify an agent who has acted unlawfully or in breach of duty.[1395]

(4) The agent has a right of lien over the principal's property if the principal has not satisfied his or her liabilities to the agent. The right is to retain the property until payment, not to sell the property.[1396]

§6. CONTRACTS BY AGENTS

275. The question to be considered now is whether the principal or the agent is capable of suing, or of being sued, by the third party with whom the agent has completed the contract. There are three possible cases. First, the agent may not only disclose to the third party the fact that he or she is a mere agent but may also name the principal. Second, he or she may disclose the fact of the agency but withhold the name of the principal. Third, he or she may conceal both facts, in which case the third party will believe that the contract is with the agent personally and that nobody else is interested in the contract. These distinctions are relevant both as to whether the principal is bound by the agent's actions and as to the personal liability of the agent.

I. Disclosed Principal

276. Where an agent makes a contract on behalf of and within the authority of a named principal, the general rule is that the contract is the contract of the principal, not the agent, and only the principal can sue or be sued.[1397] Normally, the agent possesses no rights and incurs no personal liability under the contract. But this normal rule is always subject to the parties' contrary intention.[1398] There may be an express term that the agent be a party, or the intention may be inferred from all the surrounding circumstances.[1399]

The same principles apply if the name of the principal is not disclosed. The general rule is that the agent drops out, but once more, whether he or she does so or not depends essentially upon the intention of the parties. However, in this case, an intention that the agent shall be a contracting party may more readily be inferred. It is relevant to consider the description of the parties in the body of the contract and whether the agent is referred to at any point as agent. Sometimes, a person may sign a contract in a dual capacity, as agent and also in a personal capacity.[1400]

1395. *New Zealand Farmers' Co-operative Distributing Co Ltd v. National Mortgage and Agency Co of New Zealand* [1961] NZLR 969.
1396. A lien may be exercised only over tangible goods, not digitized material: *Your Response Ltd v. Datateam Business Media Ltd* [2014] EWCA Civ 281.
1397. *Montgomerie v. United Kingdom Steamship Association* [1891] 1 QB 370.
1398. *Ibid.*
1399. *The Swan* [1968] 1 Lloyd's Rep 5.
1400. *Contributory Mortgage Nominee Ltd v. Harris Road (No. 10) Ltd* (2005) 22 NZTC 19,850; cp *Trotter v. Avonmore Holdings Ltd* (2005) 8 NZBLC 101,646.

II. Undisclosed Principal

277. Where an agent, having authority to contract on behalf of another, makes the contract with a third party in his or her own name, concealing the fact that he or she is an agent, the agent normally can sue and be sued on the contract in the ordinary way.[1401] So a person who signs a contract personally without an express limitation on the authority to do so will always be personally liable to the other party.[1402] However, the third party may later find that he or she is dealing with an undisclosed principal. In this case, subject the qualifications set out below, the undisclosed principal also may sue and be sued in his or her own name.[1403] The doctrine of the undisclosed principal 'is an anomalous legacy of eighteenth and nineteenth century jurisprudence, which survives in the modern law on account of its antiquity rather than its coherence'.[1404]

This right of action possessed by or against the undisclosed principal is subject to certain limitations. First, the authority of the agent to act for the principal must have existed at the time of the contract.[1405] Second, if the contract, expressly or by implication, shows that it is to be confined in its operation to the parties themselves, the possibility of agency is negatived, and no one else can intervene as principal.[1406] Whether this is the intention of the parties is a matter of construction of the contract.[1407] Furthermore, an undisclosed principal cannot rely on the doctrine in *Hedley Byrne & Co Ltd v. Heller & Partners Ltd*[1408] to recover damages for loss suffered in reliance on a negligent misstatement made to its agent by a third party.[1409]

It has been held in England that the third party must elect whether to sue the agent or the principal.[1410] However, Thomas J has suggested that it might be possible for both the newly discovered principal and the agent to be liable, depending on the terms of the contract.[1411]

III. Payment to the Agent

278. It may happen that either the principal or the third party settles with the agent, who, however, by reason of bankruptcy or fraud, fails to pass the money on

1401. *Rebnik Properties Ltd v. Dobbs* [2020] NZHC 3494 at [102].
1402. *Insight Legal Trustee Co Ltd v. Stokes* [2013] NZCA 138 at [38].
1403. *Siu Yin Kwan v. Eastern Insurance Co* [1994] 2 AC 199.
1404. *Playboy Club London Ltd v. Banca Nazionale del Lavoro SpA* [2018] UKSC 43, [2018] 1 WLR 4041 at [12] per Lord Sumption.
1405. *Keighley, Maxsted & Co v. Durant* [1901] AC 240 at 251.
1406. *Dillicar v. West* [1921] NZLR 617 at 629; *Siu Yin Kwan v. Eastern Insurance Co Ltd* [1994] 2 AC 199 at 207.
1407. *See* for example *New Zealand Bloodstock Finance Ltd v. Diamond Stud Ltd* [2010] NZCA 423.
1408. [1964] AC 465; *see* para. 100.
1409. *Playboy Club London Ltd v. Banca Nazionale del Lavoro SpA* [2018] UKSC 43, [2018] 1 WLR 4041.
1410. *Clarkson Booker Ltd v. Andjel* [1964] 2 QB 775; *Playboy Club London Ltd v. Banca Nazionale del Lavoro SpA* [2018] UKSC 43, [2018] 1 WLR 4041 at [12].
1411. *Fowler (L C) & Sons Ltd v. St Stephens College Board of Governors* [1991] 3 NZLR 304.

to the creditor. The question then arises whether the payer is liable to pay over again. There are two separate cases. The first is where the principal, having instructed his or her agent to buy goods or services, pays the purchase price to the agent, who fails to pay the seller. The second is where the principal instructs his or her agent to sell goods; the agent sells to a buyer and receives payment, but does not pay the principal.

In the first case, the general rule is that the principal remains liable to the seller, provided at least that the agent was known by the seller to be acting as an agent.[1412] The seller, however, may be estopped by his or her conduct from taking advantage of this rule. If the seller's conduct clearly showed that he or she looked to the agent alone for payment and thereby induced the principal, after the debt became due, to settle with the agent, no action can afterwards be brought against the principal.[1413]

In the second case, whether the buyer is liable to pay over again depends upon whether the agent is authorized to receive the purchase money. If he or she possesses this authority, the buyer is discharged from further liability; if not, the liability remains. The general rule is that an agent authorized to sell is not authorized to receive payment.[1414] The buyer, therefore, who seeks to avoid a double payment, must prove that the authority existed in fact. If the principal has not expressly authorized the agent to accept payment, the buyer must prove that what he or she did was the usual and well-recognized practice in that particular type of agency, or that the agent had ostensible authority to receive the money,[1415] or that the principal had ratified the payment to the agent.[1416]

§7. Dispositions of Property by Agents

279. Where an agent makes an unauthorized disposition of the principal's money or property to a third party, the principal can maintain as against the third party an action for conversion, or a proprietary action to recover money, or an action for money had and received. If the money or property has become intermingled with the third party's own money or property, no common law tracing remedy exists. However, tracing in equity may be available.[1417]

The principal's right to recover property may be denied if the principal has held out the agent as having authority to act in respect of the title to the property, thereby misleading the third party, and the agent deals with the property as though he or she were actually authorized to do so. The third party gains a good title and the principal is estopped from denying it.[1418] A good title also is conferred where a mercantile agent is with the consent of the owner in possession of goods or the

1412. *Irvine v. Watson* (1879) 5 QBD 102; affd (1880) 5 QBD 414: *Chamberlain v. Donovan* [1950] NZLR 850; *Fowler (L C) & Sons Ltd v. St Stephens College Board of Governors* [1991] 3 NZLR 304.
1413. *See Sopwith Aviation and Engineering Co Ltd v. Magnus Motors Ltd* [1928] NZLR 433.
1414. *Butwick v. Grant* [1924] 2 KB 483.
1415. *Butwick v. Grant* [1924] 2 KB 483.
1416. *McEwan v. Johnstone* [1918] NZLR 49.
1417. *Re Hallett's Estate* (1880) 13 Ch D 696.
1418. Contract and Commercial Law Act 2017, s. 149(2); *see* para. 303.

documents of title to goods, and makes a sale or other disposition of the goods when acting in the ordinary course of business of a mercantile agent.[1419]

§8. Rights of Third Party Against Principal

I. Right to Enforce the Contract

280. As we have seen, a third party has the right to enforce the contract between him or her and the principal if made by an agent with the principal's authority, whether actual or apparent. Conversely, if a person acts as agent without any authority, or in excess of authority, the principal (apart from ratification) is not liable at all in the first place and is not liable for the excess in the second. However, whether the principal can avoid liability in this way is likely to turn on the extent of the agent's apparent authority.[1420]

II. Right to Treat Agent's Knowledge as That of Principal

281. Information supplied to an agent is imputed to the principal if the information is received in the course of a transaction in which the agent is acting for the principal and the agent has a duty to communicate the information to the principal.[1421] Knowledge acquired before or independently of the particular agency normally is not imputed to the principal, but there are exceptions to this rule. One is where a principal engages an agent with the intention of 'purchasing' the agent's previously acquired knowledge, or because the agent is 'an agent to know', who already has knowledge of a particular business.[1422] Another is where the third party is aware that the information has not been, or will not be, passed on to the principal.[1423] And formerly there was a fraud exception, where knowledge would not be imputed where the agent suppressed disclosure out of self-interest, it being outside the scope of the agent's duties to give and receive notice of his own fraud.[1424] But in *Nathan v. Dollars & Sense Finance Ltd,*[1425] the Supreme Court rejected this view. It considered that the question did not depend upon the imputation of the agent's knowledge to the principal; rather, the question was one of vicarious liability. If the agent's fraudulent conduct had a sufficiently close connection to the task which had been authorized, then on the application of ordinary rules of vicarious liability, the

1419. *Ibid.*, s. 297; *see* para. 303.
1420. *See* para. 271.
1421. *Blackley v. National Mutual Life Association of Australasia Ltd* [1972] NZLR 1038; *Hickman v. Turn and Wave Ltd* [2011] 3 NZLR 318, at [192] (appeal allowed on a different issue in *Hickman v. Turner and Waverly Ltd* [2013] 1 NZLR 741).
1422. *Jessett Properties Ltd v. UDC Finance Ltd* [1992] 1 NZLR 138.
1423. *Blackley v. National Mutual Life Association of Australasia Ltd* [1972] NZLR 1038; *Waller v. Davies* [2005] 3 NZLR 814.
1424. *Waller v. Davies* [2005] 3 NZLR 814.
1425. [2008] 2 NZLR 557; applied in *Burmeister v. O'Brien* [2008] 3 NZLR 842.

principal would be vicariously responsible for it.[1426] So there was no fraud exception because it was the act rather than the knowledge of the agent which was critical.

§9. Rights of Third Party Against Agent

I. Agent's Liability on the Contract

282. As we have seen, where the principal is undisclosed, the agent becomes party to the contract which has been made. In such a case, the agent is liable for breach in the ordinary way. But if the agent is only an intermediary, then the third party suing on the contract must bring his or her action against the principal.

II. Breach of Warranty of Authority

283. A person who represents that he or she has the authority to act for another is deemed to warrant that such authority does in fact exist. If it does not, so there is a breach of this implied warranty, the 'agent' will be liable for the loss suffered by the person who is induced in reliance on the warranty to enter the transaction in question. So in the leading decision in *Collen v. Wright,*[1427] a land agent who made an agreement for a lease for an unauthorized period was liable to the third party for costs incurred in attempting to enforce the agreement by an unsuccessful action for specific performance. This liability is founded on a collateral contract between the supposed agent and the third party. On the one side, there was a promise that the authority existed, and on the other that a lease would be taken.

Apart from any liability in contract, an agent who misrepresents his or her authority may be liable in tort. If the agent knows that he or she possesses no authority to act as agent, but nevertheless makes a representation to the contrary and in consequence causes loss to the other contracting party, he or she may be sued for deceit. It is arguable that the agent might similarly be liable if he or she is negligent in representing that such authority has been conferred, but it has been held that a policy reason for denying a duty in tort was that there was an existing liability in contract for breach of a warranty of authority.[1428] A further basis upon which an agent may be held personally liable, even without negligence, is for misleading or deceptive conduct in breach of the Fair Trading Act 1986.[1429]

1426. *See*, in particular, *Bazley v. Curry* [1999] 2 SCR 534; *Lister v. Hesley Hall* [2002] 1 AC 215; *S v. Attorney-General* [2003] 3 NZLR 450; *Various Claimants v. Catholic Child Welfare Society* [2012] 3 WLR 1319. Note *Hockley Mint Ltd v. Ramsden* [2018] EWCA Civ 2480, [2019] 1 WLR 1617 (principal vicariously liable for deceit of agent if, but only if, the agent's deceitful conduct was within his actual or ostensible authority).

1427. (1857) 8 E & B 647; considered in *Kavanagh v. Continental Shelf Co (No. 46) Ltd* [1993] 2 NZLR 648; *SEB Trygg Liv Holding Aktiebolag v. Manches* [2006] 1 WLR 2276.

1428. *Kavanagh v. Continental Shelf Co (No. 46) Ltd* [1993] 2 NZLR 648.

1429. *Goldsbro v. Walker* [1993] 1 NZLR 394.

§10. Termination of Agency

284. 282 In general, the parties to a contract of agency, as with any contract, may agree to bring their relationship to an end or may terminate in accordance with the terms of the contract. If the contract is silent on the matter, it is a question of construction as to whether or how it is terminable.[1430] The court may well conclude that it is terminable on reasonable notice.[1431] Agency also may be determined if the authority of the agent is renounced by the agent or revoked by the principal. As a general rule, authority may be revoked even if it is agreed by the contract to be irrevocable.[1432] However, there can be no revocation without the agent's consent where the agent has been granted authority to act on the principal's behalf for the purpose of protecting some interest of the agent.[1433]

If one or other party wrongfully repudiates the contract, ordinary principles apply, and the contract is determined only on the acceptance of the repudiation by the other.[1434] However, this is likely to be a case where the innocent party in practice is obliged to accept the repudiation.[1435]

Agency may be determined by operation of law. There are a number of possibilities:

(1) When the transaction undertaken has been performed, the relationship of principal and agent is terminated. The same applies where the period fixed for the duration of the agency has expired.
(2) The death of either the principal or the agent determines the agency.
(3) Mental incapacity of one of the parties also determines the relationship. However, an incapable principal may remain liable for what the agent has done in his or her capacity as agent, for having been held out as having authority, the agent can continue to exercise it until the third party becomes aware of the principal's incapacity.[1436]
(4) The bankruptcy of the principal terminates the agency as from the time of the first act of bankruptcy within the three months preceding the presentation of the bankruptcy petition.[1437] However, if an agent for a bankrupt principal deals after the adjudication with a third party acting in good faith and providing

1430. *Marr v. Parkin* [2014] NZHC 3269 (agency to bid at an auction remained in force only so long as it was viable that the principal could raise the necessary finance).

1431. *See Paper Reclaim Ltd v. Aotearoa International Ltd* [2007] 3 NZLR 169, concerning the question of reasonable notice following the termination of a long-standing relationship between the parties to a joint venture; and *see Gu v. Du* [2011] NZCA 577 (reasonable notice of termination of listing agreement with real estate agent not less than fourteen days).

1432. *Angove's Pty Ltd v. Bailey* [2016] UKSC 47, [2016] 1 WLR 3179 at [6].

1433. *Smart v. Sanders* (1848) 5 CB 895; *Angove's Pty Ltd v. Bailey* [2016] UKSC 47, [2016] 1 WLR 3179 at [7]. In the case of a power of attorney, it is possible to render the authority irrevocable in some circumstances under the Property Law Act 2007, s. 21.

1434. *Gunton v. Richmond-upon-Thames LBC* [1981] Ch. 448.

1435. *See* para. 215.

1436. *Drew v. Nunn* (1879) 4 QBD 661; but cp *Yonge v. Toynbee* [1910] 1 KB 215, which held that the agent was personally liable for breach of a warranty of authority which the agent no longer possessed; and *see SEB Trygg Liv Holding Aktiebolag v. Manches* [2006] 1 All ER 437.

1437. Insolvency Act 2006, ss 101 and 102.

valuable consideration, and there is no intervention by the Official Assignee, the transaction will be valid.[1438] In principle, the bankruptcy of the agent does not terminate the agency, but as this affects the agent's capacity, it will in practice do so.

(5) The contract between principal and agent can be terminated by supervening illegality or frustration.

1438. *Ibid.*, s. 113.

Chapter 2. Bailment

§1. Introduction

I. Nature of Bailment

285. Bailment denotes the relationship between two parties, the bailor and the bailee, where the bailee accepts possession of goods belonging to the bailor.[1439] The goods are held subject to the express or implied condition that they should be redelivered to the bailor on the termination of the bailment or otherwise dealt with according to his or her directions.[1440] A bailment commonly will be contractual, but may also arise in the absence of a contract, as where there is a gratuitous loan of property to another or where property is found by another.[1441] A bailment may even be involuntary, as where unsolicited goods are sent to the bailee.[1442] And it is not necessary that the owner of goods should act willingly in transferring possession to the bailee.[1443] In the case of a contractual bailment, the rights and duties of the bailor and bailee are determined primarily by the terms of the contract concerned. Examples of the bailment of goods for reward include contracts for the deposit, storage or safekeeping of goods, contracts of lease, hire or hire-purchase, contracts for the carriage of goods, and contracts involving goods pledged or pawned as security. Many common transactions of bailment are also regulated by the requirements of statute, such as hire-purchase[1444] and the carriage of goods.[1445]

II. Transfer of Possession

286. Before there can be a bailment, there must be a transfer of possession of the goods from the bailor to the bailee. The bailor must intend to give legal possession to the bailee. In determining this question, a difficult distinction may need to be drawn between a bailment and a licence. The issue has arisen in the context

1439. *See generally* Palmer *Bailment* The Law Book Co, 3rd ed. 2009.
1440. *See Coggs v. Bernard* (1703) 2 Ld Raym 909, 92 ER 107.
1441. In *Yearworth v. North Bristol NHS Trust* [2009] 3 WLR 118 the Court was attracted to the view that an action in bailment was sui generis.
1442. For the rights and obligations of the bailee in these circumstances, *see* the Fair Trading Act 1986, ss 21A–21D.
1443. *Duggan v. Governor of Full Sutton Prison* [2004] EWCA Civ 78 (confiscation of unauthorized items from a prisoner would constitute a bailment of the goods).
1444. *See* the Credit Contracts and Consumer Finance Act 2003 and the Consumer Guarantees Act 1993; *see generally* Holderness (ed.), *Butterworths Introduction to Commercial Law* Ch. 31 (5th ed., 2016).
1445. The international carriage of goods by sea from a New Zealand port to a port outside New Zealand is governed by Part XVI of the Maritime Transport Act 1994, which incorporates the Hague Rules into the law in New Zealand. The international carriage of goods by air to and from New Zealand is governed by Part 9A of the Civil Aviation Act 1990, which incorporates into New Zealand law the international rules represented by the Warsaw Convention and the Guadalajara Convention. The domestic carriage of goods within New Zealand falls under the provisions of Part 5, subpart 1 of the Contract and Commercial Law Act 2017 (formerly the Carriage of Goods Act 1979). *See* Holderness (ed.), *Butterworths Introduction to Commercial Law* Ch. 17 (5th ed., 2016).

of an owner who leaves a car in a parking lot. In one case, the plaintiff paid a fee and parked his car on the defendant's land, and later the car was stolen. It was held that there had been no transfer of possession and no bailment.[1446] But in another case, the plaintiff had regularly parked his car in the defendant's parking lot, paying a monthly fee, and on arrival the car was parked where indicated by the parking attendant or left for the attendant to park, with the ignition key left in the vehicle to enable the attendant to move it. The relationship here was that of bailor and bailee.[1447]

These cases indicate that a key factor in deciding whether the bailee has possession is the extent of control over the goods exercised by the bailee. For example, a defendant who had contracted to store a launch on a cradle in a boatshed and who controlled access to the shed was a bailee, although an agent of the owner also had access in order to carry out maintenance of the launch.[1448]

The position may be different in the case of fixtures. So the hiring of loading machinery fixed to the floor in a shed was not a bailment of chattels. The relationship between the hirer and the user of the shed was that of licensor and licensee.[1449]

§2. Rights and Duties of a Bailee

I. Rights of a Bailee

287. There are two main rights of a bailee:

(1) The bailee has the right to possession of the goods bailed during the period of the bailment.
(2) As between the bailee and a third party, the bailee is deemed through possession to have absolute and complete ownership of the goods.[1450] The third party cannot raise the defence of *jus tertii* – that the bailee is not entitled to possession because he or she is not the true owner.[1451] So, probably, a bailee can sue a person who converts the bailed goods for the full value of the goods, irrespective of the extent of the bailee's own loss or whether the bailee is liable to the bailor.[1452] But the Court of Appeal, without discussion, has regarded the point as moot.[1453] Assuming full damages are recoverable, and the bailee recovers the converted goods, the measure of damages is the value at the date of the conversion, less the value of the goods when recovered.[1454]

1446. *Ashby v. Tolhurst* [1937] 2 KB 242.
1447. *Shorters Parking Station Ltd v. Johnson* [1963] NZLR 135.
1448. *Shipbuilders Ltd v. Benson* [1992] 3 NZLR 549.
1449. *Southland Harbour Board v. Vella* [1974] 1 NZLR 526.
1450. *The Winkfield* [1902] P 42.
1451. *Berg v. Anglo Pacific International (1988) Ltd* (1988) 1 PRNZ 713 at 716.
1452. *The Winkfield* [1902] P 42.
1453. *Cuff v. Broadlands Finance Ltd* [1987] 2 NZLR 343 at 346.
1454. *Trailways Transport Ltd v. Thomas* [1996] 2 NZLR 443.

II. Duties of a Bailee

288. The duties of a bailee are as follows:

(1) The bailee must return the bailed goods or deal with them in accordance with the instructions of the bailor when the purpose of the bailment is completed. Wrongful denial of the owner's rights will constitute a conversion of the goods by the bailee.[1455] For example, a finder of goods may be liable in conversion to the true owner for failing to take care in delivering the goods to the wrong person.[1456]

(2) Formerly, the standard of care imposed upon a bailee taking custody of goods differed according to the nature of the bailment: a gratuitous bailee was liable only for gross negligence in the care of the goods, while a bailee for reward was liable for ordinary negligence. The distinction is no longer drawn, and a bailee is required to take reasonable care in all the circumstances of the case.[1457] It is relevant to take into account the nature of the bailment, the nature of the goods and the expertise of the bailee. For example, a warehouse-keeper storing newsprint in a warehouse was expected to show the degree of care which might reasonably be expected from a skilled warehousekeeper acquainted with the risks.[1458] However, the bailee's responsibility may be diminished where the bailor becomes patently aware of the risks of goods being stored in a particular way.[1459] And the bailee is not liable for damage to goods caused without negligence on his or her part.

(3) Where goods are lost, destroyed or damaged while in the bailee's custody, the burden is on the bailee to show that appropriate care was taken or that the loss or damage was not caused by his or her negligence.[1460] If the bailee can discharge this onus, it does not matter that the bailee cannot explain exactly how the loss occurred. But if the bailee leaves it doubtful whether the damage was due to his or her fault, the plaintiff should succeed.[1461]

(4) The bailee naturally must comply with the terms of the contract of bailment as regards, for example, the manner and performance of the contract and whether performance may be delegated.

(5) By section 28 of the Consumer Guarantees Act 1993, where services are supplied to a consumer, there is a guarantee that the service will be carried out with reasonable care and skill. This section can apply to services supplied by a bailee.

1455. *See generally Todd on Torts* para. 11.3 (9th ed., Thomson Reuters 2023) (by C Hawes).

1456. *Helson v. McKenzies (Cuba St) Ltd* [1950] NZLR 878.

1457. *Houghland v. RR Low (Luxury Coaches) Ltd* [1962] 1 QB 694.

1458. *Wilson & Horton Ltd v. A-G* [1997] 2 NZLR 513 at 526.

1459. *Skyway Service Station Ltd v. McDonald* [1986] 1 NZLR 366 at 370.

1460. *Petersen v. Papakura Motor Sales Ltd* [1957] NZLR 495 at 498–499; *EMI (New Zealand) Ltd v. Holyman & Sons Pty Ltd* [1976] 2 NZLR 566 at 575; *Southland Hospital Board v. Perkins Estate* [1986] 1 NZLR 373; *Wilson & Horton Ltd v. A-G* [1997] 2 NZLR 513 at 526.

1461. *Wilson & Horton Ltd v. A-G* [1997] 2 NZLR 513 at 526.

§3. RIGHTS AND DUTIES OF A BAILOR

I. Rights of a Bailor

289. The rights of a bailor may be summarized as follows:

(1) The bailor has the right to have the goods bailed returned to him or her or disposed of according to his or her instructions once the purpose of the bailment has been achieved. The bailor can sue the bailee for conversion if his or her right to possession is denied, for breach of any obligation imposed by contract on the bailee, and for negligence.
(2) Bailor cannot normally sue a third party during a bailment for a fixed term, as the bailor is not entitled to possession. However, a bailor with an immediate right to possession may sue third parties who have acquired the goods and converted them to their own use. So, for example, the bailor can bring an action where there is a bailment at will that can be terminated at any time,[1462] or where the seller in a hire-purchase transaction has acquired the right to repossess goods in consequence of a breach of the hire-purchase contract by the buyer.[1463] The bailor can also sue where his or her reversionary interest in the property has been destroyed or permanently damaged.[1464]

II. Duties of a Bailor

290. The main duties of a bailor are as follows:

(1) The bailor of goods for reward must give undisturbed possession to the bailee. In addition, apart from common law principle, certain duties as to title are imposed by statutes which apply generally to contracts for the supply of goods, including contracts involving bailment for reward. Where goods are supplied to a 'consumer' within the meaning of the Consumer Guarantees Act 1993, there are guarantees that the supplier has the right to sell, that the goods are free from any undisclosed security and that the consumer has the right to undisturbed possession.[1465]
(2) At common law, the bailor must supply goods which are fit and suitable for the purpose for which they are bailed;[1466] and once again various duties of general application which can apply in the present context are imposed by statute. In particular, the Consumer Guarantees Act 1993 imposes guarantees in favour of consumers of acceptable quality, fitness for purpose, compliance with description and compliance with sample.[1467]

1462. *Manders v. Williams* (1849) 3 Exch 339.
1463. *North Central Wagon and Finance Co Ltd v. Graham* [1950] 1 All ER 580.
1464. *Mears v. London & South West Railway Co* (1862) 11 CBNS 850, 142 ER 1029.
1465. Consumer Guarantees Act 1993, s. 5; *see* para. 316.
1466. *Smith v. Stockdill* [1960] NZLR 53; *Southland Harbour Board v. Vella* [1974] 1 NZLR 526.
1467. Consumer Guarantees Act 1993, ss 6–10; *see* para. 316.

(3) It has been held that a gratuitous bailor must warn the bailee of defects in the goods of which the bailor is aware.[1468] But ordinary principles of negligence can in any event apply.

1468. *Coughlin v. Gillison* [1899] 1 QB 145 at 149; cf. *Fraser v. Jenkin* [1968] NZLR 816 at 824.

Chapter 3. Gaming and Wagering Contracts

§1. Wagering Contracts

I. Definition

291. A wagering contract is one where two parties have agreed that one or other will win something of value depending upon the outcome of some future event, such as a horse race or football match, or upon the correctness of some assertion as to a matter of past or present fact, such as the name of the star actor in a named film. If the parties have no interest in the outcome of the event, or the truth of the assertion, other than the winning or losing of the valuable item, the contract is a wagering contract.[1469] A contract of insurance may be distinguished from a wagering contract by the fact that the contract involves a party with an 'insurable interest' – that is, a party whose rights to property or income are affected by the outcome of the specified event on which the insurer is required to pay. Thus, a contract which provides for the payment of money if a nominated house burns down is an insurance contract if the money would be paid to the owner of, or a person with an interest in the continued existence of, the house. However, if the money was to be paid to a person who has no connection with or interest in the house it is a wagering contract.[1470]

II. Status

292. New Zealand law now distinguishes between legal and illegal wagering or gambling contracts. Some gambling contracts are permitted by statute, and such contracts are enforceable by law.[1471] Gaming contracts not permitted by statute are illegal, although there is the possibility of seeking relief from the consequences of illegality under the Contract and Commercial Law Act 2017.[1472]

III. Contracts Collateral to Wagering Contracts

293. In general, contracts ancillary to illegal gambling will also be illegal under the Gambling Act and indeed will involve the commission of a criminal offence.[1473] Special mention should be made of contracts for the provision of credit to gamblers by persons conducting gambling. Such provision of credit is unlawful unless it is by a casino licensed so to provide credit.[1474] As with other contracts involving conduct made illegal by the Gambling Act, there is the possibility of relief under the

1469. *Carlill v. Carbolic Smokeball Co Ltd* [1892] 2 QB 484.
1470. In some cases the need for an insurable interest has been removed by statute, but an insurance contract which is in essence a wagering contract will be void: Insurance Law Reform Act 1985, ss 6 and 7.
1471. Gambling Act 2003, s. 14.
1472. *See* above paras 147, 151 and 157–160.
1473. Gambling Act 2003, s. 14.
1474. Gambling Act 2003, s. 15.

Contract and Commercial Law Act 2017, but such relief is likely to be refused because granting it would frustrate the purpose of the statute.[1475]

1475. Gambling Act 2003, s. 14. Relief was refused on this basis in *Xiao v. Sun* [2018] NZHC 536 at [441]. For a discussion of the illegality provisions of the Contract and Commercial Law Act 2017 *see* above paras 147–160.

Chapter 4. Sale of Goods

§1. Introduction

294. The Contract and Commercial Law Act 2017 lays down specific rules relating to the sale of goods. In addition, a contract for the sale of goods is governed by the general rules of contract law. Accordingly, it is necessary to supplement the provisions of the Act by the rules and principles of the common law and of statute which are common to the law of contract generally and applicable to the sale of goods.

In England, the common law of sale was codified in the Sale of Goods Act 1893. Its drafter, Sir Mackenzie Chalmers, did not intend to effect any significant change in the then-existing law. The original English Act was adopted in New Zealand in the Sale of Goods Act of 1895, which was then re-enacted in 1908. This Act has now been re-enacted in Part 3 of the Contract and Commercial Law Act 2017. In the UK, the Act presently in force is the Sale of Goods Act 1979, which differs in certain respects from the NZ Act. However, many provisions are the same, and English authority remains influential in New Zealand.

The 2017 Act provides, in section 201(2), that the general principles of the common law continue to apply save insofar as they are inconsistent with the express provisions of the Act. So it is clear that common law principles concerning, for example, the innominate term[1476] and quantification and remoteness of damage[1477] can apply in the context of contracts for the sale of goods. However, section 201(2) does not refer to the principles of equity, and in *Riddiford v. Warren,*[1478] the Court of Appeal suggested that the principles of equity might not apply. But in *Thomas Borthwick and Sons (Australia) Ltd v. South Otago Freezing Co,*[1479] the Court of Appeal recognized that there exists a residual equity applicable to contracts for the sale of goods in cases where the provisions of the Act are not inconsistent with it.

Part 3 of the 2017 Act also exists alongside other statutory regimes. Two of these require special mention:

(1) In most respects, the remedies regime in Part 2, subpart 3 of the Contract and Commercial Law Act (formerly the Contractual Remedies Act 1979) leaves contracts governed by Part 3 unaffected.[1480] In particular, the rules laid down in Part 2, subpart 3 concerning cancellation for misrepresentation, repudiation or breach[1481] do not apply to contracts for the sale of goods.[1482] So the scheme

1476. *See* para. 305.
1477. *See* paras 237–247.
1478. (1901) 20 NZLR 572. *See also Re Wait* [1927] 1 Ch. 607; *Cutelli v. Brian Cotter Motors Ltd* (1993) 5 TCLR 500.
1479. [1987] 1 NZLR 538.
1480. The exceptions are the limits on the power to disclaim liability for certain statements in s. 50 of the 2017 Act (as to which *see* para. 178), and the provision for the recovery of damages for misrepresentation in s. 35 (as to which *see* para. 107).
1481. As to which *see* paras 210–220.
1482. Contract and Commercial Law Act 2017, s. 59(e).

of remedies in Part 3 depending on the classification of contractual terms into conditions and warranties continues to apply.[1483]

(2) The Consumer Guarantees Act 1993 imposes certain statutory guarantees in consumer transactions and provides for a scheme of remedies for failure to comply with them. The Act applies to the exclusion of Part 3 of the Contract and Commercial Law Act.[1484] It is considered in more detail in Chapter 5 below.

§2. Sale of Goods Legislation

I. Definition of a Contract for the Sale of Goods

295. A contract of sale of goods is a contract whereby the seller transfers or agrees to transfer the property in goods to the buyer for a money consideration, called 'the price'.[1485]

'Goods' are defined as including all kinds of movable personal property other than money or things in action.[1486] Dollar notes and coins are not goods unless they are sold as antiques or as having some special or unique feature.[1487] The definition also provides that 'goods' includes emblements, growing crops, and things attached to or forming part of the land which are agreed to be severed before sale or under the contract of sale. The sale of a house for removal from the land can be a sale of goods.[1488] 'Goods' do not include choses in action, which are personal rights of property which can be enforced only by action and not by taking physical possession. Examples are shares in companies and intellectual property rights.

The consideration or price paid or to be paid must be money. This means that the consideration must be measured in money, and it is not necessary that it be provided in the form of money. For example, the sale of a car where another is given in part-exchange is still a sale of goods. The price may be fixed by the contract, or may be left to be fixed in a manner thereby agree, or may be determined by the course of dealing between the parties. Where the price is not so determined, the buyer must pay a reasonable price. What is reasonable is a question of fact.[1489] However, if the terms provide that the parties are to agree on a price and they do not, it may then be that they have no contract at all.[1490]

A contract for the supply of work and materials may be a contract for the sale of goods or it may be a contract for the supply of a service. Broadly, the test is whether the substance of the contract is for the provision of goods or for the supply of skill

---

1483. *Finch Motors Ltd v. Quin (No. 2)* [1980] 2 NZLR 519; *Moodie v. Agricultural Ventures Ltd* [1998] 3 NZLR 129.
1484. Contract and Commercial Law Act 2017, s. 198.
1485. Contract and Commercial Law Act 2017, s. 120.
1486. *Ibid.*, s. 119.
1487. *Money World New Zealand 2000 Ltd v. KVB Kunlun New Zealand Ltd* [2006] 1 NZLR 381.
1488. *Oldfield Asphalts Ltd v. Grovedale Coolstores (1994) Ltd* [1998] 3 NZLR 479; cp *Lockwood Buildings Ltd v. Trust Bank Canterbury Ltd* [1995] 1 NZLR 22.
1489. Contract and Commercial Law Act 2017, ss 129, 199.
1490. *May and Butcher Ltd v. R* [1934] 2 KB 17.

and labour.[1491] But where a contract involves the provision of both goods and services, however, it may be classified, the goods must be reasonably fit for their intended purpose.[1492] Furthermore, in the case of consumer contracts for the supply of services, statutory guarantees as to reasonable care and fitness for purpose also apply.[1493]

The Act distinguishes between a sale and an agreement to sell. Where the property in the goods is transferred from the seller to the buyer, the contract is called a 'sale'; but where the transfer is to take place at a future time or subject to a condition the contract is an agreement to sell.[1494] A sale creates a right in rem, whereas an agreement to sell creates merely a right in personam. In the latter case, the innocent party to a breach of contract has no property right in the goods and is limited to a claim for damages.

II. Formation of the Contract

296. No special formalities are required. A contract of sale may be made in writing (either with or without seal), or orally, or partly in writing and partly orally, or may be implied by the conduct of the parties.[1495]

III. Passing of Property in Goods and Risk

297. Goods may be existing, future, specific or unascertained. These distinctions are important particularly in relation to the question of risk and the passing of the property in the goods. Existing goods are those which are owned or possessed by the seller at the time of the contract, whereas future goods are those to be manufactured or acquired by the seller after the making of the contract.[1496] A present sale of future goods operates as an agreement to sell the goods.[1497] Specific goods are goods identified or agreed on at the time a contract of sale is made.[1498] Unascertained goods are not defined, but are goods not so identified and agreed on.

Where there is a contract for the sale of specific or ascertained goods, the property in them is transferred to the buyer at such time as the parties intend, having regard to the terms of the contract, the conduct of the parties and the circumstances of the case.[1499] However, in the case of a sale of unascertained goods, no property

---

1491. *Art Direction v. Needham* [1977] 2 NZLR 12; *Whyte v. Owl Electrical Ltd* (1995) 6 TCLR 299.
1492. *Young and Marten Ltd v. McManus Childs Ltd* [1969] 1 AC 454.
1493. *See* para. 317.
1494. Contract and Commercial Law Act 2017, s. 123.
1495. *Ibid.*, s. 125.
1496. *Ibid.*, s. 126(1).
1497. *Ibid.*, s. 126(3).
1498. *Ibid.*, s. 119.
1499. *Ibid.*, s. 144: *Swindle v. Matakana Estate Ltd* [2012] 1 NZLR 806.

is transferred unless and until the goods are ascertained.[1500] So if goods are part of a larger bulk, no property can pass unless there is severance from the bulk.[1501]

Section 146 of the Contract and Commercial Law Act sets out a number of rules which are presumptions for ascertaining the intention of the parties as to when property is to pass. They operate subject to any evidence indicating that the parties had a different intention. The rules are calculated to diminish uncertainty as to whether property has passed in cases where the parties have not otherwise made their intentions clear. They are robust, designed to enable both contracting and third parties to rely on them.[1502]

A. Specific Goods

298. Specific goods are governed by section 146, Rules 1, 2, and 3. Rule 1 provides that where there is an unconditional contract for the sale of specific goods, in a deliverable state, the property in the goods passes to the buyer when the contract is made, and it is immaterial whether the time of payment or the time of delivery, or both, is postponed.[1503] Rule 2 provides that where there is a contract for the sale of specific goods, and the seller is bound to do something to the goods for the purpose of putting them into a deliverable state, the property does not pass until such thing is done and the buyer has notice of it.[1504] Under Rule 3, where there is a contract for the sale of specific goods in a deliverable state, but the seller has to weigh, measure, test or do some other act or thing with reference to the goods for the purpose of ascertaining the price, the property does not pass until such act or thing is done and the buyer has notice.[1505]

B. Unascertained Goods

299. The passing of property in unascertained goods is governed by section 143 and section 146 Rule 5. We have seen that under section 143, property in unascertained goods does not pass unless and until the goods are ascertained. Section 146 Rule 5 applies once the goods have been ascertained. The rule states that where there is a contract for the sale of unascertained or future goods by description, and goods of that description and in a deliverable state are unconditionally appropriated to the contract either by the seller with the assent of the buyer or by the buyer with the assent of the seller, the property in the goods thereupon passes to the buyer. Such

1500. *Ibid.*, s. 143.
1501. *Re Goldcorp Exchange Ltd* [1994] 3 NZLR 385.
1502. *Swindle v. Matakana Estate Ltd* [2012] 1 NZLR 806.
1503. Goods are in a 'deliverable state' when the buyer would under the contract be bound to take delivery of them; *see Underwood v. Burgh Castle Brick and Cement Syndicate* [1922] 1 KB 343; *Philip Head & Sons Ltd v. Showfronts Ltd* [1970] 1 Lloyd's Rep 140.
1504. *See* for example *Boys v. Rice* (1908) 27 NZLR 1038 (seller to shear sheep); *Farley v. Loughnan* [1917] NZLR 588 (seller to dock lambs).
1505. *See* for example *Farm Products Co-operative v. Belkirk Poultry Farm Ltd* [1965] NZLR 1012 (sale of poultry at a price to be fixed by valuation).

assent may be express or implied and may be given before or after the appropriation is made.[1506] This rule, like the others, is subject to any different intention of the parties.[1507] So once goods have been ascertained, the property may pass without an unconditional appropriation if that is what the parties intend.[1508]

Rule 5 also sets out a particular instance of unconditional appropriation. It provides that where the seller delivers the goods to the buyer, or to a carrier or other bailee (whether named by the buyer or not) for the purpose of transmission to the buyer, and does not reserve the right of disposal, the seller must be treated as having unconditionally appropriated the goods to the contract. Such appropriation will occur only where goods which are selected as intended for the buyer are delivered for transmission to the buyer.[1509]

C. Sale or Return Contracts

300. Sale or return contracts are covered by Rule 4. It provides that where goods are delivered to the buyer on approval or 'on sale or return' or other similar terms, the property passes to the buyer either:

(a) when the buyer indicates approval or acceptance to the seller or does any other act adopting the transaction; or
(b) if the buyer does not indicate approval or acceptance, but retains the goods without giving notice of rejection, then if a time has been fixed for the return of the goods, on the expiration of that time, and if no time has been fixed, on the expiration of a reasonable time.[1510]

D. Reservation of Property

301. Section 147 of the 2017 Act states that the seller may reserve the right of disposal of the goods until certain conditions are fulfilled. Reservation or retention of title clauses are commonly used to avoid the loss to the seller which might otherwise occur on account of the bankruptcy or insolvency of the buyer. They are called 'Romalpa clauses', after the influential decision of the English Court of Appeal in *Aluminium Industrie Vaassen BV v. Romalpa Aluminium Ltd.*[1511] Such clauses may provide, for example, that the seller is to retain ownership of the goods until payment, or that the seller is entitled to the proceeds if the goods are sold to

1506. For discussion of 'unconditional appropriation', *see Donaghy's Rope and Twine Co v. Wright Stephenson and Co* (1906) 25 NZLR 641; *Carlos Fiederspiel v. Charles Twigg and Co* [1957] 1 Lloyd's Rep 240; *MJN McNaughton v. Thode* [2012] NZHC 982. For implied assent, *see Pignatoro v. Gilroy & Son* [1919] 1 KB 459.
1507. Contract and Commercial Law Act 2017, s. 145.
1508. *Re Staplyton Fletcher Ltd* [1995] 1 All ER 192.
1509. *Healey v. Howlett & Sons* (1917) 116 LT 591.
1510. For discussion of how the buyer may intimate rejection of the goods, *see Atari Corp (UK) Ltd v. Electronic Boutique Stores (UK) Ltd* [1998] 1 All ER 1010.
1511. [1976] 1 WLR 676.

a sub-buyer, or that the seller has the ownership of new goods manufactured from the original goods, or that the buyer holds the goods or their proceeds or resulting mixtures on trust for the seller.

A Romalpa clause which simply reserves property until payment is usually effective.[1512] Where the seller is entitled to recover goods, but they have been wrongfully sold, the seller is entitled to the proceeds of sale by way of damages for conversion.[1513] Further, where the terms of the contract make the buyer the bailee or agent of the seller with regard to subsales, there may be an equitable right of tracing with respect to the proceeds of sale.[1514] However, where the contract contains a more complex reservation of property clause which purports to extend to new goods manufactured from the goods supplied, it may be construed by the courts as a charge which is void against the buyer's creditors for non-registration under the Companies Act 1993.[1515] A key question is whether the goods have retained their original character or have been converted into something else. In *Pongakawa Sawmill Ltd v. New Zealand Forest Products Ltd,*[1516] the Court of Appeal held that logs which had been converted by the buyer into sawn timber retained their essential character, and so the seller's Romalpa clause was effective. On the other hand, in *ICI NZ Ltd v. Agnew,*[1517] it was held that plastic pellets lost their original identity when they were made into containers. The test was one of common sense: pellets and containers had their own obvious identities. It did not matter that the containers could have been converted back into pellets.

These principles apply only as between a buyer and seller. Where third parties are involved the Personal Property Securities Act 1999 applies because a reservation of property clause is a security interest within that Act.[1518]

E. Risk

302. Section 148(1) and (2) of the 2017 Act provide that unless otherwise agreed, the goods remain at the seller's risk until property in them is passed to the buyer, but when the property is transferred, the goods are at the buyer's risk, whether delivery has been made or not. But where delivery has been delayed through the fault of either buyer or seller, the goods are at the risk of the party in fault as regards any loss which might not have occurred but for such fault. This linking of risk and property is subject to any contrary intention of the parties. The parties may make express provision on the matter, or the circumstances may show that risk and property should pass at different times. An obligation placed on a party to insure can be a strong indication that that party should bear the risk.[1519] Again, a

1512. For example, *see Pongakawa Sawmill Ltd v. New Zealand Forest Products Ltd* [1992] 3 NZLR 304.
1513. *Len Vidgen Ski & Leisure Ltd v. Timaru Marine Supplies (1982) Ltd* [1986] 1 NZLR 349.
1514. *Aluminium Industrie Vaassen BV v. Romalpa Aluminium Ltd* [1976] 1 WLR 676.
1515. *Re Bond Worth Ltd* [1980] Ch. 228 so held in relation to the UK companies legislation.
1516. [1992] 3 NZLR 304.
1517. [1998] 2 NZLR 129.
1518. *See* para. 304.
1519. *Donaghy's Rope and Twine Co v. Wright Stephenson and Co* (1906) 25 NZLR 641.

provision that a particular party bears the risk may indicate that property is not vested in the party, as it would be unnecessary if that party did have property in the goods.[1520]

By section 148(3), the duties or liabilities of either seller or buyer as a bailee of the goods of the other party are unaffected by section 148. The ordinary obligation of a bailee is to take reasonable care in all the circumstances of the case.[1521]

F. Perishing of Goods

303. Specific goods which have 'perished' are subject to special rules. Section 127 of the 2017 Act provides that a contract for the sale of specific goods is void if the goods without the knowledge of the seller have perished at the time when the contract is made. Section 128 provides that if there is an agreement to sell specific goods and subsequently the goods, without any fault on the part of the buyer or seller, perish before the risk passes to the buyer, the agreement becomes void when the goods perish. This section appears to constitute a statutory form of the common law doctrine of frustration.

Goods may be held to have perished if they have been physically destroyed.[1522] They may also be considered to have perished even where they are not destroyed if they are so damaged as to no longer answer to the description under which they were sold.[1523] One test is whether the nature of the goods has been so affected that they have ceased to have those qualities which led to the parties entering into the contract for their disposition.[1524]

IV. Sales Without Title

A. Nemo Dat Quod Non Habet

304. The maxim *nemo dat quod non habet* means that no one can give a better title to goods than he or she possesses. The rule is encapsulated in section 149 of the 2017 Act, which provides that, with some exceptions, where goods are sold by a person who is not the owner, and who does not sell them with the authority or consent of the owner, the buyer acquires no better title to the goods than the seller had. So the rule protects the true owner of the goods. However, in the following circumstances, it does not apply and a bona fide buyer is protected instead:

1520. *Re Anchor Line (Henderson Bros) Ltd* [1937] Ch. 1.
1521. *See* para. 287.
1522. *Oldfield Asphalts Ltd v. Grovedale Coolstores (1994) Ltd* [1998] 3 NZLR 479.
1523. *Rendell v. Tunbull* (1908) 27 NZLR 1067 (potatoes unfit for human consumption); *Asfar v. Blundell* [1896] 1 QB 23 (dates impregnated with sewage). In *Barrow, Lane and Ballard Ltd v. Phillips and Co Ltd* [1929] 1 KB 574 it was held that the subject matter of a contract to sell 700 bags of nuts was an indivisible whole which 'perished' when 109 bags disappeared.
1524. *Oldfield Asphalts Ltd v. Grovedale Coolstores (1994) Ltd* [1998] 3 NZLR 479.

(1) The true owner may be precluded from denying the seller's authority to sell.[1525] The basis for this exception is estoppel. For example, the owner may represent to a third party, expressly or impliedly, that another has the right to deal with the goods.[1526] However, mere inaction or silence will not usually constitute conduct which can give rise to an estoppel.[1527]

(2) A sale in the ordinary course of business of a mercantile agent who is in possession of goods with the consent of the owner confers a good title on a purchaser who takes in good faith without notice of any lack of authority of the agent.[1528]

(3) Where a seller of goods has a voidable title, but the title has not become void at the time of sale, the buyer acquires a good title to the goods, provided the buyer buys them in good faith and without notice of the seller's defect of title.[1529] So where a contract is voidable for fraud, but the fraudulent buyer resells the goods before the original owner avoids the sale, the innocent buyer gets a good title.[1530] Conversely, if the original sale is void *ab initio*, as where there is a mistake in the identity of the purchaser, a later innocent purchaser stands in no better position than the fraudster.[1531] But arguably the provisions governing mistake in Part 2, subpart 2 of the 2017 Act could give relief in these circumstances.[1532]

(4) A seller who continues in possession of goods after selling them can pass a good title to a second purchaser who takes in good faith without notice of the previous sale.[1533] The exception can apply even where the seller in possession sells the goods in circumstances amounting to theft from the first buyer.[1534]

(5) Where a seller retains property in goods, but a buyer obtains possession of the goods with the consent of the seller, then a sale to an innocent third person who takes without notice of the original seller's rights has the same effect as if the person making the delivery or transfer were a mercantile agent in possession of the goods with the consent of the owner.[1535] This exception operates to validate a sale as if the buyer in possession were a mercantile agent: it does not require that his conduct be that of a mercantile agent.[1536] The words 'consent of the owner' have been interpreted as meaning 'consent of the

1525. Contract and Commercial Law Act 2017, s. 149(2).
1526. *New Zealand Securities and Finance Ltd v. Wrightcars Ltd* [1976] 1 NZLR 77.
1527. *Moorgate Mercantile Co Ltd v. Twitchings* [1977] AC 890.
1528. Contract and Commercial Law Act, s. 297. By s. 296, a mercantile agent is an agent who has in the ordinary course of the agent's business as an agent authority to sell goods, or to consign goods for the purpose of sale, or to buy goods, or to raise money on the security of goods.
1529. Contract and Commercial Law Act, s. 151.
1530. *Lewis v. Averay* [1972] 1 QB 198. An owner who cannot communicate with a rogue must take all reasonable steps to avoid the sale: *Car and Universal Finance Co Ltd v. Caldwell* [1965] 1 QB 525.
1531. *Shogun Finance Ltd v. Hudson* [2004] 1 AC 919.
1532. *See* paras 125–132.
1533. Contract and Commercial Law Act, s. 153.
1534. *Sigglekow v. Gibbs* [1990] 3 NZLR 503.
1535. Contract and Commercial Law Act, s. 154.
1536. *Jeffcot v. Andrew Motors Ltd* [1960] NZLR 721.

seller', for otherwise, a title could come into existence as goods passed along a chain of buyers even though no title passed at the time of the first sale.[1537]

(6) Nothing in the Contract and Commercial Law Act affects the validity of any sale under special common law or statutory power of sale or the order of a Court of competent jurisdiction.[1538] There are many statutes conferring powers of sale on persons such as District Court registrars and bailiffs, sheriffs, pawnbrokers, and others.

B. Personal Property Securities

305. The exceptions to the *nemo dat* regime do not apply to goods which are subject to a perfected security interest under the Personal Property Securities Act 1999. This Act creates a broad and comprehensive system relating to security interests in personal property, including the creation and enforceability of security interests, the determination of priority among security interests and between security interests and other interests and the enforcement of security interests (other than in consumer goods). The PPSA provides for the creation of an electronic register of security interests and deals with the method and effect of registration of those interests. The result is a scheme of uniform rules for all security interests in personal property. The details are beyond the scope of this work.[1539]

V. Terms of the Contract

A. Conditions, Warranties and Innominate Terms

306. The obligations created by a contract are not all of equal importance. Section 132 of the 2017 Act classifies contractual promises by reference to two categories – *conditions* (important terms, breach of which entitles the innocent party to terminate the contract) and *warranties* (less important terms, breach of which entitles him or her to damages, but not to termination). Whether a stipulation is a condition or a warranty depends on the construction of the contract. A condition, broadly, is an essential term that goes to the root of the contract. A warranty, by contrast, is collateral to the main purpose of the contract.[1540] It is primarily for the parties to set their own value on the terms that they impose upon each other. Where a term is broken, the courts will endeavour to ascertain that value. A stipulation may

1537. *Elwin v. O'Regan and Maxwell* [1971] NZLR 1124; *National Employers Mutual General Insurance Association Ltd v. Jones* [1990] AC 24.
1538. Contract and Commercial Law Act, s. 149(4)(b).
1539. *See further* Holderness (ed.), *Butterworths Introduction to Commercial Law* Chs 25 and 26 (5th ed., LexisNexis 2016).
1540. Contract and Commercial Law Act, s. 119.

be a condition although called a warranty in the contract.[1541] Again, the parties' use of the word 'condition' is not necessarily conclusive, for they may not have intended to use it in a technical sense.[1542]

In *Hong Kong Fir Shipping Co Ltd v. Kawasaki Kisen Kaisha Ltd,*[1543] the English Court of Appeal acknowledged that very often the question of whether a party can terminate a contract for breach of a term will depend not on the status of the term itself, but rather on the seriousness of the breach. So there is a third category of 'intermediate' or 'innominate' terms. If the breach of a term, itself of apparently minor significance, caused severe loss or damage, the injured party might be able to treat the contract as discharged.

B. *Implied Terms*

307. In addition to the terms provided in contracts for the sale of goods by the parties themselves, the 2017 Act implies into such contracts various terms which apply unless the parties contract out of them, and classifies them as conditions or warranties:

(1) There is an implied condition that the seller has or will have the right to sell the goods,[1544] an implied warranty that the buyer shall have and enjoy quiet possession of the goods,[1545] and an implied warranty that there are no undisclosed encumbrances.[1546] In the case of a breach of the implied condition as to title, the buyer can recover the purchase price on the grounds that there has been a total failure of consideration.[1547]
(2) Where there is a contract for the sale of goods by description, there is an implied condition that the goods shall correspond with their description, and if the sale is by sample as well as description, it is not sufficient that the bulk corresponds with the sample if the goods do not also correspond with the description.[1548] Sales of unascertained goods must necessarily be by description.[1549] A sale of specific goods is by description so long as it is sold not

1541. *Ibid.*, s. 132(4).
1542. *Schuler AG v. Wickman Machine Tool Sales Ltd* [1974] AC 235.
1543. [1962] 2 QB 26.
1544. Contract and Commercial Law Act, s. 135(1)(a). The subsection is not limited to a right to pass property: *Niblett Ltd v. Confectioners Materials Ltd* [1921] 3 KB 387 (no right to sell goods which infringed another's trademark).
1545. *Ibid.*, s. 135(1)(b). The subsection covers the case where a third party acquires the right to disturb the buyer's possession after the sale: *Microbeads AG v. Vinhurst Road Markings Ltd* [1975] 1 WLR 218; and *see Great Elephant Corp v. Trafigura Beheer BV* [2012] EWHC 1475 (Comm).
1546. *Ibid.*, s. 135(1)(c).
1547. *Rowland v. Divall* [1923] 2 KB 500; *Butterworth v. Kingsway Motors Ltd* [1954] 1 WLR 1286.
1548. Contract and Commercial Law Act, s. 136.
1549. *Taylor v. Combined Buyers Ltd* [1924] NZLR 627.

merely as the specific thing but as a thing corresponding to the description.[1550] As a general rule, the description of goods relates to their identity and not their quality.[1551]

(3) Where the buyer, expressly or by implication, makes known to the seller the particular purpose for which the goods are required, so as to show that the seller relies on the buyer's skill or judgment, and the goods are of a description which it is in the course of the seller's business to supply (whether or not the seller is the manufacturer) there is an implied condition that the goods are reasonably fit for the purpose: provided that in the case of a contract for the sale of a specified article under its patent or other trade names, there is no implied condition as to its fitness for any particular purpose.[1552] The implied condition is limited to persons in the way of business, as distinct from private persons.[1553] The expression 'particular purpose' is not limited to some special purpose, but includes the general purpose itself.[1554] The purpose for which goods are required will often be easily implied. Any general purpose need not be stated, but there must be express communication of some special purpose.[1555] Where goods have several purposes, they should be fit for any one of them of which the seller is aware.[1556] The buyer must rely on the seller's skill and judgment, but this may frequently be implied.[1557] However, there may be no breach where a buyer takes a risk in buying a novel product.[1558]

(4) Where goods are bought by description from a seller who deals in goods of that description (whether the manufacturer or not), there is an implied condition that the goods are of merchantable quality: provided that if the buyer has examined the goods, there is no implied condition as regards defects which the examination ought to have revealed.[1559] The cases show different approaches to the meaning of 'merchantable quality', taking into account saleability, acceptability and usability.[1560] A helpful summary is that 'merchantable quality' means 'commercially saleable under the description by which the goods

---

1550. *Grant v. Australian Knitting Mills* [1936] AC 85.
1551. *Ashington Piggeries Ltd v. Christopher Hill Ltd* [1972] AC 441 (poisonous herring meal still herring meal); *Finch Motors Ltd v. Quin (No. 2)* [1980] 2 NZLR 519 (statement that a car was suitable for towing a boat not part of the car's description).
1552. Contract and Commercial Law Act, s. 138.
1553. *Ashington Piggeries Ltd v. Christopher Hill Ltd* [1972] AC 441 at 476.
1554. *Taylor v. Combined Buyers Ltd* [1924] NZLR 627.
1555. *Slater v. Fining Ltd* [1996] 3 All ER 398.
1556. *Henry Kendall and Sons v. William Lillico and Sons Ltd* [1969] 2 AC 31; *Ashington Piggeries Ltd v. Christopher Hill Ltd* [1972] AC 441. But sometimes, where goods of a uniform kind have a wide range of uses, this may lead to a finding that a seller cannot ensure that they will suit all purposes: *see Hamilton v. Papakura District Council* [2002] 3 NZLR 308.
1557. *Grant v. Australian Knitting Mills* [1936] AC 85 at 99; cp *Hamilton v. Papakura District Council* [2002] 3 NZLR 208.
1558. *Superior Minerals Ltd v. Watt* (2006) 11 TCLR 668.
1559. Contract and Commercial Law Act, s. 139.
1560. *See* especially *Taylor v. Combined Buyers Ltd* [1924] NZLR 627; *Bristol Tramways Carriage Co Ltd v. Fiat Motors Ltd* [1910] 2 KB 831; *Henry Kendall and Sons v. William Lillico and Sons Ltd* [1969] 2 AC 31; *BS Brown and Son Ltd v. Craiks Ltd* [1970] 1 WLR 752: *Feast Contractors Ltd v. Ray Vincent Ltd* [1974] 1 NZLR 212.

are sold'.[1561] As regards the relevance of the price, the parties are of course free to fix such price as they choose, but goods may nonetheless be unmerchantable if saleable at a substantially lower price.[1562] Whether goods are new or second-hand is another important consideration.

(5) An implied warranty or condition as to quality or fitness may be treated as being included in the contract of sale by the usage of trade.[1563] Any such custom or usage must be notorious, so the parties must be taken to have known of it and intended that it form part of their contract, it must be certain and it must be reasonable.[1564]

(6) In the case of a contract for sale by sample, there is an implied condition that the bulk corresponds with the sample, that the buyer shall have a reasonable opportunity of comparing the bulk with the sample, and that the goods are free from any defect, rendering them unmerchantable, which would not be apparent on reasonable examination of the sample.[1565] Whether the bulk corresponds with the sample is essentially a factual question. Exact correspondence is likely to be necessary.[1566]

VI. Performance of the Contract

A. *Seller's Duty to Deliver*

308. It is the duty of the seller to deliver the goods.[1567] Delivery is the voluntary transfer of possession from one person to another.[1568] The goods should be put into the custody or control of the buyer, or the buyer should be able to obtain their custody or control.[1569] Whether it is for the buyer to take possession of the goods or the seller to send them to the buyer is a question depending on the contract, express or implied, between the parties.[1570]

Where the seller delivers a quantity of goods less than he contracted to sell, the buyer may reject them, but if the buyer accepts them, they must be paid for at the contract rate.[1571] If the quantity is larger than agreed, the buyer may accept the goods included in the contract and reject the rest, or may reject the whole. If the

1561. *Finch Motors Ltd v. Quin (No. 2)* [1980] 2 NZLR 519 at 524.
1562. *BS Brown and Son Ltd v. Craiks Ltd* [1970] 1 WLR 752.
1563. Contract and Commercial Law Act, s. 140.
1564. *Woods v. NJ Ellingham & Co Ltd* [1977] 1 NZLR 218.
1565. Contract and Commercial Law Act, s. 142.
1566. *E & S Ruben Ltd v. Faire Bros and Co* [1949] 1 KB 254. A photograph of goods did not amount to the provision of a sample: *Donners v. Taylor Preston Ltd* [2011] NZCCLR 17.
1567. Contract and Commercial Law Act 2017, s. 156.
1568. *Ibid.*, s. 119.
1569. *Pro Machining Ltd v. Bunny Buster Firearms Ltd* [2010] NZCCLR 14.
1570. Contract and Commercial Law Act 2017, s. 158. For certain rules which apply apart from any agreement, *see* ss 159–163.
1571. *Ibid.*, s. 164(1); *Farley v. Loughnan* [1917] NZLR 588; *Moodie v. Agricultural Ventures Ltd* [1998] 3 NZLR 129.

buyer accepts the whole of the goods, he must pay for them at the contract rate.[1572] Where the seller delivers the contract goods mixed with goods of a different description, the buyer may accept the goods which are in accordance with the contract and reject the rest or may reject the whole.[1573]

Unless otherwise agreed, the buyer of goods is not bound to accept delivery by instalments.[1574] Where delivery by instalments has been agreed, and there is a defective delivery of one or more instalments, it is a question depending on the terms of the contract and all the circumstances whether the breach constitutes a repudiation of the whole contract or whether it gives rise to a claim for compensation but not to treat the contract as repudiated.[1575]

Where the seller is to send the goods to the buyer, delivery to a carrier must, unless the contrary is proved, be treated as being delivery to the buyer.[1576] However, the contract which the seller makes with the carrier must be reasonable, and if it is not, the buyer may decline to treat the delivery to the carrier as delivery to the buyer or may hold the seller liable for any loss or damage in the course of transit.[1577]

B. Buyer's Duty to Pay

309. It is the buyer's duty to pay for the goods in accordance with the terms of the contract.[1578] Unless otherwise agreed, payment and delivery are concurrent conditions,[1579] so generally payment will be due at the time the seller is ready and willing to deliver.

C. Acceptance

310. Unless otherwise agree, any right to reject the goods is lost once the buyer has accepted them.[1580] The buyer's only remedy thereafter is to claim damages.

Acceptance occurs when the buyer indicates to the seller that he has accepted them, or when the goods have been delivered to the buyer and the buyer does any act in relation to them which is inconsistent with the ownership of the seller, or after the lapse of a reasonable time and the buyer retains the goods without indicating to the seller that the buyer has rejected them.[1581] However, where goods are delivered

1572. *Ibid.*, s. 164(2). If the excess is trivial the *de minimis* rule may be applied: *Shipton, Anderson & Co v. Weil Bros & Co* [1912] 1 KB 574.
1573. *Ibid.*, s. 164(3); *Re Moore & Co and Landauer Co* [1921] 1 KB 73.
1574. *Ibid.*, s. 165.
1575. *Ibid.*, s. 166; *Maple Flock Co Ltd v. Universal Furniture Products (Wembley) Ltd* [1934] 1 KB 148; *Hammer and Barrow Ltd v. Coca-Cola* [1962] NZLR 723.
1576. *Ibid.*, s. 167(1).
1577. *Ibid.*, s. 167(2) and (3); *Thomas Young & Sons Ltd v. Hobson & Partners* (1949) 65 TLR 365.
1578. *Ibid.*, s. 156.
1579. *Ibid.*, s. 157.
1580. *Ibid.*, ss 133(2), 13(3).
1581. *Ibid.*, s. 170.

to the buyer which he has not previously examined, he is not deemed to have accepted them until he has had a reasonable opportunity of examining them for the purpose of ascertaining whether they conform with the contract.[1582] What constitutes a reasonable examination depends on all the circumstances, and the buyer will be taken to have accepted the goods if he or she uses them for a period longer than that required for reasonable examination.[1583]

VII. Remedies

311. The normal remedies available to the innocent party on a breach of contract by the other apply in the case of a contract for the sale of goods. The Contract and Commercial Law Act reflects these general rules.

A. *Seller's Remedies*

312. Accordingly, the seller has an action for the price[1584] and for damages for non-acceptance.[1585] The measure is the estimated loss directly and naturally resulting, in the ordinary course of events, from the buyer's breach of contract.[1586] This amounts to a statutory restatement of the first limb of the rule in *Hadley v. Baxendale*.[1587] Damages under the second limb are recoverable as well.[1588] The Act also confers on the unpaid seller certain remedies of a real nature. These are a lien on the goods or a right to retain possession for the price;[1589] where the buyer is insolvent, a right to stop the goods in transit even after parting with possession,[1590] upon which the seller may retain possession until the buyer pays;[1591] and a right of resale in certain circumstances.[1592]

1582. *Ibid.*, s. 169.
1583. *Taylor v. Combined Buyers Ltd* [1924] NZLR 627.
1584. Contract and Commercial Law Act 2017, s. 191. An action for the price cannot be maintained in circumstances other than those set out in s. 191: *FG Wilson (Engineering Ltd v. John Holt & Co (Liverpool) Ltd* [2012] EWHC 2477 (Comm): and *see Pala v. BTC Group Ltd* [2015] NZCA 487.
1585. *Ibid.*, s. 192(1).
1586. *Ibid.*, s. 192(2). Where there is an available market for the goods the measure is prima facie the difference between the contract price and the market price at the time when the goods ought to have been accepted or when there was a refusal to accept: s. 192(3). As to the meaning of 'available market', *see WL Thompson Ltd v. Robinson (Gunmakers) Ltd* [1955] 1 Ch. 177; *Charter v. Sullivan* [1957] 2 QB 117; *Lazenby Garages Ltd v. Wright* [1976] 1 WLR 459; *Air Studios (Lyndhurst) Ltd v. Lombard North Central plc* [2012] EWHC 3162. Where there is no available market the court must do the best it can: *Butler v. Countrywide Finance Ltd* [1993] 3 NZLR 623 at 629.
1587. (1854) 9 Exch 341; *see* para. 244.
1588. Contract and Commercial Law Act 2017, s. 196.
1589. *Ibid.*, s. 174(1)(a). The right is lost once the seller loses possession: *United Plastics Ltd (in Liq) v. Reliance Electric (NZ) Ltd* [1977] 2 NZLR 125; *Somme Ltd v. Central House Movers Ltd* [2012] NZAR 295.
1590. *Ibid.*, s. 174(1)(b). As to the duration of the transit, *see* s. 179; as to how stoppage may be effected, *see* s. 182.
1591. *Ibid.*, s. 178.
1592. *Ibid.*, s. 174(1)(c). For the extent of the power, *see* ss 189, 190; *Ward Ltd v. Bignall* [1967] 1 QB 534; *Reid Motors Ltd v. Wood* [1978] 1 NZLR 319.

B. Buyer's Remedies

313. The buyer has an action for non-delivery,[1593] the measure being the estimated loss directly and naturally resulting, in the ordinary course of events, from the seller's breach of contract.[1594] This once again reflects the common law. Special damages similarly are recoverable. The court may, if it thinks fit, direct that the contract be performed specifically, without giving the defendant the option of retaining the goods on payment of damages.[1595] The remedy is discretionary and will not normally be awarded where damages are an adequate remedy. Where there is a breach of warranty by the seller, or the buyer elects or is compelled (by having accepted the goods) to treat any breach of condition as a breach of warranty, the buyer can set up the breach in diminution or extinction of the price, or can seek damages.[1596]

VIII. Contracting Out

314. The parties to a contract for the sale of goods are free to contract out of the provisions of the 2017 Act. The Act provides that where any right, duty or liability would arise under a contract of sale by implication of law, it may be negatived or varied by express agreement or by the course of dealing between the parties, or by usage, if the usage is such as to bind both parties to the contract.[1597] In other fields, however, this freedom has been heavily curtailed.[1598] In particular, it is not possible to contract out of the guarantees which apply in the case of consumer transactions under the Consumer Guarantees Act 1993.[1599]

1593. *Ibid.*, s. 193(1).
1594. *Ibid.*, s. 193(2). Where there is an available market for the goods the usual measure is the difference between the contract price and the market price at the time when the goods ought to have been delivered or when there was a refusal to deliver: s. 193(3). The measure here is not the price at which the promised goods could have been sold but the price which the plaintiff would have had to pay in order to replace them: *J & B Caldwell Ltd v. Logan House Retirement Home Ltd* [1999] 2 NZLR 99; *Hughes v. Pendragon Sabre Ltd T/A Porsche Centre Bolton* [2016] EWCA Civ 18.
1595. *Ibid.*, s. 194.
1596. *Ibid.*, s. 195(1)–(3). In the case of breach of warranty of quality, the usual measure is the difference between the value of the goods at the time of delivery and the value they would have had if they had answered to the warranty: s. 195(5). The rule is subject to the overriding general principle that the buyer must prove an actual loss, even if the goods are defective: *McSherry v. Coopers Creek Vineyard Ltd* HC, Christchurch, CIV 2004-409-001888, 21 Dec. 2004 (no loss shown where defective goods sold on normal terms without complaint by purchasers). Compare *Idas Group Ltd v. Syntech New Zealand Ltd* [2014] NZHC 3188.
1597. *Ibid.*, s. 197. The courts take a strict approach to the construction of words that purport to contract out of the Act: *see* for example *The Mercini Lady* [2010] EWCA Civ 1145; *Salmare SpA v. Union Maritime Ltd* [2012] EWHC 3537 (Comm); *Herbert Construction Co Ltd v. Carter Holt Harvey Ltd* [2013] NZHC 780; and *see generally* para. 174 above.
1598. *See* paras 176–181.
1599. *See* para. 322.

Chapter 5. Consumer Contracts

§1. Introduction

315. The law in New Zealand relating to the provision of goods and services to consumers was changed and reformed with the passing of the Consumer Guarantees Act 1993. The Act sets out a number of guarantees in respect of the supply of goods and services to consumers, some of which are familiar and some of which are new. A right of action for non-compliance can be asserted against a supplier and, significantly, in some circumstances against a manufacturer. There are also some new remedies. The provisions in Part 3 of the Contract and Commercial Law Act 2017 concerning, broadly, conditions and warranties, the implication of terms and remedies for breach of warranty do not apply where the 1993 Act applies.[1600]

§2. The Consumer Guarantees Act 1993

I. Application of the Act

316. The crucial conditions that must be met for the Act to apply are that there be a 'supply'[1601] of 'goods'[1602] or services[1603] in 'trade'[1604] to a 'consumer'. In the

1600. Contract and Commercial Law Act 2017, s. 198.

1601. 'Supply' in relation to goods means supply by way of gift, sale, exchange, lease, hire, or hire-purchase, and in relation to services means provide, grant or confer. A 'supplier' is a person who in trade supplies goods to a consumer by transferring the ownership or possession of the goods pursuant to a contract of sale, exchange, lease, hire or hire-purchase to which that person is a party, or transferring ownership by way of gift, or transferring ownership or possession as directed by an insurer, or who supplies services to a consumer or a group of consumers (whether or not the consumer is a party or the consumers are parties to a contract with the person): Consumer Guarantees Act 1993, s. 2(1). The definition goes on to include a person who acts in trade as agent for another, whether or not that other is supplying in trade. Accordingly, contrary to the normal agency rule, an agent acting in a purely representative capacity might be liable for failure of a guarantee: *see Walters v. Barrington Charters Ltd* (2010) 9 NZBLC 102,822.

1602. 'Goods': '(a) means personal property of every kind (whether tangible or intangible), other than money and choses in action; and (b) includes goods attached to, or incorporated in, any real or personal property; ships, air-crafts and vehicles; animals, including fish; minerals, trees, and crops, whether on, under, or attached to land or not; non-reticulated gas; water and computer software; but (c) does not include a whole building, or part of a whole building, attached to land unless the building is a structure that is easily removable and is not designed for residential accommodation; *ibid.*, s. 2(1)'.

An incomplete building is not within the definition; *Jackson v. McLintock* (1998) 8 TCLR 161. In *Carter Holt Harvey Ltd v. Minister of Education* [2015] NZCA 321 a manufacturer of allegedly defective building cladding submitted that it was not liable as a manufacturer where the goods it supplied were used to produce a different product, and that what had been supplied were the whole or parts of whole buildings. However, the Court determined that whether liability applied under one of the guarantees would ultimately depend on the nature of the supply of the goods and the circumstances in which this occurred, and this would require evidence and careful examination at trial. The manufacturer appealed to the Supreme Court, but not on this point: *Carter Holt Harvey Ltd v. Minister of Education* [2016] NZSC 95, [2017] 1 NZLR 78.

By ss 7A and 7B, gas (other than non-reticulated gas) and electricity are not 'goods' under the Act but are subject to the guarantee of acceptable quality in s. 6 (as to which *see* para. 316).

core definition, a 'consumer' is a person who acquires from a supplier goods or services of a kind ordinarily acquired for personal, domestic or household use or consumption, and not for the purpose of resupplying them in trade or consuming them in the course of a process of production or manufacture, or repairing or treating in trade other goods or fixtures on land.[1605] The effect is that a sale in the course of a business of non-consumer goods is governed by the Contract and Commercial Law Act, and of consumer goods by the Consumer Guarantees Act.

The meaning of goods or services of a kind which are 'ordinarily acquired for personal, domestic or household use or consumption' was considered by the Court of Appeal in *Nesbit v. Porter*.[1606] The question arose in relation to a multi-use four wheel drive utility vehicle, where the evidence showed 80% use of the vehicle for business purposes and 20% use for private purposes. The court held that the majority or dominant purpose was not determinative, and it was necessary to ask whether there was a personal use as a matter of regular practice or in the ordinary or usual course of events or things. It was a question of fact and degree whether goods were ordinarily acquired for personal use when only a proportionately small number was acquired for that purpose, and on the facts the Act was held to apply.[1607]

Goods which are acquired for the purpose of resupply in trade are excluded from the Act only if the resupply is to take place in the course of the business of the purchaser. So an accountant who bought a vehicle with the intention of leasing it to his practice was not resupplying it in trade: his business was accountancy, not the leasing of motor vehicles.[1608]

Ordinarily personal goods which are acquired for a business but not for the purpose of resupplying or consuming them in trade also fall within the ambit of the Act. This covers, for example, domestic furniture used in an office or a refrigerator in a tea room.

1603. 'Services': '(a) includes any rights, benefits, privileges, or facilities provided by a supplier; and (b) includes these being provided under contracts for the performance of work (including work of a professional nature), contracts for the provision in trade of facilities for accommodation, amusement, the care of persons or animals or things, entertainment, instruction, parking or recreation, contracts of insurance, contracts between a bank and a customer, contracts for the provision of credit, contracts for the supply or in relation to telecommunications and water, and a contract relating to (but not for) the supply of gas and electricity, other than line function services: *ibid.*, s. 2(1)'.
1604. Nothing in the Act applies in any case where goods or services are supplied otherwise than in 'trade': *ibid.*, s. 41(1). 'Trade' means any trade, business, industry, profession, occupation, activity of commerce, or undertaking relating to the supply or acquisition of goods or services; *ibid.*, s. 2(1).
1605. *Ibid.*, s. 2(1).
1606. [2000] 2 NZLR 465.
1607. *See also Kaori Ltd v. Shrinkforce Shrink Wrap Services Ltd* [2012] NZHC 3204 (provision of shrinkwrapping services to protect hull of super yacht during work on the yacht not a service ordinarily required for personal, domestic or household use).
1608. *Kerry Stone Ltd v. Knowles* (2006) 11 TCLR 768.

II. Guarantees in Respect of the Supply of Goods

317. The guarantees which are required of the suppliers of goods to consumers are similar to the conditions which are implied in contracts for the sale of goods by the Contract and Commercial Law Act 2017. Thus, there is a guarantee that:

(1) the supplier has the right to sell the goods, that they are free from any undisclosed security and that the consumer has the right to undisturbed possession;[1609]
(2) if the supplier is responsible for delivering the goods, they will be received by the consumer within the agreed period, or if no delivery time has been agreed, within a reasonable time;[1610]
(3) the goods are of acceptable quality;[1611]
(4) the goods are reasonably fit for any purpose that the consumer makes known, expressly or impliedly, to the supplier;[1612]
(5) where goods are supplied by description they correspond with their description;[1613]
(6) where goods are supplied by reference to a sample or demonstration model they correspond with the sample or model and the consumer will have a reasonable opportunity to compare the goods with the sample;[1614] and
(7) where the price of goods is not determined or left to be determined the consumer need pay no more than a reasonable price.[1615]

The Act also provides for certain guarantees imposed only on the manufacturer and not on the supplier. Thus where goods are first supplied to a consumer in New Zealand, there is a guarantee that the manufacturer will take reasonable action to ensure that facilities for the repair of and supply of parts for the goods are reasonably available for a reasonable period.[1616] The obligation can be avoided if the manufacturer takes reasonable action to notify the first consumer, at or before the

1609. Consumer Guarantees Act 1993, s. 5.
1610. *Ibid.*, s. 5A.
1611. *Ibid.*, s. 6. Goods are of acceptable quality if they are as: (a) fit for all the purposes for which goods of the type in question are commonly supplied; and (b) acceptable in appearance and finish; and (c) free from defects; and (d) safe; and (e) durable as a reasonable consumer fully acquainted with the state and condition of the goods would regard as acceptable, having regard to; (f) the nature of the goods; (g) the price (where relevant); (h) any statements made about the goods on any packaging or label on the goods; (i) any representation made about the goods by the supplier or manufacturer; (j) all other relevant circumstances of the supply of the goods: s. 7(1). There is special provision for defects specifically drawn to the attention of the consumer and for where goods are put to some unexpected use: s. 7(2)–(4). The guarantee of acceptable quality does not mean that goods are free from all risk: *Contact Energy Ltd v. Jones* [2009] 2 NZLR 830, which considered the question in relation to claims for losses caused by fluctuations and outages in the electricity supply. The circumstances in which the Act could apply to the supply of electricity were amended following this decision.
1612. *Ibid.*, s. 8.
1613. *Ibid.*, s. 9.
1614. *Ibid.*, s. 10.
1615. *Ibid.*, s. 11.
1616. *Ibid.*, s. 12.

time the goods are supplied, that the manufacturer gives no undertaking in this respect.[1617] There is also a right of action for breach of an express guarantee given by a manufacturer in respect of goods, which guarantee is contained in a document given to a consumer with the actual or apparent authority of the manufacturer in connection with the supply of the goods to the consumer.[1618]

III. Guarantees in Respect of the Supply of Services

318. The Act provides that the guarantees in respect of goods are applicable whether or not the goods are supplied in connection with a service,[1619] giving statutory expression to the position at common law. It also sets out a scheme of guarantees which apply specifically to the provision of services supplied pursuant to a contract with a consumer or gratuitously. In this case, there is a guarantee that:

(1) the service will be carried out with reasonable care and skill;[1620]
(2) where a particular purpose or result has been made known to the supplier, the service, and any product resulting from it, will be reasonably fit for that purpose, and of such a nature and quality that it can reasonably be expected to achieve that result, except where the circumstances show that the consumer does not rely on the supplier's skill or judgment or it is unreasonable for the consumer to do so;[1621]
(3) if the time for the service is not fixed by the parties, it will be completed within a reasonable time;[1622] and
(4) where the price for the services is not determined or left to be determined, the consumer needs to pay no more than a reasonable price.[1623]

The thrust of these provisions is to do no more than state the previously existing position at common law or under the Sale of Goods Act 1908 (now contained in the Contract and Commercial Law Act 2017), perhaps with some clarification. Thus, the notion of a service being fit for a particular purpose receives separate treatment, having formerly been subsumed within the common law requirement of reasonable care.

1617. *Ibid.*, s. 42.
1618. *Ibid.*, s. 14.
1619. *Ibid.*, s. 15.
1620. *Ibid.*, s. 28. The obligation is to take care, not to guarantee that the service will be a success: *Jung v. Templeton* [2010] 2 NZLR 255.
1621. *Ibid.*, s. 29.
1622. *Ibid.*, s. 30.
1623. *Ibid.*, s. 31.

IV. Rights of Redress Against Suppliers of Goods

319. The Act gives a right of redress against suppliers of goods for non-performance of the statutory guarantees.[1624] A scheme of remedies then applies, under which the consumer has a number of options.

Where the failure can be remedied the consumer may require the supplier to remedy it within a reasonable time.[1625] Remedying means repairing the goods or curing any defect in title or replacing them with identical goods.[1626] If the supplier refuses or neglects to remedy or does not succeed in doing so within a reasonable time, the consumer may have the failure remedied elsewhere and charge the reasonable costs to the supplier or may reject the goods.[1627] Where the failure cannot be remedied or is of a 'substantial' character, the consumer may reject the goods or obtain damages in compensation for any reduction in the value of the goods below the purchase price.[1628]

In addition, he or she can recover for loss 'which was reasonably foreseeable as liable to result' from the failure.[1629] The test appears to be similar to that applied at common law in determining whether damage is too remote.[1630]

The right to reject goods is exercised by the consumer notifying the supplier of the decision to reject and of the grounds for rejection.[1631] In a reversal of the position under the Contract and Commercial Law Act, the consumer is required to return the goods unless, broadly, this involves 'significant' cost, in which case the supplier must collect them.[1632] The consumer can then elect to have either a cash refund of the money paid or, if reasonably available as part of the supplier's stock, goods of the same type and value by way of replacement.[1633] The replacement goods in turn are subject to the statutory guarantees.[1634]

1624. *Ibid.*, s. 16.
1625. *Ibid.*, s. 18(2)(a).
1626. *Ibid.*, s. 19.
1627. *Ibid.*, s. 18(2)(b). A consumer who elects to have work done himself without giving the supplier the opportunity to carry out the repairs cannot recover the cost of the repairs: *Cooper v. Ashley & Johnson Motors Ltd* [1997] DCR 170; *Acquired Holdings Ltd v. Turvey* (2008) 8 NZBLC 102, 107.
1628. *Ibid.*, s. 18(3). A failure to comply with a guarantee is of a substantial character if: (a) the goods would not have been acquired by a reasonable consumer fully acquainted with the nature and extent of the failure; or (b) the goods depart significantly from the description by which they were supplied or, as the case may be, from any sample or demonstration model; or (c) the goods are substantially unfit for their common purpose or for a particular purpose made known to the supplier or represented by the supplier to be a suitable purpose; or (d) the goods are not of acceptable quality because they are unsafe: s. 21.

The standard is based on reasonableness, not perfection: *Norton v. Hervey Motors Ltd* [1996] DCR 427. If the failure is substantial, the consumer should be given the option to elect between repair and cancellation: *Stephens v. Chevron Motor Court Ltd* [1996] DCR 1.

1629. *Ibid.*, s. 18(4).
1630. *See Hadley v. Baxendale* (1854) 9 Exch 341; *see* para. 240.
1631. Consumer Guarantees Act 1993, s. 22(1).
1632. *Ibid.*, s. 22(2).
1633. *Ibid.*, s. 23(1), (2).
1634. *Ibid.*, s. 23(4).

The right to reject is lost if not exercised within a reasonable time, or if the goods have been disposed of by the consumer or lost or destroyed or damaged, or if they have been attached to or incorporated in any real or personal property and cannot be detached without damaging them.[1635]

As a general rule, the obligations of the supplier are owed only to the consumer acquiring the goods from the supplier. There is an exception in the case of donees from the consumer, who may exercise any rights or remedies as if he or she had acquired the goods from the supplier.[1636] Subsequent purchasers are not covered, although they may be able to sue their vendor or, as will be seen, the manufacturer. Where the supplier is sued, he or she has no right equivalent to that of the consumer to sue the manufacturer but must maintain an action in contract against his or her own supplier, who must in turn sue down the contractual chain. If for some reason a contract action is barred or is not available the manufacturer is effectively insulated from liability.

V. Rights of Redress Against Suppliers of Services

320. A similar regime applies in the case of non-performance of the guarantees as to services. A right of redress arises, except where there is a failure to comply with the guarantees as to fitness and time for completion of services which is due to an act, default or omission of, or any representation by, any person other than the supplier or his or her agent, or cause independent of human control.[1637]

The consumer once again can require the failure to be remedied within a reasonable time or, if the supplier neglects or refuses or fails to do so, have it remedied elsewhere and charge the reasonable costs to the supplier or else cancel the contract.[1638] If the failure cannot be remedied or is of a substantial character the consumer can cancel the contract or obtain damages from the supplier.[1639]

As with goods, consequential loss also is recoverable.[1640]

A cancellation does not take effect until it is made known to the supplier or, where communication is not reasonably practicable, the consumer indicates by reasonable means his or her intention to cancel.[1641] No particular form of words is needed so long as the intention is clear.[1642] As for the effects of cancellation, the consumer is entitled to a refund of any money paid or other consideration provided unless a Court or Disputes Tribunal orders otherwise. Subject to this, the cancellation does not of itself divest a party of any property transferred or money paid pursuant to the

1635. *Ibid.*, s. 20(1).
1636. *Ibid.*, s. 24.
1637. *Ibid.*, s. 33.
1638. *Ibid.*, s. 32(a).
1639. *Ibid.*, s. 32(b). A failure is of a substantial character where: (a) the services would not have been acquired by a reasonable consumer fully acquainted with the nature and extent of the failure; or (b) the product of the service is substantially unfit for a purpose for which such services are commonly supplied or for a particular purpose made known to the supplier or the product is unsafe: s. 36.
1640. *Ibid.*, s. 32(c).
1641. *Ibid.*, s. 37(1).
1642. *Ibid.*, s. 37(2).

contract.[1643] So far as the contract remains unperformed at the time of the cancellation, no party is obliged or entitled to perform it further.[1644]

Courts and Disputes Tribunals are given wide ancillary powers to grant relief.[1645] They can, for example, vest property in any party, direct the transfer or assignment of property or the payment of money from one party to another, permit a supplier to retain all or part of any money paid or consideration provided, and order a party to do or refrain from doing any act or thing in relation to another party. However, no order can deprive a third person of any property acquired in good faith and for valuable consideration; nor can an order be made if a party has so altered his or her position in relation to property that it would be inequitable to make one.

These provisions governing the supply of services do not limit or affect any rule of law or enactment imposing on the supplier a duty stricter than that imposed in the Act, any term implied in a contract for the supply of a service, any enactment defining or restricting the obligations arising in connection with a particular service, any rule of law or enactment relating to contracts of employment or apprenticeship, and the immunity from suit of barristers or solicitors as regards the conduct of proceedings in court.[1646]

VI. Rights of Redress Against Manufacturers

321. In addition to the rights it gives against suppliers, the 1993 Act also confers on consumers a direct right of action against manufacturers where their goods fail to measure up to the statutory guarantees.[1647]

There is a right of redress against the manufacturer for failure of the guarantee of acceptable quality[1648] and of correspondence with description where the description was applied by or on behalf of the manufacturer or with the express or implied consent of the manufacturer.[1649] In each case, there is no such right if the failure is only because of the act, default or representation of any person other than the manufacturer or a servant or agent of the manufacturer, or a cause independent of human control occurring after the goods have left the control of the manufacturer.[1650] Again, the manufacturer is not liable for failure of the guarantee as to acceptable quality if the failure is due to the price charged by the supplier being higher than

1643. *Ibid.*, s. 38(1)(a), (b).
1644. *Ibid.*, s. 38(1)(c).
1645. *Ibid.*, s. 39.
1646. *Ibid.*, s. 40.
1647. A 'manufacturer' is a person that carries on the business of assembling, producing, or processing goods, and includes: (a) any person that holds itself out to the public as the manufacturer of the goods; (b) any person that attaches its brand name to the goods; and (c) in the case where goods are manufactured outside New Zealand by a foreign manufacturer with no ordinary place of business in New Zealand, the importer or distributer of the goods: *Ibid.*, s. 2(1).
1648. *Ibid.*, s. 25(a).
1649. *Ibid.*, s. 25(b). *See* for example *Carter Holt Harvey Ltd v. Minister of Education* [2015] NZCA 321 (arguable claim by building owner against manufacturer of allegedly defective weatherboards) (on appeal [2016] NZSC 95, [2017] 1 NZLR 78, but not on this point).
1650. *Ibid.*, s. 26(a)(i), (ii), 26(b).

the manufacturer's recommended retail price or the average retail price.[1651] Non-compliance with the guarantee as to repairs and parts or with any express guarantee in a document given in respect of goods likewise gives a right of redress to the consumer.[1652]

In all of these cases the consumer has a remedy in damages. They are calculated by reference to the reduction in value below the price paid or payable by the consumer or below the average retail price of the goods at the time of the supply, whichever is the lower.[1653] In cases where the manufacturer has undertaken to remedy a failure by repairing or replacing the goods, such damages cannot be claimed until the manufacturer has refused or neglected to remedy the failure or has not succeeded in remedying it within a reasonable time.[1654] The consumer may recover consequential loss where it was reasonably foreseeable as liable to result from the failure to comply with the guarantee.[1655]

The right of action against the manufacturer is not confined to the consumer who first acquires the goods from the supplier, but extends to any person who later acquires the goods from or through the consumer.[1656] This covers anyone who obtains the goods by way of gift, purchase or exchange, or takes them on lease, hire or hire-purchase. The guarantees thus run with the goods. However, the remedy does not apply to a person who acquires goods from or through a consumer unless that person also is a 'consumer' within the meaning of the Act.[1657] Consequential loss suffered by a third person without title to the goods is not covered. An action in tort for negligence remains the only remedy in such a case.

VII. Assessment of Damages

322. We have seen that consumers and recipients of gifts have rights of redress against suppliers and manufacturers for reasonably foreseeable loss or damage, including consequential losses, resulting from the failure of a guarantee under the Act. In *Contact Energy Ltd v. Jones,*[1658] Miller J accepted that the Act admitted the sharing of losses where there was more than one cause. The court's power to award the full loss was discretionary, carrying with it the power to award less. He considered that the strict liability nature of consumer guarantees did not mean that consumers could ignore reasonable steps which might prevent breaches of a guarantee or limit the damage. Consumers should protect their own interests to that extent, and had to ensure that their acts or omissions did not contribute to the failure of relevant guarantees. The Act sought to strike a balance between suppliers and consumers, and loss sharing was not inconsistent with the Act. However, whether it was appropriate in any particular case would depend upon all the circumstances. As regards

1651. *Ibid.*, s. 26(a)(iii).
1652. *Ibid.*, s. 25(c), (d).
1653. *Ibid.*, s. 27(1)(a).
1654. *Ibid.*, s. 27(2).
1655. *Ibid.*, s. 27(1)(b).
1656. *Ibid.*, s. 27(1).
1657. *Ibid.*, s. 27(3).
1658. [2009] 2 NZLR 830, at [129]–[137].

the onus of proof, in circumstances where a guarantee under the Act was breached and damage resulted, the consumer was likely to recover his or her reasonably foreseeable losses in full unless the retailer could point to evidence of another contributing cause.

VIII. Contracting Out

323. It is not generally possible to contract out of the provisions of the 1993 Act as they relate to consumer transactions.[1659] Indeed, a supplier or manufacturer who purports to do so commits an offence under section 13(i) of the Fair Trading Act 1986.[1660] This refers to making false or misleading representations about the existence, exclusion or effect of any condition, warranty, guarantee, right or remedy in connection with the supply of goods or services in trade.

Contracting out is permitted where there is an agreement in writing made between parties in trade who agree to contract out of the provisions of the Act and it is fair and reasonable that the parties are bound by the provisions in the agreement.[1661] The benefit of any such exclusion extends to the manufacturer.[1662] In determining what is fair and reasonable for this purpose, the court must take account of all the circumstances of the agreement, including, *inter alia*, the subject matter of the agreement, the value of the goods or services, the respective bargaining power of the parties, and whether all or any of the parties received advice from or were represented by a lawyer.[1663]

Of course, the Act only applies to begin within the case of consumer transactions. The exception appears to be aimed at the case where a business person buys household goods not for resupply but for use in the business, such as an employer buying a refrigerator for his or her employees' tea room, and who accordingly comes within the definition of 'consumer'.

1659. Consumer Guarantees Act 1993, s. 43(1).
1660. *Ibid.*, s. 43(4).
1661. *Ibid.*, s. 43(2).
1662. *Ibid.*, s. 43(5).
1663. *Ibid.*, s. 43(2A).

Chapter 6. Building Contracts

324. Building contracts are subject to the ordinary rules of contract law. There are several standard forms of building contract in New Zealand, the most common being *New Zealand Standard Conditions of Contract for Building and Civil Engineering Construction.*[1664] This, and most of the other standard forms, provides in detail for such matters as variation of the contract and remedies for breach. In the latter instance, the remedy provisions in Part 2, subpart 3 of the Contract and Commercial Law Act 2017 have effect subject to the express terms of the contract.[1665] Some forms of contract provide for various types of alternative dispute resolution. 'Partnering', a procedure whereby all participants in a construction project act collaboratively rather than adversarially, enhances the desire to avoid litigation: partnering is not as common in New Zealand as it is in the United Kingdom.

Certain statutes supplement the common law on building contracts:

(1) Building work in New Zealand must be carried out in accordance with the Building Act 2004. This requires that all building work must comply with the building code, and lays down an elaborate regulatory framework for building practitioners and building consent authorities. The Act is not generally concerned with issues of liability, leaving these to be determined by ordinary principles of contract and tort. However, it does lay down mandatory statutory warranties in all contracts for building work for 'household units' and contracts of sale of household units made by an 'on-seller'.[1666] The warranties require, broadly, that all building work be done with reasonable care, properly and competently and in accordance with the plans and building consents; that materials used will be suitable and, unless otherwise stated, new; that household units intended to be occupied on completion of the work will be suitable for occupation; and if the contract specifies the particular purpose for which the work is required, that the work and materials will be reasonably fit for that purpose.[1667] A right of action for breach of any of these warranties is not confined to the other contracting purchaser: a subsequent owner may take proceedings whether or not that person was a party to the contract.[1668] It is required that any contract between a current or intended owner of a residential building for work costing more than a prescribed monetary limit (currently NZD 30,000) is only valid if it is in writing.[1669]

1664. NZLS 3910 (2013).
1665. Contract and Commercial Law Act 2017, s. 34.
1666. Building Act 2004, ss 362H, 362I. A household unit is a building or group of buildings or part of a building or group of buildings that is used or intended to be used only or mainly for residential purposes and occupied or intended to be occupied exclusively as the home or residence of a single household, and does not include a hostel, boarding house, or other specialized accommodation: s. 7. An on-seller is a person who, for the purpose of on-selling the household unit, builds it or, in trade, arranges for it to be built or acquires it from a person who built it or arranged for it to be built, or acquires it in a transaction intended to defeat the purpose of the Act: s. 362H(3).
1667. *Ibid.*, s. 362I.
1668. *Ibid.*, s. 362J.
1669. *Ibid.*, s. 362F.

(2) The Weathertight Homes Resolution Services Act 2006 lays down processes for the assessment and resolution of claims by owners in respect of leaky dwelling houses. This Act and an earlier Act in 2002 were passed in response to the widespread leaky buildings problem in the building industry. The Act seeks to facilitate the resolution of leaky building claims in a number of ways: by making special provision for claims in respect of multi-unit complexes; by providing a mechanism for the assessment and evaluation of claims, remedies, lower value claims and the termination of claims; by the compulsory adjudication of claims by the Weathertight Homes Tribunal; and by providing for access to special mediation services. The Act does not alter the applicable principles of contract and tort. As regards the latter, the subsequent owner of a defective dwelling house can sue the builder, engineer, architect or local authority inspector for negligence.[1670] The owner of a commercial building also can sue.[1671]

(3) The Construction Contracts Act 2002 applies to both commercial and domestic construction contracts. It invalidates 'pay if paid' clauses, i.e. clauses which purport to make the obligation to pay conditional on the payer being first paid by someone else. It also lays down a mechanism for determining the amount of progress payments where the parties have not agreed on such a mechanism themselves, and provides a procedure for making and responding to payment claims. It sets up a statutory adjudication process for resolving disputes, although that process does not prevent the parties from submitting the dispute to another dispute resolution procedure of their own choosing, whether or not that other procedure takes place concurrently with a statutory adjudication. The adjudicator's determination is enforceable in court. The Act has effect despite any provision to the contrary in any agreement or contract.

1670. *Invercargill CC v. Hamlin* [1996] 1 NZLR 513; *North Shore City Council v. Body Corporate 188529 (Sunset Terraces)* [2011] 2 NZLR 289.

1671. *North Shore CC v. Body Corporate 207624 (Spencer on Byron)* [2013] 2 NZLR 297.

Chapter 7. Leases

§1. Definition

325. A lease arises whenever one person (the landlord or lessor) grants another (the tenant or lessee) the right to the exclusive possession of land for a period less than that for which the landlord holds the land, which period is either certain or capable of being rendered certain, with the intention of conferring on that other person an interest in the land as opposed to a personal privilege. An obligation on the tenant to pay rent is a normal, but not necessary, incident of a lease.

§2. Term of Lease

326. A lease may be for a fixed term, say a year or three years. A lease for 999 years is sometimes called, incorrectly, a lease in perpetuity. A periodic tenancy (usually weekly or monthly) is one which continues indefinitely from week to week or month to month until it is determined by the appropriate notice (a week or month as the case may be). If a tenancy is created without any express agreement as to its duration, it is presumed by section 210 of the Property Law Act 2007 to be a tenancy terminable by twenty working days' notice in writing, notice which can expire at any time. To rebut that presumption, it is necessary to prove an express or implied agreement that the tenancy is terminable in some other way.[1672]

A tenancy at will is one whereby a person occupies land as a tenant on the terms that either party can determine the tenancy at any time, with no particular period of notice being required.[1673] A tenancy at sufferance is created when a tenant holds over after the expiry of his or her term without the landlord's assent or dissent.[1674]

§3. Creation of Leases

327. A lease of Land Transfer land for a term of not less than three years must, by virtue of section 91 of the Land Transfer Act 2017, be created by a lease instrument under that Act.[1675] The legal estate does not pass to the tenant until the memorandum is registered. A legal lease of less than three years may be created by informal writing or even orally.[1676]

1672. *Beattie v. Littleton Borough* [1966] NZLR 65; *Fulton v. Woods* [2002] 2 NZLR 508.
1673. *Sangster v. Burns* [1960] NZLR 910 at 915–916.
1674. *Remon v. City of London Real Property Co Ltd* [1921] 1 KB 49 at 58; *Sangster v. Burns* [1960] NZLR 910 at 917.
1675. Land Transfer Act 2017, s. 91(1); *Domb v. Owler* [1924] NZLR 532.
1676. Property Law Act 2007, s. 208.

An agreement to lease, or an unregistered lease for three or more years, is, however, effective in equity under the doctrine in *Walsh v. Lonsdale*.[1677] To be enforceable it must be in writing under the Property Law Act 2007, but the doctrine of part performance applies so that even an oral agreement can be enforceable if there has been a sufficient act of part performance.

For a residential tenancy a written agreement is not required, but if either party wants one he or she is entitled to it.[1678]

The Public Bodies Leases Act 1969 and the Land Act 1948 contain detailed provisions regulating leases by local authorities, and the Crown, respectively.

The Te Ture Whenua Maori (Maori Land) Act 1993 contains provisions relating to leases of Maori land.

§4. Commercial Leases

I. Landlord's Obligations and Powers

328. There is both a statutory and a common law implied covenant by a landlord that the tenant will have quiet enjoyment of the premises.[1679] Such a covenant is often expressed. The long-established rule that a grantor must not derogate from his or her grant involves that a landlord must not do anything inconsistent with the letting of the premises or the purpose for which they are let.[1680] A landlord is not obliged to repair the premises unless he or she expressly covenants to do so. There is often an express covenant to keep the exterior in repair. Many leases contain a right of renewal.

The benefit and obligation of a landlord's covenants relating to the subject matter of the lease run with the land.[1681]

In every lease, there are implied two powers of the landlord:

(a) to enter at reasonable times to view the state of repair;[1682]
(b) to re-enter and determine the lease whenever rent is in arrears for twenty-one days or the tenant has breached other terms of the lease.[1683]

1677. (1882) 21 Ch D 9. This principle has survived the changes made by the Property Law Act 2007. *See Inglis v. Clarence Holdings Ltd* [1997] 1 NZLR 268 at 272 and *Chambers v. Chatfield* [2016] NZHC 1871 (2016) 10 NZBLC 99–723.
1678. Residential Tenancies Act 1986, s. 13.
1679. Property Law Act 2007, s. 218; *Kanizaj v. Bruce* [1954] NZLR 283 at 284.
1680. *Mount Cook National Park Board v. Mount Cook Motels Ltd* [1972] NZLR 481 at 496.
1681. Property Law Act 2007, s. 231.
1682. *Ibid.*, s. 218 and Sch. 3, Part 2, para. 11.
1683. *Ibid.*, s. 218 and Sch. 3, Part 2, para. 12.

II. Tenant's Obligations

329. In every lease, there are two implied obligations on the part of the tenant:

(a) to pay rent;[1684]
(b) to keep, and yield up, the premises in the condition existing at the commencement of the tenancy.[1685]

In a long-term lease the tenant will often expressly covenant to pay rates and to insure the premises. If the tenant has covenanted not to assign the lease without consent, there is an implied proviso that that consent is not to be unreasonably withheld.[1686]

The rent and the benefit of the lessees' covenants relating to the land run with the reversion.[1687] The burden of all covenants which touch and concern the land runs with the lease and binds an assignee.[1688]

§5. Domestic Leases

I. Introduction

330. The Residential Tenancies Act 1986 regulates leases and tenancies of dwelling houses, and provides a substantial measure of protection for tenants. Generally speaking, the provisions of the Act cannot be contracted out.[1689] The Act sets up a Tenancy Tribunal and mediation service to resolve problems.[1690]

II. Landlord's Obligations and Powers

331. At the commencement of the tenancy, the landlord must provide premises which are in a reasonable state of cleanliness and repair, and must maintain them in that state. The tenant has the right of quiet enjoyment and privacy, and the landlord must take reasonable steps to ensure that none of his or her other tenants interfere with that.[1691]

Unless there are special reasons, a landlord must give a tenant ninety days' notice to quit. Special reasons include requiring the premises for the landlord's, or the

1684. Property Law Act 2007, s. 218 and Sch. 3, Part 2, para. 4.
1685. *Ibid.*, s. 219.
1686. *Ibid.*, s. 224.
1687. *Ibid.*, s. 233.
1688. *Ibid.*, s. 231.
1689. Residential Tenancies Act 1986, s. 11; but the parties may expressly exclude the Act if the tenancy is a fixed-term tenancy for at least five years.
1690. Residential Tenancies Act 1986, Part III.
1691. Residential Tenancies Act 1986, s. 45.

landlord's family's own occupation, or the sale of the premises. Even then, forty-two days' notice is required.[1692] If a tenant is in breach of the agreement, the landlord can apply to a Tenancy Tribunal for an eviction order.[1693]

A tenant may apply to a Tenancy Tribunal for a review of rent.[1694] A landlord may not increase the rent more than once every six months, and must give the tenant sixty days' notice of an increase.[1695]

The landlord may, after giving notice, enter the premises during daytime to inspect the premises or do repairs.[1696] There is no power to distrain for rent,[1697] but the landlord has a statutory power with the consent of the Tenancy Tribunal[1698] to sell the tenant's goods if the tenant abandons them.

III. Tenant's Obligations

332. A tenant must:[1699]

(1) pay the rent when it is due;
(2) ensure the premises are occupied principally for residential purposes;
(3) keep the premises clean and reasonably tidy;
(4) notify the landlord as soon as possible of any damage or of the need for any repairs;
(5) leave the premises reasonably clean and tidy at the end of the tenancy.

A tenant must not:[1700]

(1) intentionally or carelessly damage the premises, or permit others to do so;
(2) use the premises for any unlawful purposes;
(3) interfere with the peace, comfort or privacy of the landlord's other tenants.

The tenant is responsible for the actions of others on the premises with his or her permission.[1701]

1692. *Ibid.*, s. 51.
1693. *Ibid.*, ss 55, 56.
1694. *Ibid.*, s. 25.
1695. *Ibid.*, s. 24.
1696. *Ibid.*, s. 48.
1697. *Ibid.*, s. 33.
1698. *Ibid.*, s. 62.
1699. Residential Tenancies Act 1986, s. 40. There are similar obligations to keep the place tidy in the Property Law Act 1952, ss 116D–116F; they apply to domestic tenancies to which the Residential Tenancies Act does not apply.
1700. Residential Tenancies Act 1986, s. 40(2).
1701. *Ibid.*, s. 41(1).

§6. AGRICULTURAL LEASES

333. There are no special rules relating to agricultural leases where the parties are private individuals. The Land Act 1948 contains provisions about the leasing for agricultural purposes of Crown Land. The lessee must reside personally on the land, and there are implied covenants that he or she will properly farm the land; will preserve timber; will clear the land of noxious weeds; will maintain improvements belonging to the Crown; and will insure all buildings belonging to the Crown. The Commissioner of Crown Lands can require other covenants, and can require improvements to be effected. It can advance money for the purpose of developing the land. The Crown can resume possession of the land if it is needed for public works; compensation must be paid. There are provisions about purchase and renewal by the lessee.

Likewise there are provisions in the Public Bodies Leases Act 1969 regulating leases by local authorities of farm land. Leases can be for terms of twenty-one or thirty-three years, and tenancies for periods of up to five years. Leases are granted after call for public applications. There are implied covenants by the tenant to farm properly and to keep the property free from pests and weeds. There are provisions for rent review, renewal, etc.

Leases of Maori Land under the Te Ture Whenua Maori (Maori Land) Act 1993 are often for farming purposes. That Act provides that the Maori Trustee may administer such leases, and may exercise powers of re-entry, distress, etc. Such a lease may not contain an option to purchase on the part of the lessee. Any assignment or sublease requires the consent of the Maori Trustee or a court-appointed agent. The Act provides for rent review, and for compensation for improvements effected by the lessee. If a lessee of farm land effects or proposes to effect improvements he or she is entitled to have a record of them made by the Maori Trustee.

Chapter 8. Contracts of Suretyship

§1. CONTRACTS OF GUARANTEE AND CONTRACTS OF INDEMNITY

I. Definition

334. A contract of guarantee will operate in a setting where there are three relevant parties – a creditor, a principal debtor and a secondary debtor or guarantor. The paradigm contract of guarantee involves a promise by the guarantor to the creditor that if the principal debtor does not pay the debt due to the creditor, the guarantor will make good the deficiency. A guarantee may be given in relation to future liabilities which the principal debtor may incur. The key feature is that the guarantor is only taking on a conditional obligation. The obligation to pay only arises where the principal debtor does not discharge his or her obligations to the creditor. However, if the debtor does default on his or her obligations, the creditor need not exhaust his or her remedies against the debtor before enforcing the guarantee unless the contract of guarantee specifically so requires.[1702]

If the contract has effect to get rid of any liability the principal debtor had to the creditor, and to substitute for that discharged liability a fresh obligation on the person contracting with the creditor, the contract is not one of guarantee but one of indemnity.

The question for the court is what effect the parties intended the transaction to have, and there is no need for the correct technical terms to have been used. However, the use of the formal terms of a guarantee will indicate a contractual intention to create a guarantee.[1703]

II. Formal Requirements

A. *Requirement of Writing*

335. The difference between contracts of indemnity and contracts of guarantee is of considerable practical importance. No special formalities are required for a contract of indemnity, but a contract of guarantee must be made in writing, and must be signed by the guarantor before the creditor can enforce the guarantee.[1704] Where the enforceability of a guarantee is in question, the first question for the court will

1702. *DFC Financial Services Ltd v. Coffey* [1991] 2 NZLR 513.

1703. *Bradley West Solicitors Nominee Co Ltd v. Keeman* [1994] 2 NZLR 111; *Jenkins v. NZI Finance Ltd* (1991) 3 NZBLC 102,199; *Trafalgar House Construction (Regions) Ltd v. General Surety & Guarantee Co Ltd* [1996] 1 AC 199 at 205.

1704. Property Law Act 2007, s. 27. The writing must contain the essentials of the obligation undertaken by the guarantor: *Brougham v. Regan* [2020] NZSC 118, [2020] 1 NZLR 315. The questions of writing and signatures are discussed at paras 92, 93.

be whether the agreement in question is truly a contract of guarantee. If that is answered in the affirmative, the court must then determine whether it meets the statutory requirements.[1705]

There is no guarantee, and therefore no requirement for writing, where the contract never involved a third party who owed a legal liability to the creditor. If A is in fact undertaking personal liability for any debt or obligation owed to B, a creditor, then there is no guarantee, because there is no third party whose defect of performance A is promising to make good. This may be the case either where there never was a third party C who was legally bound to B, or because any obligations owed by C to B have been discharged because A has taken on the equivalent liability.[1706]

The Property Law Act does not require that the consideration for the guarantee appear in the contract or note or memorandum,[1707] but it is the normal practice that it will do so.

B. Cases Where Oral Guarantee May Still Be Enforceable

336. It has been suggested, but not authoritatively decided, that a contract which gives to the creditor a remedy against the possessions of a third party, rather than the general personal liability of that third party, is not a contract of guarantee as it does not fall within the formula in the Property Law Act requiring the guarantor to 'answer for' the debt of another.[1708]

The Property Law Act requirements will probably not apply where the guarantee is not the main object of the transaction but a mere incident of it. In the case of a *del credere* agency, the guarantee is a minor part of the agency relationship and therefore falls outside the statute.[1709]

It has been held in England that where a person guarantees the discharge of a liability owed to a creditor by a third party so as to induce the creditor to give up rights over property of which the promisor is the substantial owner, the oral guarantee is binding.[1710]

These cases amount to judicial glosses on the clear words of the statute, and certainly are unlikely to be given any expanded application.

By contrast a recent High Court decision has held that if an unsigned agreement to lease is binding because there has been part performance, and the Court enforces it by an order for specific performance on the basis of part performance, the order

---

1705. *Doughty-Pratt Group Ltd v. Perry Castle* [1995] 2 NZLR 398 at 403.
1706. *Guild & Co v. Conrad* [1894] 2 QB 885; *Harburg India Rubber Comb Co v. Martin* [1902] 1 KB 778 at 784–785; *Mountstephen v. Lakeman* (1871) LR 7 QB 196; affirmed (1874) LR 7 HL 17. *See also Radius Residential Care Ltd v. Krishna* [2013] NZHC 2886.
1707. Property Law Act 2007, s. 27.
1708. *See BNZ v. Baker* [1926] NZLR 462; the point was left open in *Jenkins v. NZI Finance Ltd* (1991) 3 NZBLC 102,199.
1709. *Couturier v. Hastie* (1852) 8 Exch 40; *Sutton & Co v. Grey* [1894] 1 QB 285. For *del credere* agents, *see* para. 263.
1710. *Fitzgerald v. Dressler* (1859) 7 CBNS 374; *Harburg India Rubber Comb Co v. Martin* [1902] 1 KB 778.

for specific performance can validly compel the proper execution of an guarantee contained in the unsigned lease, with the result the guarantee then will comply with the Act.[1711]

III. Cases Where Creditor's Conduct May Render Guarantee Unenforceable

337. There are several circumstances in which a creditor's conduct may render the guarantee unenforceable against the guarantor, even though the formal requirements have all been complied with. First, there are the cases where the guarantor has entered into the transaction after being unduly influenced by another person, or where the transaction is unconscionable.[1712] Second, there may not have been adequate disclosure to the guarantor by the creditor. The creditor need not reveal details of a normal debtor-creditor relationship, but where there are unusual aspects to the creditor's underlying relationship with the debtor, these aspects must be disclosed or the creditor may be disqualified from enforcing the guarantee.[1713] Third, a creditor cannot enforce a guarantee where there has been any material change in the contract between the creditor and the debtor which has not been agreed to by the guarantor.[1714] Lastly, a guarantor's liability may be reduced where the creditor releases a security for the debt without the guarantor's consent.[1715] However, if the guarantor's legal position under the contract is not affected by the release of the security because the guarantee is to remain in force until the debt is fully paid, release of the security may not have this effect.[1716]

IV. 'Guarantees' in Consumer Transactions

338. It is very common in consumer contracts for both goods and services for the vendor of the goods or services to offer a 'guarantee' in relation to the goods or services – usually a promise to repair or replace defective goods or make good the results of defective services. Where the contract is for the sale of goods or chattels, it is normal for the retail vendor to make the promise as an agent for the manufacturer of the goods or chattels. Such promises may be enforceable under the contract or in the exercise of statutory rights, but they are not 'contracts of guarantee', and the formal requirements and principles discussed above have no application.

1711. *Chambers v. Chatfield* [2016] NZHC 1871 (2016) 10 NZBLC 99-723. For part performance *see* para. 94.
1712. *See* paras 137–144.
1713. *Scales Trading Ltd v. Far Eastern Shipping Co Public Ltd* [1999] 3 NZLR 26; *Shivas v. Bank of New Zealand* [1990] 2 NZLR 327.
1714. *Madden v. UDC Financial Services Ltd* [1996] 1 NZLR 542; affirmed (1997) 8 TCLR 92.
1715. *National Bank of New Zealand Ltd v. Murland* [1991] 3 NZLR 86; *Davis v. Bank of New Zealand* [1991] 1 NZLR 745; *China & South Sea Bank Ltd v. Tan* [1990] 1 AC 536.
1716. *Roc Mac Ltd v. Buxton* (2007) NZCPR 434.

Chapter 9. Contracts of Pledge

§1. Contracts of Pledge

I. General

339. Contracts of pledge or pawn are generally only to be encountered in pawnbroking transactions. Pawnbroking is the practice whereby a lender of money, the pawnbroker, lends money to a person by way of an interest-bearing loan on the security of some goods which are actually or constructively brought within the pawnbroker's possession.[1717] In some cases, the borrower, or pawnor, may pledge the items in question to secure some other obligation than a debt, but this is not now common.

A contract of pawn creates a special interest or property in the pawnee which entitles the continued possession of the pawned chattel or goods until the debt secured by them is discharged, at which point the property in the goods revests completely in the pawnor.[1718] It is therefore different from a lien or a chattel mortgage.

The commercial practice is centuries old, and there are a number of licensed pawnbrokers operating in New Zealand's larger cities. Their business is regulated by the Secondhand Dealers and Pawnbrokers Act 2004, but a private contract of pawn or pledge is not subject to the statute.

II. Contracts of Pledge or Pawn

A. *Things Capable of Being Pawned*

340. Contracts of pawn are a form of contracts of bailment, and the general principles of such contracts apply.[1719] While normally a contract of pawn will involve goods or chattels which can be easily transported and brought within the actual possession of the pawnee, constructive possession will suffice, for example, where the keys to a locked storage area are delivered. It is possible to pledge other forms of property, such as title deeds to real or personal property.[1720] A pledge of title deeds to property does not create a mortgage interest in the property itself.[1721]

1717. Secondhand Dealers and Pawnbrokers Act 2004, s. 3; *Coggs v. Bernard* (1703) 2 Ld Raym 909.
1718. *The Odessa* [1916] 1 AC 145 at 158–159; *Attenborough v. Solomon* [1913] AC 76.
1719. *See* Part II, Specific Contracts, Ch. 2.
1720. *Beckett v. District Land Registrar* (1909) 28 NZLR 788. Under the Mercantile Law Act 1908, s. 4, a pledge of the documents of title to goods is deemed by statute to be a pledge of the goods themselves.
1721. *Beckett v. District Land Registrar* (1909) 28 NZLR 788.

B. Rights of Parties to Contract of Pawn

341. The principal feature of a pawnbroking transaction by a licensed pawnbroker is that when the pawnee takes possession of the pledge, the pawnee will give to the pawnor a pledge ticket. The holder of the pledge ticket – who may well not be the original pawnor – is entitled to redeem the pledge on payment of the appropriate sums of money, unless the pawnbroker has been informed that the pledge ticket had been lost by, or illegally obtained from, the pawnor, or that the pledge was not lawfully in the possession of the pawnor when pawned.

The pawnee's principal rights are first to hold the pledge as security of the moneys advanced and for any interest due, and second to sell by public auction (and only by public auction) the pledge at the expiry either of the agreed duration of the pledge contract or, where no period has been agreed, at the expiry of a period fixed by the Secondhand Dealers and Pawnbrokers Act. Should the sale of the pledge produce more than the principal and interest due and any costs of sale, the pawnor is entitled to the surplus. Should there be a deficit on the sale, this remains a debt owed by the pawnor and the pawnee may pursue such other remedies as are available at law. As the pawnor is unlikely to be worth suing, legal action is unlikely.

Chapter 10. Contracts of Loan

342. While generally a transaction which is a mere loan will not be contractual in nature, because the borrower furnishes no consideration for the benefit conferred by the lender, the position is different if the borrower is furnishing consideration. This will occur most commonly in cases where the transaction involves the lending of a sum of money where the borrower promises to pay a sum which is in total greater than the sum borrowed, whether by way of periodic payments of interest or by the repayment of a greater capital sum at the termination of the loan. All such contracts for the loan of money are affected by the Credit Contracts and Consumer Finance Act 2003, which is designed to give a degree of protection to the borrower. The Act creates a regime which is in a number of important respects different from that which would apply to normal contracts:

(1) Commercial lenders have a duty to disclose to borrowers the actual costs the borrowers are incurring.
(2) Borrowers from commercial lenders have a right to cancel the contract provided this is done within a limited period after the contract was made.
(3) A party to a credit contract who alleges the contract is oppressive may seek to have the contract reopened by the court, and the court may grant relief by way of variation or cancellation of the contract.

The Act is in effect a code governing such contracts. If a contract is made or performed in breach of the Credit Contracts and Consumer Finance Act it is not thereby rendered illegal, and thus relief under the Contract and Commercial Law Act 2017 is not available.[1722]

1722. Credit Contracts and Consumer Finance Act 2003, s. 136.

Chapter 11. Contracts with the Government and Other Public Administrations

343. For the most part, there is little in New Zealand law to distinguish contracts between private individuals from those between private individuals and a government agency.[1723] Cases involving the central government, or local government, or a legally separate entity controlled by either local or central government, will be dealt with through the normal courts, and in essentially the same way as would a case between private individuals.

The right to sue the state in contract or tort was recognized in the nineteenth century and is now firmly established by statute.[1724] Indeed, it has been indicated that the ability to bring such proceedings is an essential part of a free and democratic society.[1725]

It has been suggested that central government or its agencies owe a duty of good faith to those with whom they contract, although if there is any such general duty it is apt to be displaced by specific statutory regimes which require such agencies to act in a commercial manner.[1726]

In general, there are no special rules as to the making of contracts between individuals and the state, acting through governmental departments. Such contracts have the same procedural or formal requirements as contracts between individuals.

However, where the contract is between an individual and a local body or other public or statutory authority, the position is somewhat different. Legislation does impose certain formal requirements, notably that contracts involving sums of more than NZD 1,000 must be made in writing. Agreements which do not meet these formal requirements are unenforceable and void.[1727]

Many statutes creating specific institutions have specific provisions regulating the contracts which the institution may make and the manner in which they may be made.[1728] Some difficulty attaches to contracts which involve the local body acting outside the powers conferred on it by statute. In some cases, the High Courts awarded relief under the Illegal Contracts Act 1970 (now replaced by sections 70–84 of the Contract and Commercial Law Act 2017) by way of an order validating the contract.[1729] However the Court of Appeal has suggested that agreements

1723. As to determination of any intention to create legal relations in such transactions *see* para. 76.
1724. The first such statute was the Crown Liabilities Redress Act 1871. The current law is as stated in the Crown Proceedings Act 1950. See *Todd on Torts* para. 23.1 (9th ed., Thomson Reuters 2023).
1725. New Zealand Bill of Rights Act 1990, s. 27(3).
1726. *Pratt Contractors Ltd v. Palmerston North City Council* [1995] 1 NZLR 469; contrast *Transit New Zealand v. Pratt Contractors Ltd* [2002] 2 NZLR 313 at 323; appeal dismissed [2005] 2 NZLR 233.
1727. Public Bodies Contracts Act 1959, s. 3; *Tuck Construction Ltd v. Waipa County* [1967] NZLR 987. However, under s. 3(4), a failure to sign or seal a contract will not render it invalid if the contract was made pursuant to, or gives effect to, a resolution of the public body; *see* for example *Taueki v. Horowhenua District Council* [2017] NZHC 34.
1728. By way of example only, *see* Health Research Council Act 1990, s. 35; Museum of New Zealand Te Papa Tongarewa Act 1992, s. 18.
1729. As to validation under the Contract and Commercial Law Act 2017 generally *see* paras 157–160; contrast *Mercurius Ventures Ltd v. Waitakere CC* [1996] 2 NZLR 495; *Lower Hutt City Council v. Martin* [1987] 1 NZLR 321.

which exceed the local body's powers are void not illegal, so relief under that Act will not be available.[1730]

1730. *Banks v. Grey District Council* [2015] NZCA 417, fn 20. Leave to appeal to the Supreme Court was refused: *Banks v. Grey District Council* [2015] NZSC 158.

Chapter 12. Partnerships

344. Partnership is regulated in New Zealand by the Partnership Law Act 2019. The purpose of this Act is to re-enact the Partnership Act 1908 in an up-to-date and accessible form.[1731] Part 2 of the 2019 Act sets out the nature of a partnership, and, in particular, it defines a partnership as the relationship that exists between persons carrying on a business in common with a view to profit.[1732] Part 3 sets out the rules governing the relationship of partners to third parties and to each other. Partners are jointly and severally liable to any person who is not a partner for the wrongful act or omission of any partner acting in the ordinary course of the business of the firm or with the authority of the co-partners.[1733]

1731. Partnership Law Act 2019, s. 3.
1732. Partnership Law Act 2019, s. 8.
1733. Partnership Law Act 2019, ss 23 and 25. Partners may sue or be sued in the name of their firm: High Court Rules 2016, r 4.25.

Chapter 13. Restitution

§1. The Traditional Law

345. The law of restitution formerly tended to be known as quasi-contract, because some so-called quasi-contracts were seen as based on an implied contract. But this branch of the law really concerns the provision of a remedy against those who have been unjustly enriched at the plaintiff's expense and is not about agreement between the parties. Lord Atkin once called the relevant categories of claim 'fantastic resemblances to contracts'.[1734] The law of restitution or unjust enrichment[1735] can nonetheless operate in a contractual context, although the Contract and Commercial Law Act 2017 enables the court to exercise a form of relief which means that it is unnecessary to have recourse to the common law, or even that common law is inapplicable.[1736]

However, for the sake of convenience, we shall set out the traditional categories of quasi-contract or restitution and comment on their utility in New Zealand today.

I. Money Paid by the Plaintiff to the Defendant's Use

346. If the plaintiff has been compelled to pay money for which the defendant is liable, he or she may sue the defendant for the amount so paid. The plaintiff must establish that: (1) he or she has been constrained to pay the money; and (2) it is money for which the defendant was legally liable.

II. Money Paid under a Mistake

347. The general rule has thus been stated:[1737]

> Where money is paid to another under the influence of a mistake, that is, upon the supposition that a specific fact is true which would entitle the other to the money, but which fact is untrue, and the money would not have been paid if it had been known to the payer that the fact was untrue, an action will lie to recover it back.

A number of points may be made.

First, at common law, the mistake had to be one of fact, not law. The distinction needs no longer be drawn in New Zealand. Section 74A of the Property Law Act 2007 provides:

1734. *United Australia Ltd v. Barclays Bank Ltd* [1941] AC 1 at 29.
1735. The leading work is *Goff and Jones: The Law of Unjust Enrichment* Sweet & Maxwell Ltd, London, 10th ed, 2022. The first 7 editions of this book were called The Law of Restitution.
1736. For example, the Contract and Commercial Law Act 2017, ss 24, 43 and 76.
1737. *Kelly v. Solari* (1841) 9 M & W 54 at 58 per Parke B.

(1) If relief in respect of any payment that has been made under mistake is sought in any Court (whether in civil proceedings or by way of defence, set off, counterclaim, or otherwise) and that relief could be granted if the mistake were wholly one of fact, that relief must not be denied by reason only that the mistake is one of law whether or not it is in any degree also one of fact.

(2) Nothing in this section enables relief to be given in respect of any payment made at a time when the law required or allowed, or was commonly understood to require or allow, the payment to be made or enforced, by reason only that the law was subsequently changed or shown not to have been as it was commonly understood to have been at the time of the payment.

Thus, relief is available even in respect of mistakes of law. Since the passing of the section relief has been granted in several situations, although all of them would have qualified as mistakes of fact under the old law: for example a mistaken payment made by a legal firm into a client's trust account in reliance on a fraudulent misrepresentation by a clerk of the firm;[1738] a mistaken payment of dividends by a company to the wrong person;[1739] and payment of a cheque by a teller without realizing it had been countermanded.[1740]

Second, while in many cases there has been no contractual nexus between the parties, sometimes a mistake is connected with an apparent contract between the parties. At common law, it would appear that recovery of the money in quasi-contract would lie provided the plaintiff could prove the same sort of mistake as would entitle him or her to treat the contract as void *ab initio*. In New Zealand today, a mistaken payment by a party to a contract will often be able to be dealt with under the Contract and Commercial Law Act 2017.[1741]

If a mistake of the kind specified in section 24 of the Act has induced entry into the contract, the party's claim for relief lies under that Act. However, if the mistake has arisen after the formation of the contract,[1742] and relates to its performance, the Act is inapplicable, and the common law remedies will apply. However, the relationship between the Act and common law is less clear than it should be, and it has been argued that:[1743]

> If, for example, there never was a contract because due to a misunderstanding offer and acceptance did not correspond, there does not appear to be anything the Act to prevent the mistaken promisor from relying on this point ... as the foundation for restitutionary action.

1738. *Thomas v. Houston Corbett & Co* [1969] NZLR 151.
1739. *Lambe v. Jacobsen* [1970] NZLR 1008.
1740. *Southland Savings Bank v. Anderson* [1974] 1 NZLR 118. *See also KJ Davies (1976) Ltd v. Bank of New South Wales* [1981] 1 NZLR 262 and *Westpac Banking Corporation v. Rae* [1992] 1 NZLR 338.
1741. *See* paras 125–131.
1742. Under the Contract and Commercial Law Act 2017, s. 24 the only mistakes for which relief under the Act is available are those which influence the decision to *enter* the contract.
1743. McLauchlan and Rickett [1989] NZ Recent Law Review 277 at 290, commenting on *England v. G & D Ritchie Holdings Ltd* (HC Wellington, CP 912/88, 28 Feb. 1989).

Third, section 74B of the Property Law Act 2007 provides as follows:

> Relief, whether under Section 74A or in equity or otherwise, in respect of any payment made under mistake, whether of law or of fact, must be denied wholly or in part if the person from whom relief is sought received the payment in good faith and has so altered his or her position in reliance on the validity of the payment that in the opinion of the court, having regard to all possible implications in respect of other persons, it is inequitable to grant relief, or to grant relief in full, as the case may be.

In *Thomas v. Houston Corbett & Co,*[1744] a legal firm paid GBP 840 into a client's trust account on the faith of a fraudulent misrepresentation by the firm's clerk. Since the client had relied on the payment, the court, 'balancing the equities', allowed him to retain GBP 560; it is interesting to note that while the three members of the court agreed on the outcome, they differed somewhat in their views of the equities as between the parties.

In determining whether a payment was received in good faith, the Court must have regard to the circumstances and earlier conduct of the parties. Thus, the defence was not available where a bank sought to recover funds paid out on a counterfeit cheque where the payee knew facts from which he should have known the cheque was unlikely to be valid.[1745]

Section 74B only applies when there is payment under mistake. If one party suspects the payment is incorrect, alteration of position may still be a defence to a claim for repayment, relying on common law doctrine rather than the section.[1746]

III. Total Failure of Consideration

348. At common law, if the plaintiff had paid money to the defendant in pursuance of a valid contract and the defendant then failed completely to carry out his or her part of it, the plaintiff had an option. He or she might either rest the claim on the basis of the contract and seek damages for its breach, or he or she might treat the contract as at an end and sue in quasi-contract for the return of the money.[1747]

In New Zealand today, this common law principle has lost its vitality. If there has been a failure of consideration, that will normally be because there has been a breach of contract by the other party, or because the contract has been frustrated. If the failure of consideration was caused by frustration of the contract, the frustration

1744. [1969] NZLR 151.
1745. *ASB Securities Ltd v. Geurts* [2005] 1 NZLR 464, [60]–[63].
1746. *National Bank of New Zealand Ltd v. Waitaki International Processing (NI) Ltd* [1999] 2 NZLR 211. The limits of the change of position defence in New Zealand are not fully clear. There is, for example, some difference as to whether simply spending money received may be a change of position; contrast *ASB Securities Ltd v. Geurts* [2005] 1 NZLR 464, [65] and *Karl v. ACC* [2005] NZAR 97, [33]–[35]. *See also Philip Collins Ltd v. Davis* [2000] 3 All ER 808.
1747. *Wilkinson v. Lloyd* (1845) 7 QB 27; *Mackley v. Brighton* (1914) 34 NZLR 314; *Bray v. Anderson* [1956] NZLR 347.

of contract provisions of the Contract and Commercial Law Act 2017[1748] will govern the recovery of money paid. If the contract has been broken, the innocent party will, since *ex hypothesi* the breach is fundamental, have a right to cancel under the Contract and Commercial Law Act and bring an action under section 43 of that Act claiming the return of the money. The cancellation provisions of the Act apply in place of the rule of common law governing circumstances in which a party may rescind a contract for breach.[1749]

In the case of a contract for the sale of goods, where the cancellation provisions of the Contract and Commercial Law Act 2017 do not apply, however, there may still be scope for the operation of the common law remedy.[1750]

IV. Money Paid in Pursuance of a Void Contract

349. The plaintiff may have paid money to the defendant in pursuance of a transaction which he or she thought to be valid contract, but which in truth, through the operation of some rule of law, is null and void.

At common law such money was recoverable in quasi-contract. Once again in New Zealand, statutes have changed the position – for example, in relation to contracts entered into under a mistake.[1751]

Where, however, the transaction is avoided, not by the common law but by statute, the position is more complicated. The context of the statute, its purpose and the true construction of its language, may prevent the recovery of the money. Each statute rendering a contract void, or empowering a court to declare it void, must thus be carefully construed to determine the consequences placed upon the voidness. The leading consumer protection statute, the Fair Trading Act 1986, for example, empowers a court to declare contracts void for being in breach of the Act, but preserves the right to seek relief under section 76 of the Contract and Commercial Law Act 2017.[1752]

At common law special difficulties arose where a company purported to make a contract which was ultra vires. In New Zealand, the difficult questions which arose at common law have been rendered legally superfluous: the Companies Act 1993 provides that all companies have full rights, powers, and privileges.[1753] Moreover, nothing done by a company is invalid by reason only of the fact that the company had no power to do it.[1754] The doctrine of ultra vires is thus effectively abolished as far as outsiders are concerned, although it still retains some life vis-à-vis insiders.

1748. Contract and Commercial Law Act 2017, ss 50–69. Those provisions are discussed at paras 231–232.
1749. Contract and Commercial Law Act 2017, s. 40.
1750. *Riddiford v. Warren* (1901) 20 NZLR 572. *See* para. 166.
1751. Contract and Commercial Law Act 2017, ss 21–32. *See* paras 128–131.
1752. Fair Trading Act 1986, s. 43.
1753. Companies Act 1993, s. 16.
1754. *Ibid.*, s. 17.

V. Money Paid in Pursuance of an Illegal Contract

350. At common law, the general rule was that if a contract was illegal, whether by statute or as contrary to public policy, a party could not sue to recover money if, to sustain the claim, he or she must rely on the illegality and disclose his or her guilt. However, there were certain exceptions to that rule: if, for instance, the parties were not in *pari delicto* (e.g., where one had taken advantage of the defenceless condition of the other) the more innocent might be able to recover moneys paid. This whole question is now governed in New Zealand by the Contract and Commercial Law Act 2017 which declares that illegal contracts are unenforceable and that no money paid under them may be recovered; but which nevertheless confers a discretion on the court to grant relief in a deserving case.[1755]

VI. Claims Against Wrongdoers

351. A plaintiff who has suffered loss through a wrongful act committed against him or her by the defendant, may in certain circumstances be entitled to sue the defendant in quasi-contract for money had and received to his or her use. He or she may for instance have been compelled by the improper pressure of the defendant to pay money which could not lawfully have been demanded from him or her.[1756]

VII. Claims on a Quantum Meruit

352. The common law has long provided a convenient remedy when the plaintiff seeks, not a precise sum alleged to be due, but a reasonable remuneration for services rendered. He or she is then said to sue on a quantum meruit.

Statute has in New Zealand rendered obsolete one of the common law's most frequent examples. At common law, a plaintiff could seek to recover reasonable remuneration for work done in pursuance of a contract which had been discharged by the default of the defendant: in such a case quantum meruit was an alternative to a claim in damages for breach of contract. In New Zealand, today such a case would be dealt with under section 43 of the Contract and Commercial Law Act 2017, which enables a court to direct one party to pay the other such sum as the court thinks just when a contract has been cancelled for breach. In deciding on the nature of the order the court can take into account any expenditure incurred by a party, the value of any work performed, and any benefit already conferred on the other party. It has been decided that quantum meruit does not survive the Contractual Remedies Act 1979 in this situation.[1757]

Another example of the use of quantum meruit as a quasi-contractual remedy (which still survives in New Zealand) is to be found where the plaintiff has rendered services in pursuance of a transaction, supposed by him to be a contract, but

1755. *See* paras 158–160.
1756. *Maskell v. Horner* [1915] 3 KB 106.
1757. *Brown and Doherty Ltd v. Whangarei County Council* [1990] 2 NZLR 63.

which, in truth, is without legal validity.[1758] The rationale here is similar to that employed to support an action for money paid in respect of an ineffective contract and differs from it only in the circumstance that the plaintiff sues, not for the return of a precise sum, but for a reasonable remuneration. The well-known *Craven-Ellis v. Canons Ltd*[1759] is a good example.

However, in the case of contracts rendered void by statute, the court may hold, on the construction of the statute, that no remedy lies, even on a quantum meruit.[1760]

By an extension of the principle in *Craven-Ellis v. Canons Ltd*, a plaintiff may be able to claim on a quantum meruit for work done which was to be paid for under a contract which the parties erroneously believed was about to be made. Thus, in *Dickson Elliott Lonergan Ltd v. Plumbing World Ltd,*[1761] a builder was successful in claiming reasonable payment when it had commenced work in the reasonable expectation, shared by the defendant, that a formal contract would be concluded shortly. There is some uncertainty as to the law here, particularly whether in such cases it must be shown there was a request that the work be done as opposed to knowledge that payment would be expected.[1762]

By section 124(2) of the Contract and Commercial Law Act 2017, it is enacted that:

> [I]f necessaries are sold and delivered to a person who because of mental incapacity or intoxication is incompetent to contract, he or she must pay a reasonable price for the goods.

The situation of minors contracting for necessaries, which used to be governed by the same rules, is now regulated in New Zealand by sections 85–118 of the Contract and Commercial Law Act 2017.[1763]

§2. Restitution Today

353. As was noted at the outset, this branch of the law is today dealt with under the rubric of restitution.[1764] There is growing support for a theory of unjust

1758. *See* for example *Cassels v. Body Corporate 86975* (2007) 8 NZCPR 740 (quantum meruit available to recover value of services provided by body corporate where bylaws requiring payment were invalid).
1759. [1936] KB 403. *See also Radoven v. Slater* [1952] NZLR 266; *Tipling v. TPR Printing Co Ltd* [1955] NZLR 136; *Love v. McIntyre* [1921] NZLR 339.
1760. That conclusion has been reached in respect of contracts unenforceable for lack of writing under the Public Bodies Contracts Act 1959. *See Tuck Construction Ltd v. Waipa County* [1967] NZLR 981.
1761. [1988] 2 NZLR 608.
1762. The point was discussed and expressly left open in *Morning Star (St Lukes Garden Apartments) Ltd v. Canam Construction Ltd* 8 Aug. 2006, CA 90/05.
1763. *See* para. 119.
1764. *See* in particular *Enrichment and Restitution* by Grantham and Rickett (2000). *See also* Goff & Jones, *The Law of Unjust Enrichment* (10th ed., Sweet & Maxwell 2022).

enrichment as its basis. Despite initial judicial coolness to this idea,[1765] courts in Australia,[1766] Canada,[1767] England,[1768] and New Zealand[1769] have in recent years made overt reference to it as an underlying rationale in claims of restitution.

New Zealand courts have not yet accorded it the status of a cause of action.[1770] The authors of the leading New Zealand text on restitution are cautious, and are concerned that an open-ended notion of 'unjustness' might place pressure on the law of restitution to 'collapse into an open-ended concept of fairness'.[1771]

1765. *See* Mahon J in *Carly v. Farrelly* [1975] 1 NZLR 356 at 367.
1766. *Pavey & Mathews Pty Ltd v. Paul* (1987) 162 CLR 221; *ANZ Banking Group v. Westpac Banking Corp* (1988) 164 CLR 662.
1767. *Pettkus v. Becker* (1980) 117 DLR (3d) 257 at 274.
1768. *Lipkin Gorman v. Karpnale Ltd* [1991] 2 AC 548 at 559 and 578; *Woolwich Building Society v. Inland Revenue Commissioners* [1993] AC 71 at 97.
1769. *Equiticorp Industries Group Ltd v. R* [1996] 3 NZLR 586 at 611; *Goss v. Chilcott* [1996] 3 NZLR 385 at 392; *Transpower New Zealand Ltd v. Meridian Energy Ltd* [2001] 3 NZLR 700 at 714.
1770. *Rod Milner Motors Ltd v. Attorney-General* [1999] 2 NZLR 568 at 576 applied in *Li v. 110 Formosa (NZ) Ltd* [2018] NZHC 3418 at [27]. However, without discussion of the case law, amendment of pleadings to include an unjust enrichment claim was allowed in *Pollock v. Pollock* [2019] NZHC 554.
1771. Grantham and Rickett *Enrichment and Restitution* (2000) 16.

Selected Bibliography

Abdussalam and Rickett. 'Towards a Dynamic Concept of the Remoteness Rule in Contract Law'. *JCL* 36 (2020): 157.

Ahdar. 'Remoteness, "Ritual Incantation" and the Future of *Hadley v. Baxendale*: Reflections from New Zealand'. *JCL* 7 (1994): 53.

Atiyah. *The Rise and Fall of Freedom of Contract*. Oxford: Oxford University Press, 1979.

Barton. 'The Effect of the Contract Statutes in New Zealand'. *JCL* 16 (2000): 233.

Beck. 'Illegality and the Court's Discretion: The New Zealand Illegal Contracts Act in Action'. *NZULR* 14 (1989): 389.

Benjamin's Sale of Goods. 11th edn. London: Sweet and Maxwell, 2022.

Bigwood. 'The Elements of Duress in New Zealand Today: A Case of Ockham's Razor'. *NZBLQ* 10 (2004): 326.

Bigwood. 'Undue Influence in the House of Lords: Principles and Proof'. *MLR* 65 (2002): 435.

Bigwood. *Exploitative Contracts*. Oxford: Oxford University Press, 2003.

Birks and Chin. 'On the Nature of Undue Influence'. In *Good Faith and Fault in Contract Law*, edited by Beatson & Friedmann. Oxford: Clarendon Press, 1995.

Bowstead & Reynolds. *Agency*. 22th edn, edited by Watts. London: Sweet and Maxwell, 2022.

Bridge. 'Markets and Damages in Sale of Goods Cases'. *LQR* 132 (2016); 405.

Bridge. 'The Nature of Assignment and Non-assignment Clauses'. *LQR* 132 (2016): 47.

Campbell and Halson. 'By Their Fruits Shall Ye Know Them'. *CLJ* 79 (2020): 405.

Capper. 'Banks, Borrowers, Sureties and Undue Influence – A Half-Baked Solution to a Thoroughly Cooked Problem'. *RLR* (2002): 100.

Conte. 'The Penalty Rule Revisited'. *LQR* 132 (2016): 382.

Coote. 'Consideration and Benefit in Fact and in Law'. *JCL* 3 (1990): 23.

Coote. 'Contract Forms, Consideration and Contract Doctrine'. *JCL* 14 (1999): 116.

Coote. 'The Performance Interest, *Panatown* and the Problem of Loss'. *LQR* 117 (2001): 81.

Coote. *Exception Clauses*. London: Sweet and Maxwell, 1964.

Dawson & McLauchlan. *The Contractual Remedies Act 1979*. Auckland: Sweet & Maxwell, 1981.

Day. 'Remoteness in Contract Damages'. *CLJ* 80 (2021): 29

Eldridge. 'The New Law of Penalties: Mapping the Terrain'. *JBL* (2018): 637.

Foxton. 'How Useful is Lord Diplock's Distinction Between Primary and Secondary Obligations in Contract?' *LQR* 135 (2019): 249.
Foxton. 'The Status of the Special Rules of Construction of Exemption Clauses in Commercial Contracts'. *JBL* [2021]: 205
Friedmann. 'The Performance Interest in Contract Damages'. *LQR* 111 (1995): 628.
Fuller & Perdue. 'The Reliance Interest in Contract Damages'. *Yale LJ* 46 (1936): 52.
Gardner and Murphy. 'Concurrent Liability in Contract and Tort: A Separation Thesis'. *LQR* 137 (2021): 77
Gardner. 'Being Conscious of Unconscionability in Modern Times: *Heller v Uber Technologies*'. *MLR* 84 (2021): 874
Gault on Commercial Law, Wellington: Brookers (looseleaf).
Goff & Jones. *The Law of Unjust Enrichment*. 10th edn. London: Sweet and Maxwell, 2022.
Grantham & Rickett. *Enrichment and Restitution in New Zealand*. Oxford: Hart Publishing, 2000.
Grower. 'On the Relations Between Agent and Principal'. *MLR* 81 (2018): 141.
Holderness (ed.). *Butterworths Introduction to Commercial Law*. 5th edn. Wellington: LexisNexis, 2016.
Joseph. *Constitutional and Administrative Law in New Zealand*. 5th edn. Wellington: Brookers, 2021.
Lawson. *The Law of Property*. Oxford: Clarendon Press, 1958.
Leggatt. 'Making Sense of Contracts: The Rational Choice Theory'. *LQR* 131 (2015): 454.
MacMahon. 'Rethinking Assignability'. *CLJ* 79 (2020): 288.
McFarlane and Sales. 'Promises, Detriment and Liability: Lessons from Proprietary Estoppel'. *LQR* 313 (2015): 610.
McLauchlan and Summers. 'Mitigation and Causation of Benefits'. *LMCLQ* (2018): 171.
McLauchlan. 'A Better Way of Making Sense of Contracts'. *LQR* 132 (2016): 577.
McLauchlan. 'Agreements to Negotiate in Good Faith: A Non-justiciable Contract?'. *NZBLQ* 11 (2005): 454.
McLauchlan. 'Contract Interpretation: What Is It About?'. *Sydney Law Review* 31, no. 1 (2009): 5.
McLauchlan. 'Rectification for Unilateral Mistake'. *NZULR* 18 (1999): 360.
McLauchlan. 'Reliance Damages for Breach of Contract'. *NZ Law Rev* (2007): 417.
McLauchlan. 'Remoteness Re-invented'. *OUCLJ* 9 (2009): 109.
McLauchlan. 'The New Law of Contract Interpretation'. *NZULR* 19 (2000): 147.
McLauchlan. 'Rectification Rectified?' *JCL* 36 (2020): 131
Milsom. *Historical Foundations of the Common Law*. 2nd edn. London: Butterworths, 1981.
Ming Ten Ran. 'Contractual Variations: Long Live the Doctrine of Consideration'. *CLJ* 80 (2021): 235
Mullan. 'Damages for Breach of Contract: Quantifying the Lost Consumer Surplus'. *OJLS* 36 (2016): 83.
New Zealand Law Commission Report No. 25. *Contract Statutes Review*. Wellington, 1993.

New Zealand Law Commission Report No. 47. 'Apportionment of Civil Liability'. Wellington, 1998.

Palmer. *Bailment*. 3rd edn. Sydney: The Law Book Co., 2009.

Peden. 'Policy Considerations Behind Implication of Terms in Law'. *LQR* 117 (2001): 459.

Peel. 'Loss of Bargain Damages'. *LMCLQ* [2020]: 449.

Phang. 'Doctrine and Fairness in the Law of Contract'. *LS* (2009): 534.

Ridge. 'Uncertainties Surrounding Undue Influence: Its Formulation, Application and Relationship to Other Doctrines'. *NZ Law Review* (2003): 329.

Robertson. 'The Basis of the Remoteness Rule in Contract'. *LS* 28 (2008): 172.

Rowan. 'Cost of Cure Damages and the Relevance of the Injured Promisee's Intention to Cure' *CLJ* 76 (2017): 616.

Spence. *Protecting Reliance: The Emergent Doctrine of Equitable Estoppel.* Oxford: Hart Publishing, 1999.

Spiller, Finn & Boast. *A New Zealand Legal History*. 2nd edn. Wellington: Brookers, 2002.

Tettenborn. '*Hadley v. Baxendale* Foreseeability: A Principle Beyond Its Sell-by Date'. *JCL* 23 (2007): 120.

Tiverios. '*127 Hobson Street Ltd v Honey Bees Preschool Ltd*: The Penalties Doctrine, Signalling and the Balancing of Legitimate Interests'. *NZULR* 29 (2020): 385.

Tiverios (ed.). *Contractual Penalties in Australia and the United Kingdom: History, Theory and Practice*. London: Sweet & Maxwell, 2021.

Todd (ed.). *Todd on Torts*. 9th edn. Wellington: Brookers, 2023.

Todd and Barber. *Burrows, Finn and Todd on the Law of Contract in New Zealand.* 7th edn. Wellington: Lexis Nexis, 2022.

Tokeley. 'Introducing a Prohibition on Unfair Contract Terms into New Zealand Law: Justifications and Suggestions for Reform'. *NZULR* 23 (2009): 419.

Treitel. *The Law of Contract*. 15th edn, by Peel. London: Sweet & Maxwell, 2020.

Ventakeson. 'Causation in Misrepresentation: Historical or Counterfactual? And 'But For' What?' *LQR* 137 (2021): 503

Webb. 'Performance and Compensation: An Analysis of Contract Damages and Contractual Obligation'. *OJLS* 26 (2006): 41.

Selected Bibliography

Index

The numbers here refers to paragraphs numbers.

Absolute promise, 226
Acceptance
  bilateral contracts, in, 52, 54
  communication by method stipulated, 55
  electronic communications, by, 58
  fact of agreement inferred from, 54
  generally, 50, 52
  in response to offer, 54
  machines, by, 42
  offer and, 28
  post, by, 57
  revocation of, 61
  retrospective, 51
  silence, effect of, 54
  standing offer, 40, 50
Accord and satisfaction
  cheques in full settlement, 236
  definition, 236
Account of profits, 239, 255
Advertisements
  auction, of, 38
  misleading, 103
  offer or invitation to treat, 35
  two contract analysis, 36
Affirmation, 216
Agency, *see also* Agent, Principal
  apparent, 272
  authority of agent, 270–272
  contract of, 260
  duties of parties, 273, 274
  express, 267
  formation of, 267–269
  generally, 260
  liability of parties, 280–283
  necessity, of, 269
  pre-incorporation contracts, 268
  Property Law Act 2007, agent and, 93
  ratification, 268
  rights of third parties, 282–283
  termination of, 284
Agent, *see also* Agency, Principal
  apparent authority, 272
  appointment, 267
  auctioneers, 265
  authority of, 270–272
  bankruptcy of, 284
  brokers, 263
  contracts by, 275–278
  death of, 284
  del credere, 264
  disclosed principal, 275
  dispositions of property by, 279
  duties of, 273
  express authority of, 271
  generally, 261
  implied authority of, 271, 272
  incapacity of, 284
  knowledge of, 281
  liability of, 282
  mercantile, 262, 304
  misrepresentation by, 106, 283
  payment to, 278
  principal, duties of, 274
  ratification by principal, 268
  real estate, 266
  rights of third party against, 282–283
  signature of, 93
  termination, 284
  unauthorized acts by, 279
  undisclosed principal, 277
  warranty of authority, 283
Agreement
  certainty of meaning, 66
  conditional or provisional, 68
  conduct, inferred from, 30

domestic, whether giving rise to legal relations, 75
future, 64
'global' objective view of formation, 32
government, with, 76, 343
intention to create legal relations, 71–76
objective view of, 30
sale and purchase of land, 41
subject to finance, 67
trade unions, with, 74
written, rectification of, 131
Anticipatory breach, 212, 214
Arbitration clauses
effect after cancellation, 218
generally, 182
public policy, not contrary to, 146
use in establishing contractual terms, 65
Assignment
absolute, 199, 204
bankruptcy, on, 209
bare right to litigate, 205
burden of contract, of, 208
choses in action, of, 198, 204
consideration, need for, 201
death, on, 209
equitable, 198, 200, 204
generally, 198
legal, 198, 204
liabilities, of, 208
limits on, 205–207
notice of, 202
novation, and, 208
personal contracts, of, 206
prohibitions on, 207
statutory, 199, 204
subject to equities, 203
vicarious performance, and, 208
Auction
advertisement of, 35
generally, 38

Bailment
duties of bailee, 288
duties of bailor, 290
excluding terms, 174
generally, 285
gratuitous, 285, 288
jus tertii, 287
licence compared, 286
rights of bailee, 287
rights of bailor, 289
standard of care of bailee, 288
Benefit
benefit in practice, 85
consideration, 77
substantial reduction of, 214
third party, to, 195–197
Bilateral contracts
acceptance in, 52, 54
generally, 29
Bills of Exchange Act
cheque in full settlement, 236
past consideration, 79
Breach
affirmation, 216
anticipatory, doctrine of, 211, 212
cancellation, 210
election, 215
essential term, 213
repudiation, 211
rescission, comparison with cancellation, 218
stipulation will be broken, 213
substantial breach, 214
Building contracts, 324

Cancellation of contract
affirmation compared, 216
Contract and Commercial Law Act, under, 210
effect of, 218
entitlement to cancel, 211, 225
Fair Trading Act, and, 114, 225
good and bad reason, 220
notification, 217
relief after, 218, 219
sale of goods, 223
Capacity
corporations, of, 119
drunken persons, of, 122
limitation periods, effect of incapacity, 257, 258
mentally disordered persons, of, 120, 121
minors, of, 117, 118
necessaries, 122
Certainty
machinery provisions and, 65
meaning of terms, as to, 66
requirement of, 62, 63
Cheque
in full settlement, 236
Chose in action
assignment of, 23, 198, 201

Coercion, 135, 136, 139
Collateral contracts
  construction of, 164
  generally, 37, 164
  meaning of, 37, 164
  use of, 164
Commercial custom, 167
Common law origins, 27
Composition with creditors, 86
Compromise of suit, 82
Conditional contracts
  examples, 67
  generally, 67
  obligation to seek fulfilment, 70
  subject to contract, 68
  waiver of conditions, 69
Consent
  impaired, *see* Duress, Illegal contract, Misrepresentation, Mistake, Unconscionable bargains, Undue influence
  silence as, 54
Consideration
  acts, whether amounting to, 78
  adequacy of, 81
  assignments, 201
  benefit in practice, 85
  compositions with creditors, 86
  compromise of suit, 82
  definition, 77
  discharge of public duty, 83
  duty, acts in excess of, 83
  executed, 78
  executory, 78
  existing duty as, 83–85
  Foakes v. Beer, 86
  forbearance to sue, 82
  joint promises, and, 80
  past, 79
  privity, in relation to, 80
  promise not to sue, 82
  promise to pay less than amount due, 86
  promisee, must move from, 80
  promissory estoppel, 87
  public duty, 83
  Williams v. Roffey, 85
Construction of contract
  business common sense, 187
  commercial purpose, 184
  evidential issues, 188
  matrix of fact, 184
  parol evidence rule, 163
  post-contractual conduct, 186
  pre-contractual negotiations, 185
  subsequent conduct, 185
  surrounding circumstances, 184
Consumer contracts, 20, 179, 315–323
Consumer Guarantees Act 1993
  application of, 316
  consumer, 316
  damages, 322
  exclusions from, 180, 323
  generally, 20, 315
  guarantees in relation to goods, 317
  guarantees in relation to services, 318
  goods, 316
  manufacturer's liability, 321
  sale of goods and, 294, 315
  services, 316
  supplier's liability, 319–320
  supply, 316
  trade, 316
Contract
  certainty as to, 62
  definition and elements, 15
  history in NZ, 16
  interpretation of, 183-188
  requirements as to form, 90
  tikanga Māori and, 27
Contract and Commercial Law Act 2017
  electronic transactions provisions in, 58
  generally, 16
  illegal contracts provisions in, 155-162
  minors contracts provisions in, 117-118
  mistake provisions in, 124-130
  privity provisions of, 195-197
  relief for frustration of contract under, 231-232
  sale of goods provisions in, 294-314
Contractual intention
  advertisements, 35
  agreements with the state, 76
  business agreements, 72
  domestic agreements, 75
  trade unions, agreements with, 74
Contractual mistakes under the Contract and Commercial Law Act 2017
  generally, 124
  history, 16
  meaning of 'mistake', 126, 127
  quasi-contract and, 345
  relief under, 125, 129, 130
  statutory discretion, 16, 130
  third party rights, 130

Index

Contractual remedies under the Contract and Commercial Law Act 2017
- Consumer Guarantees Act 1993, relationship with, 224
- contracting out, and, 221
- excluding and limiting terms, and, 176
- Fair Trading Act, comparison with, 225
- history, 16
- misrepresentation, remedies under, 107, 212, 213
- relief, power of court to grant, 219
- sale of goods provisions in Contract and Commercial Law Act, relationship to, 223
- savings, 222

Conveyance
- contract and, 23

Corporations
- capacity of, 119

Counter-offers
- battle of the forms, 59
- generally, 60
- rejection of offer, 45
- request for information and, 60

Court
- ouster of jurisdiction, 147

Court of Appeal, 8

Courts
- Court of Appeal, 8
- Disputes Tribunal, 11
- District Court, 10
- Employment Court, 12
- High Court, 9
- Supreme Court, 7

Crime
- contract to commit, 150

Cross-offers, 54

Damages
- *Addis v. Gramophone*, rule in, 247
- cancellation, after, 218
- chance, loss of, 237
- consequential loss, 240
- contributory negligence, 250
- date of quantification, 242
- distress, for, 247
- exemplary, 243
- expectation loss, 237
- Fair Trading Act, under, 114
- *Hadley v. Baxendale*, rule in, 244
- measure of, 237–243
- misrepresentation, for, 107
- mitigation of, 249
- penalty clauses, 181, 251
- release fees, 237
- reliance loss, 238
- remoteness of, 244–248
- restitution of benefits, 239
- *The Achilleas*, rule in, 246
- wrongful dismissal cases, 247

Death
- agent, of, 284
- assignment of causes of action on, 209
- offeree or offeror, of, 49
- principal, of, 284

Debt, part payment of, 86

Deed
- consideration not required, 18, 77
- definition, 18
- formalities, 18
- where required, 91

Deposit
- recovery of unpaid deposit, 218

Disability
- contractual capacity, effect on, 117–122
- limitation period, effect on, 257, 258

Discharge by agreement, 233–236
- and *see* Accord and Satisfaction

Disputes Tribunal, 11

District Court, 10

Document
- joinder of, 92
- signature mistakenly made, 132
- rectification of, 131

Domestic agreements, 75

Drafting styles, 26

Duress
- economic, 135
- nature of, 134, 135
- undue influence, 136–142

Election
- doctrine of, 215

Electronic transactions
- acceptances, 58
- default rules, 58
- signatures, 93

Employment contracts
- damages, 247
- restraint of trade and, 160

Employment Court, 12

English influence on New Zealand law, 27

Estoppel
- cause of action, as, 89

detriment, 89
future of estoppel, 89
misrepresentation, relationship with, 100
promissory, 88, 89
proprietary, 89
remedies, 89
Evidence
burden of proof, 99
generally, 96
oral contracts, of, 163
parol, rule as to, 97, 163
Exclusion clauses
bailment contracts, in, 174
'battle of the forms', 59
construction *contra proferentem*, 173
consumer cases, 179, 180, 323
credit contracts, 175
fundamental breach, 174
generally, 171
incorporation of, 172
insurance cases, 175
interpretation of, 173
misrepresentation cases, 177, 178
negligence, and, 173
non-performance of contract, 174
pre-contract negotiations, 177
shipping cases, 174
signature, effect of, 172
small disputes, 176
statutory control, 175–180
third parties, effect on, 194
ticket cases, 42
Express terms
oral contract, 163
partly written, partly oral, 163
written contract, 163

Fact
opinion distinguished from, 103
Fair Trading Act
avoidance, 115
contracting out, 116, 178
damages for misrepresentation, 114
in trade, 110
mental element, 112
remedies, 113
unfair terms, 179
Family arrangements, 75
Finance, subject to, 67
Forbearance to sue, 82
Form
discharge of contracts, 234
Fraud
signature obtained by, 132
third party, on, 150
Frustration
Contract and Commercial Law Act 2017, 231, 232, 348
definition, 226
discharge under doctrine, 226, 227
effects of, 231
event expressly provided for, when, 228
foreseeability of event, 229
onus of proof, 230
performance of contract radically different, 226
self-induced, party cannot rely on, 230
total failure of consideration, 348
Fundamental breach, 174
Future agreements
generally, 64
options and rights of pre-emption, 39

Gaming and wagering contracts, 291-293
Good faith
generally, 25
in negotiations, 101
Government
agreements with, 76, 343
Guarantee
consumer transactions and, 338
contracts of, 95, 334
creditor's conduct rendering unenforceable, 337
formalities required, 91, 92, 335
indemnity, distinguished from, 334
oral contract of, 336
statutory, 315–323

Hadley v. Baxendale, rule in, 244
High Court, 9
High Trees case, 88

Illegal contract
breach of statute and, 155
common law, at, 149-151
consequences of illegality, 156
contracts void but not illegal, categories of, 147, 148
course of justice, interference with, 151
crime, tort, or fraud on a third party, 150
defrauding revenue, 152
generally, 145
prejudicial to good government, 153

quasi-contract and, 351
sexual immorality, 154
Illegal contracts provisions in Contract and Commercial Law Act 2017
contracts in breach of statutes and, 155
definitions, 146
discretion to grant relief, 159
effect of illegality under, 156
history, 16
relief available, 157
jurisdiction to grant relief, 158
restraint of trade, effect on, 162
Implied contracts, 31
Implied terms
business efficacy, 170
construction, and, 170
consumer cases, 317, 318
contracts of a class, 169
courts, implied by, generally, 169–170
custom, implied by, 167
particular contracts, 170
sale of goods cases, 307
statute by, 168
Impossibility of performance, 226
see also Frustration
Inducement by misrepresentation, 104
Infants
capacity of, 117, 118
Injunction, 253, 254
Interpretation of contracts, 183-188
business common sense, 187
evidential issues, 188
matrix of fact, 184
pre-contract negotiations, 185, 186
subsequent conduct, 185, 186
Insane persons
capacity of, 120, 121
Insurance
special contract, 20
International sales of goods, contracts for,
acceptance in, 57
revocation of offer of, 46
Intoxicated persons
capacity of, 122
Invitation to treat
instances of, 35
offer distinguished from, 34

Joinder of documents, 92
Judicature Act, 86
Judiciary, 6

Laches, 259
Land
contracts to dispose of interest in, 23, 41
formalities, 90, 91
Landlord and tenant statutes, 330–332
Lease
agreement to lease, 327
agriculture, 333
commercial, 328–329
creation, 327
definitions, 325
domestic, 330–332
Maori land, 333
privity of estate, 23
term, 326
Legal relations, *see also* Contractual intention
intention to create, 71, 72
Letters of comfort, 73
Limitation of actions
acknowledgment of liability, 257, 258
background, 256
disability, effect of, 257, 258
equitable relief, 259
fraud, effect of, 257, 258
knowledge, date of, 258
Limitation Act 1950, 257
Limitation Act 2010, 258
longstop period, 258
Part payment effect of, 257, 258
Long-term contracts, 233

Machinery provisions, 65
Maintenance
agreement tainted by, 151
Maori
language, 2
population and culture, 1
Marriage
legality of contracts affecting, 148
Minors
capacity of, 117, 118
Minors contracts provisions in Contract and Commercial Law Act 2017, 16, 117, 118
Misleading conduct, 111
Misrepresentation
agent, by, 106
cancellation, 108
Contract and Commercial Law Act and, 102
damages for, 107
definition of, 102, 103

essential, 212
fraudulent, 105
half-truth may be, 103
inducement, 104, 105
knowledge of falsity, 104
materiality, 103
misleading conduct, comparison with, 111
nature of, 103
non-disclosure, 103
puffs, 103
silence, whether constitutes, 103
statement of fact, 103
statement of opinion, 103
terms, comparison with, 107
Mistake, *see also* Contract and Commercial Law Act 2017
generally, 123
money paid under, 347
rectification and, 131
Mitigation of damage, 249
Mutual promises, 15

Necessaries, 121
Negligence
concurrent liability in, 21
exclusion of liability for, 173
misrepresentation, and, 107
Negotiations
Liability, 100
breakdown of, 101
good faith in, 101
Nemo dat quod non habet, 304
New Zealand
constitutional and legal history, 3
culture, 2
geography, 1
history of contract in, 16
legal system, 4
parliament, 5
population, 1
Non est factum, 132
Notice of cancellation, 217
Novation, 208

Offer, *see also* Acceptance
advertisement of auction, as, 38
bid at auction, 38
conditional, failure of condition, 48
counter-offer as rejection of, 60
cross-offer, not creating agreement, 54
death, effect on, 49
generally, 28, 33
invitation to treat, 34, 35
knowledge of, by acceptor, 53
lapse of time, effect of, 48
rejection of, 45
retrospective, 51
revocation of, 46, 47
self-service shops, in, 33
standing, 40
termination of, 45, 48
unilateral contracts, 43
when effective, 44
world at large, to, 43
Onus of proof, 322
Opinion
distinguished from fact, 103
Options, 39
Oral contracts, 163

Parliament, 5
Parol evidence, 97, 163
Part payment acknowledgment in writing, 86
cheques in full settlement, 236
composition with creditors, 86
does not discharge debt, 86
stranger by, 86
Part performance doctrine of, 94
Partnership, 344
Pawn, contracts of
generally, 339
rights of parties to, 341
things capable of being pawned, 340
Penalty clauses, 181, 249
Dunlop test, 181
legitimate interest test, 181
Performance
illegal, 155
impossibility of, 226
part, 94
Personal Property Securities Act 1999, 305
Pledge, contracts of, 340-341
Post, acceptance by, 57
Pre-contract negotiations
evidence of, 185
exclusion of liability for, 177
promissory estoppel, 100
Pre-contractual liability, 100
Pre-emption, right of, 39
Principal, *see also* Agency, Agent
authorized acts, liable for, 270–272
bankruptcy of, 284

competency of, 268
death of, 284
disclosed, 276
duties of, 274
incapacity of, 284
imputed knowledge, 281
liability of, 270–272, 275–280
payment to agent, effect of, 278
ratification by, 268
rights of third party against, 282–283
undisclosed, 277
Privity of contract
Contract and Commercial Law Act 2017 and, 195–197
exclusion clauses and third parties, 194
generally, 189
liabilities of third parties, 190
promisee's remedy where benefit to third party, 192
rights of third parties, 191, 195–197
trusts and, 193
Privity of estate, 23
Process contracts, 36
Promissory estoppel
doctrine of, 87–89
pre-contractual negotiations, 100
waiver compared, 235
Proof, burden of, 99
Property
contract and, 23
Property Law Act 2007
assignment under, 204
deeds, 18
generally, 92-95
leases, 326–329
Property (Relationships) Act 1976
agreement under, 91
intention to create legal relations, 75
Provisional agreements, 68
Public law, 13
Public policy
contracts contrary to, 145

Quantum meruit
generally, 352
work done in anticipation of contract, 100
Quasi-contract
money paid to defendant's use, 346
money paid under illegal contract, 350
money paid under mistake, 347
money paid under void contract, 349
quantum meruit, 352
total failure of consideration, 348

Rectification of document, 131
Land Transfer Act 2017, 131
Relief after cancellation, 219
Remedies
account of profits, 239
cancellation of contract, 210–225, 252
damages, 237–251, 254
injunction, 253, 254
statutory relief, 219
specific performance, 253, 254
Remoteness of damage, 244
failure to pay money, 248
generally, 244
scope of duty, 245–246
upset and distress, 247
Representation or term, 165
Rescission, compared with cancellation, 218
Restitution
damages, 239
generally, 353
Restraint of trade
cancellation of contract, effect of, 218
generally, 160, 161
impact of legislation, 162
Retrospective agreements, 51
Revenue
contracts to defraud, 152
Revocation
of acceptance, 61
of offer of bilateral contract, 46
of offer of unilateral contract, 47

Sale of goods,
contracts for, 295
generally, 294
goods, 295
Sale of goods provisions in Contract and Commercial Law Act 2017
acceptance of goods, 310
agreements to sell, 295
application of, 294
conditions, 306
Consumer Guarantees Act 1993, and, 294, 315-323
contracting out of, 314
damages, 312, 313
delivery of goods, 308
formalities, 296

generally, 294
goods, 295
implied terms under, 307
innominate terms, 306
instalment contracts, 308
misrepresentation cases, 165
nemo dat quod non habet, exceptions to, 304
passing of property, 297–303
payment for goods, 309
performance of contract, 308–310
perishing of goods, 303
Personal Property Securities Act 1999, and, 305
price of goods, 295, 307
rejection of goods, 310
remedies of buyer, 313
remedies of seller, 312
relationship with the common law, 294
remedies in Contract and Commercial Law Act 2017, 222
reservation of property in goods, 301
risk of loss, 302
Romalpa clauses, 301
sale, 295
sale or return contracts, 300
sales without title, 304, 305
specific goods, 297, 298
terms of contract, categorization of, 306
unascertained goods, 297, 299
warranties, 306
Sale of land
contracts for, 16, 92, 206, 216, 253
Signature
non est factum, availability of, 132
electronic, 92
generally, 93
mistaken, 132
Silence
misrepresentation, as, 103, 111
offeree, by, 54
Simple contracts, 19
Specific performance, 253-254
Spouses
agreements between, 75
Standard form contract
battle of the forms, 59
history, 20
ticket cases, 42
Standing offers, 40
Statutory intervention in contract, 27, 144, 175-180
Supreme Court, 7

Tax
agreements to avoid, 152
Tenancy, *see* Lease
Tender, 35
Termination
contractual provisions for, 233
Terms
express, 163-164
implied, 166–170
uncertainty, 66
unfair, 179
Third party
Contract and Commercial Law Act 2017, rights under, 130, 157
guarantee by, 335
Ticket cases, 42
Tikanga Māori
nature of, 27
significance for contract, 27
Time
limitation of actions, 256–259
offer revoked by effluxion of, 48
Tort
action for misrepresentation, 100, 107
negligence, 21
relation to contract, 21
Trade unions
agreements with employers, 74
Trust
contract and, 24
privity and, 193

Uberrimae fidei, 103
Uncertainty as to terms, 62
Unconscionable dealings
adequacy of consideration, 81
generally, 143
gifts, 143
statutory unconscionability, 144
Undisclosed principal, 277
Undue influence
classes of, 137
effect of, 141
Etridge decision, 139
generally, 136
imputed, 142
manifest disadvantage, 138
presumption of, 139
proof of, 140
surety cases, 142

unconscionable bargains and, 143
Unfair terms, 179
Unilateral contracts
acceptance of, 52
consideration for, 78
generally, 29
offer in, 43
revocation of offer, 47
Unjust enrichment
damages for, 240
generally, 353

Variation of contract
consideration for, 85
third party cases, 196
waiver compared, 235
Void contract
generally, 147
money paid recoverable, 349
ousting jurisdiction of courts, 147
prejudicing status of marriage, 148
restraint of trade, 160–162
wagering contracts, 291

Wagering contracts, 291
Waiver
communication, of, 56
conditions, of, 69
promissory estoppel compared, 235
variation compared, 235
Williams v. Roffey, 85
Writing, need for, 92, 335

www.ingramcontent.com/pod-product-compliance
Lightning Source LLC
Chambersburg PA
CBHW071425230926
51846CB00001B/123
9789403511580